Eros and Ethos

Volume 1: A New Theory of Sexual Ethics
Or, The First Eudaimonistic Sexual Ethic

by Jason Stotts

Copyright © 2018 Jason Stotts. ALL RIGHTS RESERVED.
Copyright registered in the United States and Canada.

This book contains material protected under International and National Copyright Laws and Treaties. Any unauthorized reprint or use of this material is prohibited. No part of this book may be reproduced or transmitted in any form or by any means, electronic or mechanical, including photocopying, recording, or by any information storage and retrieval system, without express written permission from the author.

Any requests for reproduction or republication, in part or whole, should be directed to the author via his website at
http://JasonStotts.com/contact/
or his email address: Jason@JasonStotts.com.

First Edition (Version 1.1)
Publisher: Erosophia Enterprises (Hamilton, Ontario, Canada).
Date of first publication: February 9th, 2018.

Paperback ISBN: 978-1-7751752-0-9
eBook ISBN: 978-1-7751752-1-6

Cover image: "Pygmalion and Galatea" by Jean-Leon Gerome. Image in public domain in the United States {{PD-US}} and in Canada {{PD-Canada}}.

To Truth, above all else.

Acknowledgements

Throughout this project there was one man who stood unfailingly behind it, encouraging me at every step, and without whom it likely would not have happened. Thank you, Tom, for your support. It made a world of difference.

I want to thank Patrick Ryan for his very thoughtful feedback on a draft of the manuscript. His comments and criticisms had a large role in shaping the project and made it much better.

I also want to thank my wife for many things, but two things that are especially relevant here. First, for challenging me on the initial question that would lead me to challenge everything I knew about sexuality, ultimately leading to this book. Second, for her editorial skills and comments on the penultimate version of the book that pushed it to be much better than it otherwise would have been. This book would not have been nearly as good without her.

I want to thank Robert Garmong for his comments and insights on an early version of the manuscript, which helped me to start down the path on the right tone and style.

I want to thank Rachel Miner, Tom Jones, and Donna Paris for their help with copy-editing.

I also want to thank everyone else who had a part in making *Eros and Ethos* better in some way, including: Joseph Pearson, Tim White, William Green, Sandra Daugherty, Jennifer Snow, John Drake, Alan T. Moore, and Scott Johnson.

A special thank you to Joseph Pearson for his design work on the cover and on the websites JasonStotts.com and ErosandEthos.com.

Lastly, I want to thank the readers of my blog *Erosophia* for always challenging me to be better.

Table of Contents

INTRODUCTION — I

CHAPTER 1: EUDAIMONISM — 1
1. The Passionate Life — 2
2. Human Nature and the Foundation of Ethics — 8
3. Principled Ethics — 12
4. Rational Egoism — 20
5. Values, Purpose, and Hierarchy — 24
6. Universal Values and the Virtues — 33
7. Character — 50
Summary and Conclusions — 54

CHAPTER 2: EMOTIONS AND SENTIMENTS — 58
1. What is an Emotion? — 59
2. The Emotional Process — 63
3. Sentiments — 74
4. Beliefs and Philosophy — 86
Summary and Conclusions — 91

CHAPTER 3: EROTIC LOVE — 93
1. Challenging the Old Paradigms of Love — 94
2. The Nature of Erotic Love — 102
3. What Kind of Person is Capable of Love? — 114
Summary and Conclusions — 116

CHAPTER 4: RELATIONSHIPS — 118
1. The Erotic Relationship — 118
2. Friendship versus the Erotic Relationship — 128
3. Marriage — 130
4. Divorce — 134
Summary and Conclusions — 137

CHAPTER 5: SEXUAL ATTRACTION & FANTASY — 139
1. The Origins of Sexual Attraction — 140
2. The Nature of Sexual Attraction — 147
3. Fantasy — 157
Summary and Conclusions — 160

CHAPTER 6: SEXUAL IDENTITY — 162
1. Sexual Orientation — 162
2. Societal Sex Roles — 175
3. Erousia — 188
4. Sexual Identity — 199
Summary and Conclusions — 201

CHAPTER 7: SEX AND THE GOOD LIFE — 203
1. Sexual Pleasure — 204
2. The Nature of Sex — 211
3. Integrating Sex — 219
Summary and Conclusions — 230

CONCLUSION: THE SEXUAL ETHICS REVOLUTION — 233
1. A Revolution Against the Past — 233
2. A Revolution for the Future — 237
3. A Philosophy for Life — 243

BIBLIOGRAPHY — 247

ABOUT THE AUTHOR — 251

ENDNOTES — 252

Introduction

*When it comes to erotic health, nothing is more important
than the interplay of eros and ethics.*[1]
~ Jack Morin

*The question of whether a [moral] code is good or bad
is the same as the question
whether or not it promotes human happiness.*[2]
~ Bertrand Russell

We do not learn for school, but for life.[3]
~ Seneca

There are many ideals about sex in the world. Even if we could not immediately name them, we all have an idea of what they are or at least have a vague idea of some people who represent them. There is the woman who has a high sex drive, but who feels guilty about her desires and tries to resist them. The man who really enjoys masturbating, but who feels guilty about it. The woman who has sworn off masturbation entirely. The man whose life goal is to have as much sex as possible. The parents who see their young child touching her genitals and shames her for this, telling her that children should not be sexual. The priest, monk, or nun who has given up sexuality entirely for religious reasons. All of these people hold different ideas about sex and different ideals for sex. Even people who do not manage to live by these ideals often still hold them as ideals. These ideals fit into three broad camps: those who *resist* sexuality, those who *abstain* from sexuality, and those who *indulge* in sexuality. Interestingly, and perhaps surprising to some, these people have all been influenced by an ancient, but still critically important, debate about the nature of sex and its role in human life.

Unfortunately, this ancient debate has not been kind to sexuality. Broadly, the history of ethics can be classified into three primary camps regarding sexuality: the "Resistant," the "Abstinent," and the "Indulgent." While these three camps all have different ideals about the role of sex in a human life, they are united in that their ideals will not help us to live happy lives that include sex in healthy ways, as we shall see. The only way to fix the attitudes that plague our culture is to address the philosophy head on—to provide a new approach to sexual ethics that integrates sex into what it means to live well. This is precisely what we will do in this book. However, we must briefly look to the past to get a better understanding of these debates before we can move forward, so that we may avoid their pitfalls and understand where we fit in, or fail to fit in, the debates.

The Resistant camp is the tradition of resisting emotions, appetites, and desires—especially sexual ones. In its modern incarnations, it gives rise to rules about which sexual acts we should do and which sexual feelings we should allow ourselves to feel. The best example of this was put forth by Plato in the *Phaedrus* (253d), where he used the metaphor of a charioteer pulled by two strong steeds: a beautiful white purebred stallion (reason) and an ugly black stallion (the "passions" or emotions). Plato claims that in order to maintain our chosen path, we must tame the black stallion of emotions as much as possible so that the two horses work together. If the black horse cannot be tamed, then it will pull the chariot astray. Plato even uses sex as his quintessential case of strong passions, and so his moral psychology relies on sex to get off the ground. Unfortunately, he simply stipulates, without justification, that resisting the passions is virtuous and says that the white horse of reason also loves "self-control" (253e) and is controlled by his "sense of shame" (254a). Thus, the Resistant camp regarding sexuality was born, as well as the idea that we should feel shame when we give into our "base desires for sex."

The essence of this camp is still common today in the idea that we should only engage in sex in moderation, and even then, only certain kinds of sexual acts are permissible. This school really caught its stride in Thomistic Catholicism (Catholicism as influenced by Thomas Aquinas), which stipulated that the only acceptable form of sexuality was vaginal penetration by a penis, for the purpose of reproduction, in a marriage sanctioned by the church, when both partners were fertile and capable of producing children. Even so, a person is not supposed to enjoy it too much or too frequently.[i] This idea is still prevalent today, whether its religious underpinnings are evident or not, as the idea that enjoying sex too much is somehow unhealthy or dangerous and therefore sexuality should be resisted.

---

[i] Seneca, although he predates Aquinas (and all of Christianity), shares the same idea in *On Marriage*: "Indeed, any love of someone else's wife is disgraceful, but so is excessive love of one's own. The wise man ought to love his wife deliberately, not passionately. He controls the impulse to pleasure and is not led headlong to intercourse. Nothing is more disgusting than to treat one's wife like an adulterer." (from Nussbaum, *Therapy of Desire*, p. 473; Trans. Nussbaum). Stoics can be found in both the resistant and abstinent camps.

The Abstinent camp comes from the tradition of rule-based moral systems that call for us to abstain from sex. This is in order to build a certain constitution such that we can always be ready to obey rules and do our duty. In this camp, it is not merely that we should *resist* some sexual urges while others are okay; rather, we should try not to experience sexual desires at all and we certainly should not act on them. This, too, is exemplified by Plato, who took a dualist position and believed that people are truly immortal souls[i] trapped in prisons of the flesh. He believed that to be able to return to the perfect realm (or "heaven"), we must abstain from the corruption of the soul by the body, with its appetites and emotions, as far as possible. Plato is not subtle about this and says in the *Phaedo* that: "The body keeps us busy in a thousand ways because of its need for nurture. [...] It fills us with wants, desires, fears, all sorts of illusions and much nonsense [...] and it is the body and the care of it, to which we are enslaved." (66c). He also writes: "The soul is polluted when it leaves the body, having always been associated with it and served it." (81b).[ii] Insofar as a person does give into their bodily impulses, they pollute their soul and weaken their constitution.

The essence of this camp is still common today in the idea that we should abstain from sex in order to remain in control of ourselves and to be ready to do our duty. Moreover, we should resist most desires and emotions, so as not to have potential conflicts with our duty. Within this camp, to whom we owe the duty varies—whether to a god, the state, or the *Volk*. One of the best examples of this camp is Saint Augustine, another of the fathers of the Catholic Church. He is known for his hatred of sexuality and for being one of the major forces in turning Christianity away from sexuality.[iii] Augustine thought that sex was always to be avoided, so that one could maintain a "pure" soul and always be ready to do the Christian God's bidding (presumably Augustine cared little if one was ready to do Zeus's or Shiva's bidding). Some versions of Stoicism (an ancient Greek/Roman school of philosophy/religion) also advocated abstinence from sexuality to cultivate *apatheia*,[iv] or a sense of internal peace uncorrupted by emotions or strong desires. Kant as well pushed for abstinence

---

[i] Unless talking about someone else's theory, we will use the terms "soul," "mind," and "spirit" interchangeably throughout to mean that aspect of a person that thinks, feels, desires, *etc.*

[ii] More broadly, Plato is thoroughly misanthropic: "nothing among human things is worth much seriousness." (*Republic*, 604b12; trans. Nussbaum, from *The Therapy of Desire*, p. 92)

[iii] Augustine, to be fair, appears to have the support of Jesus himself: "Jesus replied, 'Not everyone can accept this word, but only those to whom it has been given. For there are eunuchs who were born that way, and there are eunuchs who have been made eunuchs by others—and there are those who choose to live like eunuchs for the sake of the kingdom of heaven. The one who can accept this should accept it.'" (The Christian Bible, New International Version, *Matthew* 19:11-12)

[iv] Cicero, for example, is clearly in the abstinent camp: "For just as it is a moral offense to betray one's country, to use violence against one's parents, to rob a temple, which are evils in result, so too to fear, to grieve, to have erotic desires are each of them a moral offense, even without any result." (Cicero *De Finibus*, 3.32, Trans. Nussbaum. As found in *Therapy of Desire*, p. 365)

from sexuality, going so far as to equate masturbation to self-murder[i] and saying that "[Sex] is a principle of the degradation of human nature."[4] In whatever form, the idea that we should forgo sex in order to maintain a dutiful constitution is still very common today (as with the idea that athletes should avoid sex so as to not "weaken" themselves).

While these two camps differ on the role that sex should play in life, whether a very restricted one or none at all, they are united in that they believe that sex is harmful. Thus, they give us no guidance about how to integrate sex into our lives in healthy and life-affirming ways. Yet, most people desire to have sex in their lives and so many often seek refuge in the third camp: the Indulgent camp.

The Indulgent camp comes from the tradition of hedonism. This camp holds that the only good thing is pleasure and so a person should do whatever they can in order to maximize their pleasure. This camp is exemplified by Aristippus (a follower of Socrates) and the Cyrenaic hedonists, who believed that pleasure is intrinsically good and that immediate pleasure ought to be our only moral aim. This school embraces sexuality enthusiastically and without any reservation whatsoever. Indeed, it says that we should have sex with whomever, whenever, wherever, however, we can, as long as it is pleasurable. If we return to Plato's metaphor of the charioteer, where the Resistant camp picked the white horse, the Indulgent camp accepts the conflict, but chooses the black horse instead.

The Indulgent camp never achieved widespread popularity. Yet, throughout history, it has had its adherents and resurgences: in more recent memory, France had its "Libertine" movement and the U.S. had the sexual revolution of the 1960's and 70's which advocated "free love." Even when there is not a large movement, individuals and small groups are sometimes drawn to the Indulgent camp, thinking that they have found the secret to a good life. One of the most common ways this manifests today is radical subjectivism about sexuality: they believe that since pleasure is both intrinsically good and the goal of morality, whatever feels good to them is moral. They believe that there is no way for one person to judge the pleasures of another and no standard to use besides pleasure.

Much like the Resistant and Abstinent camps, the Indulgent camp offers

---

[i] "But it is not so easy to produce a rational proof that unnatural, and even merely unpurposive, use of one's sexual attribute [masturbation] is inadmissible as being a violation of duty to oneself (and indeed, as far as its unnatural use is concerned, a violation in the highest degree). The *ground of proof* is, indeed, that by it a man surrenders his personality (throwing it away), since he uses himself as a means to satisfy an animal impulse. But this does not explain the high degree of violation of the humanity in one's own person by such a vice in its unnaturalness, which seems in terms of its form (the disposition it involves) to exceed even murdering oneself. It consists, then, in this: That a man who defiantly casts off life as a burden is at least not making a feeble surrender to animal impulse in throwing himself away" (Kant. *The Metaphysics of Morals* (Trans. Mary Gregor), p. 425)

us no advice about how to incorporate sexuality into our lives in a healthy way. Indeed, the imperative to indiscriminate indulgence is no advice at all to someone who wants to live a good life: it is too myopic and neglects much of what it is to be human, while also failing to bring about the pleasure it so desperately craves. Worse, though, is that there is an inherent irony in the Indulgent camp. However, this will not clearly manifest until we have presented our views and so we will return to these objections against the Indulgent camp in the Conclusion.

Having seen the three primary responses to sexuality throughout history, a person could quite reasonably be exasperated. What if a person finds value in sexuality and wants to enjoy it in healthy ways? For this person, the history of ethics has little of use to offer.

That changes now.

The major theme of this book is that sexuality is not a lapse in moral strength, a corrupting influence, or an area of our lives with respect to which morality is neutral; rather, sexuality is an important expression of our ethical lives (this will be fully elaborated in Chapter 7). Moreover, we are particularly able to express our moral selves through sex in a way that not many other things can rival, since sex brings so much of ourselves to bear. In my view, virtue does not lie in rules subjugating our appetites, desires, and emotions, but in aligning these with our conscious ends so that we can flourish and, at the same time, feel good about doing so (which has the added benefit of creating meaning in our lives, a point we will explore in Chapter 1). By becoming integrated into our happiness, our appetites and desires become expressions of our moral ideals and help to drive us towards the best life open to us. Moreover, by integrating our emotions into our ethical framework we can have much richer and more rewarding lives than we could have otherwise.

Sexuality, then, does not stand in opposition to morality, but rather is one of the most powerful driving forces behind our flourishing and moral development. Or, it can be, *if* we integrate it into our lives in the right ways. Thus, *Eros and Ethos* presents a new option for how we should view sexuality: not as something to distrust and ward against with rules, but as an important moral facet of our lives, through which we can express our moral selves.

My project here is both new and radical: to create the first system of ethics that shows the deep value that sexuality has for a good life. I am going to show how sexuality can be integrated into our lives in healthy and life-affirming ways. To do this, I am going to create the first eudaimonistic sexual ethic. By "eudaimonistic,"[i] I mean that it involves the rich sense of happiness of a good and full life. We will sometimes simply use the word "happiness," but in English that word has come to mean something more like the feeling of joy or contentment and has lost its richer and deeper meaning. Eudaimonism is not

---

[i] Eudaimonistic is pronounced: you-die-moan-ist-ic.

only the correct morality for human life, but it also leads to the best kind of sex life possible, as we shall see. I will also need to create a new conception of moral psychology and a new theory of emotions and sentiments that will underpin much of the later work (which is the subject of Chapter 2). All of this will be clearer as we proceed through the book.

A few editorial comments. First, *Eros and Ethos* is being published in three volumes due to its length and a natural split between volumes. The present volume, Volume 1, deals with the more theoretical work of creating the first eudaimonistic sexual ethic. In Volume 2, we will apply this theory to particular topics to show its usefulness and how it can answer previously intractable problems, such as abortion, "non-traditional" relationships such as polyamory, and "kinks." We will find that the answer to many of these questions is nuanced and that whether they will benefit or harm our life largely depends on how we engage in them. Volume 3 will be a collection of essays that grew out of the writing of *Eros and Ethos*, but could not find a proper place in Volume 1 or 2. They either expand upon ideas in earlier volumes or attempt to clarify them. It is my intention that after all three volumes are completed and published, an omnibus edition will be published that combines all three volumes into a single book. To this end, chapter numbering will be continuous between volumes.

Second, some comments about formatting. I have put clarifying comments in footnotes (designated by Roman numerals) and reserved endnotes for references (designated by Arabic numerals). Thus, the reader need only to turn to the endnotes if they wish to find references and no commentary will be missed by not doing so. Each chapter has a summary and conclusion at its end and certain readers may wish to read these first, in order to have an overview of the chapter before diving into its details. Quotations, especially epigraphs, are not an unqualified endorsement of an author and should merely be construed to show that I agree on that particular point or that I think the author makes a point particularly well. I do not intend to speak for any other authors and I certainly do not intend to let them speak for me.

One final remark with respect to the style of the book. In contrast to some authors who equate obscurity and confusion with profundity, this book has been written with clarity as one of its primary goals. Nietzsche says that: "Whoever knows he is deep strives for clarity; whoever would like to appear deep to the crowd strives for obscurity. For the crowd considers anything deep if only it cannot see to the bottom."[5] It is my firm belief that philosophy should help us to clarify problems and help us to live good human lives. Philosophy is for *living* and understanding the world around us in the deepest ways. In order to do this, it must have clarity as one of its primary goals.

One of the marks of good philosophy is that if we were to ask ourselves the question before we read the philosopher's answer, it would seem incredibly complicated. But, once we read their answer, it becomes clear (if not simple). That is, the mark of a good philosopher is making complicated ideas relatively easy to understand. The opposite, muddying of the waters to make them appear deep[6], will bring no value to our life or improve our understanding of the world. Such tactics prey upon insecurity and ignorance, or as Aristotle more eloquently says: "conscious of their ignorance, they admire those who proclaim some great thing that is above their comprehension."[7] Clear thinking leads to a better life and that is something that we should all desire.

With that, I welcome you to our philosophical journey. You fellow lovers of wisdom who burn with curiosity and are driven to understand the world as deeply as you can, this book was written for you.

Jason Stotts
February, 2018

Volume 1: The Theory

*For the future of civilization
a new and better sexual ethic is indispensable.
It is this fact that makes the reform of sexual morality
one of the vital needs of our time.*[8]
~ Bertrand Russell

*Sex lies at the root of life,
and we can never learn to reverence life
until we know how to understand sex.*[9]
~ Havelock Ellis

*Let nobody put off doing philosophy when he is young,
nor slacken off in philosophy because of old age.
For nobody is either too young or too old
to secure the health of the soul.
And to say that the proper time for doing philosophy
has not yet come, or has already gone by,
is just like saying that the time for eudaimonia
has not yet come or has already gone by.*[10]
~ Epicurus

Chapter 1: Eudaimonism

*The problem of determining what sexual morality would be best
from the point of view of general happiness and well-being
is an extremely complicated one.*[11]
~ Bertrand Russell

*What gives our lives meaning is not anything beyond our lives,
but the richness of our lives.*[12]
~ Robert Solomon

How should a person live? This is *the* question of Ethics. Each of us must figure out how to create a rich and meaningful life for ourselves; which, for many of us, will include sexuality. We should approach this inquiry not dispassionately, but with a sense of wonder and joy. We should take on this task not as a duty, but with reverence for what we can make of our lives. To do this, we are going to need the right kind of ethics—but we should not get ahead of ourselves.

In this chapter, we are going to inquire into ethics in order to lay the foundation for the rest of our undertaking in the later chapters. We must start, not with the question of which ethical system to pick, but with the question of whether it makes sense to pick one at all. If life were ultimately meaningless, then our entire inquiry would be in vain. Yet, if meaning is possible, then surely we will want to aim to have meaningful lives, no matter where else our inquiry may take us. However, showing that meaning is possible merely sets the stage for ethics, but it does not answer the question of why we might want it. In order to answer this question, we must take a closer look at the nature of ethics. Since we are human we will need a human ethic, so it would also be a good idea to take human nature into account (if we can learn anything about it). If this is successful, then we can turn to see which particular kind of ethic may serve us best in our goal. We will find that eudaimonism is uniquely capable of handling the task.

1. The Passionate Life

*That it will never come again
is what makes life so sweet.*[13]
~ Emily Dickinson

The Meaning in Life

We all want our lives to have meaning: to have meaning in life is a real human need.[i] Yet today, all too many people are searching for meaning and failing to find it. Some people try to find meaning in how much money they make or in possessions, thinking, presumably, that once they are rich or have the nicest house or car, that they will have meaning in life. Others are searching for meaning after leaving religion and finding nothing but a cold, indifferent universe. Others simply know that something crucial is missing from their lives, even if they do not know what it is.

It is true that the question "What is the meaning of life?" cannot be answered. Fortunately, this is not because it is too complex; rather, it cannot be answered because the question itself is fundamentally misguided.[ii] The proper question is not "what is the meaning of life" — a question that implies life needs something outside of human existence to give it meaning — but "how do I go about *creating* meaning *in* my life?"[iii]

In order to try to understand this more useful question, it is helpful to consider the opposite case: what would it mean for someone's life to be *without* meaning? This is often said of someone who is unambitious, unfocused, and without purpose. Meaning, in this context, means roughly "purpose." Having a purpose means choosing some end we want to achieve and then working to achieve it. Indeed, this act of setting ends and working to achieve them *is* creating meaning in life.[iv] Aristotle thought this choice of ends was of critical

---

[i] We will return to this idea of human needs in more depth in Chapter 2.

[ii] The problem with the question is that this sense of meaning is dependent on the concept of life; meaning could not exist outside of a framework of life. To ask what the meaning of life is, is to ask a person to step outside of the necessary framework and attempt to justify the concept on some other basis besides life. This, however, is impossible. It is similar to "What is the meaning of Checkmate (outside of the context of chess)?" The concept of checkmate only makes sense in the context of chess, just as the concept of meaning only makes sense in the context of life; outside of its context, the concept is empty. Meaning is not something that can be found outside of life and applied to it.

[iii] Would we really want the meaning of our life given to us? Do we not want to create it ourselves? Is not that the uniquely human opportunity: to have a life of our own choosing?

[iv] This is the primary way we create meaning, but it is not the only way in which we create meaning in life. There are lots of other important ways in which we create meaning, such as: participating in social institutions (*e.g.*, marriage), rituals (*e.g.*, daily routines, seasonal traditions), relationships (*e.g.*, familial, romantic, friendship), and milestones in life (*e.g.*, coming of age ceremonies, graduations).

importance for ethics:

> We must enjoin every one that has the power to live according to his own choice to set up for himself some object of the good life to aim at [...] with reference to which he will then do all his acts, since not to have one's life organized in view of some end is a mark of much folly.[14]

If we want to create meaning in our life, then we must identify ends *and seek to achieve them*. It is the very process of identifying ends and seeking to achieve them that is the primary way we give meaning to our lives. Hunter S. Thompson made this same point well: "To let another man define your own goals is to give up one of the most meaningful aspects of life — the definitive act of will which makes a man an individual."[15] This runs counter to the idea that we have to *find* meaning in life, as though life is hiding it from us. The fact is that there is no intrinsic meaning in life: we are not predestined to do any particular job, have any necessary goals, or play any particular roles.

This process of choosing ends for our lives and then working to achieve them also involves *valuing*. Valuing has two related senses that we must bring together: the objective and subjective. The first sense, the objective sense, is when we judge that a thing would beneficial in our lives.[i] This judgement we call *evaluation* and it must be based in the facts about our human nature and the particulars of our life, as well as aimed at the end of happiness.[ii] This judgement must be scrupulously rational and made within our full context of our knowledge, if it is to aid us in living well. This is the objective sense of value.[iii] On the other hand, the *act* of valuing, or subjective valuing, is when a person *chooses* to care about some ends as important in their life. Of course, that we subjectively value something does not, in fact, make it a value in the objective sense. Conversely, that we objectively value something does not mean that we will subjectively value it (unless we want to commit ourselves to Socrates' mistaken path that to know right is to love it and do it).[16] Indeed, with subjective valuing a person can be right or wrong: a person might be wrong that something is an objective value or it may be an apparent value (something

---

i Tara Smith makes this point particularly well: "Something's being a value depends on its serving a life-enhancing function for a being engaged in the struggle to survive. [...] The requirements of survival are set by reality; what is valuable is valuable by virtue of its capacity to contribute *to* a specific person, *for* his life. This is the core of value's objectivity." (*Viable Values*, p. 101)

ii Evaluation is a form of teleological reasoning, specifically about an individual's happiness. Other forms of teleological reasoning would have other ends.

iii In order for something to be objectively valuable to me, I must *know* that it is because I have used good judgement in my evaluation. The other sense of "objective," that requires a god's-eye view, is illegitimate, because there is no such non-situated view to be had.

which appears to be a value, but which is not).[i]

Ideally, we will work to achieve alignment between our subjective values and objective values: that is, we will choose to care about things that are actually good for us. If we fail to align our subjective valuing with objective values, then we will be acting in a self-defeating manner since we will be choosing to value things that are not beneficial to our life. Indeed, there is a deep irony to "valuing" when subjective values are not aligned with objective values, as we will be choosing to care about things that do not make our lives better or even make our lives worse. Thus, we can say that proper valuing requires subjective valuing to be aligned with objective values, if we care about our lives.

To return to our larger point, valuing is a choice and it is through this choice that we create emotional significance and meaning in our lives.[ii] The act of choosing to value something, choosing to care about it in our lives, is *ipso facto*[iii] choosing to create meaning in our lives. Life is the end that values seek to achieve and human nature sets the conditions on which it can be successfully achieved (we will return to this in the next section).[iv]

Creating meaning in life comes from *choosing* to care about our lives and what happens to us. Underlying every choice we make in life is the most fundamental choice of all: to live.[v] For any choice, the ultimate answer to "why" must be that we choose to live. Of course, we can make the choice to die. Barring that momentous and irreversible choice, every choice we make is evidence of our desire to live: even if we choose to live badly, we still choose to live. There is no middle ground here, nor can we abstain. As Sartre said: "choosing not to choose is still a choice."[vi] One either chooses to live and lives or chooses to die and dies: there can be no middle ground.[vii]

This choice to stay alive is not enough if we are seeking happiness. But

---

[i] The term "apparent value" comes from Aristotle, see: *NE*, III.4.

[ii] It is important to point out that the ways in which we *create* meaning in life can be different than the ways in which we *experience* meaning in life.

[iii] Latin for "by that very fact."

[iv] It is also important to point out that there also exist, in addition to values, antivalues, and avalues. Antivalues are those things that negatively impact our lives. Avalues are those things that do not impact our lives either positively or negatively (which makes them rather unimportant).

[v] I credit Tara Smith for this point, which I took from her lecture: "To Imagine a Heaven—And How 'Sense of Life' Can Help You to Claim It." The choice to live is not some mystical choice. It is not made once and then forgotten, but it is a *perpetual choice* that underlies every other choice we make.

[vi] Paraphrase as frequently used by Ron Santoni, whom I had the pleasure of knowing at Denison University as an undergraduate. Although we rarely agreed, his passion for philosophy and for life was always admirable: he is a man who truly *cares*. Quote from Jean-Paul Sartre's "Existentialism is a Humanism." Original: "In one sense choice is always possible, but what is not possible is not to choose. I can always choose, but I must know that if I do not choose, that is still a choice."

[vii] Which is, emphatically, not to argue that all of our choices *successfully* help us to live. The point is not about the success of our choices, but about what it means about us *that we are choosing*.

happiness cannot be aimed at directly: happiness is not a discrete thing that, once acquired, is held forever. Happiness arises from living a certain kind of life: it is a kind of activity, a thing that we *do*, and not a passive state or a thing we *have*. This is the existential element of happiness. Of course, happiness is also a self-reflective state of consciousness about how one is living. This is the psychological element of happiness. Happiness is, thus, both an activity and a state, depending on which aspect we focus on. We will soon look at some of the central things that constitute happiness, but for now it is sufficient to focus on how our central purpose in life[i] goes a long way to structuring our lives, making meaning possible, and helps us to direct our effort at happiness.[ii]

When we choose a central purpose in life, this is also a choice about who we want to be and how we want to structure our lives. This is simpler than it might seem: if I choose to become a philosopher, I make a choice that will structure much of the rest of my life. The implications of this self-chosen end, our central purpose in life, extends to every aspect of our lives and we often, if not usually, consider other choices and aspects of our lives with regard to this end. For example, if I had a book deadline looming, then I would not choose to go on vacation if it might make me miss my deadline. While choosing to value something and giving it emotional significance is how we create meaning in life, our central purpose helps us to decide which things to value. Our central purpose in life is incredibly important for creating meaning. Without it, we will have conflicts between our values and we will not know which things will truly help us and which things will not (we will return to the discussion of central purpose in life shortly).

Yet, even given all this, have we not stumbled right into the fear we were trying to avoid after all? If there is no intrinsic meaning in our lives and we are mortal, how can we ever come to have meaning knowing that we will someday die and it will all be for nothing?[iii] If we can die, then our values will die with us and our lives will be rendered ultimately meaningless. This concern is at least as old as Plato; it is the idea that only that which is eternal can have value. However, just because life ends does not mean that values are impossible and

---

[i] I credit Ayn Rand for this idea: "A *central purpose* serves to integrate all the other concerns of a man's life. It establishes the hierarchy, the relative importance, of his values, it saves him from pointless inner conflicts, it permits him to enjoy life on a wide scale and to carry that enjoyment into any area open to his mind; whereas a man without a purpose is lost in chaos. He does not know what his values are. He does not know how to judge. He cannot tell what is or is not important to him, and, therefore, he drifts helplessly at the mercy of any chance stimulus or any whim of the moment. He can enjoy nothing. He spends his life searching for some value which he will never find…" (*Playboy Interview*).

[ii] Conversely, a lack of a central purpose in life is a major contributor to psychological problems such as anxiety and depression.

[iii] This is, broadly, the Existentialist fear. Existentialism is a broad philosophic movement that is rightly concerned with questions like freedom, meaningfulness of life, and authenticity. Among its philosophers are Nietzsche, Sartre, and Camus. As we will see, however, we must reject their answers as mistaken, especially in the realm of meaningfulness.

life is without meaning. As Aristotle says: "What is white for many days is no whiter than that which is white for a single day; so the good will not be more good by being eternal."[17] Values do not have to last forever to be real values: just because things end, does not mean that they are not good or valuable while they exist.[i] This, then, is the answer to the fear that death destroys the very possibility of values or meaning in life: just because something ends, does not mean that it is not real.

More importantly, we can only have values and meaning *because* we are alive and will eventually die. We have already seen that the concept of value is intimately tied to life and, consequently, meaning can only be found *in* life: the dead have no values, nor could they have values. In what way can a dead body be benefited? It is nonsensical to apply values to inanimate things: what could be of value to a rock?[ii] Values apply only to living things: the concept of value is empty outside of life. Therefore, we only wind up with a meaningless life if we fail to create meaning for ourselves.[iii] Or, to put it positively: o*ur life will only be meaningful if we make it so.*

The Motivation of Meaning

We have been alluding to this in the foregoing, but it is time to explicitly address it: we cannot achieve meaning in life through abstract reasoning alone. We have to be engaged in our lives and we have to *care* about the outcomes. That is, we have to become *emotionally invested* in ourselves in order to have meaning in life. The philosopher Robert Solomon said, "It is because we are moved, because we feel, that life has a meaning."[18] It is our emotions that allow us to experience the reality of our values: for better or worse. When we have our subjective values aligned with our overall goals in life, then we have not only created meaning, we are also able to *experience* it as well.[iv]

This is one of the most important, and yet most overlooked, aspects of emotions: emotions can help to motivate ethics. Contra the Stoics who thought that the reasonable person should live a cold life of dispassion (*apatheia*), our emotions can help motivate us to become better than we would be otherwise:

---

[i] While obviously each of us desires to maximize the good in our lives, we should not let this desire blind us to the value found in things that do not last forever and thereby lose the world to our (mistaken) ideal of it.

[ii] Values presuppose desires, which presuppose life. See, for example: "And how can one suppose that there is desire where there is no life? One should consider seriously about this and not assume without reasons what it is not easy to believe even with reasons." (Aristotle, *Eudemian Ethics* I.8.1218ª27)

[iii] Robert Solomon says that: "The meaninglessness of life is in fact a projection of our own sense of worthlessness onto the world" (*The Passions*, 53). The existentialist worry is, in fact, a form of self-confession.

[iv] We will investigate emotions at length in Chapter 2.

our emotions can become a driving force for living well.[i] Our emotions are responses to our beliefs and the more important the beliefs are to us, and the more deeply integrated into our self they are, then the more powerfully we will experience our emotional responses to them. For most of us, our ethical beliefs are exactly this kind of deeply held belief: thus, we will have strong emotional responses to our ethical beliefs. This allows us to *experience* the reality of ethical beliefs in our lives.

Consider the implications of this: if our personal philosophy is well integrated and self-consistent, then our emotions will be congruent with our philosophy. If we truly believe that to live well is the good in life, then we will feel joy at the thought of our living well and feel sadness at the thought of our not living well. We will feel anger at injustice, pride when we are being virtuous, and shame when we fail to live up to our own principles. And we will love when we find the person who embodies our values. Our emotions provide us with a very literal motivation to live well.

Unfortunately, many people will not experience this connection between their emotions and ethics, since they hold inconsistent beliefs and do not always even know why they believe the things that they believe. This means that they will have emotional responses to beliefs that do not fit with their conscious conception of who they are; that is, emotional responses that are "wrong" for them. Since the emotional process is capable of operating on any of our beliefs, it follows that if we have inconsistent beliefs, then we will have inconsistent emotions (see Chapter 2). Luckily anyone can achieve unity in their beliefs through introspection (perhaps with the help of a psychologist or psychotherapist) and a dedication to always understanding the justification for their beliefs and how any particular belief fits in with the rest of their conceptual framework. Those who are willing to do this and to achieve unity in their beliefs will be able to experience the reality of their ethical beliefs in the form of their emotions.

By experiencing the reality of our beliefs (in particular our ethical beliefs) through our emotions, we have a continuous motivation to live well. Our emotions become a constant advocate of our beliefs, rewarding us for living well and punishing us for living badly. Of course, this assumes our beliefs are good. Otherwise, this can create a vicious cycle as our emotions can reward us for living badly if doing so is consistent with our beliefs and (false) values. Our emotional mechanism does not know good from evil: it only knows to reward us for living consistently with our beliefs. In order to know whether our emotional mechanism is helping us to live well, we need to have the right kind

---

[i] To the extent that the Stoics advocate *ataraxia* (serenity), we can endorse this goal. But to achieve this by radically limiting the scope of our values to our own virtue, and giving up the external world, is too great a cost and would destroy the possibility of happiness. So, we must reject their method. To the extent that the Stoics advocate *apatheia* (indifference), or lack of any strong emotion, we must reject this as even a desirable end.

of philosophy—specifically, the right kind of ethics.

If we can achieve this tight integration of our emotions and our ethics, we can come to live *passionately* ethical lives: rich, fulfilled, moral lives full of meaning. The kind of life where, at the end of our last day, we will be able to look back at our life and be proud. Furthermore, the connection that we establish between our philosophy and emotions will have deep implications for our ability to love (Chapter 3) and have relationships (Chapter 4), for our sexual attraction (Chapter 5), and even our sexual identity (Chapter 6). After all, our sexuality is an important part of a human life and, thus, it will play an important role in making life meaningful for most of us (we will return to this point later in the book). Let us turn now to human nature and see the connection between it and ethics.

2. Human Nature and the Foundation of Ethics

Learn to value yourself, which means:
to fight for your happiness.[19]
~Ayn Rand

Our inquiry into ethics must begin with a single question: "What is it to live a good human life?"[i] It is vitally important that we know, really and concretely, what it would mean for us to live a good life. We must be able to imagine a real and vivid picture of what our life would look like if it were going well.

This is why I am a eudaimonist. Eudaimonism is a moral system concerned with living a full and rich human life. The closest word in English is "happiness," but this has come to mean something more like the feeling of joy or contentment. Although I will still use the word happiness, know that I mean something richer than its common usage: I mean living a rich and flourishing life as a person. For a eudaimonist, morality is not about following the rules of an imaginary father-figure, sacrificing ourselves for others, or blindly doing our duty; that is, it is not primarily other-oriented at all. Rather, for the eudaimonist, morality is about an individual making good choices and developing his character, in order to live the best kind of life open to him. This is important to remember because someone who comes from a religious tradition or even takes the loose ideas about morality from their culture, will be thinking of morality in a way that is completely different than how we will be using it here.

---

[i] Of course, there is an earlier meta-ethical question of why we should inquire into Ethics at all, on which point I agree with Ayn Rand that: "The first question that has to be answered, as a precondition of any attempt to define, to judge or to accept any specific system of ethics, is: *Why* does man need a code of values? Let me stress this. The first question is not: What particular code of values should man accept? The first question is: Does man need values at all—and why?" (*VOS*, "The Objectivist Ethics," 13). We need ethics because we can die and a good life is not guaranteed.

At least for now, we must try to let go of our previous ideas about morality and have an open mind for our inquiry.[i]

Eudaimonism has been around for thousands of years, well before most of the current religions came onto the scene. Aristotle was one of the first eudaimonists[ii] and there is a eudaimonist tradition stretching all the way through the present to Ayn Rand, who helped to refine the ideas of eudaimonism into a more consistent system.[iii] While our account of eudaimonism is grounded in these philosophers, it is not the same as either: our account of eudaimonism is new.[iv]

The core idea of eudaimonism is the idea that morality is a set of principles to help an individual live a good human life: not to just achieve pleasure in the short run or to sacrifice the present for the future, but to live a rich life that is multi-faceted and encompasses the many things a person needs to live well. Some of the things that a person needs to be truly happy are: rationality and the other virtues, friends, love, money, a productive career[v], and health.[20] Some of these things, like money, are merely necessary for happiness, while others are both necessary for happiness and part of it. Aristotle called these latter things "constitutive of happiness," because these things make up or *constitute* what it is to live well.[21] Happiness is not something *apart* from these things, happiness *is* these things: happiness is like the image that emerges from the completed puzzle. While the things that make up happiness are largely within our control, there is certainly a degree of moral luck with some of them and sometimes we may fail even though we acted as well as we could have.[vi] Nevertheless, even in these cases where we fail due to circumstances outside

---

[i] We will treat the terms "ethics" and "morality" as synonymous and consider them to mean the branch of philosophy that deals with human action and what humans *should* do.

[ii] Although Aristotle is frequently described as doing "virtue ethics," this is a deceptive misnomer. Aristotle is clear that we should "call things after the ends they realize" (*De Anima*, 416^{b}22) and the end of Aristotle's Ethics is *eudaimonia*, not virtue. Thus, Aristotle does *eudaimonistic ethics*, not virtue ethics. This is more than mere semantics: the goal of Aristotle's ethics is not simply to be virtuous, but to be virtuous *in order to live well*.

[iii] This is not to discount work by Julia Annas or other recent eudaimonists, but merely to say two things: 1) I do not fall into that part of the eudaimonist tradition and 2) I think that part of the Eudaimonist tradition suffers from some internal contradictions. The contradictions are particularly glaring with communitarian and altruistic eudaimonists. Annas even goes so far as to claim that "Ethics is fundamentally about the good of *others*, not my good." ("Virtue Ethics and the Charge of Egoism," *Morality and Self-Interest*, p. 205)

[iv] While I take the overall structure of my account of eudaimonism from Aristotle, he lacks a good account of the motivation for ethics and has no basis for his views on virtue. Rand has a much better overall view of ethics, including her views about rationality and virtue, but has a thin account of happiness and that of which it is comprised. Part of my goal is to take the best that each of them has to offer and to refine it with my own contributions.

[v] This should be thought of as producing values in life, whether or not it makes money.

[vi] "Moral luck" is simply the recognition that we do not have full control over all situations and that many of the things that happen in our lives, even things that have significant impact, are beyond our control.

our control, a good character enables us to weather these bad times more easily than we would have otherwise.[i]

Now, someone may be wondering what this has to do with sex. Remember that we are trying to understand sexual ethics and how to incorporate sex into our lives in such a way that we are able to achieve the best kind of life possible. In order to do that, we must first understand ethics more broadly and what it would mean to live a good life. How can we understand what it could mean to integrate sex into our lives in such a way as to achieve the best kind of life possible, if we do not even understand what a good life might be in the first place?

We must ground our ethical inquiry in human nature, if we hope to construct a system of ethics for human life, as opposed to a good horse life or a good cat life. While some people hear the term "human nature" and think of excuses for otherwise dubious actions (*e.g.*, "How could we expect him not to cheat on his wife? It's only human nature."), others think that even identifying human nature is impossible. Yet, we can identify human nature and doing so will help our inquiry. Just because people have the capacity to act in almost any way they see fit, to construct societies that are radically different from each other, and even have drastically different lifestyles from each other, does not mean that there is no underlying human nature. Indeed, comparing these different cultures can actually help us to see the things that *are not* essential to human nature and thus bring us closer to understanding it.

In order to identify human nature, we need to understand the fundamental attribute that explains the other things we know about humans. Unlike other animals, our means of survival is not primarily physical: humans do not have larger claws than other predators, nor bigger teeth, nor wings with which to fly. The human means of survival is our mind, specifically our faculty of reason.[ii] It is reason that underlies all of our most fundamental and distinctly human characteristics: from our ability to form concepts and hence language, to our ability for judgements and evaluation, to logic, science, and technology.[iii] Indeed, this very book, the homes we live in, and how we get to work every day are all products of reason. Broadly, we should understand reason as that faculty of our consciousness that helps us to understand and interact with reality.[iv] As such, it is of the utmost importance in ethics: ethics is about how to live a human life and reason is our primary faculty for interacting with the world outside ourselves, the world in which we have to live.

---

[i] We will return to this point in the section "Character and Happiness" later in the chapter.

[ii] I take this point from Ayn Rand's "The Objectivist Ethics" in *The Virtue of Selfishness*.

[iii] It is not that reason is unknown in other animals, but our capacity is so greatly different from any other animal's that it should be understood as a qualitative difference arising from an extreme quantitative difference.

[iv] A discussion of the precise nature and limits of reason, while interesting, is beyond the scope of this book.

Yet, it is not reason alone that defines human nature. This might lead us to the absurdity of claiming that humans are merely our "souls" *a la* Descartes. Importantly, we are *embodied* rational agents or, as Aristotle says, we are the *rational animal*. The fact that we have bodies of a certain sort is an essential fact of humans. We are integrated beings of both mind and body and inseparably so: we are born embodied, we live embodied, and die embodied.[i]

The fact that we are embodied entails that we die. This is one reason why people are so afraid to admit our embodiment. These people are afraid because, to return just briefly to our discussion from the last section, they worry that the fact that we will ultimately die makes life meaningless. However, as we have already seen, life does not cease to have meaning if it eventually ends. Indeed, quite the opposite. Values and meaning *require* our eventual death: it is only *because* we can die that our lives can have meaning.

Consider that all of a person's reasons for action come from a need to get something done: we need to eat to not starve, we need to go to work to earn money, we need money to buy food to eat, *etc*. All of these can be reduced down to this: we want to keep living. If our continued existence was guaranteed, if we were immortal and death were impossible, then there would be no reason to take any action at all.[ii] To see why this is so, let us hypothesize an immortal demon. Would this demon need to eat or drink? No, it cannot die. It might choose to eat or drink, but it would not *need* to do so and would have no reason to do so. Would anything ever be urgent to it? No, it has no needs at all, and so would never need anything urgently. An immortal demon would have no reason for taking any action ever: nothing could be good for it (help its life) or bad for it (harm its life), because it cannot die. Help and harm presuppose life and death. The ultimate impetus for all purposeful action is the desire to live and if we remove this impetus, then we destroy the foundation for any meaningful action as we have removed the very possibility of any *reason* for action.[iii] Thus, if this demon existed, it could not help but have an empty and meaningless existence.[iv] It would be the same for any being that could not die.

Death is a necessary part of life: all living things die. Without death, there could be no values, because values are things that benefit our lives. Or, to put it differently: if we could not die, then we could not have values because nothing could benefit or harm us (as in the case of the immortal demon).

---

[i] Thus, we must reject dualism—the view that our mind is separable from our body. See Volume 2, Chapter 10 for a more detailed inquiry into this point.

[ii] Immortality should be contrasted with the case of immortability, where a being does not die unless killed (as opposed to most living things which age and die). This case would be entirely different because the immortable being would still die and values would still be possible.

[iii] Which is not to say that all actions *actually* further one's life. Clearly human beings can act in ways that are counter to their survival, but it is that survival that gives ultimate meaning to action.

[iv] For this reason, if gods existed, we should pity them for the absurdity of their meaningless existence.

Without death, there could be no such thing as living well (and definitely no reason to seek it). Death is not the antithesis of *ethics*; death is the *impetus* of ethics. Death *creates* the possibility of values and meaning. Thus, we are lucky that we will eventually die. *Memento Mori.*

We should celebrate our eventual death, because it gives the possibility of meaning to our lives. Given that we are mortal and our lives are finite, every moment we are alive is precious.[i] However, humans are not born knowing which actions will help them to live a good life and achieve happiness and which actions will bring them to ruin or death. We are not born with this knowledge, but that does not make it any less critical for our success in life. It is also the reason why we must have ethics: the guidance of what kinds of ends are good is important for us, since we need to act to live and we only have one life. While we could try to live through trial and error, we are much better served living by the principles of ethics so we do not have to repeat the mistakes from which others have already learned. It is not that we could not perhaps stumble upon the right way to live, but why waste our lives in this endeavor if we already have clear principles to help us achieve our values in life? Thus, our need for ethics arises from our very nature and is motivated by our desire to live.

3. Principled Ethics

Existence is to all men a thing to be chosen and loved.[22]
~ Aristotle

We have already said that eudaimonism is uniquely capable of handling sexual ethics; yet, it is not simply that it helps us to achieve good and rich lives that makes it so. Rather, eudaimonism approaches sexual ethics in a way no other ethical system can. In this section, we will see more broadly why this is, before moving onto a more in-depth analysis of eudaimonism later in the chapter.

---

[i] I connect this with Nietzsche's idea of the eternal recurrence and whether we would choose to affirm the choices we are making if we had to repeat them over and over through eternity. For the person who loves his life, this would be a blessing; for the wicked person, it would be a curse:

"What, if some day or night a demon were to steal after you into your loneliest loneliness and say to you: 'This life as you now live it and have lived it, you will have to live once more and innumerable times more' ... Would you not throw yourself down and gnash your teeth and curse the demon who spoke thus? Or did you once experience a tremendous moment when you would have answered him: 'You are a god and never have I heard anything more divine.' If this thought were to gain possession of you, it would change you, as you are, or perhaps crush you. The question in each and every thing, 'Do you want this once more and innumerable times more?' would weigh upon your actions as the greatest stress. Or how well disposed would you have to become to yourself and to life to *crave nothing more fervently* than this ultimate eternal confirmation and seal?" Nietzsche, *The Gay Science*, §341.

Rules or Principles

One of the major differences between eudaimonism and most other ethical systems is that it relies on moral principles, not rules. A "rule" is always a command, usually of the form "You must…" or the more archaic "Thou shalt…" (*e.g.*, "You must not lie"). A rule is absolute and irrespective of context; for example, Kant argued that even if a person could save the life of their beloved by lying to a murderer, they must not lie.[i] A principle, on the other hand, gives general guidance to a person that they must then apply to their own life. A principle might be of the form "Honesty is important because it preserves our connection to reality and we need this to successfully live in the world." A principle does not command that we be honest; instead, it tells us why it is important and we must decide how to apply that to our lives ourselves.

A principled system of ethics does not attempt to create universal rules to be applied to any situation without consideration of the context or the consequences. Rather, principled ethics operate *conditionally* (*i.e.*, they take the form "do X, if Y") and are to be applied by the agent to particular situations. In our example of honesty above, a person would only do this (*e.g.*, be honest) if they wished to live. There is no *command* in the principle for the agent to be honest.

The conditional nature of principles is unique to eudaimonism: one need only do X, if one desires Y.[ii] Since eudaimonism is designed to guide human life, its conditional nature is based upon the agent's desire to keep living: our conditional ethics is of the form "do X, if you wish to live." This serves as a continual reminder that the choice to live is not a one-time choice, but a perpetual choice evidenced in our every action. At the same time, it is also a recognition that we are free in our choices, that there is no such thing as intrinsic morality just out in the world. Sexual ethics cannot rely on a rule-based system because we cannot know the future and sexuality is much too dependent on the individuals involved to create broad rules.[iii] Instead, eudaimonism gives individuals the framework to understand what a good choice would be and the tools to make that choice, letting the individuals in question apply it to their own lives.

It is a person's desire to live that "binds" them into a eudaimonist ethic:

---

[i] See Immanuel Kant's: *"On a Supposed Right to Tell Lies from Benevolent Motives."*

[ii] In her essay "Causality Versus Duty," Ayn Rand puts the point thus: "Reality confronts a man with a great many 'must's,' but all of them are conditional; the formula of realistic necessity is: 'You must, if—' and the 'if' stands for man's choice: '—if you want to achieve a certain goal'." *Philosophy: Who Needs It*, p. 99.

[iii] We will deal with the practical application in depth in Volume 2. However, as a broad point, consider the wide variety of human sexual expression. How could anyone construct a rule that could cover such a diverse phenomenon? Rules would only be appropriate if humans were all alike and had identical preferences and desires.

which makes sense, since it is also the motivating force behind eudaimonism.[i] There could be no such thing as a commandment in eudaimonism or even a moral imperative, at least that did not end in "if you want to live." Now, lest it be thought that this is no more than a fancy kind of subjectivism, eudaimonism does not endorse any kind of action whatsoever. There are limits placed on the kinds of moral behavior and these are set by human nature and the requirements of a good human life. It is important to understand that for a eudaimonist, to live and to live well is the same thing: living organisms are either flourishing or they are declining. There is no middle ground.[ii] An animal that is "merely alive" is an animal nearly dead. Living implies living well.

Now, although eudaimonism is based in human nature, this gives us only general information about which things benefit humans and which things hurt us. It does not say anything about the ends a person ought to choose for their life, including their central purpose in life. It does not tell us to be doctors as opposed to librarians. It does not tell us to enjoy hiking instead of playing the piano. It does not tell us to own dogs or cats. Although we will discuss this point more fully shortly, eudaimonism only gives the broad strokes, such as: we need a productive career, we need healthy hobbies, and pets can bring joy into our lives. Human nature sets the standard by which we judge actions broadly, but the specific purpose of ethics is an individual's happiness, and our nature can tell us nothing specific about that.[iii]

---

[i] Someone might object here that if a person did not want to live, then they would exempt themselves from ethics. This is true in one sense, but not in another. It is false because the person is human and ethics is based in the reality of human nature, so the principles still apply to him and others can even judge him accordingly for the purpose of determining whether his actions will be detrimental to *their* lives. However, it is true in the sense that a person who truly did not wish to live would either commit suicide or let himself die from inaction. Either way, ethics can have no binding force on a dead person.

[ii] Rand makes this point beautifully in "The Objectivist Ethics" from the *Virtue of Selfishness:* "The maintenance of life and the pursuit of happiness are not two separate issues. To hold one's own life as one's ultimate value, and one's own happiness as one's highest purpose are two aspects of the same achievement. Existentially, the activity of pursuing rational goals is the activity of maintaining one's life; psychologically, its result, reward and concomitant is an emotional state of happiness. It is by experiencing happiness that one lives one's life, in any hour, year, or the whole of it. And when one experiences the kind of pure happiness that is an end in itself—the kind that makes one think: 'This is worth living for'—what one is greeting and affirming in emotional terms is the metaphysical fact that life is an end in itself." (p. 32)

[iii] Human life is the standard of ethics, but the purpose is each individual's happiness. The difference between the standard and purpose is this: the standard provides the objective criteria of judgement based on the reality of human nature, while the purpose of ethics is the application of this by an individual to his life in order to help him achieve happiness (I follow Rand in this distinction, as in *VOS,* 27). This is how objectivity can be combined with conditional principles in order to achieve an ethic that is both rooted in metaphysical fact and able to achieve normativity, while also being targeted at the individual's happiness, without being subjective.

Positivity and Normativity

The fact that eudaimonism is a conditional system of principles, which come into play only if we choose to live, is very important. If we were to base ethics simply on the facts of human nature and then attempt to dictate right and wrong from this, we would run smack into a classic philosophical problem, first identified by David Hume, called the "is/ought dichotomy." According to the dichotomy, it is not possible to construct an ethical system — a system of "oughts" — from a set of facts. This is not too hard to see. For example, if we were to tell someone not to eat fatty foods, then they could reasonably ask "why not?" There can be no answer to this question without reference to some end that they want to achieve. We might say that they should not eat the fatty foods because they are high in calories; but, what if they are a wrestler, like Milo, who is trying to gain weight? Our advice will lead to the opposite of what they want to achieve. If the statement is to have moral import, it must be conditional on their ends; or, if we want a person to care about something, we must give them some reason to care.

It is possible to create an objective system of ethics based on fact, but the facts themselves cannot be the origin of the binding force of morality, or what is called "normativity."[i] This can easily be seen if one simply asks "why?" of any normative claim based *simply* on facts. However, we can still create a normative system from positive facts through the use of these conditional principles.[ii] We cannot say "you should do X" and leave it at that, because someone could easily rejoin "why?" and we would have no response. We *can* say: "you should do certain actions, if you wish to live" or "You should not eat so much that it harms your health, if you wish to live well." Although the requirements of human life are objective facts, the normativity enters from the agent's desire to achieve the end in question: morality only arises once we choose to live.[iii]

Phronesis

In eudaimonism, it is up to the individual to apply the principles to his life in ways that will be beneficial to him.[iv] Because principles are general, they do

---

[i] Nietzsche, in *Beyond Good and Evil* (epigram 108), makes this same point: "There are no moral phenomena at all, but only a moral interpretation of phenomena."

[ii] Some people worry that this means we could have no moral reason to choose to live. This is true. To say that there is a moral reason to live would be to beg the question. Yet, all is not lost. While we cannot have "moral reasons" to choose to live, we can still have reasons and desires to do so: we might simply enjoy being alive, want to explore the world, or be engaged in projects, *etc.*

[iii] All normativity is, thus, teleological in nature.

[iv] Someone might object that this account of principles goes against the common usage of "principled" which takes it to mean "unyielding and rigid," in the way that we have described

not apply directly in every case, nor are they meant to.[i] Principles are designed to be sensitive to context; that is, they are sensitive to the situation in which the person acts. For example, it is a general principle that a person should never fake reality either to themselves (*e.g.*, evading or repressing) or to another (*e.g.*, lying). Now, let us return briefly to our Kantian example and suppose another murderer turns up at our door. Let us say that this murderer wants to know if our best friend has taken refuge at our house. If we tell him the truth: that indeed, our best friend is there hiding from the murderer, then the murderer will kill him (and likely us for harboring him). If we lie to the murderer, he will leave to continue looking for our best friend and we both will be safe. If we merely remain silent, the murderer will kill us, then search our house, likely finding our friend and killing him anyway.

So, what do we do? Obviously, we lie (we might also consider moving to a place with fewer murderers). Lying is, in this context, the *moral* thing to do. In fact, to tell the truth in this context would be *immoral*. Why? Because morality is supposed to help us live a good life and friends are an important part of this: morality is not a noose to be hung around our neck, but a torch to guide our way through the darkness. The prohibition on faking reality is very important, because once we lose touch with reality, then we have made it extremely hard, if not impossible, to live well. But, there is little danger of that from this single lie to the murderer. Indeed, telling the truth to the murderer would be a great injustice: aiding a murderer is immoral and it is even worse to sacrifice our values and harm our long-term interests by giving up our friend for the sake of a rule.[ii]

As this example illustrates, a principled ethics requires us to think about moral principles, our life and context, and how we should best apply these principles to our life in order to live well. Aristotle called this *phronesis*, or practical wisdom, but it is no more than being active and engaged with our life and thinking about our actions and how they affect our flourishing.[iii] Aristotle thought that *phronesis*[iv] was foundational to virtue: "virtue [is] that which is in accordance with practical wisdom."[23] This is because virtue is the cultivated dispositions of character necessary for achieving a good life (we will explore this in depth below), but they are acquired, as well as practiced, through *phronesis*. That is, while someone might tell us that honesty is a virtue and tell us

---

rules. Perhaps so. The principled person is not rigid in the sense that he refuses to consider options or alternatives; he simply sees the context of his life and refuses to betray it or act against it.

[i] In Volume 2, we will explore the "eudaimonist rubric" as an aid to *phronesis* in thinking about how to deal with practical issues in sexual ethics.

[ii] To make matters even worse, it is, to borrow from Anscombe, a rule without a rule-giver (see her essay "Modern Moral Philosophy").

[iii] We will be using "*phronesis*" and "practical wisdom" interchangeably.

[iv] *Phronesis*, for Aristotle, is not simply teleological reasoning, although it is a kind of teleological reasoning, but reasoning specifically about how to live a good life. (*NE*, VI.5.1140a25).

what that means in general, applying this to our life is done by *phronesis*. We need to understand the principle of honesty, including its practical benefit, and then apply this principle to the specific context of our life. It is the wisdom and judgement of how to apply principles correctly to our life that constitutes *phronesis*.

Importantly, none of the virtues are things that we can simply choose once and consider ourselves to have achieved them: they are ongoing choices that we must make to be a certain kind of person and live a certain kind of life. This means that even once we acquire the disposition to be honest, we will still need *phronesis* to apply this to our life. Part of this process relies on experience and the knowledge we gain from it, including: integrating our experience into our existing framework of knowledge, thinking critically about our experiences and whether our actions had the outcomes we predicted, and seeing the connections between our experiences and our overall aims and goals. In this way, *phronesis* is also very important to evaluation and identifying values in our lives. *Phronesis* is a skill, and like any skill, we must purposefully practice it if we wish it to improve.

Phronesis is incredibly important for eudaimonism. Indeed, one would not be able to even attempt to practice eudaimonism without some skill with *phronesis*. Luckily, this is a skill we all already have, at least in some degree. We all have experience trying to live by our beliefs and seeing how this plays out in the world: Did we judge correctly? Did we achieve our ends? Were there factors that we did not anticipate or were outside our control? If we think about how to bring our beliefs into the world successfully and practice them, then we can improve our skill with *phronesis* and, at the same time, come to live better lives. Now that we have seen how *phronesis*, or practical wisdom, works, let us contrast this with a rule-based system of ethics to show just how radical this really is.

Rule-based Systems

Historically, most systems of ethics have been constructed as set of rules. Whether these are rules from a god, rules from a divinely appointed king, rules from some abstract "moral law," or even rules from society, they are all systems of rules. (In contrast, remember that the binding force of eudaimonism comes from our *choice* to live). Here, let us focus just on those sets of rules that also purport to be moral rules.

There are different motivations behind these theories, but they are united in that they assume that only rules could have any kind of binding force on a person[i] and that it is necessary for us to be in possession of answers to ethical

---

[i] Anscombe, in her brilliant essay "Modern Moral Philosophy," makes the point that the idea that rules and duty have a unique "moral force" is a relic of the Christian perversion of ethics through divine command theory. It did this by conflating morality with divine legislation and, if a person violated this divine moral "law," then he was evil *in toto* (a "sinner" or completely

situations before they arise. There are two possible reasons ultimately motivating a rule-based ethic: that individual people are incapable of discovering moral truths and applying them to their own life (*phronesis* is impossible or prohibitively hard) or, more simply, that the one who makes the rules is capable of doing a much better job than "regular" people would be, so he should, therefore, be able to make the rules. Of course, he who makes the rules is the ruler. Much as a parent can set rules for a child and punish them if they disobey, the ruler takes on the role of parent to his children (or subjects) and creates rules for them to live by, since, of course, they are incapable of doing it for themselves.

The ultimate force behind these allegedly moral rules is just that: force. We must obey the rules or we will be *punished*. Sometimes this punishment is very straightforward and direct, like Socrates being put to death by the Athenian Democracy, and sometimes the punishment is amorphous, like a deity who will allegedly punish us sometime after our death. No matter where on the spectrum of rule-based ethical systems, it is force that sits behind them. Any rule that is not contingent on something the individual cares about necessarily implies force; else how could the individual be compelled to act? In this way, the ultimate justification of these kinds of ethics is a threat: do it or be punished. This is no real system of ethics: might does not make right, even if someone can compel us to act how they choose. Moral rules are designed to serve the ruler, not the ruled.

However, it is worse than this. Even if a ruler was to impose upon us the duty of acting perfectly virtuously under the harshest punishments and we were to comply, this would still not lead to happiness. We must be the motive power of our own happiness or we will end up with, at the very best, a thin façade of happiness. Happiness is not simply copying certain activities and hoping that happiness will then arise. Happiness is a way of being engaged with our life and the experience of it going well. Thus, even in the best possible case a rule-based ethic cannot bring about happiness and history shows that the best-case scenario is rare. For this reason, all rule-based systems of ethics are illegitimate and, since they are simply systems of force, they are not systems of ethics at all.

There is a further problem with nearly every system of rule-based ethics.[i] These systems of moral rules claim to be absolutely true, irrespective of the context. For example, according to Christians, we can memorize a small set of rules (*e.g.*, their "ten commandments") and, through these, have prepackaged answers to any situation, because the answers do not change based on the situation. According to the Christian ten commandments, there are no situations where lying is moral: "thou shall not lie," not "thou shall not lie, unless…".[ii]

"evil person") and a moral outlaw of the worst kind. He was a categorically bad person.
[i] Except, perhaps, Utilitarianism.
[ii] The "ninth commandment" of Christianity is often given as "thou shall not lie," even though

Unfortunately, this commitment to the absolute nature of the rules requires the commitment to another, sometimes hidden, thesis: the consequences of the rules are irrelevant. A universal rule is equally valid no matter the context and since the same action will have different outcomes in different contexts, those who advocate universal rules must be indifferent to the consequences if they wish to insist on the rule's universality. To return to our example of the murderer looking for our best friend, if there is a rule such as "thou shalt not lie," then lying is simply wrong and we should not lie in *any* situation; not even if a small lie would save the life of our best friend and maybe our own as well. But, we might ask, why should we not lie to save our friend? Why must we tell the murderer where our friend is hiding when he asks, simply to avoid lying?

At this point the rule advocate can answer in one of two ways: it is intrinsically wrong or it is wrong because a moral authority has declared it wrong. The former is begging the question: to be *intrinsically* immoral means that something is immoral *because* immorality is part of its nature. If that sounds like nonsense, it is because it is. In the latter case, an action is right or wrong based solely on the judgement of the authority; but by what standard does the authority himself judge?[i] Ultimately, a system of moral *rules* is self-contradictory: its authority inevitably reduces to "because you will be punished if you do not" and this is no moral justification at all.[ii] A system of ethics based on rules will invariably prove to be inimical to human life, as some outcomes will improve one's life, while other outcomes will impede or damage one's life: in reality, different actions will have different outcomes in different situations. If we care about human life, ethics cannot be constructed as a system of rules.[iii]

---

it is actually "Thou shalt not bear false witness against thy neighbour" in the King James version of their Bible (Exodus 20:16). I am using the more straightforward and common understanding of it in my argument here, although my argument would apply, *mutatis mutandis*, to any moral rule.

[i] This is fundamentally the problem of Plato's *Euthyphro*.

[ii] Now, a system of rules can be perfectly appropriate in the law, but the law does not claim to be a moral system. Rules give very clear guidance and this is very useful for the law and for the citizenry knowing what is permissible and not permissible. However, even here, the rules of the law should be sensitive to the principles from which they arise. For example, if the law says "An adult may not have sex with anyone less than 18 years old" and two 17-year-olds are in an intimate relationship, they should not be considered to be committing a crime because one of them happens to have a birthday before the other. The law should be sensitive to the deeper principles here about consent and coercion.

[iii] One might, understandably, suppose here that Kant provides a counter-example to this. Yet, one would be mistaken. While Kant initially portrays his ethics to be grounded in the nature of a rational agent (whatever this is), he ultimately reveals himself to be doing no more than putting a thin veneer over Christian ethics in the guise of "reason." He is forced, when pushed on why we should be moral, to conclude that both the Christian God and an immortal soul are both necessary so that his God can assure that those who are virtuous will be rewarded: "the existence of a cause of nature, distinct from nature, which contains the ground of this connection, namely the exact correspondence of happiness with morality" (*Critique of Practical*

Principled Ethics

Eudaimonism, being based on *principles* instead of rules, is a radical departure from most conceptions of ethics. Rule-based ethics are great for condemning certain actions or others for performing these actions, but they are not helpful for living well. In contrast, eudaimonism is not primarily about how to judge others, but about how to lead the best life possible. For most people, this radical departure will take much thought to get used to, since judgemental ethics has been dominant in our culture. Yet, it is liberating to be free of worry about what everyone else is doing and to focus on our own personal life. This does not mean that we will never need to morally judge another, but that it would only be done in the context of our own happiness and not as one of the primary purposes of ethics. Our new ethical focus puts an individual's welfare at the center of the stage and tells him to make the most of his life, if he so chooses.[i]

It should now be clear, if we recall the Introduction, how different our position is from those of our predecessors in the history of Philosophy: we do not think that we have a duty to cultivate dispositions in order to obey moral rules, nor do we think that our emotions are things to be resisted (although we will have to wait for Chapter 2 for a full exposition of this latter point). We reject both the concepts of "duty" and of "moral rules" as being illegitimate and of having no connection to morality at all. As a consequence of this fundamental moral difference, *Eros and Ethos* presents a new option for how we should view sexuality: not as something to ward against with rules, but as an important moral facet of our lives through which we can express our moral selves, as we shall see.

4. Rational Egoism

The good man should be a lover of self.[24]
~ Aristotle

Self-defeating Egoism

In the last section, we said that eudaimonism is uniquely capable of handling sexual ethics and this is partly because eudaimonism puts the focus of ethics on an individual's welfare and tells him to make the most of his life. This is an

---

Reason, 5:125). Kant is ultimately, as Nietzsche says, a couched Christian and his entire ethical system ultimately rests on "God said so."

[i] It would be impossible for a rule-based system to be composed of rules that put an individual's happiness first, because it would be impossible to construct rules to account for the wide variety of human lives and experiences. While principles can handle this kind of variety, rules cannot be constructed to do so: their rigidity prohibits it.

egoistic enterprise. Unfortunately, when many people hear "egoism," they think of the person who is willing to walk over piles of bodies just to achieve his ends, whatever they may happen to be. However, this is not egoism at all, as we shall see.[i]

Egoism, in its essence, is simply the idea that a person should act in his own interest. It might appear that egoism says nothing about the ends that a person should pursue; however, if the egoist were to pick self-defeating ends that were contrary to his life, then these would not be egoistic ends. There is a contradiction if an alleged egoist chooses ends that are not consistent with his long-term life and interests. This limits the scope of ends that the true egoist can pursue: any end which works against his happiness would be irrational and, therefore, not egoistic. For example, imagine a person who says he wants to live in a good world and bemoans that the world is getting worse. Yet, he is unkind to others arbitrarily. He snaps at them, rudely cuts people off while driving, and generally behaves narcissistically, as though only he matters in the world. What is wrong with his actions is not that he is acting egoistically to achieve his own interests (he is, in fact, *not* achieving his own interests), but rather that the he is acting irrationally. A person who wants to live in a good world, and a reasonable person should want this, should not take the kinds of actions that cause the world to become worse (even on a small scale). Thus, an actual egoist would not act like that because he has a personal interest in the world being a good and benevolent place. The person above is acting neither rationally nor egoistically. This highlights a critically important point: *rational egoism is the only coherent form of egoism*.[ii] The "egoist" who does whatever he likes simply because he wants it is no egoist at all.

This tension between real egoism and fake, or self-defeating, egoism is one reason why Rand attacked the common cultural idea of "selfishness." She explained that she wanted to reclaim the idea of selfishness and to break the "package-deal" that selfishness had become: our culture had illegitimately packaged the idea of rationally acting to achieve a good life together with the idea of engaging in whatever irrational whim may strike us.[iii] This is a problem

---

[i] I take "egoistic" and "selfish" to be completely synonymous with each other and will use them interchangeably.

[ii] Both Rand and Aristotle make this point. Aristotle, for example, says: "Therefore the good man should be a lover of self (for he will both himself profit by doing noble acts, and will benefit his fellows), but the wicked man should not; for he will hurt both himself and his neighbors, following as he does evil passions." (*NE*, IX.8.1168^{a}10). It should also be clear from this that I am against Nietzsche's idea of egoism, insofar as Nietzsche has coherent positions on anything.

[iii] Rand considered the contemporary usage of "selfish" to be a package deal, which is an informal fallacy that she identified. The fallacy is done by "equating opposites by substituting nonessentials for their essential characteristics," which leads to the real differences being obliterated. For more on the "package-deal," see her essay "How to Read (and Not to Write)," *The Ayn Rand Letter*, p. 117. For more on the issue of selfishness, see *The Virtue of Selfishness*, "Introduction" and "The Objectivist Ethics."

because being truly selfish, being a real egoist, entails working to live the best kind of life that we can.[i] This precludes being irrational and arbitrarily harming others. The person who goes about making the world worse is no egoist.

To Condemn Egoism is to Destroy Morality

Eudaimonism, striving to live well, is fundamentally egoistic: choosing to live is a selfish choice, as is choosing to pursue happiness. Above we said that the purpose of ethics is to help an individual live the best life open to him. This is the core of egoism: I want a good life. Egoism is choosing to strive for the best life open to us and to make the most of the life we have. It is a commitment to ourselves to be the best we can and to not be passive with our lives. If we want to be happy, it is imperative that we act to pursue this: passivity does not lead to happiness. Happiness is only possible to the rational egoist.

Given this, consider what it would mean to condemn egoism. Since egoism simply means actions concerned with one's own interests and one's own life, to condemn egoism is to condemn an individual for daring to choose his own course in life and to live by his own judgement. The problem with this, as Rand correctly identifies, is that: "the doctrine that concern with one's own interests is evil means that man's desire to live is evil."[25] To say egoism is evil, regardless of how we go about achieving it, is to say that it is the very *pursuit* of our lives itself that is evil. But since we must take action to live, to *simply* condemn selfishness as evil is to condemn human life as evil.

If a person cannot morally pursue his own interests, then having a healthy sex life is out of the question. A person cannot attempt to construct a healthy sex life *entirely*, or even principally, on the basis of his partner's pleasure or desire. Imagine a couple attempting to have sex doing it *only* for each other and disregarding their own pleasure and enjoyment. Sex would become an unpleasant chore: an undesirable duty to perform simply for our partner. Healthy sex is necessarily selfish.

At this point we could reasonably ask why anyone would condemn an individual for simply acting in his own self-interest if his goals are rational. The problem comes from the clash of two diametrically opposed ethical systems: egoism and altruism.[ii] In egoism, the focus is the individual and the pursuit of his own personal happiness: an individual is properly the moral beneficiary of his actions. In altruism, the focus is others: it is *only* others who are the appropriate moral beneficiary of an individual's actions.[iii] Consequently,

---

[i] This is one of the largest differences between the ideas of selfishness as advocated by Nietzsche and Rand.

[ii] The term "altruism" was coined by the philosopher August Comte to be the antonym of egoism and means literally "other-ism."

[iii] The most immediate example of altruism for most people in the English-speaking world is Christian ethics.

altruism does not draw a distinction between an individual acting in his own rational self-interest and an individual acting irrationally to achieve his apparent self-interest; to an altruist, both are simply cases of an individual who should be acting for the good of others. Indeed, the altruist often conflates an egoist rationally acting for his own happiness and what we have called false egoism in order to paint both as bad and thus commits the fallacy of the package-deal. This conflation of the pursuit of irrational and rational ends is too obvious to be merely accidental: it purposely obscures the essential nature of each kind of action. In order to justify his position, the altruist must disregard all consequences of actions and instead focus merely on the beneficiary of the actions; otherwise it is not possible to lump the rational and irrational kinds of egoism together. Thus, because of the prevalence of altruism, good or evil stopped being a measure of whether an action benefited a person's life and instead gauged only *whom* the action was done for.

This change in emphasis from the benefit that an action has for an individual to *who* the beneficiary of the action is causes some interesting paradoxes. It culminates in the idea that the only thing that can be truly good is a good (*i.e.*, other-directed) will, regardless of the consequences. To the consistent altruist, for example, if our will is to aid another, and we inadvertently end up killing them, we are not only morally blameless for their death, since consequences are irrelevant, but also we should be praised for our good will.[i] The absurdity of this, to anyone concerned with life, should be shockingly apparent: *both* our intentions (will) and the outcome of our actions matter. Of course, there will be situations where we intend to do good things, but the outcome is not what we intended. But, we do not ignore the outcome: we judge the action by both the intention and the outcome. For example, we would not judge a nurse who accidently gave the patient the wrong medicine and killed him to be a murderer, since she did not intend to kill him. However, we also would not think her blameless: she did, in fact, kill someone (even if she lacks *mens rea*[ii]). To think that her simple good will is enough to exonerate her action is atrocious, but if we ignore the consequences of actions, as altruism must, we are led inevitably to exoneration. Since we live in the real world, the consequences of our actions matter.

---

[i] I agree with Nietzsche that Kant is merely a couched Christian who takes their position to its logical conclusions. For example, Kant says: "Nothing in the world—indeed nothing even beyond the world—can possibly be conceived which could be called good without qualification except a *good will*." From "First Section: Transition from the Common Rational Knowledge of Morals to the Philosophical," *Groundwork of the Metaphysic of Morals*.

[ii] "*Mens rea*" is a legal term meaning "guilty mind" that signifies a person acted with intent to commit a crime and did not do so accidentally.

Philanthropic Egoism

There is one other important point we need to consider. Egoism has typically been thought of as pursuing ends that do not include others: it is thought of as misanthropic. Yet, the conception of egoism that precludes others as being part of one's good is an impoverished one and is not consistent with rational egoism. The rational person is capable of incorporating others into his life. Moreover, we have already said that for most of us, happiness is impossible without love and friendship. These relationships entail an expansion of the self to include these others. We will talk about this in depth in Chapter 3 when we discuss erotic love, but the rationally selfish person can incorporate another person into his hierarchy of values and pursue another's good as his own by caring about his partner and internalizing his partner's values as his own. For example, in a good marriage, a husband acting to benefit his wife is also benefiting himself since his wife is a value to him, he values her ends, and her happiness directly impacts his.

We shall soon see that not only can a rationally selfish person value another person in this way, but also that certain kinds of relationships with others are *necessary* to achieve happiness. For example, both friendship and romantic relationships require one to incorporate another person into one's own happiness. Moreover, a good sex life contributes to the life of both partners: through it each can become better than they were on their own. For those that have sex properly integrated into their lives, it can help them to achieve happiness in a way not otherwise possible.

The final strike against the claim that egoism is misanthropic is the fact that only the egoist can truly be benevolent. The egoist does not have an obligation to act for the sake of others, so his benevolent actions are truly free and uncoerced (although, as we have shown, the very idea of an unchosen obligation is incoherent). The altruist, on the other hand, will constantly be under the strain of sacrifice and will grow to resent others who may not be sacrificing as much for him as he does for them. This resentment, which is inevitable under altruism, poisons any possibility of true benevolence.

So, is egoism misanthropic? Not if it is done correctly.

5. Values, Purpose, and Hierarchy

Soon we shall breathe our last.
Meanwhile, while we endure,
while we are among human beings,
let us cultivate humanity.[26]
~ Seneca

Most of us want to be happy. We want to live good and meaningful lives, have good friends and lovers, and enjoy our time while we are alive. These desires are good; but, how do we actually go about living good lives? We need a system of ethics.

Ethics is the science of living well and provides us with principles to help us work to achieve our happiness. But, how do we generate these principles? And how can we use these principles to give us concrete guidance in our lives? The principles that we will examine will be based on our choosing to live good human lives and they will all be aimed at helping to achieve this in reality. This section will pull together much of the groundwork we have laid in the previous sections to show how it all comes together into a cohesive whole that will help us to live the best life possible.

We have already seen how choosing to live makes ethics both possible and necessary, and that this is not one momentous choice, but is evidenced in our every choice and action. We have discussed how our choice to live entails certain things due to human nature, but we have not yet seen how this generates specific virtues. We have discussed that ethics must be principled and conditional, but we have not fully explored values. We have discussed how this is all egoistic, but we have not discussed how to really concretize it in our lives. Finally, all of this will hang on creating a certain type of chosen self, character, and setting ourselves up to both want to live well and enjoy it emotionally, which is how we experience the meaning of our lives. Let us turn now to filling in these gaps and seeing how it all comes together into a rich whole.

Central Purpose in Life

We must start by revisiting the idea of the central purpose in life and flesh it out to see its pivotal role in ethics and its practical utility in everyday life. In order for ethics to be helpful, we need, as Aristotle says, to set up some ideal of the good life at which to aim. Luckily, eudaimonism—and remember we are seeking *human happiness*, not the happiness appropriate to a tree or dog—can be aimed at any rational end. This is because flourishing is principally concerned with the *how* of living. The goal can be any rational end and the specific goal that a person chooses for their life will be determined by the kind of life they want to lead. This end will be a person's central purpose.[i]

For example, eudaimonism says that friends are important to a good life, but it does not say with whom we should be friends. Or, eudaimonism says that for most of us a good lover is important in life, but it does not specify if we should prefer brunettes, someone of the same sex, a family-man, or tall women. Or, eudaimonism says that a productive purpose is necessary in life, but it does not matter if we wish to be a philosopher or a chef, as long as we go about it

---

[i] Remember that happiness is not something that we can find in the world and then keep forever. Happiness arises from living a certain kind of life. Thus, we must aim at this. The core around which happiness revolves will be our central purpose in life.

the right way. These choices can be perfectly healthy and rational choices, as opposed to the man who enjoys the "excitement" of raping an unwilling woman or the woman who has as many children as possible so that she can attempt to birth meaning and a sense of self into the world. Eudaimonism does not tell us what, precisely, we should pursue in life, but it does help us to see the kinds of things that we need and then allows us to choose our own ends and goals. A central purpose is one of these things that a person must have, but it can be any rational end.

For most people, their central purpose in life will be their productive career. It is important to note that "productive" here means "producing values" and not "producing money." While money is a value, it is certainly not the only value. Thus, it should be read as inclusive of ends such as research, parenting, and others, as long as they are pursued seriously and they create value in a person's life. A person's productive career may not be their primary source of income and they may need to have another job or jobs to support themselves at it until they reach financial sustainability with their productive career (if they can at all). If a person is merely working a job to get by and the work that they really love, identify with, and that creates value in their life is unpaid, then it is that latter thing that is their productive career. Now, it should not be surprising that a person's central purpose is their productive career, because there is a great value for anyone in being independent and using their mind to deal with reality. In fact, a person's experience of using their mind to create values and be efficacious in the world is a sort of existential proof of their mental efficacy. Moreover, because people identify so strongly with their central purpose in life, being efficacious here has a large impact on their existential orientation and their ability to feel efficacious in the world overall (we will return to this point in Chapter 2), which means that their central purpose plays an important role in their mental health.

A person's central purpose, via productive career, is how they bring into reality many of their other values.[i] It also allows them to structure their lives in such a way that they can see the effects of their various actions on their overall lives and whether they are working to achieve their values. If a person does not have a single overarching purpose in their lives, then they have no way to understand how to best use their time and where to best place their efforts.[ii] However, a central purpose is not, by itself, sufficient for a rich life. Once a person has chosen the overall course of their life, their central purpose, they

---

[i] This should be obvious, but values entail action in the world to achieve them. Otherwise, we do not truly value the thing or else we lack the integrity to be true to our values (all other things being equal).

[ii] I do not know precisely how many purposes a person can hold as central purposes, but it is certainly a small number. I might be the kind of person whose central purpose is to be a philosopher, but also a good husband, and father. However, the more I take to be "central," the more conflicts I will have and the harder it will be to actually achieve *any* of my values.

need to elaborate the other values that will make their life meaningful and rich, as well as help them to achieve their central purpose.

Variations in Values

A person's central purpose is the keystone of their hierarchy of values: it sets the structure of a person's hierarchy of values and allows it to function.[i] The hierarchy of values is, just like its name suggests, a hierarchical ordering[ii] of a person's values, which are of two different *types*. The first and most important type of values is "core values," which define a person's identity (and which also includes their central purpose in life). The second type of values is "peripheral values," values that enrich a person's life, but which do not define them. While we need not know where every particular value is in the hierarchy or what type of value it is, we must have clearly identified core values so that the hierarchy can function correctly and help us to achieve these, since they are a big part of our happiness.

There are also three fundamentally different *kinds* of values. The first is "universal values," which are the necessary conditions for happiness and are universal to all people because they are based in, and necessitated by, our shared human nature. The second is "constitutional values," which are necessary for a particular person's happiness based on their unique constitution.[iii] The third is "personal values," which a person chooses to help to give happiness its richness, but whose role in happiness is not necessary. Before we continue our discussion of the hierarchy of values, it is important to pause briefly to examine these ideas, because we cannot understand the hierarchy of values until we better understand values, and the hierarchy of values is important to our quest to live well.

Core values are those values that define a person; they are the values that are *sine qua non* for a person. For example, let us say that our central purpose in life is to be a concert pianist, but we also care deeply about our spouse, our kids, developing our character, reading, target shooting, and being active in defense of liberty. Let us say that we care about these things so much that they make up a part of our identity: without these things, we would cease to be the

---

[i] The concept of "hierarchy of values" at use here is from Ayn Rand. Although the hierarchy of value is a very important ethical concept for Objectivism, Ayn Rand does not explain it in great detail in any of her writings. For some of her discussions, see: *Introduction to Objectivist Epistemology* 44; *The Virtue of Selfishness* 25, 44-46; and *Playboy's* "Interview with Ayn Rand" (March 1964).

[ii] This ranking is ordinal rather than cardinal, such that it focuses on the *relative* position of the values.

[iii] There is a wide variety of constitutions and many of these will culminate in a happiness that is roughly equivalent. However, certain constitutions will lead to an impoverished kind of happiness, compared to what is generally possible for humans. In these cases, the person should still try to live the best life open to them, to the extent that they are able.

same person. These, then, are our core values: things that we care about so much that they make up the core of our identity. If we were to somehow remove one of these values from a person, they would cease to be the same person (which is not to say that values can never change). Core values will vary quite a bit from person to person and can be made up of universal values, constitutional values, or personal values.

Peripheral values are those values that enrich a person's life, but do not define their identity. This is quite the wide spectrum of values between those that are very important to a person to more trivial pleasures. Peripheral values can range from games a person enjoys playing, particular foods they enjoy, or books of which they are fond. It is important to note that these things must still be objective values and further a person's life in order to be values at all. However, we should not take the requirement that they further a person's life as some rationalistic rule, but instead acknowledge that there are many ways a person's life can be improved and this will include things such as leisure and rest. Moreover, not every action a person takes needs to be in service to their central purpose in life and attempting to do so would certainly rob life of its richness and joy. We must understand a person's values in the full context of their life and being able to do so is one of the great advantages of the hierarchy.

Universal values are the necessary conditions for happiness and are universal to all people because they are based in, and necessitated by, human nature. That is, they are those things that are necessary to live a rich and fulfilling human life (we will explore them in detail below) and, as such, they do not vary from person to person. We can be said to hold the universal values when we care about them and work to achieve them in our lives, whether or not we practice them perfectly. As long as a person cares about the value, conscientiously works to achieve the value, and works to correct any mistakes, then they hold the values. The universal values that any particular person holds will be those values from the set of universal values that they have chosen to care about and work to bring about in their lives.[i]

We must work to actualize all of the universal values if we want to achieve happiness.[ii] Indeed, the process by which we actualize these universal values is what we call *virtue*. At the same time, we can actualize these universal values in different ways, as long as the particular way we choose to actualize the value fulfills the role of the universal value in question. To be more concrete, truth is a universal value and honesty is the virtue by which we achieve this value, but

---

[i] It is important to understand that we can value *processes* or *ways of living* that are ongoing over the course of our life. Indeed, this is common: if I say that I value honesty, I am not saying that I have now "achieved honesty" and can stop worrying about it. Rather, I am saying that I have cultivated the disposition to be honest and will continue to work to be honest in the future as well.

[ii] The universal values are necessary for happiness, but do not constitute it. The virtues are the activities by which we achieve the universal values and it is these that constitute happiness. This is because happiness is the *activity* of living well.

the particular way we exercise this virtue will depend on our judgement (which highlights the necessity of *phronesis* for our account). For example, there can be a legitimate disagreement about whether honesty requires that we tell other people what we think even when not asked: such as, without being solicited, we tell the partner of a sibling exactly what we think of them. While many people would think that honesty does not require it, and tact demands that we not do so, some people might think that it is required for honesty (perhaps if they are young or socially inept). However, if directly asked such a question, a person can deflect it or refuse to answer, but they cannot lie. There can, thus, be legitimate disagreements about how to best practice a virtue. Moreover, this also highlights the utility of the hierarchy. Lying is bad because it damages a universal value (our ability to interact with reality), but our exact course of action may depend on our other values and their relative importance. As we saw, we may even *need* to lie to save the life of our friend from the Kantian murderer.

Constitutional values are necessary conditions for a particular person's happiness, based on their constitution.[i] That is, certain things might be necessary for an individual's happiness due to their particular nature, but without being common to all humans like universal values because of variations in individual constitutions.[ii] For example, having children is a constitutional value for some people, because happiness would not be possible to these people without having children. At the same time, other people may be differently constituted such that they may deliberate about the choice or choose not to have children at all and are still able to achieve happiness. Sex, too, may be a constitutional value: most of us would consider sex so important that we would not want a life devoid of it, but some people can live happy lives without it. This highlights the fact that not everyone is exactly the same and differences in our individual constitutions can lead to variations in what is necessary for us to achieve happiness.

Personal values are those things that we choose to contribute to the meaning of our lives and help give happiness its richness, but whose role in our happiness is not necessary. For example, what we choose to do for leisure is completely open to our choice as long as it ultimately helps us to live well, whether this is hiking, reading, target shooting, making models, *etc.* It is worth stressing again that in order to qualify as a value at all, a thing must contribute to our life in some way; it is not enough that we merely subjectively value it (or

---

[i] A person's constitution may be physical or it may be psychological. Indeed, our psychological constitutions may be so deeply ingrained and intractable as to be effectively unchangeable (at least without professional psychological help). For example, wanting to have kids may be so deeply psychologically ingrained as to be indistinguishable from a biological drive.

[ii] A person's happiness depends in part on their constitution and so they must seek happiness in accordance with this, unless an aspect of their constitution is harmful (*e.g.*, conflicts with the universal values) and then they must seek to change that element if they want to be happy.

else it is merely an apparent value). Personal values are not a license for irrationality.

Understanding the distinctions between the various kinds of values helps a person to understand what things are most important in life and where to put their energy in order to live the best kind of life possible. Moreover, it helps us to understand how to populate our hierarchy of values. Let us return now to that topic.

Structuring the Hierarchy

We said above that the structure of a person's hierarchy of values is set by his central purpose in life and this allows him to understand how his other values fit into his life, so that he is always aiming to live the best life possible to him. Now that we have explored what kinds of values constitute the hierarchy, it should be obvious that a person must understand his core values and peripheral values (as well as whether these are universal, constitutional, or personal), in order to know how to integrate them into his hierarchy. Our hierarchy of values allows us to focus on which values are the most important to us and helps us to work to achieve these first. In essence, it brings clarity to our values and helps us to prevent sacrifices (surrendering a higher value for a lesser value or non-value[i]). To take a simple example, let us say that a lesbian values her relationship with her wife and is very happy with her, but is propositioned by a very attractive woman. Let us assume that a sexual encounter with this woman would be exciting and enjoyable to her. Let us also assume that her wife would not approve. How is she to decide what to do? She can utilize her hierarchy of values to see that her relationship with her wife is more important than an affair and she can choose accordingly. Even if the idea of a hierarchy of values sounds complicated, it is something that we all use in our decision-making already and we are merely making it more explicit and understandable.

While we all naturally use the hierarchy as adults, we were not born with one, nor do we see infants creating them. Creating a hierarchy of values is a conscious choice and something that we must do, and constantly redo, as we grow and our values change. Creating and maintaining our hierarchy of values in the real world is a messy, iterative process that starts in childhood. Most of us start with different hierarchies that may or may not be related to each other and are usually in narrow contexts. For example, a child might have a hierarchy of leisure activities (such as reading, playing with Legos, or playing video games) and a hierarchy of people he likes (such as his sister, cousins, or parents) and although both have to do with how he likes to spend time, there might be no

---

[i] Following Rand's definition of sacrifice: as in "The Ethics of Emergencies," *The Virtue of Selfishness*, p. 45. Giving up what is important to us for something less important, or not important at all, is no way to achieve a good life.

connection between them. Moreover, his different hierarchies might use different (or even undefined) standards, making them incommensurate. To add to the messiness, consider that when we are young, most of us do not know what we want out of life. Because of this, we often have to revise our hierarchies as we grow and our interests change.

These problems can be easily resolved by choosing a central purpose in life, because it serves as the keystone for our hierarchy of values and gives it structure. This structure helps us to integrate our lesser values so that they help us to work towards our goals; that is, by serving as the goal of the hierarchy, our central purpose in life works to keep our actions focused on achieving the thing that makes our life worth living and is our highest aspiration.[i] In this way, our central purpose in life defines who we are and what we want out of life.

Once we have a firm idea of our central purpose in life, we can begin to construct the hierarchy from the top down. This is not to say that this is how we come to have a hierarchy of values historically, but that we must do this process sometime as an adult when we are figuring out our identity and direction in life. This often involves the young adult's crisis: "What should I do with my life?" Once our central purpose is established, next comes our core values, because these are the values that define us and which we have chosen to provide the richness of our lives. These values do not merely complement our quest for our central purpose in life: they also help to bring meaning into our lives and provide happiness with its richness and depth. We seek our core values also as ends in themselves and not simply for the sake of happiness: that is, even if we found that happiness was closed to us, we would nevertheless still seek these values.

Finally, we round out the structure of the hierarchy with our peripheral values. Peripheral values add to our happiness and the richness of our lives, even though they are neither ends in themselves nor do they define us. Yet, they are still pleasant pursuits that we enjoy and which contribute to our lives. By creating our hierarchy thus, we will be able to see the overall structure of our values and how to prioritize different values.

---

[i] Someone might ask here whether we should not have happiness as our highest value. The question, however, is misplaced. We cannot aim to achieve happiness as though it were a goal and once we arrived, we would be happy. Happiness is not a passive state, but is defined by the right kinds of activity. This is very similar to pleasure. As Aristotle notes in the *Nicomachean Ethics*, we do not aim to do pleasure itself; but pleasure arises from performing an activity well ("without activity pleasure does not arise" 1175a20. Aristotle's idea of pleasure is elaborated in the *Nicomachean Ethics* VII 11-14 and X 1-5). The case is the same with happiness: we cannot shoot for happiness as our goal and expect to ever achieve it. We must, instead, aim to live a certain kind of life.

Utility of the Hierarchy

The creation of the hierarchy of values is an important ethical process that should be undertaken consciously at some point as an adult and then actively maintained and even changed as our values and goals change. Broadly, the hierarchy of values helps us to direct our actions at our goals, including our central purpose, and keep the overall context of our values. There are three primary ways to utilize the hierarchy of values: prevent sacrifices, prevent conflict, and maximize our values.

The hierarchy of values helps us to *prevent sacrifices* by allowing us to see whether a course of action will help us to achieve our values without endangering any of our other values. It is important that we have the hierarchy for this because we cannot judge one value in isolation from the rest of our life and values. It is not enough to know that something will improve or retard our life right now—we must also know how it impacts the overall course of our lives.

The hierarchy also helps us to *prevent conflicts* between values, by helping us to see which is more important and thus work towards one over the other. For example, it may seem that a person has a conflict in her values if she cannot both engage in her favorite hobby and also spend as much time with her children as they would like. Yet, there is a sense in which it is impossible for there to be a true conflict between values, since all values adhere to the standard of life and thus are aimed at the same end (in our example, both the person's hobby and spending time with her children contribute to her happiness). Since they are aimed at the same end, a true conflict between them is impossible, since the end will determine which value better fits the situation. Nevertheless, it is still possible that we will not be able to achieve two values together due to time or other constraints: maybe we simply do not have the time to pursue our hobby and spend as much time as we would like with our children. The hierarchy helps us see this and prevent this kind of conflict by helping us to prioritize one over the other.[i]

At the same time, the hierarchy can also be used to help us *maximize our values* in a slightly different way, where we try to make decisions that bring all of our values into play and only silence one of them in our deliberation if no such path is possible.[ii] On this approach, instead of choosing one or the other, we try to find a way to achieve both by rethinking the situation, reconceptualizing the problem, or reconsidering how to actualize our values, *etc*. To return to our above example, perhaps this person could introduce her children to her hobby and get them interested in it, so that she could both enjoy her hobby *and* time with her children. This would obviate the apparent conflict

---

[i] This, of course, means that we are eschewing a one-size-fits-all answer and that each individual will need to decide these things for himself, utilizing *phronesis*.

[ii] I credit Patrick Ryan with this third approach to using the hierarchy of values.

and allow her to maximize her values. Both ways of using the hierarchy can be important and help guide us to the best kind of life possible.

Thus, we can see the hierarchy of values has many benefits, the greatest of which is that it helps us to always be working towards our central purpose in life and our most important values. In this way, the hierarchy of values is a great tool to help guide us on the path to happiness. In life, we must choose to be purposeful and pursue our values if we want our lives to be meaningful. The hierarchy of values is also a powerful tool for *phronesis* as it helps us to see concretely how to apply ethical principles in the full context of our lives and values.

6. Universal Values and the Virtues

> *We are inquiring not in order to know what virtue is,*
> *but in order to become good,*
> *since otherwise our inquiry will be of no use.*[27]
> ~ Aristotle

Universal Values as Underlying Virtue

Let us turn now and take a closer look at the universal values and their corresponding virtues. Each of these plays a different and important role in human happiness and its absence will damage our ability to achieve happiness. Unfortunately, not all of the things that we need to be happy are directly controllable.[i] In such cases we must simply do the best we can to achieve or acquire them and work to minimize the damage that their absence causes. Luckily, though, we can identify certain ways of living that will help us to achieve these universal values: the virtues. It is the virtues, or the ways of living that achieve these universal values, which are partly constitutive of happiness.

Throughout the ages, different philosophers have identified different "virtues," although usually no reason is given to explain *why* something is a virtue. For example, Aristotle identifies virtues as being habits of actions that are the mean between extremes: liberality is the virtue with respect to giving and taking money and it is a mean between deficiently giving money, which is meanness, and giving away too much money, which is prodigality.[28] Aristotle elaborates a robust account of the doctrine of the mean, primarily in Books II-IV of the *Nicomachean Ethics*. He also accounts for other kinds of virtues that arise from certain constitutions, such as pride,[29] and those things about which

---

[i] It is vitally important, as Epictetus identified thousands of years ago, to be aware of which things are in our control and which things are not (*Handbook*, p. I). Or, to follow William Irvine, to be aware of the things over which we have no control, over which we have some control, and over which we have complete control (*A Guide to the Good Life: The Ancient Art of Stoic Joy*, p. 89).

there is no good mean, such as adultery.³⁰ Yet, he does not explain why we should consider the mean between extremes to be virtue in the first place.

In contrast, our eudaimonistic account bases virtue, not in the doctrine of the mean, but in human nature and the human condition. We can say more about virtue than that it is simply what a good person should do, or that it is inherently fine or noble, or that it brings honors. We can say that what makes something a virtue is that it helps us to achieve the universal values in life and helps us live well. Virtue is a kind of self-perfection that helps us to achieve happiness.

Virtue is one of the major ways in which we concretize ethics in our lives and get practical guidance. The virtues offer specific guidance in life; for example, the virtue of justice is giving a person what is their moral due, whether positive or negative, and helps us to see how we should interact with others in the world. It is important to note that, like happiness, the virtues are not things a person can simply achieve once and then be set for life. The virtues are *ways of living* and need to be recurrently chosen and affirmed: "being virtuous" means actively living virtuously. It is not a passive state. Moreover, the activity of virtue, being virtuous, is part of what constitutes the activity of happiness, or being happy. Virtues are, thus, cultivated dispositions of character for achieving a good life by means of realizing the universal values.

While the virtues are critically important for understanding how to live well, a person could live a completely virtuous life and still fail to achieve happiness. This is because not all of the things that make up happiness are in our control, such as friendship and love. It is not enough that we, individually, act correctly. We also need certain kinds of relationships with others. This is because humans are, as Aristotle says, social animals.[i] There is a great value for humans in living socially, because part of our human nature is social and we naturally desire to share certain kinds of connections and values.[ii] Indeed, the person stranded on the desert island would have only an impoverished life open to him, being cut off from all other people. Certain kinds of relationships, such as friendship or loving relationships, provide a kind of spiritual value that is necessary for a rich human life. Aristotle even goes so far as to say that the person who could live without others must be either a beast or a god.³¹

Living in certain kinds of social arrangement is valuable both for practical reasons and spiritual reasons. For instance, consider how much we gain by sharing our labor and specializing. This allows us to do the kinds of work we

---

[i] Although ζῷον πολιτικόν (*zoon politikon*) is commonly translated as the "political animal," this should be understood as meaning that we live in a *polis* (or city) and, thus, are social (*Politics*, I.2.1253a1). I think "political animal" confuses the issue as the English translation in this context, given the contemporary usage of the term "political."

[ii] One of the greatest values of society is the dissemination of knowledge to later generations, especially through the medium of books, so that knowledge is not lost and we can constantly look to improve our situation, instead of reinventing discoveries already made.

find important and valuable, while still collectively getting everything we need produced and created. For these reasons, living socially is one of the best ways for a person to maximize their chance at happiness. Unfortunately, living in a bad society is worse than living in no society: the state can be the greatest danger to happiness if it goes awry and deviates from the path of simply protecting individual rights and freedom. Nevertheless, a society of good people each setting out to virtuously achieve their own happiness will be a society of peace and prosperity and will not have major conflicts.[i]

Let us now turn to the universal values of happiness and the virtues by which they are achieved, in order to concretize our discussion. We will not elaborate every one of these universal values, but we will discuss several of the most important of these.[ii] However, we will not discuss love or sex here, since they are constitutional values and we discuss them in depth in their respective chapters.

The virtues are the means of achieving the universal values, which are responses to facts about human nature and reality. Thus, our choice to live a good life entails certain things due to our human nature. The virtues work together to create the kind of character necessary to achieve the universal values and, thereby, a good life. Moreover, there are many overlaps between universal values, virtues, vices, and corruptions. For example, self-esteem requires that we know we are worthwhile, but this requires things like being purposeful and efficacious in the world, while pride requires that we practice and have come to habituate many of the other virtues. This is not a failure of clarification or identification, but a recognition that these things are all interconnected for a person as important parts or ways of living well. Thus, the identified aspects below of the universal values, virtues, vices, and corruptions represent the primary elements and should not be thought of as exclusive and exhaustive.

In the following, we will identify the universal values and explain why they are necessary for happiness. We will then identify their corresponding virtue and explain how the virtue achieves the value. However, sometimes people go awry and make poor choices and so we will also consider the corresponding vices and corruptions of the universal values.

Reason and Rationality

The universal value of *reason* comes from the recognition of the fact that reason is the primary human means for interacting with reality and our only

---

[i] This is beyond the scope of this work, but see Rand's "The 'Conflicts' of Men's Interests" in *The Virtue of Selfishness* for one example of this. I hope to return to questions of politics at a future date.
[ii] There are also other things, such as money, that are necessary for happiness, but which are not constitutive of happiness.

source of knowledge: reason is our fundamental means of survival.[i] It is reason that underlies all of our most fundamental and distinctly human characteristics: from our ability to form concepts and hence language, to our ability for judgements and evaluation, to logic, science, and technology. Indeed, this very book, the homes we live in, and how we get to work every day are all products of reason. Broadly, we should understand reason as that faculty of our consciousness that helps us to interact with, and understand, reality. As such, it is of premier importance in ethics: ethics is about how to live a human life and reason is our faculty for interacting with the world in which we live. Let us, however, never forget that we are *embodied* rational beings, *rational animals*, lest we end up in absurdity by claiming that we are *simply* rational beings (*a la* Kant).

The virtue of *rationality* is a commitment to the excellent use of our faculty of reason. In practice, it means committing ourselves to objectivity, clarity, and focus. It means never accepting anything other than reason, such as faith or wish, as a basis for a belief. It means living our lives in a state of full conscious awareness, with frequent introspection and critical evaluation of our own ideas to identify and correct errors. It means holding reason as an absolute in our minds. For example, it means not putting our health at risk in a sexual situation simply because we are aroused and desire sex, but requires us to keep the larger context of our life in mind. The goal of rationality is: a life untroubled by contradictions, a life lived in the world as it really is instead of some fantasy realm, a life lived with clarity of thought. The goal of rationality is a life lived according to reason: a *human life*. Without the virtue of rationality, happiness is impossible to achieve.

Because rationality is our faculty of engaging with reality and other virtues are likewise responses to different aspects of reality, rationality may be considered to be the primary virtue. Yet, it would be wrong to attempt to reduce the other virtues to rationality. Each virtue requires careful cultivation to achieve its value and to reduce them all to rationality is to lose the richness of the virtues, without any clear gain. Thus, while rationality underlies the other virtues, they cannot be reduced to it.

Of course, there is also a vice associated with reason and that is *irrationality*. Irrationality is failing to adhere to reason and takes one of two forms: the first is substituting desires, wishes, emotions or whims in the place of reason, while the second is failing to think correctly. The first way is clear enough; it is the second that requires elaboration. The ways to think incorrectly are manifold and include such things as: paying inadequate attention to reality (*e.g.*, being out of focus), fallacious reasoning (*e.g.*, *ad hominem*, appeal to authority), cognitive distortions (*e.g.*, catastrophizing, personalization), biases (*e.g.*, confirmation bias, negativity bias), and problematic coping strategies (*e.g.*, addiction, religion). This

---

[i] This point, that reason is our fundamental means of survival, is Rand's ("The Objectivist Ethics," p. 22). I likewise follow Rand in emphasizing the importance of rationality for happiness. Indeed, my account of the virtues follows hers closely at points.

must suffice for an overview of irrationality, because as Aristotle says, "It is possible to fail in many ways [...], while to succeed is possible only in one way."[32] Indeed, it would be impossible for us to completely elaborate all of the ways that it is possible to be irrational. It is important to note that not all of these are the result of a person's actions (*e.g.*, the biases), but one should take care to learn about these things and either ward against them or attempt to correct them.

The corruption of reason is *misology*[i] (or hatred of reason). This arises when someone wants to believe something that they know to be irrational and, in order to justify this desire, attacks reason.[ii] This is most common with mysticism[iii] because if a person does not evade their knowledge that they are being irrational, then they must attack reason in order to justify their beliefs.[iv] Indeed, mysticism reduces to no more than the proposition that if a person wants something to be true and believes that it is true, that it is, therefore, true. But this is not the way the world works. Our minds do not have direct causal efficacy and no amount of wishing can directly change the world.[v] It is possible to change the world, but only by acting in it and according to the laws of nature (*i.e.*, Bacon's dictum that "Nature, to be commanded, must be obeyed").[33] When mystics are confronted by reality's refusal to conform to their desires, many grow to hate reason in a fit of childish petulance. The joke, sadly, is on them: by setting themselves against reality, they are doomed to fail and they will pay the penalty with their happiness and perhaps even their lives.[vi]

Purpose and Productiveness

The universal value of *purpose* comes from the recognition of the fact that a human life requires structure if it is to achieve happiness and that we must impose this structure ourselves by picking some end around which to organize our lives (our central purpose) and by which we can organize our values. This, as we have already shown, not only lays the foundation for meaning in life, but also allows us to experience the sentiment of purpose and *feel* that our lives have purpose.[vii] Purpose is what we will call a "fundamental psychological

---

[i] I take this term from Plato's *Phaedo* (89d), trans. Grube.
[ii] Alternatively, they could *evade* their knowledge that they are being irrational, which is likely more common.
[iii] We will explore the idea of mysticism in Volume 2, Chapter 9, but its core idea is that the law of identity (A is A) is mutable in some respect, whether that is because of a "god," "mystic forces," "the occult," *etc.*
[iv] This is the very move that Kant makes attempting to justify his secularized version of Christian ethics: "I had to deny *knowledge* in order to make room for *faith*." (*Critique of Pure Reason*, Bxxx). Kant's whole project is to destroy reason to make room for his mysticism.
[v] This point is made exceptionally well by Rand and her idea of "Primacy of Consciousness" (as found in "The Metaphysical Versus the Man-Made," *Philosophy: Who Needs It*, p.24).
[vi] Compare with the idea of "misology" in this chapter and of the divided soul in Chapter 6.
[vii] Conversely, without a purpose, our lives are doomed to be meaningless and we will likewise

need"[i] and it is a response to the question: "Is there some point to my life?" We all want to feel as though there is some reason for our lives and since there is no external reason to be found, we must create it ourselves. By choosing a purpose, we give meaning to our lives. Purpose is, thus, important for its own sake as well as for its contributions to meaning and happiness.

The virtue of *productiveness* is the commitment to achieve the goals that we have set for our life. Productiveness is how we bring our values into the world and this is one of the major means by which we create meaning in our lives. We have already explored the connection between our central purpose in life (ideally, our career) and meaning. However, productiveness has deeper ties to meaning, because it is how we actualize our values in the world and it is through the creation of values that we come to have meaning in life. At the same time, since life requires activity, or rather *life is activity*, productiveness is also an important part of how we achieve a rich and happy life. Aristotle made this point in a spectacular way in one of the culminating books of the *Nicomachean Ethics*:

> Existence is to all men a thing to be chosen and loved, and that we exist by virtue of activity (*i.e.* by living and acting), and that the handiwork *is*, in a sense, the producer in activity; he loves his handiwork, therefore, because he loves existence. And this is rooted in the nature of things; for what he is in potentiality, his handiwork manifests in actuality.[34]

We must be productive because we love existence and our lives, and productiveness is our way to bring our values into reality.[ii]

The vice associated with purpose is *parasitism* and it arises from a lack of purpose or aimlessness. The aimless person will not have a central purpose in life, because they do not want anything out of life. They seek, not to achieve a good life, but to not die—and these are radically different things. Since there is nothing they want out of life, they have no real values and would have no drive to achieve them if they did. Consequently, they become parasites that seek to live off the productiveness of others. Values do not just exist in the world: they must be created.[iii] A person who is unwilling to do this for himself must become

---

feel this.
[i] See Chapter 2 for a full discussion of fundamental psychological needs.
[ii] If, in perhaps a not too distant future, we end up with a society of autonomous robots doing all of our labor, this will not make productiveness any less important. Indeed, by divorcing labor and the maintenance of our lives, it will make productiveness all the *more* important. We will simply need to be productive about other ends: instead of earning our basic sustenance, we will have to be productive in achieving rich human lives.
[iii] This point is formulated beautifully by Per Bylund, a professor of entrepreneurship at Oklahoma State University. He says: "What causes poverty? Nothing. It's the original state, the default, and starting point. The real question is: What causes prosperity?" (Twitter, Nov.

a parasite upon those who do. Yet, this position, in addition to harming his victims, destroys the possibility of a meaningful life for the parasite. It is, thus, untenable for all involved.

The corruption of purpose is *entitlement*. Even worse than the parasite, who may at least have the decency to be chagrinned by his need, is the person who thinks that they have a right to have others live for his sake: the entitled person. The parasite passively defaults into his position because he has no values and drive. The entitled person actively wants to sacrifice others to himself, believing that his life is somehow more valuable than theirs. This is a complete corruption of purpose because this person is not creating meaning in his life through creating value in the world, but attempting to rob other people of their lives and values. Sadly, the joke is on the entitled person, because they will forever close themselves off from happiness on that path.

Self-Esteem and Pride

The universal value of *self-esteem* comes from the recognition of the fact that "man is a being of self-made soul"[35] and that to live is a choice. Self-esteem is another fundamental psychological need and it is an affirmative response to the question: "am I worthy to live?" Everyone has some conception of their own self-worth. A good self-esteem comes from creating a good self. Moreover, self-esteem is a feedback loop: as we do good things and come to see ourselves as good, we are motivated to become better (and vice-versa). In order to be motivated to live well, we must think of ourselves as worthy to live and we can only do this by choosing to live and creating the kind of self that is worthy of living.[i]

The virtue of *pride* is the practical implementation of our choice to live and is a kind of "moral ambitiousness,"[36] or the commitment to achieve a good life.[ii] Pride is about the overall way we live, which includes the other virtues. It

---

[15] 2015, https://twitter.com/PerBylund/status/665900726388785153). Ultimately, the "economic pie" must be baked by someone and, like Aesop's grasshopper, those who do not create values have no claim on those who do.

[i] The fundamental core of self-esteem is our always choosing to be rational and live well. It cannot be based on outcomes or perfection in all things, because the only thing in the entire world over which we have complete control is ourselves. If we set goals for ourselves that dictate outcomes where we have only some control over events or no control at all, then we will inevitably, and necessarily, fail and we set the stage for mental health problems. This is irrational and no path to happiness.

[ii] I understand Rand's idea of moral ambitiousness to be the same as Aristotle's conception of the lover of self who wants to be the best person he (morally) can be: "if a man were always anxious that he himself, above all things, should act justly, temperately, or in accordance with any other of the excellences, and in general were always to try to secure for himself the honorable course, no one will call such a man a lover of self or blame him. But such a man would seem more than the other a lover of self." (*NE*, IX.8.1168b25) [Aristotle is also contrasting two different kinds of egoism, or self-love, in the passage and saying that irrational

is for this reason that Aristotle calls pride "the crown of the virtues,"[37] since we cannot be proud without them.[i] Pride, however, is not guaranteed even to a person of otherwise complete excellence who is doing his best to achieve a good life. If our impetus for excellence lies solely in our derivative desire for the praise of others or our desire to avoid punishment or censure, then we can never achieve pride. We can only achieve pride by practicing virtue and seeking moral perfection.

The vice associated with self-esteem is *hubris*, which is a kind of false pride. While pride is acting to live a good life and thereby achieving self-esteem (or knowing that we are worthy to live), hubris is more concerned with cultivating the perception of this. To be more precise, hubris is when a person feels that they are worthy of great things, even though they have not earned them, or that they are morally great, even though they have not cultivated virtue or tried to live well. Hubris is a kind of illusion, about which a person tries to convince themselves, and which manifests in a desperate sort of over-confidence or arrogance. The hubristic person does not feel proud or self-confident, but is desperate to be *perceived* as such, because the hubristic person needs the perceptions of others to confirm his illusion. Hubris is, therefore, a kind of derivativeness. The hubristic person believes that if only others would perceive him as being proud, then he must be so and, by this fact, must be living well. Hubris is, thus, the desire to *seem to be*, rather than to be, worthy of a good life.

The corruption of self-esteem is *ressentiment*[ii], which is, in Ayn Rand's perfect formulation, "hatred of the good for being good."[38] This is the hatred felt by a person who sees someone who he judges as better than himself and, instead of wanting to work to become better, wants to destroy the better person.[iii] As long as the better person exists, the inferior person sees him as a slap in the face, showing that the inferior person could have been otherwise.[iv]

---

egoism is, at best, a defective kind of egoism.]

[i] Pride also has a retrospective component in the recognition of our achievements and progress on our path to living well. This is the *feeling* of being proud.

[ii] I take this term from Nietzsche who uses the French word for resentment to signal that there is more at work here than simple resentment. We will return to *ressentiment* in Volume 2, Chapter 10. (*On the Genealogy of Morals*, "First Essay: 'Good and Evil,' 'Good and Bad'," section 10, p. 19.)

[iii] This can also be tied to Carol Dweck's idea of a "fixed mindset," from her book *Mindset*, in that some people believe that they are as good as they will ever be and improvement is not possible. These people will be more likely to experience *ressentiment* for those who are better than them, because they will feel that it is not possible for them to be as good. However, as Dweck points out, a mindset is changeable.

[iv] One common response from the person who feels *ressentiment* is to act as though they do not actually care about the values in question as a way to attempt to preserve their psychological dignity. This is much like the "hipsters" of today who think that if they first ridicule themselves, then they will be spared the ridicule of others. This is different than nihilism because this person actually does care about values, but is trying to protect themselves from pain by acting as though they are indifferent. (An excellent example of this is Aesop's "The Fox and the Grapes.")

Ressentiment is a hatred of those who have made themselves worthy to live, because the hater has not. It is important to point out that it is not hatred of those who have divergent values, but of those who one actually regards as good, either consciously or subconsciously, and therefore is one of the most perverse[i] and evil things that a human can feel.

Truth and Honesty

The universal value of *truth* comes from the recognition of the fact that the unreal can be of no benefit in life and that any severance between our mind and reality is disadvantageous to living well. Things exist (which we collectively call reality), these things have a definite identity (they are what they are and are not what they are not), we get information about them through our senses, and come to understand and know them through reason. When our beliefs correctly correspond to reality, they are true. Truth is correspondence to reality.[ii]

The virtue of *honesty* is a strict adherence to reality in our own mind and in our communication with others; the former is sometimes called "intellectual honesty," while the latter is typically just called honesty. The goal of honesty is to prevent any disconnect between our thoughts and reality, thus reducing the chance for error and helping to maximize our cognitive efficacy. In this way, honesty is very much aligned with rationality and integrity, even though honesty is usually thought of only in terms of interactions with others.[iii]

The vice associated with truth is *dishonesty*. Dishonesty, like honesty, can be in our own mind or with other people. In the former case, we attempt to deceive ourselves, while in the latter case we attempt to deceive others. In both cases, we attempt to gain something through falsehood: we might feel a little better because of a lie we tell ourselves or we might seek a spiritual or material gain by lying to another. For example, one person might lie to another to manipulate them into having sex when they would not otherwise.[iv] Every act of dishonesty creates a world of deception that we must maintain and our efforts to this end will permeate our thoughts until the lines between reality and

---

[i] Perversion will be a particularly useful concept in Volume 2, where we will give a full account of it. Let us foreshadow here that we will take perversion to be: a corruption or distortion of something that is good (life-affirming) that makes it evil.

[ii] Given that this is not a treatise on epistemology, we will leave aside the many tricky questions here as beyond the scope of our present inquiry.

[iii] Honesty entails what Ayn Rand calls the "Primacy of Existence," which is: "the axiom that existence exists, *i.e.*, that the universe exists independent of consciousness (of *any* consciousness), that things are what they are, that they possess a specific nature, an *identity*. The epistemological corollary is the axiom that consciousness is the faculty of perceiving that which exists—and that man gains knowledge of reality by looking outward." ("The Metaphysical Versus the Man-Made," *Philosophy: Who Needs It*, p. 24)

[iv] Deceiving a person to get them to have sex with us is a kind of coercion and fraud and represents a kind of rape if the person would not have otherwise done so. We will explore nonconsensual actions around sex in Volume 2, Chapter 9.

fantasy begin to blur.[i] This reduces our ability to effectively engage with reality and, as a consequence, it is always at least the liar that is harmed by his lies.

The corruption of truth is *self-deception* or willfully losing touch with reality. This can happen directly or indirectly. Indirect self-deception is when we intend to deceive others, but through engaging in webs of deception, we lose sight of the truth and are ourselves deceived. Direct self-deception can be either attempting to deceive ourselves that something we know to be true is false or that something we know to be false is true.[ii] The most common form of the former is a futile attempt to create a false sense of self-esteem by trying to erase our failings. The most common form of the latter is mystical thinking where we attempt to deceive ourselves that if we believe something to be true, it is, by this fact, true: such as "if I wear this special pair of socks, my favorite sports team will win."[iii] Both of these are accomplished by repetition of the lie and purposefully ignoring all contradictory evidence, until we are no longer sure what is real.[iv] This destroys the possibility of certainty and conviction, because we can no longer tell which of our beliefs is real if our self-deception is successful.[v] When we deceive ourselves, reality becomes our enemy and we must actively work to defeat it, in order to uphold our world of lies. All of these are ways of setting our minds against reality and this destroys our ability to live well.[vi]

---

[i] Ayn Rand says of dishonesty that: "An attempt to gain a value by deceiving the mind of others is an act of raising your victims to a position higher than reality, where you become a pawn of their blindness, a slave of their non-thinking and their evasions." (*For The New Intellectual*, 129). This is because now, instead of focusing on reality, the liar must pander to his lies in order not to be caught in his deception.

[ii] We should contrast self-dishonesty, which is telling ourselves something that is false so that we feel better but without the intention that we actually believe it, with self-deception, which is telling ourselves something that is false *with the intention that we come to believe it*.

[iii] Of course, mystical thinking includes all forms of mysticism and faith. We will return to these topics in Volume 2, Chapters 10.

[iv] Sadly, this is often done to us as children as in religious indoctrination.

[v] The sad irony is that self-deception rarely convinces us completely, because we always remember that we have lied to ourselves (even if we cannot remember about what), and so we give up certainty and conviction for a rather paltry prize.

[vi] Ultimately, all forms of self-deception reduce to a single proposition: that some consciousness has causal efficacy in the world and, so, whatever that consciousness believes is, by this fact, true (since it *creates* reality)—whether this is my consciousness or a god's. This is what Ayn Rand calls the "Primacy of Consciousness," which is "the notion that the universe has no independent existence, that it is the product of a consciousness (either human or divine or both). The epistemological corollary is the notion that man gains knowledge of reality by looking inward (either at his own consciousness or at the revelations it receives from another, superior consciousness)." ("The Metaphysical Versus the Man-Made," *Philosophy: Who Needs It*, p. 24)

Unity of Self and Integrity

The universal value of *unity of self* comes from the recognition of the fact that humans exist as a unity and, although we have a mental aspect and a physical aspect, that these are inseparable.[i] Thus, any attempt to artificially divorce the mind from the body, whether in thought or action, leads to an internal schism and, ultimately, to becoming our own enemy (as we shall see with its corruption). When we have unity of self, we experience internal peace and tranquility.[ii]

The virtue of *integrity* is the commitment to achieve and maintain our unity of self. We do this in two ways: the commitment to the careful cultivation of our values and beliefs, which leads to unity of soul (which we will return to in Chapter 5), and the commitment to live by our values and work to actualize them. The cultivation of our values and beliefs is the commitment to never hold irrational or contradictory values and beliefs. We do this by practicing rationality as well as carefully cultivating our values and beliefs and making sure that they are consistent with our central purpose in life.[iii] The latter case, living by our values and working to actualize them, is the commitment to identifying our values and understanding their relative importance to us (which is the function of the hierarchy of values) and then acting to bring our values into the world (which is related to productiveness).[iv] We do this by formulating principles and then acting by them to actualize our values. If our values are life-affirming, then many of our moral principles will be the virtues.[v]

When we successfully practice integrity, when we align our values and beliefs with our central purpose and conscious goals and then work to achieve them, all of our emotions will be consistent with our ends and we will be motivated by our emotions to pursue our goals (we will explore this more in Chapter 2). This facilitates achieving our values.

One consequence of this view of integrity is that if a person values

---

[i] We discuss the mind/body problem at length in Volume 2, Chapter 10.

[ii] Contra the Stoics, internal peace is achieved not by giving up the world, but by aligning our values and beliefs with our conscious purposes. This is true internal peace and tranquility. This will be explored in Chapter 2.

[iii] For this reason, the person who holds irrational beliefs cannot have integrity and neither will he achieve tranquility. Any commitment to the irrational will necessarily cause internal schisms as the person attempts to hold beliefs that contradict each other and the facts of reality: "integrity" to irrational beliefs would be impossible. Yet, even so, we might respect that a person is working hard to be consistent, but lament that they have chosen bad ends to achieve (such as the man who believes his religion and works very hard to live by its tenets).

[iv] It is imperative to understand that the careful cultivation of our beliefs and values must *precede* their actualization. Integrity is not commitment to our principles *because* they are our principles, but because they will help us to achieve tranquility and live a good life.

[v] If our values are not life-affirming, then we will necessarily end up in contradictions, as we would at least sometimes be forced to take actions to further our lives as well as those that harm our lives.

something, they must work to actualize it in reality. If they do not, this is a failure of their integrity. If a person says that they love someone, they must take certain actions in the world to achieve this end. It would also be a failure of integrity to have sex with someone with whom we shared no values and who was not a value to us, because this would be an attempt to divorce sex from our values and this would harm our chances at long-term happiness (as we shall see).[i]

The vice associated with unity of self is unnamed and is often just called a lack of integrity, but we shall call it *internal discord*. This can happen when a person either fails to cultivate values (or cultivates them incorrectly) or when they fail to live by their values. A person can fail to cultivate values for many reasons, such as: lacking purpose, acting irrationally, acting only by their whims, and failing to utilize the hierarchy of values. A person can also fail to live by their values for many reasons as well, such as: fear to act on them, failure to consider the full context of their life when deciding to act, failure to use the hierarchy to understand the importance of their values, or even *akrasia*.[ii] Regardless of the reason, the result is a state of internal discord. This destroys the possibility of tranquility and sets the stage for sentimental problems, as we shall see in the next chapter.

The corruption associated with unity of self is also unnamed, but we shall call it *auto-enmity*. It is becoming our own enemy due to being pulled in contrary directions by having conflicting values and beliefs, which give rise to conflicting emotions and sentiments. This is the danger that Plato warned against with his metaphor of the black horse of the passions that we discussed in the Introduction: that our emotions will pull us in various ways and so we will be unable to go where we actually wish and must constantly fight against ourselves. This, of course, destroys our ability to be purposeful and live according to our values, destroys the possibility of feeling good for doing what we believe is right, and destroys any chance we have at tranquility—the sum of which destroys any chance at happiness.

Responsibility and Independence

The universal value of *responsibility* comes from the recognition of the fact that our lives are our own and if we want to achieve certain ends, then we must act to do so. A good life is not achieved by passivity, but through action. One of our greatest responsibilities is the creation of our own self through our actions and choices and, ultimately, through creating the right kind of character.

---

[i] This is not to say that "casual sex" is necessarily immoral, but it can be. This is a question to which we will return in Volume 2.

[ii] "*Akrasia*" is the Greek word for "weakness of will" and is the etymological origin of the English word "crazy." In short, it is when one knows better, but acts badly. Or, when one knows the good, but does not do it.

The virtue of *independence* is the commitment to always act on our own judgement and take responsibility for our choices.[i] This is done in two ways, which we will differentiate for the sake of clarity. We will deal with the existential manifestation of this first and deal with the psychological aspects of it below. Existentially, it is choosing our values according to our own judgement about what is best for our lives and then acting on them. That is, the independent person will be deliberate about his values and pursue them intentionally. If he values his sexual partner, it means that he judges that he contributes to his happiness, and it means that he will intentionally act to create a good relationship with him and then continue to work to keep their relationship strong.

The vice associated with responsibility is *dependence*, which is failing to be responsible for ourselves and expecting that others will take over responsibility for our lives. Much like the parasite that fails to be productive and create values in his own life, although for different reasons, the dependent person expects others to create for him while he merely consumes the fruits of their labor. Besides destroying his own potential for happiness, the dependent man is treating others unjustly, expecting them to sacrifice themselves for him. This is, emphatically, not to say that helping others through an emergency or crisis is immoral; nor is it to say that a person needing help in an emergency or crisis is destroying his character. Rather, it is to say that the kind of person who chooses not to be responsible for himself is vicious and closing himself off from happiness.

The corruption associated with responsibility we shall call *misautarkeia* and it is the hatred of independence. The misautarkic person failed to become responsible for himself, but instead of simply being dependent upon others, grows to hate independent people. This is because independent people exist in stark contrast to him and show his moral failures in relief. Misautarkeia is, then, an instance of *ressentiment* and of hatred of the good for being the good, specifically with respect to independence.

Reality-Focus and Psychological Independence

The universal value of *reality-focus* comes from the fact that only reality exists and we must work to maintain our connection to it. This is a precondition of truth, because truth involves our beliefs corresponding to reality correctly and, if we want any chance of this, we must actively maintain our mind's connection to reality.

The virtue of *psychological independence* is the commitment to maintain our

---

[i] This has significant implications for mental health because an "internal locus of control," or a sense that we are in control of our life, is one of the keys to resilience. Resilience is the measure of how well a person can cope with trauma: the more resilient we are, the more we can handle without being broken by it.

direct connection to reality and this entails actively working to maintain this connection as well as never privileging anything over this connection, such as our desires or the opinions or desires of other people.[i] Thus, the psychologically independent person does not look to others to determine his self, but picks his path carefully and sticks with it. If he enjoys sex with men, then he will have sex with men, even in the face of social censure. If he has a specific kink, he will be clear with others about his sexual needs and desires and will not let others shame him about this. The psychologically independent person concerns himself with others only insofar as others can be a value in his life, but never as his primary concern. The person who loves another and puts this above everything else, such that the love eclipses the rest of his soul, has thrown into darkness all that makes him worthy of love. True love, as we shall see in Chapter 3, builds upon a person's greatness without destroying any of the things that makes him what he is: true love is an impetus to become even greater. Indeed, it is only the psychologically independent person, the person who does not *need* another, who is truly capable of love. This is not to say that the psychologically independent person disregards others: others can and should play an important role in his life, but merely that he cannot allow others to judge for him, make his choices, or to determine his self.

The vice associated with psychological independence is *derivativeness*, which is living a life defined by others.[ii] Instead of maintaining a firm connection with reality as the independent person does, the derivative person is only concerned with the wishes, desires, expectations, *etc.*, of other people. To the derivative person, there is nothing more important than the feelings of other people and this leads him to prioritize their approval over his own judgement and to eventually replace his judgement with their approval. His world becomes, not reality, but the feelings of others and so he goes through life trying to conform to their feelings. Sadly, the derivative person never asks what they really want out of life and simply goes through the motions of living.[iii] This leads the derivative person to, as Thoreau might say, "lead lives of quiet desperation"[39] as they try to live according to the wishes and whim of everyone else, like poor

---

[i] This is very much related to one aspect of rationality, but important enough to be its own virtue. We should not be surprised at the overlap of virtues, since they are all means of living well and the ways to go about this are finite.

[ii] Ayn Rand calls this "second-handedness," which is when one "regards the consciousness of other men as superior to his own and to the facts of reality. It is to a [second-hander] that the moral appraisal of himself by others is a primary concern which supersedes truth, facts, reason, logic." (*The Virtue of Selfishness*, p. 165 [substituting "second-hander" for her older, but synonymous, term "social metaphysician"])

[iii] It is even more tragic when derivative people end up vying for each other's approval and create a system where everyone is trying to conform to each other's feelings, but where no one has any standards and, thus, no reason for their feelings. This creates a vicious circle of needing the empty approval of those who have no standards by which to judge. This systematic mess often runs on the empty ideas of platitudes and passed-down information and regulates those who diverge through shamenorming (see Chapter 6 for more on shamenorming).

toy boats adrift in a river of the feelings of others.

In contrast, the psychologically independent person maintains a firm connection to the world. While he has a place for others in his life, he still sets his own course. The contrast can perhaps best be seen with a metaphor: Imagine a moral mirror that showed all of our choices stretching out behind us. If we looked at each one, would we find that we made the choice because we thought it was the right thing to do based on our own values and judgement, or would we find that we chose what other people wanted us to choose? Would we find that we were living our own life or would we find that we were living a pale reflection of life, trying to conform to other people's feelings and desires? Would this moral mirror reflect our true self or a thin image of how others thought we should be? That is the difference between a derivative life and a psychologically independent life.

The corruption associated with psychological independence is *power-lust*, which is a more pernicious form of derivativeness.[i] Just as with the derivative person, the power-luster's world is constituted by the feelings of other people. However, unlike the derivative person, the power-luster does not want others to simply approve of him: he wants to rule them. The power-luster believes that if he rules other people, then he *ipso facto* rules reality, since his reality is constituted by their feelings. The joke, sadly, is on him: happiness is closed to those who constitute their world through other people. Thus, he may gain the power to rule, but in so doing will close himself off from happiness.

Meaning and Authenticity

The universal value of *meaning* comes from the recognition of the fact that meaning is not found in life, but must be *created* by us, and that it is necessary for both living well and our mental health. Yet, a meaningful life is not easily achieved. It requires achieving other universal values such as responsibility, reality-focus, purpose, and unity of self, as well as their corresponding virtues. Through achieving these foundational values for meaning, we lay the groundwork that makes meaning possible.

The virtue of *authenticity* is the commitment to *purposefully* living by our values in order to create meaning; that is, authenticity is the purposeful pursuit of a meaningful life. Much like pride requires other virtues to be in place before being possible, so too does authenticity; it requires, among others, independence, psychological independence, productiveness, and integrity. That is, we must live by our own judgement and choose values that will lead to our happiness, which is independence. We must keep our minds firmly focused on reality, letting neither our own wishes or desires nor those of others come between our judgement and reality, which is psychological independence. We

---

[i] I take the term "power-lust" from Rand (*The Romantic Manifesto*, p. 116).

must organize our life around a central purpose and then work to achieve it, which is productiveness. And we must carefully cultivate our values and beliefs and commit to live by them and work to actualize them, which is integrity. While it is true that these virtues work together to create meaning in life, this is not their primary end. In contrast, the end of authenticity is a meaningful life and its focus is how we live our life.

While the goal of all of the virtues is the habituation of action into a good character, such that we need not consciously deal with every situation, with authenticity this is even more pronounced. While authenticity can be done consciously, it is most effective as a subconscious habit. Indeed, once authenticity is internalized and habituated, it gives us the *experience* of authenticity. The experience of authenticity is an existential mood (see Chapter 2) and it allows us to experience the reality of living our lives according to our values and for our own sake. Authenticity is a way of being oriented to the world and of feeling that our lives matter because we have made them matter and we do this by identifying our values and working to achieve them. In this way, authenticity is a joyful celebration of our humanity and our individuality; that is, it is a celebration of our lives.

The vice associated with meaning is *inauthenticity* and it is a failure to create a meaningful life. It can have elements of many vices, depending on the person, but always includes derivativeness and internal discord. This is because the inauthentic person failed to create their own self by putting things before their own rational judgement (derivative) and failing to cultivate and live by their values (internal discord). Because of this, the inauthentic person has no meaning in life and this leads them to be disengaged with their life, since there is little point to meaningless action. Sadly, the inauthentic person usually knows that there is something missing in their life and they experience a deep sense of being unfulfilled: their life has lost its significance or, more accurately, they have failed to make their life significant. To break out of this trap of meaninglessness, a person must create a good character and work to achieve the virtues that underlie authenticity. They must face reality, use their own judgement, create their own self, and passionately pursue their values. They must be active in the pursuit of their own life. They must embrace the necessity of choice and responsibility for their life. It is only through this that they can make their life meaningful.

Because authenticity is the joyful living of one's life by one's own values, it is, by its very nature, a transgressive act in a derivative world. In a world full of people living lives they do not enjoy, acting like people they really are not, and giving up their lives in myriad ways that they do not even realize, the authentic person is the only real one in a world made up of the shadows of empty lives. He is, thus, often as hated as the person who has seen the sun and returns to the cave.

The corruption associated with meaning is *nihilism*. The nihilistic person knows that they have failed to achieve values in life or to create a meaningful life, but instead of working to fix this, believes that their best course of action is to destroy all values, thinking that "if I cannot have meaning and values, no one can." Thus, the nihilist wants to *destroy* for the sake of destruction. He wants to destroy values *because* they are values. He wants to ruin people's lives in an effort to show that their lives are empty, like his own. He wants to radically recreate the world in his own empty image. Nihilism is the metaphysical expression of ressentiment.[i]

Phronesis

Now that we have investigated some of the most important of the virtues, let us return briefly to the issue of *phronesis*. We said, following Aristotle, that *phronesis*, or practical wisdom, is reasoning about how to live a good human life and that it is foundational to virtue. We also said that virtue is acquired through, as well as practiced by, *phronesis*. We are now in a position to see how this is so.

Phronesis involves learning how to apply principles in our lives. This process requires us to keep the full context of our lives in mind when making choices and has both deductive and inductive elements. We start by taking the general principle, such as honesty, and applying it to our lives.[ii] We see, for example, that when we do not fake reality, we are better able to engage with the world as we are dealing with it as it is and not how we might want it to be. We see how this operates in our own particular context and we learn from this and are able to increase our understanding of the general principle. As we continue to do this throughout our lives, we increase our understanding of both the general principle as well as its application to our lives. Of course, we will sometimes make mistakes in our understanding of a general principle or in what actions we should take to concretize it. For example, perhaps we subordinate honesty to someone else's feelings and lie to them and say that we love a gift when we do not. This might lead to us receiving more gifts of that kind, since the person reasonably believes that we liked the gift. These are great opportunities to identify our errors and to learn from them in order to live better lives. In this case, we should not be rude and tell them that we hate the gift, but be kind and explain that it is not the right kind of gift for us, but that we appreciate their kindness nonetheless. This allows them to better know what kind of gift we might want in the future and also that we appreciate their giving us a gift at all. It is only through coming to have these kinds of experiences in applying the general principles to our lives that we come to fully understand

---

[i] There are many other universal values, virtues, vices, and corruptions, but more would be tedious here. See Volume 3, Chapter 22 for more.

[ii] A person who had no contact with other humans would have to start inductively and ascertain what works and what does not. Luckily, most of us will not need to attempt to inductively arrive at ethics.

them and how they benefit us. *Phronesis* is a skill that all adults have, to at least some degree, since we engage in applying our general principles and seeing how they work throughout our lives.

7. Character

> *Man is a being of self-made soul.*[40]
> ~ Ayn Rand

The Created Self

Living well is not only about virtue and achieving the right kinds of values, but also about creating the right kind of character. Character is the source of moral actions that we do without deliberation and it is the result of the choices, beliefs, and values that we have internalized as right and as our own.[i] That is, character is our habituated dispositional nature. It is the summation of the principles by which we live and the moral choices we have made; in this sense, our character is our created moral self. For these reasons, Aristotle believed that character was one of the most important constitutive goods of happiness:

> For if the good life consists in what is due to fortune or nature, it would be something that many cannot hope for, since its acquisition is not in their power, nor attainable by their care or activity; but if it depends on the individual and his personal acts being of a certain character, then the supreme good would be both more general and more divine, more general because more would be able to possess it, more divine because happiness would then be the prize offered to those who make themselves and their acts of a certain character.[41]

Our character is what we have chosen to become. For this reason, we look to the character of others if we want to judge them and whether they will benefit or harm our life. Looking to a person's actions out of context does not tell us who he really is. But, if we look to his patterns of action, his reasons for action, and the principles that he believes, then we can see who he really is. Our character is the culmination of all of our moral beliefs and past actions. Our character is our real and enduring self. This is why Rand says that: "Man is a being of self-made soul." Each of our choices influences who we are as people: we both make the choices and are made by them. We are, in this way, self-made.

This is not to say that every action we might take will be consistent with

---

[i] See Chapter 2 for more on internalization.

our character. There are two primary situations where there might be an incongruity between our action and character: when a person has a good character, but takes a bad action or when a person has a bad character, but takes a good action. In the latter case, we would praise the person if they were trying to change their character for the better. In the former case, there can be a number of reasons why we act inconsistently with our character, such as weakness of will (*akrasia*), tiredness, intoxication, *etc.*, or we might simply have made a mistake in judgement.

Regardless of why a person acts "out of character," we can say that the one-off action has less effect on the course of our lives than our habitual actions. This is not to diminish that even a one-off action can have catastrophic consequences, but to emphasize that living well happens over time and so we must take care to cultivate a good character so that we can take the right actions throughout the course of our lives. These discrete actions can be moral or immoral, but our character and our habitual action over the long term make all the difference in our lives. This is perhaps clearer with an example. People sometimes have sex with people that they do not know well after a night of drinking. Doing this once will not destroy our character or our ability to have deeply intimate relationships. Yet, if we are the kind of person who habitually gets drunk and has sex with whoever is around, it does show something bad about our character and it will erode our ability to have deeply intimate relationships (as we shall see).

Virtue versus Self-Restraint

True virtue entails cultivation of certain kinds of beliefs and emotional responses such that a person *desires* to do the virtuous thing; which, of course, reduces the likelihood of these "out of character" actions.[i] Virtue is, thus, a cultivated habit to desire to do the right thing and then choosing to act to do the right thing. In contrast to this is the person of self-restraint, who is able to control himself and do the right thing, but struggles against his own desires or emotions to do so. The virtuous person has his beliefs in line with his conscious philosophy and, *ipso facto*, has his emotions in line with his goals: he has true unity of soul and his internal world is tranquil (this will be fully explained in Chapter 2). The person of self-restraint is able to control himself and do what needs to be done, but instead of having tranquility, has internal turmoil.

The vast difference between self-restraint and virtue can perhaps best be seen with a metaphor. The person who has never rowed a boat before might pick a point to head to and then row one oar and then the other.[ii] If so, his boat will never be heading in the right direction as it will first be pointing one way

---

[i] Moreover, the virtues entail a certain kind of emotional response to their instantiation; for example, the honest person will enjoy seeing honesty in others and will despise dishonesty.

[ii] Whether this is how all neophyte boaters behave is not the point.

and then the other and, even if he does eventually get there, he will struggle the entire time. In contrast, the person who knows how to row a boat will row both oars together and thereby achieve a straight line towards his goal without struggle. A better example might be of the "dry alcoholic" who is currently not drinking, but who struggles against his urges purely through self-restraint versus the person who dealt with the real underlying problems and who no longer desires to drink in unhealthy ways.[i] These examples show the difference between self-restraint and virtue.[ii] Moreover, because self-restraint involves constantly struggling against ourself, there is always the danger that we will fail to reign in our desires and then do the wrong thing. This makes self-restraint unstable and leads a person to self-doubt and anxiety, since they know that failing to be restrained is always a real possibility.

Yet, for those who were not raised well and who did not internalize good moral messages as they grew and matured or who have simply made mistakes, self-restraint may be a necessary step to becoming virtuous. During the process of changing our beliefs for the better, as we come to internalize better ideas and change our emotions as a result, self-restraint is necessary. However, self-restraint should not be a goal, but merely a stepping-stone to virtue and internal unity.

Our Most Precious Creation

Thus, a good character is not only about doing the right things, but, more importantly, it is about *wanting* to do the right thing and *feeling* good about doing the right thing. Moreover, character is also about wanting to *not* do the wrong thing and feeling bad about it if one does. It is for this reason that Aristotle says: "Excellence of character is concerned with emotions and acts."[42] This is because character is a cultivation, not just of our dispositions to action, but of our desires. We do this by having the right kinds of values and beliefs and integrating them into our hierarchy of values. By having well-formed values and beliefs (rationality) and by integrating them with our conscious goals (integrity), we come to desire to live by (authenticity) the values we have chosen for ourselves (independence) and then actually take the actions in the world to achieve these values (integrity). This integration gives us the desire to live well and to feel good about living well. Moreover, because we are living by our

---

[i] This is the failure of "Alcoholics Anonymous": it treats alcoholism as an irreducible "primary disease" and does not deal with the real underlying problems. Sadly, the person who is "helped" by AA is left with only self-restraint and will never experience the tranquility of a unified soul until they actually deal with their underlying psychological problems.

[ii] The person who has achieved virtue will experience internal unity and tranquility. The person who is merely self-restrained will always feel at odds with himself and experience internal discord, such as Plato described with his metaphor of the black horse of the passions and the white horse of reason and their struggle against each other. This is, incidentally, the exact same metaphor that Nietzsche uses with his Apollonian (reason) and Dionysian (passions) divide.

values, we will experience the meaningfulness of our lives. It is for these reasons that character is perhaps the most important component of happiness, because it ties together our values, our emotions, and our decision to live into a cohesive package that helps us to achieve these things and feel good about it. *A good character is the most important key to living well and being happy about it.*

Overall, we can say that happiness is a robust thing that includes many different pieces that must all come together in the right ways and character is one of the most important of these. This is certainly true. But each of the pieces that make up happiness is separately valuable as well and the result is the best thing we can hope to achieve. It cannot be "found in" achieving specific values, but emerges from the activity of living well. It is, like pride, partially self-reflective understanding of how our life is going. Happiness cannot be found in sex, or a career, or a partner, or any other particular thing. There is no single thing the achievement of which can give us happiness. Living a certain type of life *creates* happiness: it can never be passively brought about, but must be actively created.

Yet, even if a person could live a completely virtuous life, create good character, and achieve their values, they might still fail to achieve happiness. Consider the example of Priam, the King of Troy, and father of Hector and Paris. Priam had been happy before the siege of Troy, the death of his son Hector at the hands of Achilles, and the fall and ruination of his city. Even though Priam was happy before all these ills befell him, he was certainly not happy after. Even so, as Aristotle notes, he will have lived a better life than if he had not been virtuous and developed a good character:

> Now many events happen by chance, and events differing in importance; small pieces of good fortune or of its opposite clearly do not weigh down the scales of life one way or the other, but a multitude of great events if they turn out well will make life more blessed (for not only are they themselves such as to add to the beauty of life, but the way a man deals with them may be noble and good), while if they turn out ill they crush and maim blessedness; for they both bring pain with them and hinder many activities. Yet even in these nobility shines through, when a man bears with resignation many great misfortunes, not through insensibility to pain but through nobility and greatness of soul.
>
> If activities are, as we said, what determines the character of life, no blessed man can become miserable; for he will never do the acts that are hateful and mean. [...] And if this is the case, the happy man can never become miserable – though he will not reach *blessedness*, if he meet with fortunes like those of Priam.[43]

Priam's virtue and the character he developed could not prevent events outside his control, such as Paris abducting Helen from Agamemnon and the resulting war. Yet, they allowed him to bear these events much better than he would have been able to otherwise. There is much that can be taken from a person and which might destroy the possibility of his happiness, but, at the very worst, we are left with our virtue and character to weather the storm. This is no paltry consolation prize. A good person will not become truly miserable, because he will always be able to take solace in his achievements, including those in his own soul, and these cannot be taken away.

It is worth pointing out that happiness is not a thing that can be achieved in the same way that someone can run a marathon once and then be said to have achieved their goal of running a marathon. Happiness is *living well* and this is an ongoing process. The goal is not to achieve happiness at the end of our days, but to *live well* right now and throughout the course of our life. For this reason, we must make the goal of every day to live well so that we can live happy lives. That this also allows us to bear even the worst of times is a bonus.

Let us conclude our discussion of character by addressing one of Glaucon's worries from *The Republic*, which is roughly this: "What if we could simply *appear* to be good instead of being good, such that we had all the benefits of virtue and none of the problems associated with vice, yet with all of the gains of vice? Would not this be best?"[44] To him, we can now clearly respond that there is a fundamental difference between simply *appearing* to be good and actually being good. The person who acts viciously, regardless of how others view him, destroys the possibility of happiness in his own soul. This is reminiscent of the Christian idea: "For what would it profit a man if he gains the whole world and forfeits his soul?"[45] Whatever it is that this man gains through his vice, it is no human life. And his loss is the most precious thing of all: happiness, a life well-lived.

Summary and Conclusions

*What you need now
is not to return to morality,
but to discover it.*[46]
~ Ayn Rand

We opened the present volume by noting in the Introduction that the history of philosophy has been characterized by three primary responses to sexuality: resistance, abstinence, and indulgence. We showed there that philosophers were united in the belief that sexuality stood in opposition to reason, although their responses to this were different: the Resistant and Abstinent camps took sexuality to be opposed to morality, while the Indulgent camp thought that sexuality and pleasure exhausted morality. Yet, we are already beginning to see that sex does not stand in opposition to reason or morality and this will become more and more evident throughout the following chapters. Moreover, we have also seen how rule-based systems are not truly ethical systems at all, but merely systems of commands backed by punishments. We can, thus, dispense with the misguided advice of the Resistant and Abstinent camps if what we want is a good life, since they do not share that end. (We shall return to the issue of the fatal error of the Indulgent camp in the Conclusion.)

However, we will need some ethical guidance if we want to live well and learn how to integrate sex into our lives in a healthy way. This is why we had to start by creating the philosophic foundation on which to rest our new theory of sexual ethics. Our new account of eudaimonism has the subtlety and richness necessary to support our account of sexual ethics, as we shall see. In order to get this level of subtlety and richness, we had to inquire into a number of different areas to understand their connection to happiness.

We started by asking whether any such inquiry could be worthwhile or whether it was as pointless as sex without the friction. We found that meaning is indeed possible, if we take care to integrate our emotions and philosophy together. We saw how this allows us to experience the reality of our philosophy through our emotions, which also lets our emotions motivate our philosophy so that we can *create* meaning in our lives. Thus, we saw that if we want meaning in our lives, we must work to create it.

Since our inquiry into ethics was focused on us, as humans, living a good life, we had to begin with a single question: "What is it to live a good human life?" We saw that since reason is our means of survival and of interacting with and understanding the world around us, our picture of the good life must include reason at its core. However, we also saw the danger of focusing exclusively on reason (to the exclusion or suppression of our emotions) and so ended up agreeing with Aristotle that we are rational animals. Of course, since we admitted our embodiment, we also acknowledged our mortality. We saw, however, that far from derailing our project, it was the fact that we can die that created the possibility of meaning in our lives. Our mortality not only motivates ethics, but also makes it both possible and necessary.

We also saw that if ethics is to help us live well, it cannot simply be a system of rules that is imposed on us from outside to control us. Rather, it must be a freely chosen system whose only normativity arises from the choice to live. For this reason, we saw that it cannot be composed of rules at all, but of principles whose moral force comes from their contribution to our end of living well. Additionally, we saw that ethics cannot include just any ends, but only ends compatible with living a good human life: that is, ethics cannot be subjective.

We then noticed that this account of ethics, since it was fundamentally concerned with helping an individual live a good human life, is egoistic in nature. We saw that egoism is not simply doing whatever one wants, since this would be self-defeating and not in a person's interest, but rather is choosing to live a good life and taking the actions necessary to do so. Because of this, we saw how the scope of ends was limited to those that actually improve a person's life (which includes relationships with other people). For these reasons, we concluded that rational egoism is the only coherent kind of egoism and that to simply condemn egoism is to condemn human life.

From there, we turned our attention to the question of values, because we saw that the ends of eudaimonism (*i.e.*, its specific aims), are not given to us, but must be chosen. We saw that this meant that happiness is like a broad outline that we must arrange to our purpose and fill in with our values, including our core values and peripheral values. On the other hand, we saw that there are some values, the universal values, which are necessary for happiness for anyone, constitutional values, which are necessary for a person's happiness, but depend on their constitution, and others like personal values, which give richness to happiness.

Since we realized that the universal values were necessary for everyone, we had to inquire more closely into their nature and how they fit into happiness. We saw that each of the universal values was a response to some fact about reality and human nature. Moreover, we discovered that the virtues were the means by which we achieve these universal values and, therefore, that they partly constitute happiness. Thus, we focused on some of the most important virtues for happiness and cultivating a good character, such as rationality, productiveness, and pride.

Finally, we saw that cultivating a good character is one of the most important parts for achieving happiness. We saw that this involves having the right habits, including the virtues, but also in having well integrated beliefs and values such that we desire to do the right thing and feel good about doing so. We saw that this allows a person to live well, not only in the moment, but also throughout the course of their life, while also helping them to deal with anything that might come their way, even the worst of circumstances.

Overall, we saw in this chapter that our conception of ethics is radically different in kind from the mistaken rule-based systems, because it has human happiness as its end. If we want to achieve a good life, we need an ethical system that can not only point us in the right direction, but that can help us to achieve an integration of our emotions in order to live *passionate* ethical lives full of meaning. Luckily for us, we have precisely this in eudaimonism. Eudaimonism is a moral framework whose goal is an individual's happiness, understood as flourishing in a rich human life, across all its aspects. The advantage of eudaimonism is that it combines a moral system aimed at helping us live a good human life with the added benefit of the emotional integration that allows us to experience the reality of our ethical beliefs, culminating in a rich life that's full of values and meaning. Eudaimonism's close integration with emotions results in us feeling good when we are being moral and living well, giving rise to a strongly virtuous circle. If we want to live the best kind of life possible, the ethical framework we will need is a *eudaimonistic* one, which is uniquely constituted to handle this task.

We have now seen that ethics is about living a good human life and how eudaimonism accomplishes this. So, it is time to begin our inquiry into the nature of sexuality so that we can understand how to integrate these two things together. Indeed, we must be careful, as we progress, to make sure that our analysis is always rooted in our knowledge of ethics and our passion for life. To begin to understand sexuality, and the role of sexual ethics, we must begin with the most basic concepts and build our knowledge hierarchically, so that we can be assured that our later knowledge is as indubitable as the foundation upon which we will build. Consequently, we shall turn next to emotions, which we will need to understand in order to understand love and sexual attraction, which will underlie our later chapters. It is important to keep our eudaimonist framework in mind throughout the rest of the book, because our account of sexual ethics will be firmly rooted in it.

Chapter 2: Emotions and Sentiments

*Emotions are the automatic results of man's value judgements
integrated by his subconscious; emotions are estimates
of that which furthers man's values or threatens them.*[47]
~ Ayn Rand

*At the heart of every emotion is a set of
fundamental ontological and evaluative commitments, [...]
a micro-metaphysical and ethical system, a bit of philosophy,
which it is appropriate for us, as philosophers, to make clear.*[48]
~ Robert Solomon

Understanding emotions can be incredibly difficult: in fact, understanding emotions is so hard that they have been traditionally considered to be impervious to reason and analysis.[i] Emotions can be so interesting and complex that entire plays have been written revolving around a single emotion, as is the case with Shakespeare's *Othello* and jealousy. Some of the most complicated and interesting emotions center around love and sex. Consider the man who wants to have a threesome and who knows his wife will only consent if it is with another man. He may be afraid to see her have sex with another man because

---

[i] For example, Plato's psychology treats the passions as innate and irreducible, in addition to being opposed to reason. Recall, from the Introduction, how in the *Phaedrus* (253d) he uses the metaphor of a charioteer who must fight against the black stallion of the passions so that he does not overpower the white purebred of reason. Moreover, Plato would agree with the standard Greek idea that it is the sight of a beautiful male youth that stirs sexual desire for a Greek and that this passion is innate and irreducible. Yet, if the sight of a young man necessarily stirred desire and this was innate, then all humans, or at least all human males, should feel desire for beautiful male youths. However, today young men are not the objects of the lust of (most) older men, but rather it is women that now serve as the primary ideal of beauty—a concept completely foreign to the Greek mind. This presents a radical problem for the idea of it being innate or irreducible. (Incidentally, Sigmund Freud simply copied Plato's tripartite soul, but renamed the parts "Id" (it), "Ego" (I), and "Super Ego" (above-I), and in this way is a mere derivative of Plato.)

he might feel jealous or he may worry that he may not feel the same toward her afterwards. Let us say that his desire to have the threesome outweighs his worries and he goes through with it. He finds that he is incredibly turned on by watching his wife have sex with another man, but now feels a deep sense of unease and is not sure what that means about him or if it means he does not really love her. Or, consider the woman who is really into submission and really enjoys it, but feels deeply conflicted about what this means for her as an independent woman and wonders whether she could ever find the kind of man to whom she would want to submit.

How can we make sense of these very confusing emotional reactions that people can have around love and sex? To understand what is going on in these cases, we need to understand emotions: what they are, where they come from, and how they can conflict with each other and even with our rational convictions. That is precisely what we are going to do in this chapter. It is only through understanding the deeper operation of emotions that we can hope to grasp these interesting and complex examples or, indeed, understand emotions in our own lives.

More broadly, we must understand and integrate emotions into our lives in the right way if we want to live rich and meaningful lives. That is, we need to cultivate emotions that are in line with our conscious goals if we want to live well and be able to experience this. It is not merely that we need to understand emotions in order to understand sexuality, which is important—we must understand them as a practical matter, if we want to be happy.

1. What is an Emotion?

An emotion, perhaps such as love, hate, joy, or sorrow, is one of several different kinds of psychological phenomena (among which are also thought and perception). In order to flesh out exactly what emotions are, it is important to first understand what emotions are not. This is an important step for studying the elements of our inner lives, as it is not always easy to introspect on subtle differences between the things that go on inside us. Therefore, let us turn briefly to perception and thought to see how these differ from emotions.

Emotions are a Unique Psychological Phenomenon

Unlike emotions, perception is the way that we directly experience the world. When we "look out at the world," we do not see some green here, some white and blue there, and some movement over that way. Rather, we see green grass, clouds in the sky, and some birds flying by. We experience all of this together as one giant perceptual field in which we can identify particular entities.[i] Now, whether we can identify what we are seeing or not, we still perceive the world as being made up of discrete entities and are able to understand it as such. Thus, we can understand perception as the way that we experience the external world, the "out there," in terms of whole entities and not merely in terms of disconnected colors and shapes.[ii] Perception is our faculty for experiencing the world outside ourselves.[iii] Emotions, on the other hand, do not tell us about the outside world directly, but about our *assessment* of the outside world (there are other kinds of emotions as well, as we shall see). For example, let us say that we perceive a sunny spring field coming alive after a long winter and because of this, and other things going well in our life, we feel *joy*. We do not *perceive* joy in the field; we *feel* joy about what we are perceiving. The joy comes from our assessment of the scene and of how our life is going, not from the scene itself. If this same field were the place where our lover died suddenly, then our emotional reaction to it would be radically different, even though the field would not change, nor would our perception of it.[iv] We will return to this point later, once we have a better understanding of emotions.

Unlike emotions, thought uses various faculties of our minds (such as abstraction, differentiation, logic, teleological reasoning, *etc.*) to help us to deal with information about the world, which helps us to function within it. In this respect, thought is a completely different type of psychological phenomenon from both emotions and perception. While thought may operate on information from perception, a person can never think with his perception (*e.g.*, a man cannot think *with* his taste, but he can think *about* his taste. The salient point is that thought is its own separate category of mental phenomena. Emotions, on the other hand, are not a kind of thought, but seem to be a response to our beliefs, which are formed by our thoughts.[v] For example, we might decide that we need to repair a fence in our yard and think about what the most efficient way to do this would be: should we buy lumber,

---

[i] To be clear, that I *know* the identity of the existents (*e.g.*, clouds) is a function of conception, not perception. That I perceive the existents *qua* entities is a function of perception and not of conception.

[ii] In contrast, sensation is the material provided by our proper sense faculties (*e.g.*, sight, touch, hearing, taste, and smell), which is why they are called "sense-ation."

[iii] Perception is self-evident and indubitable, if the mind and sense faculties are correctly functioning. I cannot be wrong *that* I perceive something, although I can be wrong about *what* I perceive if I *misconceive* it.

[iv] Of course, my *experience* of the field would change because we often get lost in ourselves and experience the world through our *surreality*; that is, through the lens of our internal life. For example, if I am depressed, this will color my experience of the world. Our perception, however, does not change even if we lose sight of it by focusing on other things in our surreality. (See Volume 3, Chapter 21, "On Surreality.")

[v] I do not intend to give a full epistemological account of belief formation here, as it is much beyond the scope of our concern.

a hammer, and nails ourselves? Should we hire someone to do it? If we decide to do it ourselves, think about the best way to do it, and then fix our own fence, we might then feel a deep sense of satisfaction at doing the work ourselves. Thought would help us to know what to do; the emotion of satisfaction would be a response to having done it.

Emotions are Responses to Values and Beliefs

Now that we know that emotions are their own unique category of psychological phenomena, we must move on to our next question: what are emotions? For example, we can list things we believe to be emotions, such as love, hate, shame, *etc*. But, what is it that makes all these things emotions? What unites them in being emotions as opposed to something else like perceptions or thoughts? Our next step is to find that which links together these things we are calling emotions.

Since emotions are not things that exist in the outside world, we cannot look to their physical constitution to find their nature. Instead, we need to introspect, look inward, at those things that we already believe to be emotions and see if we can identify any similarities among them. Since each emotion clearly feels different to us (*e.g.*, love feels different than shame or disgust, but we think all of these are probably emotions), we must look past their affective qualities (how they *feel* to us) if we are to discover some commonality among them. In order to analyze the deeper level of emotions, we have to identify the underlying process that gives rise to the emotions that we experience. To do this, let us look at some examples of emotions. In them, we shall see that there is a deep connection between emotions and beliefs, which we will need to explore.

First, let us imagine parents who have just lost their son. We would assume that they are grief stricken because most parents value their children and we tend to feel sadness when we lose our values (the more valuable the object lost, the more intense our feeling of sadness). However, what if their son was a suicide bomber and they believe that this means that he is guaranteed entrance into the most cherished realm of the afterlife and, further, that they will now be welcomed as well? If this were the case, the parents might feel very different, perhaps even happy. On the other hand, what if they feel conflicted about this because while they profess belief in their religion, they actually harbor doubts?

Second, let us imagine a young woman who comes from a poor family, but who has worked hard in college, including at side jobs while in school, to support herself in achieving her dream of getting into medical school and becoming a doctor. Now let us imagine that she gets the call from the admissions department of the very last school that she had applied to, from which she had yet to hear, and the admissions officer mistakenly tells her that she has been rejected. She believes that she has been rejected from every medical school and is despondent. She feels as though her dreams are crushed and that all of her hard work has been in vain. She commits suicide. What if, however, the admission officer had not made a mistake and, consequently, our hopeful medical student believed that she had been admitted to medical school and that she was on her way to achieving her dreams? Clearly, she would not feel despondent. In fact, she would likely feel joy and pride.

Third, let us say that two men, John and Dave, are best friends and have been for many years. Let us now imagine that John comes home to find Dave having sex with his wife, Sarah, and he becomes extremely angry. John feels angry because he believes he has been betrayed by two people that he trusted and loved. But that is certainly not all: there is a whole web of other beliefs that lead to John's anger. For example, John must also have a belief that marriage means that a spouse will not have sex with others. Let us say that, instead, John and Sarah were in an established and healthy open (*i.e.*, non-monogamous) relationship and they had discussed Sarah being intimate with Dave beforehand. If that were the case, John would not have been angry, because there would have been no breach of trust and no betrayal. Instead, John would likely be happy and aroused. John's response will be very different depending on what he believes.

Fourth, let us say that we have a friend, Sally, who is utterly overcome with grief by the loss of a particular button. We would likely find this to be silly or not understandable. We would probably question her about her reasons for being so distraught over such a small and apparently valueless object. Unless she could provide some compelling reason for holding this particular button in such high regard, we would consider her behavior irrational, because we expect a level of rationality from emotions. Yet, if we imagine that this particular button was her grandmother's, who has just died, then it is more understandable. It is even more understandable if we learn that her grandmother carried this button with her through her time in a National Socialist (NAZI) death camp as a token of good luck and it was given to Sally by her grandmother on her deathbed. If this were the case, we would think her response perfectly reasonable: it turns out that it is a particularly valuable button to her for sentimental reasons. What leads us to expect rationality in her emotional response? We expect that the emotion parallels the value the object had to our friend and since a button does not usually warrant debilitating grief, we would think this asymmetry between her esteem of the button and her response to be irrational. It is the same if we change our example to any emotion where a seemingly trivial object elicits a powerful emotion.

Through these examples, we have seen a clear connection between beliefs and emotions, even though historically emotions have been thought to be beyond analysis. Perhaps it is the immediacy of the emotional response or perhaps it is due to poor introspective skills; either way, few people recognize the role of belief in emotions until it is pointed out to them. Yet, once the connection to their beliefs is elucidated, most people are able to introspect on their own situations and see that it is indeed operative in their own lives. To say that belief is operative in emotions is merely to find a starting point. Yet, even so, it allows us to provide a tentative definition that we can use to push our analysis deeper. Our tentative definition of emotion is: emotions are a kind of mental phenomenon that operate as a response to our beliefs. Yet, we need to know more to understand how emotions work, so let us turn to the emotional process itself.

2. The Emotional Process

We saw in the above examples that beliefs change our emotions. Or, to be more precise, our emotions are *responses* to our beliefs.[i] The connection is more complicated, however, than the idea that any one particular belief directly causes any particular emotion. The belief "I am now holding a pen" is not by itself sufficient to cause an emotional response. On the other hand, the belief that "I am now holding the pen with which I will sign my beloved wife's death certificate," might cause an emotional response. Our emotions are rarely, if ever, responses to single beliefs. Rather, they are responses to our network of antecedent, or past, beliefs.

In order to better understand emotions, let us now analyze the emotional process in detail so that we may better understand its operation. The emotional process has three phases: the *identification phase*, the *evaluative phase*, and the *response phase*. We will discuss each in turn and then revisit our provisional definition in light of the new information. It is important to remember, however, that although we can conceptually break down the process of emotions, this process is still *experienced as a single, discrete, and instantaneous response*. A person never experiences the emotional process in terms of its component phases.

Identification Phase

The first step of the emotional process is the *identification* of something that will serve as the object of the emotion, whether that is an entity, action, or state of existence.[ii] Our emotions are not activated by our immediate experience of a thing, but only when we form a belief about that thing, which starts with the conceptual identification of the thing, such as "this X is a Y." This

---

[i] As Robert Solomon says, "The objects of the emotions are objects of [...] the world as we experience it." (*The Passions*, p. 115). Our emotions are not direct responses to things in the world, but to our *beliefs* about them.

[ii] Of course, our emotions can also be responses to our memories or imaginations. Our emotions can even have other emotions as their objects. We will turn to these more complicated cases in the next section.

identification provides the object of the emotion, to which the emotional process responds.[i] The simple perception or imagination of an entity, action, or state of existence that does not involve identification cannot serve as the object for an emotion as it would be a cognitive blank[ii]: we cannot feel anything about something that we know nothing about. It is not until we are able to form the concept of the thing in question, or recognize it as an instance of a previously formed concept, that it can serve as the object of an emotion. If a thing is not conceptually identified, at least on some level, it cannot cause an emotional response.[iii]

While conceptual identification is necessary, it need not be consciously performed. Indeed, most conceptual identification (*e.g.*, "this" is an X) is automatically done by our subconscious: we do not have to consciously pick out "cars," "trees," or "road" when we go for a walk and only become consciously engaged in this process when our subconscious cannot make the identification on its own. Because of this, we sometimes experience emotions without initially being able to consciously identify the object. For example, a person walking alone at night may start to feel afraid, although there is nothing around them that they consciously recognize as a threat; that is, although they feel afraid, there is no conscious object of the emotion. This indicates that the identification of the object of the emotion was made subconsciously. In this case, perhaps their subconscious linked their walking down a dark street at night to a similar event in their past where they felt unsafe or they believed that such an act would be unsafe because of things they have been told about the area. What is important here is that we may not consciously know the object of an emotion, but that does not mean that it has not been identified as this can happen in our subconscious.

The object of the emotion, whether identified consciously or subconsciously, does not need to be external to us; we can, and often do, have emotional responses to our own memories, imagination, thoughts, and beliefs.[iv] Indeed, our emotions can even be the object of our emotions (which would be

---

[i] This should not be understood as appealing to Cartesian representationalism. Rather, it is just an acknowledgement that we do, in fact, respond to our beliefs about the world and not to the way the world truly is. While the object of my belief *should* perfectly match the world, I am sometimes *wrong* about my assessment of the world or even my identification of things in it. We lack any sort of epistemic guarantee of our beliefs. We will return to this point shortly.

[ii] I first encountered this useful term in Leonard Peikoff's book *Objectivism: The Philosophy of Ayn Rand*.

[iii] Of course, we can feel fear because we have encountered something we do not know, where "something we do not know" actually serves as the object of the emotion. In this case, our fear is not about the thing itself, but about our lack of knowledge about it.

[iv] Cognitive Behavioral Therapy (CBT) operates on this very premise: that often our emotional responses stem from our automatic thoughts and that if we can change these automatic thoughts, then we can change our emotional responses. Of course, in CBT, the automatic thoughts are just the tip of the iceberg. My theory here, however, perfectly meshes with this idea and, I believe, even explains it in a more robust way, as we shall see.

a second-order emotion): *e.g.*, a person might be annoyed at his feelings of insecurity, and this whole thing can be the object of an emotion (which would be a third-order emotion), *e.g.*, a person being frustrated with his annoyance at his feelings of insecurity.[i]

At the same time, the object of an emotion can actually be false, as long as we believe that it is true or fear it being real enough to believe it is at least probable. This is because emotions are not responses to the world, but to our beliefs about it and our beliefs can be true or false. This is related to our emotional responses to fiction. Even though we know it is not real, we suspend disbelief in order to immerse ourselves in the story. This suspension of disbelief is us treating the story as though it were real.

To return to our major point, conceptual identification is necessary for the emotional process to begin.

Evaluative Phase

To understand the evaluative phase, let us start with an example. Let us say that a woman comes home from work early to find two cars in her driveway, one of which she knows is not her husband's. She opens the door and sees clothes strewn about by the couch and a couple of empty lowball glasses. She heads upstairs and hears the noises of people having sex. She opens the door to the bedroom and finds her husband in bed with another woman. She feels…what? Disgust? Anger? Shame? Or does she feel aroused? Excited? Or, perhaps, indifferent? Relieved that she can finally get the divorce?

From the example, we would not know what the woman would feel, because we do not know her evaluative framework. We do not know whether she will view the situation as good for her life or bad for it. Let us say that she believes that an open relationship would be optimal for her and her husband, that she values the love and stability of their existing relationship, but also values the excitement and variety of new sexual partners, and expects that they will enjoy their polysexual[ii] lifestyle together. If this is the case, she is going to feel excited about her discovery (as long as they had discussed this possibility in advance). To understand what the woman in our example will *feel*, we need to understand much more about her. Specifically, we need to understand her values and beliefs.

Our emotions are responses to our values and beliefs. In this way, conscious evaluation sets the stage for the evaluative phase of the emotional response, since it is the ultimate source of most of our values. Let us, then, briefly return to the topic of conscious evaluation, before we look further at the evaluative phase.

---

[i] Although interesting, second-order and third-order emotional responses are outside the scope of the present work.
[ii] For more discussion of polysexuality, see Volume 2, Chapter 13.

Conscious evaluation, as we have already seen in Chapter 1, is a kind of judgement about whether a thing would be a value or antivalue to a person; that is, whether a thing would promote the life of a person or whether it would be detrimental to the life of a person.[i] If we judge the thing to be a value, then we must fit it into our hierarchy of values, so that we can understand how it fits into the broader context of our life. We must also judge whether to pursue the value or work to avoid the antivalue: a thing might be a real value to a person, might be compatible with their hierarchy of values, and yet they should not pursue it if doing so would cause them to sacrifice something more valuable. It is important to remember that we have no guarantee of certainty about values and people do not always accurately judge what is best for their life. Sometimes people subjectively value things that are not objective values. However, any values or antivalues will function in the emotional process, whether they are real or apparent.[ii] Yet, as we have seen, for emotions to actually serve our lives and help us to create meaningful lives, they must be based on objective values.

The idea of *antivalues* requires more discussion. Just as their name suggests, antivalues are the opposite of values: they are things that harm our lives or make them worse. We did not focus on antivalues in Chapter 1 because they are more important for emotions than ethics, since ethics tells us what to do in order to live well (it is positively oriented). However, antivalues are important for understanding emotions because our evaluations sometimes tell us that a thing will be detrimental to our living well and we retain this in the form of an antivalue. Our subconscious retains both our values and antivalues in our evaluative framework and they both come into play in our emotions. To return to our example from above, if the woman walking in on her partner valued their relationship being monogamous and held an antivalue that being betrayed hurts her life (perhaps from being cheated on in the past), then we can predict that she will experience a strong negative emotional reaction, since one of her values is being threatened and one of her antivalues is happening.[iii]

Frequently, values and antivalues go together, but this is not necessarily so. We sometimes form values without any corresponding antivalues (*e.g.*, a person who has never been cheated on likely does not have a specific antivalue against it) and sometimes we form antivalues without any corresponding values (*e.g.*, a person who has a very negative existential orientation[iv] will likely have formed many antivalues without many corresponding values because he

---

[i] As a reminder, there is also the class of avalues, things that are morally neutral and neither help nor harm our life. This class is small and unimportant.

[ii] This explains how a person can have contradictory emotions: because they are coming from contradictory values that he holds. We will return to this point later in the chapter.

[iii] Without this antivalue in place, she may feel a strong negative reaction, but she might also feel nothing in the moment, as she would have to process what happened before having an emotional response.

[iv] We will defer discussion of existential orientation until the next section.

focuses only on negatives). Holding antivalues is important for emotions because it prevents the need to reevaluate unnecessarily. Moreover, holding well-formed and clear antivalues facilitates quicker evaluations and stronger emotional reactions, as we shall see.

We have seen that values and antivalues are involved in our emotional responses and we have seen how conscious evaluation functions, but we have yet to come to a real understanding of how this connects with emotions. Certainly, it is not the case that just because we consciously hold a value or antivalue that our emotions will respond to it. So how do we get from having values and antivalues to emotions? The connection comes through *internalization*.

What does it mean to "internalize" a value or antivalue? It means that we accept it as part of ourselves, which means that we accept it as something that will influence our choices and behavior. If we internalize honesty as a value, for example, then this means we accept that we should be honest and that this should influence our behavior. Insofar as we resist this, we have not fully internalized it as a value.[i] However, internalizing is not always, or perhaps not even usually, a conscious process. Internalization is an automatic subconscious process that can happen as the result of wanting to consciously internalize a value, but it can also happen without any conscious input. Indeed, we internalize all sorts of messages passively through the culture in which we live and from the ideas to which we are exposed (as we will see with "shamenorming" in Chapter 6). Moreover, as we grew up and matured, we internalized many beliefs and values, some actively and some passively. All of these have an impact on our identity. To paraphrase Ayn Rand: If there is any truth in the myth of a great judge who records everything, it is to be found in our subconscious, from which nothing can be hidden.[49] Our subconscious retains these values and beliefs that we internalize, whether we did so actively or passively. Internalization is not usually quick as we often take a while to fully accept something as true. On the other hand, we sometimes internalize new values and beliefs quickly if they fit with the values and beliefs we already hold.

The values we *purposely* choose to internalize and work to achieve are a major part of our character. Yet, all of our values and antivalues, even those we internalized passively, partly constitute our identity because they all end up in our evaluative framework. Everything in the evaluative framework, not simply the values that we have chosen purposefully and put into our hierarchy of values, comes into play in the emotional process.

A person's evaluative framework contains all of their values and antivalues, as well as some of their beliefs. More specifically, the evaluative framework contains a person's *moral* beliefs about what is good and evil, about

---

[i] Which is not to take the Socratic position that *akrasia* is impossible (*Protagoras*, 358d: "no one willingly goes after evil or what he thinks to be evil"), but merely to say that if we really believe it, then we will usually act according to it, all other things being equal.

the standard of judgement used to understand this, and about how to apply this to our lives. It contains a person's idea of virtue, their moral principles, and their beliefs about how their life should go. To be clear, our evaluative framework does not contain the processes or the ability to judge itself. Rather, it contains the results of these things: our evaluative framework contains our values, antivalues, judgements, and beliefs. Our evaluative framework is largely the result of our conscious philosophy that has been internalized and it simply stores these things to be used in our subconscious evaluation.

Now that we have seen the function of the evaluative framework and how conscious evaluation sets the stage for the evaluative phase, it is time to see how this actually works. The evaluative phase operates through what might be called subconscious evaluation, but which is more precisely called *subconscious correspondence*. This is because our subconscious does not, itself, have the power of judgement or evaluation *per se* (which are conscious faculties). Rather, our subconscious compares the object of the emotion with our evaluative framework to see if anything there is *relevant* or *corresponds* to the object of the emotion.[i] By making a comparison to relevant internalized values and beliefs in our evaluative framework, our subconscious can give us an immediate evaluation of the object of the emotion. Thus, in the *evaluative phase* of the emotional process, our subconscious compares the identified object of emotion to our relevant internalized values and beliefs in order to be able to give us immediate evaluative information in the response phase.

In order to judge relevance between the identified object of the emotion and our internalized values and beliefs, our subconscious searches for past instances where the object of the emotion has occurred before. It tries to find values or beliefs related to the same object or similar objects to use these in the response phase. At the same time, it also takes into account the context of the object of the emotion and looks for similar instances in the past where the situation was the same or similar, whether or not the object of the emotion is the same. If it finds a direct match (the exact object of emotion or context), then it will consider this to be relevant and will use the values or beliefs associated with it to provide the basis for an emotional response.

If our subconscious is not able to find a direct match, but is able to find a similar instance, then it will use this as the basis of the response, although this will lessen our response, as we will feel uncertain of the emotion. If our subconscious can find no relevant past instances, then this will stop the

---

[i] Lest it be objected that the subconscious does have the power of judgement, because we sometimes have beliefs that we do not remember consciously forming, it should be recalled that the ways in which we come to have beliefs are many and complicated. This includes passively accepting them from other people or the culture. In these cases, the subconscious merely checks to see if the new belief is concordant with our existing beliefs and, if it is, simply accepts it. If it does not match our pre-existing beliefs, then the subconscious will likely reject it (even if it is, in fact, true). This process relies on similarity of belief, not judgement.

emotional process and we will experience no response. In order to find relevance, our subconscious looks for similarity with our internalized values and antivalues. In cases where our subconscious can find no match, the conscious mind will have to make a judgement about whether it is bad or not and then the emotional process will continue from that point.[i] Subconscious correspondence is, then, more a process of scanning our internalized values and beliefs for similarity to the current object (including its context) in order to automatize our ability to react to situations immediately through our emotions, instead of having to consciously deliberate about every situation we encounter.

One of the ways that we can facilitate subconscious correspondence is by having a well-formed hierarchy of values. While subconscious correspondence is capable of utilizing anything in the evaluative framework, it starts with those values and beliefs that we identify with most strongly. A well-constructed hierarchy of values allows subconscious evaluation to function more efficiently because it establishes a relationship of the relative importance of our values, and our subconscious uses this to facilitate its search for relevance. Of course, the better integrated our values are to our overall life and the fewer discordant values we hold, the better this works. If we do not have a well-formed hierarchy, the process of subconscious correspondence simply turns to the broader evaluative framework.

Even if our hierarchy of values is well-formed, subconscious correspondence does not solely rely on our hierarchy of values and may pull in other values and beliefs from the evaluative framework, even those that are discordant. To be clear, "discordant" here does not simply mean discordant with a person's hierarchy of values, but can also mean discordant with their conscious convictions and sense of their own personal identity. Let us return, briefly, to our example from above of the woman finding her husband in bed with another woman. She might consciously think of herself as the kind of person who is okay with her partner having sex with others and think that jealousy is an emotion that she should not experience. Yet, if she has internalized cultural beliefs that monogamy is the only right way to have a relationship, then this discordant belief could cause her to feel conflicted or even jealous when confronted with the reality of the situation. Discordant beliefs can cause us to have weak emotional responses or cause discordant emotional responses that do not fit with our conscious beliefs about what we should be feeling.

Since many people have at least some discordant values and beliefs, whether from having an inconsistent philosophy, making a mistake, accepting apparent values, passively internalizing beliefs, *etc.*, our subconscious can even find *contradictory* relevant values and beliefs. If we continue with our example, if

---

[i] The emotional process will continue if, and only if, the conscious judgement is consistent with the antecedent network of beliefs. If it represents a shift or break with past beliefs and value judgements, the emotional process will not continue until that new judgement is internalized.

the woman had only recently come to believe that sex outside her relationship could be morally permissible, but still held the belief that monogamy was the only way for a relationship to be successful, then her subconscious correspondence could return contradictory beliefs. While we cannot consciously hold contradictory beliefs for long without being aware of this tension, we are capable of doing so subconsciously because our subconscious does not process the beliefs. It merely stores them and uses them in certain processes, such as here in subconscious correspondence. In this case, it can stall the emotional process or end up with the person feeling competing emotions, such as the woman feeling excited to find her partner with another woman while feeling scared that relationship might fail.

Since our subconscious correspondence compares the object of the emotion to our values and beliefs, it should come as no surprise that this is naturally self-directed and, thus, self-interested. On the other hand, emotions are responses to our values and if we value other people, then our emotions can include them as well.[i] Nevertheless, emotions are primarily self-directed. If, once the object is identified, a person is not able to see a relationship to himself, then the emotional process will end. This holds even with emotions like empathy, which seems naturally other-interested. There are two ways that the emotional process can be activated by others: the first is when a person can imagine the same thing happening to himself and the second is when a person already has a pre-established relationship with the other person in question. Empathy is a feeling-together-with another person. In the case of empathizing with a stranger, we can empathize if, and only if, we can at least imagine the same misfortune befalling us. If we cannot "put ourself in the other person's shoes," then empathy will not arise.[ii] On the other hand, if the person in question already has an established relation to us, as in the case of a friend or family member, then we need not "put ourself in their shoes" as the person in question is already part of our value hierarchy and thus any harm to them is an indirect harm to us as their happiness is partly constitutive of our own (to the degree to which we value them). The process of understanding the object's connection to our life and its impact on our life is the process of evaluation in

---

[i] We will return to this point later when we discuss integrating others into our lives, specifically with regard to friends and lovers.

[ii] This "putting oneself in the shoes of another" need not be even quasi-literal. I could feel empathetic for a woman who has just had a miscarriage, even though as a male I could never literally experience this. This is because I can understand that her miscarrying means the termination of her yet unborn child and that this is a terrible loss. I need not literally know what it is like to experience this loss in order to know that it is terrible. A person might argue that someone could not understand the *depth* of a person's suffering who has lost a child, unless he has also lost a child. This may, indeed, be true. But, empathy does not need a literal construal of "putting oneself in another's shoes" in order to make sense. It is sufficient that I understand that another sees something as a loss and could imagine the feeling of loss in my own life. There is a real way in which all losses are similar.

a nutshell.

Because the subconscious is incapable of actual evaluation, if it were met with an entirely novel experience, it would be unable to process it. This is hard to imagine, because it is hard to imagine something about which we have no experience or even relevant experience. A person who has never seen a cougar or tiger in person, but has some idea that large cats can be dangerous, will still feel fear when confronted by a cougar hunting them in the dark, even though they have never seen a cougar. This is because we can generalize from our knowledge about large cats in general to the specific kind of large cat now hunting us. However, let us imagine a knight in the early medieval period. If someone were to point a modern rifle at him, the knight would not know to be afraid. The knight would have no idea what the rifle was: it would just look like someone pointing a weird stick at him. How can a knight be harmed by this weird stick with his armor and shield? Of course, we know that the bullet would go right through the knight's armor, but he does not. The knight would not know to fear the rifle, because the rifle is completely alien to him. Until he learns what it is and what it is capable of, he cannot have an emotional reaction to it. It would be the same if we pointed the gun at an infant: until the infant learns what a gun is, it will not fear it (please do not do this).

Thus, we can now see that the evaluative phase uses subconscious correspondence to compare the identified object of the emotion against relevant internalized values and beliefs to form an instantaneous evaluative response. The stage is set for the evaluative phase by conscious evaluation, but it relies on subconscious correspondence to function. Emotions are morally oriented and we can see this because they rely on our evaluative framework to set the stage for our emotional responses. Emotions help us to live well, as long as we do the work of forming the right values and beliefs, internalizing these, and working to root out discordant and contradictory values and beliefs.

Response Phase

Once our subconscious has located relevant internalized values and beliefs, we will have an emotional response. In terms of the response itself, it is completely outside of our control[i]: we can neither directly cause it to happen, nor stop it from happening.[ii] However, a question arises here about what, exactly, an emotional response is. Many people tend to think of emotional

---

[i] This is why a person cannot be judged for their emotional responses. However, we can be judged for failing to properly cultivate our values and beliefs as well as not working to change emotions that are not aligned with our happiness.

[ii] There is also no doubt that it is possible to repress or evade our emotional process: not completely and not indefinitely, but for at least a time and to some degree. However, it is impossible to do this in one isolated area only: if we repress the emotional process, then it is effected across the board.

responses simply in terms of their affective states (*i.e.*, how they feel in the body). For example, some people think that anger feels hot, that they "see red," and that it involves a rush of adrenaline, tensing of the muscles, *etc.*, and this is all we can say of anger because this is all that anger is.[i] However, saying that an emotion is just an affective response presents many problems. For example, we cannot distinguish emotions based on affective states alone: if we know only that our heart is racing and we feel tense, we cannot determine what emotions we might be experiencing (if any). We might be angry or scared. We might be about to confront a person who is assaulting someone else and feel *both* brave and nervous.

On the other hand, we often experience emotions without feeling any affect at all. Let us say that we have a longstanding hatred for an enemy of ours who has harmed us repeatedly in the past. When thinking of this person, we will experience hatred, but it is unlikely that we will have a strong affective response. Of course, we could cause ourselves to have a strong affective response for this person if we recalled to mind the various ways in which this person has harmed us in the past. But, we can feel hatred without that. Or, consider that when we say that we love our spouse, we do not usually mean that we are feeling a particularly strong affective response when we think of them or any affective response at all. Yet, this does not mean that we do not love them. All of this is inconceivable if we tie emotions too strongly to affective states. But, if we do not tie emotions to affective states, then what are they?

Emotions are a kind of understanding of a person's relationship to the object, a form of automatic evaluative awareness based on their internalized values and beliefs, that allows a person to *experience* their values and beliefs, so that they can immediately know whether the object will be beneficial or detrimental to their life. In this way, emotions are automatized evaluations that orient us to the world. However, emotions are more than simply the immediate awareness, since it is obvious that they persist across time. They persist through time by forming part of our identity as well as being manifestations of it: that is, our being the kind of person who hates wickedness comes from our values and beliefs, which cause certain emotions that allow us to experience the reality of these values and beliefs, which in turn reinforce them in our identity. Moreover, as we have already said, our emotions allow us to create meaning in life by being able to experience our values.

None of this is to say that emotions do not often, or even usually, involve affective states. But, it *is* to say that emotions do not *necessarily* involve affective states and that it creates insurmountable problems to try to tie them too closely together, not the least of which is that it contradicts our actual experience of emotions (*e.g.*, being in love without always feeling love's affects).[ii] Emotions

---

[i] We will return to this point when we discuss physicalism in love in Chapter 3.
[ii] This is why Robert Solomon says that: "feeling [affect] is the ornament of emotion, not its

should be primarily identified with being oriented to the object in a certain way, but always with the *potential* for affective response.

That emotions always have the potential for affective response can be seen if we consider that we can always activate the affective response of an emotion that we already have by thinking about the reasons that we hold the emotion and letting the affective response happen. For example, when a person says that she loves her wife, she is saying that she is oriented to her wife in a certain way. But, she is not reporting that she has a specific affective state at any time. Now, however, she could bring on the affective state by thinking about the reasons that she loves her wife, specific memories that are particularly symbolic, and their history together. Through doing this, she can activate the affective state and experience it. Thus, emotions are a way of being oriented to the object and with a potential affective response to it.

Emotions

Now that we understand the emotional process and how it operates, we are ready to give a better definition of emotions. Our original tentative definition was: "emotions are a kind of mental phenomenon that operate as a response to our beliefs." This is still true, but not very instructive. Our revised definition is this: Emotions are a form of automatic evaluative awareness that orient us to their objects and are experienced as a cognitive conviction and often with attendant affect. Underlying this is the emotional process, which we have seen is a very specific automatic process of identification, evaluation, and response.

The emotional process, however, is *not* a truth-generating process. It cannot tell us anything about the world itself; it can only tell us about our own values and beliefs, to which it is a response. This is the reason why Rand said that: "emotions are not tools of cognition."[50] This is very important to understand because many people think that their feelings do, in fact, tell them something objectively true about the world.[i] However, since our emotions are responses to our values and beliefs, if our values and beliefs are not objective, then our emotions will not be proper responses to the world. This is not to say that an emotion *could never* be a correct response to the world; it is just that we have no direct way of knowing this, as there is no truth-tracking function built into emotions. Unless we took the emotion that we are experiencing and consciously tried to identify the values and beliefs to which it was a response, we will have no way of even knowing whether or not the emotion is consistent with our overall beliefs, let alone true, because of the issue of discordant and

---

essence." (*The Passions*, p. 97). I, however, think this is too strong because emotions are always *potentially* affective.

[i] This mistake is often labeled "intuition." See Volume 3, Chapter 19 for a full discussion of intuition and intuitionism.

contradictory values and beliefs. Thus, we cannot use our emotions as *tools* of cognition, although they are certainly appropriate *objects* of cognition; that is, we cannot think *with* our emotions, but we should certainly think *about* them, and this can be quite beneficial.

One final thing to consider about response phase is an emotion's *scope*, which refers to the *breadth* and *depth* of the values and beliefs to which it is a response. Breadth refers to the range of different parts of a person's self that come into play through the values and beliefs to which the emotion is a response: a broad scope will impact many different values and beliefs from different parts of a person's life, while a narrow scope will only impact a few. Depth, on the other hand, refers to the degree to which a person considers any particular value or belief constitutive of their identity: a deep scope comes from a response to those values that constitute a person's core values, while an emotion with shallow scope will be a response to those peripheral values that are not so closely tied to their identity. For example, a man's love for his wife should encompass his most deeply held values, beliefs, and even his conception of who he is as a person. The values and beliefs to which his love is a response are both broad and deep in scope: it is a response to his core values that go all the way to the heart of his identity. Emotional responses that are broad in scope we experience as "expansive" emotions, while emotional responses that are deep in scope we experience as "profound" emotions.

3. Sentiments

We have seen how emotions, such as love, hatred, anger, *etc.*, operate and we now have a solid understanding of the emotional process. However, in our above discussion of emotions, we glossed over a distinction between related mental phenomena that have different experiences and different impacts on our psychological life. We did this in order to first get a firm grasp of emotions, since they are more familiar and because they serve as a good paradigm of the related phenomena. However, emotions are but one kind of *sentiment*,[i] which are united in that they share the same underlying process that we have been discussing (and, given that they are united in this process, it should more properly be called the "sentimental process"). Moreover, we will have to update our definition to reflect this more nuanced view: Sentiments are a form of automatic evaluative awareness that orient us to their objects and are experienced as a cognitive conviction and often with attendant affect. Underlying this is the sentimental process with its very specific automatic

---

[i] Although I use the term "sentiments" to connect all those things that result from the "emotional process," this should not be construed as a connection to the tradition of Sentimentalism that comes from David Hume or Adam Smith. Indeed, I take the opposite view (that emotions and reason are intimately connected), as opposed to the Sentimentalist view that they are necessarily in opposition.

process of identification, evaluation, and response.

Sentiments range from emotions, to moods, to existential moods, and to existential orientation and are distinguished from each other by their objects and responses. The type of object is different for each kind of sentiment: while emotions have a definite object, the object for a mood is how things are going right now (this could be today or this week), the object for an existential mood is how our life is going overall, and the object for an existential orientation is the entirety of ourselves, other people, and reality. Because the objects of the sentiments differ in kind, the responses are different in kind as well. Sentiments with broader objects *potentially* lead to more of the evaluative framework being involved and, thus, to the response having a larger impact on us in terms of orienting us to the object. Even so, it is important that we stress that it is potentially the case, because some emotions like love will have a larger impact on us than some moods like being excited.

At each stage, as the object and the response to it becomes broader, the sentiments become more encompassing and play more of a role in a person's life and identity. In general, the more abstract the sentiment (*i.e.*, existential orientation), the more intricate its connection to the scope of our values and beliefs; however, even simple emotions can be quite intricate in the values and beliefs to which they are a response. Through understanding the sentiments, we will set ourselves up to understand things like sexual attraction and love at the deepest level.

Emotions

We have already discussed emotions at length, but it is worth pointing out some things about their objects and responses to help more easily compare emotions to the rest of the sentiments. In the case of emotions, the object of the emotion is always definite, although it can range from things in the world and their actions, to other emotions (*e.g.*, annoyance at loving an ex-partner who treated us badly).

Although the object of emotion is definite, it still might have a very complex web of values and beliefs to which it is a response, so the responses might still be expansive and profound. With erotic love, for example, the object of emotion is always a person and it draws from experience with friends, expectations about love and a good partner, past romances, *etc*.

In addition to the object of the emotion being definite, so is the response to the object; *e.g.*, "Frank hates John." Depending on the reasons why Frank hates John, the hatred could be expansive and profound or it could be narrow and shallow, if, for example, he hated him because he did not like his orange hair. The salient point is that emotions are distinguished by having a definite object and response and, in this case, Frank will be oriented in a very specific way towards John.

Moods

In the case of *moods*, such as joy, sorrow, or excitement, which are sentiments with slightly larger scopes, the object of emotion is typically a state of existence instead of a specific object. However, the state of existence here is very delimited; *i.e.*, the object is what is happening around me today or this week. The object of moods is indefinite in the sense that there is no unitary object, but rather different factors come together to make the object. For example, we are not having a good day and feeling joy merely because we slept well, worked out, ate a good lunch, or talked to an old friend we have not seen in a while. Instead, we are experiencing joy because all of these good things happened and they collectively culminate in the response of our mood.

This is because joy is a mood of well-being that has as its object the belief that "things are going well right now," where "right now" means today or this week, but not the overall course of our life. Even in the case where joy seems to have a specific object, for example that we finished a big project at work, if the overall situation were different and things had been going very poorly that day, we would not feel joy, but maybe simple accomplishment at this fact. Moods are about how our life is going right now.

Since moods have as their object states of existence, their responses tend to be broader than emotions. Our mood of joy, for example, having as its object how our day is going, has a broader response that encompasses more things. Joy orients us towards the state of existence and positively disposes us to the objects. Moreover, because the response is broad, it tends to color our responses to other things at the same time: we are less likely to let minor annoyances bother us when we are in a good mood and more likely to do so when in a bad mood.

Existential Moods

Existential moods,[i] like moods, have an indefinite object, but they have a larger scope than moods. Existential mood has as its object the way our overall course of life is going and whether we think it will lead to happiness or not.[ii]

---

[i] I was introduced to the term "existential mood" by Patrick Ryan, who got it from Matthew Ratcliffe. However, there is no similarity in our views (at least, as far as I can tell from reading "Depression, Guilt, and Emotional Depth" and "The Phenomenology of Existential Feeling," because Ratcliffe seems to have no well-defined view at all). I, thus, beg Ratcliffe's forgiveness for using the term, but it seemed that someone should.

[ii] We can sometimes directly experience how our lives are going through an "existential moment"—a moment of perspective where we are able to see the course of our lives through a particularly meaningful event or through a work of art that concretizes our values for us. An existential moment arises when our values are on the line and the more fundamental the value is to our identity, the more likely we will be to experience an existential moment. Achieving a high value or losing a high value are both common times to have the experience of an

This is much more foundational for our identity than a mood because it takes into account the overall course of our life, as opposed to a mood which is simply about how our life is going *right now*. There are many existential moods, such as depression, anxiety, ennui, malaise, *etc.*, on the negative side, and happiness (the felt aspect), tranquility, contentment, pride, satisfaction, hopefulness,[i] *etc.*, on the positive side. These are all about the overall course of our life and have this as their object.

The actual judgement of how our life is going is made consciously and this judgement is used as one of the beliefs in the formation and continuation of the existential mood.[ii] While this may seem to be a rare event, it is a judgement that we all make all the time. For example, a man facing adversity and being crushed by it might internalize the belief that his life is not going well and he is powerless to do anything about it. If this persists, these beliefs will be reinforced and this may lead to depression. Of course, the exact beliefs to which the existential moods will be a response will vary from person to person depending on their context: not everything that would cause depression in one person would cause it in another (this is primarily a function of existential orientation, but is also impacted by how a person conceptualizes the events of his life).

The responses of existential moods are pervasive and affect a person across their identity. In fact, our existential moods make up a part of our identity: *e.g.*, "no matter what happens, he is unflappable and always seems at peace," indicates contentment or tranquility. Indeed, a person's existential moods are often a major way that they are thought of and understood by others, and even understand themselves.

Existential Orientation

In the case of existential orientation, like existential mood, the object and response to it is also indefinite and broad. Yet, for the existential orientation, its scope is even larger: indeed, as large as it can be. The object of the existential orientation is our view of ourself, our view of others, and of the very nature of the world itself. Let us call this *existential orientation* because it is the fundamental way a person orients himself towards existence. It is deeper and more pervasive than an existential mood and influences everything about us from our emotions, to our judgements, to the way we carry ourselves and interact with

---

existential moment.

[i] There is a fundamental difference between being hopeful that my team may win a sporting event (a mood) and a cultivated disposition of hopefulness towards how our life is going (an existential mood).

[ii] As a psychological matter, existential moods are also marked by patterns of thought that serve to reinforce and perpetuate them. This is true for both the positive existential moods as well as the negative existential moods. The latter are also usually marked by epistemic fallacies that lock people into them, which are called "cognitive distortions" by CBT.

others. It is, in a real sense, the foundation of the "style" of our soul.[i] We are going to look more closely at existential orientation because it is important for understanding emotions, moods, and existential moods as well as love and sexual attraction.

In order to get to existential orientation, we must start with Rand's idea of "sense of life," from which it grew. Rand thought that sense of life had as its object two different and fundamental views: our beliefs about the nature of the world and our beliefs about the nature of ourselves.[51] Sense of life is a response to questions like: Is the world knowable to us? Are we capable of effective action? Is the world the kind of place where effective action is even possible? Is our fate open to our action or determined by things outside our control? *etc*. These questions are united in their attempt to understand the nature of the world and of ourselves.

Sense of life ultimately comes down to the question: "Is life open to us?" This leads to there being two fundamentally different kinds of sense of life, depending on the answer. The first, a malevolent sense of life, is when a person believes that the world is unknowable, that it is not the kind of place where success is possible, that he is incapable of efficacious action, and that choice is an illusion; it is, in short, the belief that life is not open to him. The second, a benevolent sense of life is when a person believes that the world is knowable, that it is the kind of place where success is possible, that he is capable of efficacious action, and that choice is real; it is, in short, the belief that life is open to him. Sadly, Rand's idea of sense of life is underdeveloped and this is about as far as it goes.[ii]

Rand thought that sense of life was foundational to a person and held at the very deepest levels. Moreover, she believed that a person's sense of life impacted them at every level and helped to shape who they were as a person. In this way, it served as a sort of "leitmotif" of a person.

Our account of existential orientation generally agrees with Rand's idea that this deepest level of response must be based in a person's fundamental views of the world and himself, but further develops the underlying account of how this works. In order to flesh this out, we need to turn first to the Cognitive Behavior Therapy idea of "core beliefs" as elaborated by Aaron Beck.[iii] In CBT, the idea of core beliefs is as follows:

---

[i] We will explore this idea in depth in Chapter 5.

[ii] Although she does some very interesting work applying it, as in "Art and Sense of Life" and "Philosophy and Sense of Life" in the *Romantic Manifesto*.

[iii] Aaron Beck, along with Albert Ellis, is the father of CBT. Core beliefs and intermediate beliefs should be distinguished from regularly-held conscious beliefs, in that they operate below the level of consciousness (*i.e.* in the subconscious) and impact how we *experience* ourselves and the world.

> Beginning in childhood, people develop certain ideas about themselves, other people, and their world. Their most central or *core beliefs* are enduring understandings so fundamental and deep that they often do not articulate them, even to themselves. The person regards these ideas as absolute truths—just the way things "are."[52]

These core beliefs are what sense of life is trying to capture: those deep-seated and unarticulated beliefs that underlie our view of everything and constitute our conception of the nature of existence or, as Beck says, "just the way things are." However, Beck is right that, as opposed to the two categories of the nature of the self and the nature of the world in sense of life, that there are actually *three* fundamental categories: views about oneself, views about others, and views about the nature of the world.[i]

These three categories are not only the categories of the core beliefs, but also of the *fundamental psychological needs*, to which core beliefs are a response. To be more precise, core beliefs are responses to the fundamental psychological needs, which arise because of the need to *understand* the nature of our selves, other people, and the world in which we live. There are many fundamental psychological needs that give rise to core beliefs. Among these are: the need for personal identity, psychological continuity, intimacy, meaning, safety, whether moral action is possible, whether I am a moral person, *etc.*[ii]

These needs are fundamental because they lay the foundation for a person's entire worldview and impact every level of their sentiments: they are fundamental to the very self. Some of these needs are also fundamental in the sense that a person must understand certain things in order to be able to act in the world. It is hard to elaborate these needs in conceptual terms, because they begin prior to the maturation of our conceptual faculty (that is, in childhood) and this framework underlies our understanding of everything. One useful shorthand is to think of the needs in terms of questions that need to be answered. For example, we all have a fundamental psychological need for safety that we can think of in terms of the question: "Am I safe?" This need starts immediately after birth, long before an infant or child can even understand the concept of safety. Nevertheless, infants and young children have a sense of this through bonding with their caregivers and the attachment they form with them: the child either *feels* safe or does not. As adults, we can think about this process

---

[i] Arguably, Rand's statement "A sense of life is a pre-conceptual equivalent of metaphysics, an emotional, subconsciously integrated appraisal of man and of existence" (RM, 25) could be taken to include all three categories, but her usage does not track this, *e.g.*, "Every choice and value-judgment implies some estimate of himself and of the world around him—most particularly, of his capacity to deal with the world." (RM, 25).

[ii] I do not intend this list to be exhaustive, but to show some of the fundamental psychological needs that give rise to the questions to which core beliefs are a response. An exhaustive set of fundamental psychological needs is outside of the scope of this book.

as the child's mind integrating information such as: "Am I healthy?," "Am I in pain?," "Are my needs being met?," "Is someone watching out for me?," or "Am I in danger?". From this, the child forms a rudimentary core belief to which his feeling of safety is a response. However, it would be a radical misunderstanding to think of this in the same way that an adult might make a conscious judgement of safety, or lack thereof, when walking through an area with high crime after dark. The fundamental psychological need is for safety *as such*, the very possibility of safety, and not safety in this moment.

We naturally and automatically form responses to the fundamental psychological needs, although this is not done consciously. We start this process as infants, from the moment our minds begin to work, and continue through childhood, as we begin to purposefully engage with the world, forming and reforming our conclusions as we go. When we reach adulthood, this process continues unabated, although we can indirectly affect it with effort (which is a major goal of psychotherapy). Consider even something so basic as object permanence that we learn as infants. It is not as though we abandon this as adults. Rather, it forms part of our conception of the nature of the world: objects will not simply disappear when we are not viewing them (contra *esse est percipi*).[i] Our view of the nature of the world is composed of myriad observations and conclusions that we reached as we learned about the world; such as we learn that hot things can burn and cause pain, objects tend to fall to the ground, and day always follows night. From these things, we learn that the world is predictable and understandable. This we hold as part of our core belief related to the nature of the world.

While, again, the fundamental psychological needs are not questions, it is useful to conceptualize them as such to aid in our understanding. For example, with regard to core beliefs about the self, we can understand them as though they were responses to such questions as: "Am I worthy of love?," "Am I capable of effective action?," "Am I capable of knowing the world outside myself?," "Am I capable of creating purpose in my life?," and "Can I learn and increase my abilities or am I as good as I will ever be?".[ii] There are also corresponding core beliefs in the other categories. For example, "Am I capable of knowing the world outside of myself?" also entails "Are other people?" and "Is the world the kind of thing that is capable of being known?" If the world is mutable, if it can simply change for no reason, then we are not capable of truly knowing it. If other people are unable to look out at the world and know it, then that is an important thing to know as well. It is important to remember, again, that the question is just a tool to consciously understand a psychological

---

[i] Latin for "to be is to be perceived." From (Bishop) George Berkeley, who believed that existents depended on being perceived, so posited a god to look on and save things from disappearing.

[ii] Some exceptional work on this particular question has been done by Carol Dweck and her theory of "Mindsets."

need. For example, with the question "Am I worthy of love?" the need here is to feel worthwhile. Self-worth is a real human need and its lack can contribute to significant psychological problems, such as depression.

Self-worth is a core belief and we all have some sense of whether we consider ourselves worthwhile and whether others do as well. However, it is not as though we consciously hold this belief in conceptual form as a clear and fully articulated belief. Core beliefs are held subconsciously as more of a positive or negative "sense" of the thing.[i] This sense is dichotomous and held as an affirmation or denial: *e.g.*, a person either holds a positive sense that they are worthwhile or a negative sense that they are not worthwhile, with no middle option. Because these core beliefs are not consciously held, a person may not be aware of their own beliefs.

Existential orientation also varies in intensity in how it is experienced by a person. In general, a person's existential orientation is a constant baseline that he experiences day in and day out. This experience is very low in intensity and is constantly present, so he usually does not turn much attention to it. There are times, however, when a person's existential orientation response becomes very intense and he cannot help but turn his attention to it. This happens when high values are at stake: when a person has achieved a high value or has lost a high value. For instance, imagine a man on his wedding day, overcome by the many sentiments that such an event evokes: joy at the momentous event in his life being achieved, pride in winning a worthy spouse for himself, and hope for their shared future. All of these emotions will well up inside him during the moment when he sees his future wife for the first time on their wedding day, yet at the same time he will also have an existential orientation response to this momentous event and he will feel, perhaps in a quiet moment after the ceremony has been completed and he is alone with his new wife, that his life is going well and that he is achieving the things that are important to him in his life: that *this is how life should be*. Whenever there are high values gained or lost, a person will have an existential orientation response to this and its intensity will vary based on the degree of the value involved.

One of the places where existential orientation becomes very important is in terms of a person's personality: existential orientation is that indescribable something, the *"Je ne sais quoi,"*[ii] that makes two people different from each other, even if they share the same ideas, backgrounds, wishes, *etc*. Existential orientation is one of the core components of a person's personality. For example, we can imagine two women with the exact same job, from similar backgrounds, with the same ambitions, and even with the same general set of beliefs (*e.g.*, they both believe in classical liberalism). However, let us say that the two women have a very different fundamental outlook on life: one is very

---

[i] It is worth pointing out that a person's existential orientation is not quantifiable in terms of some kind of core belief calculus.
[ii] The phrase *"Je ne sais quoi"* is French for "I know not what."

optimistic and looks forward to a challenge, whereas the other is very pessimistic and feels that any sort of challenge is an assault to her self-esteem. This difference is based on their existential orientation: on how they view their ability to achieve goals. Perhaps the optimistic woman believes that the world is the kind of place where effective action is possible and that she is the kind of person who is capable of efficacious action while the other woman believes that the world is the kind of place where effective action is not possible or that she is the kind of person who is incapable of efficacious action. Either way, it should be obvious that these women's personalities will be very different.

Existential orientation can manifest in fundamental personality in lots of ways, such as in the person who thinks that he is fundamentally good but that the world is fundamentally bad, and so are other people, and so attempts to cope through sarcasm. Or the woman who views herself and the world as fundamentally good, but other people as generally incompetent, but who expects them to try, and so is optimistic. To be clear, a person's fundamental personality *is* the expression of a person's existential orientation. While there might be some small natural disposition (*i.e.*, temperament) with which babies are born, this merely sets the stage for the existential orientation to develop, but does not determine the existential orientation.

While a person's conscious philosophy plays a large role in his personality, and his existential orientation, it is a person's existential orientation that we respond to when we make instant judgements about a person when we first meet them: whether a person is friendly or hostile, someone we would like to get to know or someone we would rather not waste our time on, or perhaps someone who is a potential friend or lover. Insofar as there is any truth in the idea of our "first impressions" of a person being able to tell us much about them, or of the idea of "love at first sight," the truth comes from our recognition of their existential orientation and our recognition of its compatibility with our own. Existential orientation provides that "spark" that people talk of when they know that they "just fit"—it is the basis of interpersonal "chemistry." We recognize it based on our own experiences with other people; how people hold their bodies, comport themselves, in the way they gesture and talk, and all the various subconscious cues that people give off. Even though most of us could not explain how we are able to tell so much about a person when we first meet them, we know that we do. Existential orientation is how this works: we are responding to their existential orientation and learning about them from it.

In order to really show existential orientation and its impact, let us turn to a fictional example.[i] In *The Count of Monte Cristo* by Alexandre Dumas, we can see the issue of existential orientation play out perfectly through the character of Edmond Dantès. The story opens with a young sailor who is doing well for

---

[i] I am purposefully omitting many details and even characters in order to focus on the issue of existential orientation. Please refer to the original for the full story.

himself and is proud of it. His life is going the way he wants and he will soon be marrying his beloved Mercédès. During this time, Dantès has a very benevolent view of the world and believes it to be the kind of place where efficacious action is possible, where other people are good, and where he himself is acting well.

Unfortunately, he is conspired against by a trio of blackguards: one of the men on the ship (Danglars) is jealous of him for his successes, Mercédès's cousin (Fernand) wants to marry her instead, and a prosecutor (Villefort) wants to protect his family name for political reasons. Because of their treachery, Dantès ends up in a terrible prison, Le Chateau D'If. There, he spends many years growing bitter at the injustice of having his life robbed from him. He seeks nothing but revenge and it grows to completely consume him. Six years after he is imprisoned, he meets an old priest (Faria) who was trying to escape through a tunnel, but went the wrong way. The priest takes him under his wing and teaches him all manner of things. He also tries to turn Dantès away from his darkness, but Dantès cannot be swayed: he is consumed by the need for revenge. Eventually, 14 years after he was originally imprisoned, Dantès escapes and seeks out a great treasure that the priest told him about. With this treasure, he transforms himself into "The Count of Monte Cristo" and begins to plan his revenge. During this time, his existential orientation has turned darker: Dantès has come to view other people as hostile to him and the world itself as indifferent to evil. To cope with this, he takes up the mantle of divine justice and intends to help those people who were good to him and to smite those who harmed him

The first thing Dantès does in his new persona of the Count of Monte Cristo is to seek out information about what has happened to the men who hurt him. In the process, he finds out that his father starved to death during his imprisonment. He also learns that his former employer, who always treated him fairly, is near ruin. He saves him and his business. After showing kindness to those who were kind to him, he seeks out the three who unjustly imprisoned him. He finds that they have all prospered and goes forward with nothing but revenge on his mind. This period is especially dark for Dantès, since he finds that his father has died and sees nothing in the world but good people being punished and evil people prospering.

Through a complicated and intriguing series of events, Dantès ends up ruining Danglars, disgracing Fernand, and driving Villefort insane. Each time, he destroys everything dear to a person before the final blow and when there is nothing left to them, he reveals his real identity so that they may know that justice was served.

Dantès's experiences changed him deeply. He went from having a very benevolent and positive existential orientation to having a much darker existential orientation. He came to view the world as coldly indifferent and most other people as deeply vicious. He came to view the world as a place where the good is punished and evil rewarded. It is not until he has had his revenge on those who betrayed him and Haydee, with whom he falls in love, is able to impress upon him that he is letting them destroy him completely by allowing them to change his view of the world, that he is able to go off with her to reclaim his once-held benevolence and recreate his life.

Through this story, we can see the connection between a person's existential orientation and their experiences and beliefs. We can see how their personality was molded and why it ends up the way it ends up. Let us now turn to one final aspect of existential orientation.

The greatest challenge for most people regarding existential orientation is the difficulty of pinning down their existential orientation in order to think about it. Indeed, for any but those who have trained themselves in introspection, it might be nearly impossible. Even for those of us who are very good at introspection, thinking about our own existential orientation is still hard. The problem is that it is a response to the totality of our life and thus its object is all existence. Trying to hold this in conscious thought is anything but simple. However, since it is the monumental events in our life that have the biggest impact on existential orientation and the achievement or non-achievement of our highest values, if we focus on these events, then we can get a good idea of our existential orientation and why it is oriented the way it is.

We have now explored existential orientation enough for our purposes here and have a good grasp of it and its role in life. It is important to understand existential orientation, since it has been so frequently overlooked and yet is so vital in personality and interpersonal relationships, especially in sex and love (as we shall see).

Before we conclude this section, let us raise one interesting connection regarding existential orientation. One of the origins of the idea of gods can be found in existential orientation. Because our existential orientation is experienced as an instantaneous sum, like our emotions or intuitions, some people think that this gives us information about the world. They then take the false step of anthropomorphizing their existential orientation and thinking that it is out in the world. For example, the person who is inefficacious in the world and whose life is not going well, might develop an anthropomorphic view of existence where it is hostile to him. The view can manifest in many different ways: "the gods are against me," "the fates are cruel," "the world is out to get me," *etc.* The important idea is that the person is imagining that existence (or some omnipotent, unknowable being) has agency and is averse to his success. This belief is self-serving as it allows a person to feel content in his ineptitude and failure; after all, how could he have been expected to succeed when existence itself is hostile to him? On the other hand, a person who has a positive view of the world and who comes to think of existence as being friendly towards him and helping him achieve his values might generate the idea of a benevolent god as an explanation. Unfortunately, people tend to think of anything that happens as being caused by an agent, even when the thing in question is indubitably not (earthquakes, tornadoes, *etc.*), and thus people tend to think about existence itself as personified. It is this misstep of anthropomorphizing existence that is the root of the superstitions of gods and fates.

Sentimental Interaction

One last question that we should explore is how the sentiments impact one another. We should start by noting that a person only has one existential orientation, because existential orientation encompasses a person's most fundamental views on everything, and so could never experience multiple or conflicting existential orientations. With existential moods, a person can only experience one at a time as well, because it is about how our life is going overall. It is not possible for it to be going different ways *overall*. With moods, however, it is possible to have conflicting moods if we are currently experiencing one mood, but something changes and another mood starts to arise. Lastly, with emotions, it is obviously possible to experience multiple emotions at once, even emotions that conflict with each other, and we have all had this experience.

At the same time, our deeper sentiments will impact our other sentiments: existential orientation will impact all other sentiments, but is not directly impacted by the other sentiments. Existential orientation will set our base sentimental state which will impact which existential moods we are likely to experience, as well as which moods, and which emotions.[i] This is not to say that it will *determine* them, but it will dispose us to either more positive or more negative sentiments.

It is likewise the case with existential moods: they will impact our moods and emotions, but are not directly impacted by them. When we experience an existential mood like depression, it colors our moods and emotions. This does not mean it is impossible to experience joy or love while depressed, but they are colored by the depression and it effects their affective response: we tend to feel our positive moods and emotions less fully when we are in a negative existential mood. At the same time, a negative existential mood heightens negative moods and emotions and we will feel these more strongly during negative existential moods. It is the same for the positive existential moods: positive existential moods heighten positive moods and emotions and lessen negative moods and emotions. This is one of the reasons why sentiments are so important for ethics: cultivating a positive existential orientation and positive existential moods leads us to feel our living well, our eudaimonia, more fully and to better weather the harms and downfalls of life. We will discuss how to do this by careful

---

[i] It is because the object of an existential mood is a part of the object of existential orientation, and not the other way around, that their ability to influence each other is asymmetrical.

cultivation of certain beliefs and philosophies in the next section.

It is also the case that moods will impact what emotions we are likely to feel: if we are in a joyful mood, then we are less likely to feel sad from a setback or a minor disappointment. On the other hand, because moods have as their object the way things are going right now, it is possible for an emotion to disrupt a mood in a way that does not happen with existential moods or existential orientation.

Of course, there is a feedback mechanism between our sentiments and beliefs and as our beliefs change, so will our sentiments as we internalize the beliefs. Because of this, our sentiments can impact each other through the belief process, even if they do not impact each other directly. For example, a single instance of rejection of romantic interest will not impact our existential orientation, but repeated rejection may lead us to believe that we are unlovable. If we internalize this belief, it could impact our existential orientation, because this is the kind of core belief from which the existential orientation stems.

Finally, we cannot ignore the role that our physiology plays in this process. A person's body can contribute to emotions and mood: for example, when a person is tired, they are more prone to become irritable or frustrated, not because their beliefs change, but because their physiology has changed. Moreover, changes in or to our bodies can affect our existential moods or existential orientation, depending on how we conceptualize and internalize this. For example, a person who had some sort of bodily defect or injury and internalized the belief that this somehow makes them less of a person or that happiness was now closed to them, could have this effect their existential moods or even their existential orientation. While the sentiments are primarily about values and beliefs, it would be absurd to ignore our bodies and treat ourselves only as minds.

4. Beliefs and Philosophy

> *We will not even be in a position to understand much less to change ourselves until we have learned to accept this responsibility, to view the passions as our own and our doing.*[53]
> ~ Robert Solomon

If happiness is our goal, we must work to have a philosophy that is in accordance with it. This entails a responsibility to manage our beliefs and values and, through them, our sentiments. To do this, we need to first understand what philosophy is and how it connects with our beliefs.

Philosophy

Originally "philosophy" meant a love of wisdom and learning, from the combination of the Greek *philos* (love) and *sophia* (wisdom).[i] Today, philosophy has come to mean the field that asks the most fundamental, or foundational, questions about the world and our place in it. Science, and the specific sciences (biology, chemistry, physics, *etc.*), have taken over inquiries into their areas and so "natural philosophy" as an inquiry into the specific problems of the world is dead.[ii]

Philosophy, as a unique field, is today composed of five primary branches: *Metaphysics*, which is the study of the nature of existence (or "What is there?"); *Epistemology*, which is the study of human knowledge (or "How do we know?"); *Ethics*, which is the study of human action (or "What should we do about it?"); *Politics*, which is the study of human social arrangements (or "How should we live together?"); and *Aesthetics*, which is the study of beauty or art (or "What is beauty?"). A "philosophy" is a system of beliefs, usually encompassing these primary branches and either the work of a single major philosopher (*e.g.*, Aristotelianism, Kantianism, Objectivism, *etc.*) or a tradition of philosophy (*e.g.*, Utilitarianism, Scholasticism, Pragmatism, *etc.*).

Everyone has a philosophy, whether they recognize this or not. There are two kinds of philosophy that a person can hold: a formal philosophy or a personal philosophy. A formal system of philosophy is a unique and integrated system of beliefs by a philosopher or tradition in philosophy. A person who is either a direct follower of a philosophy or who fundamentally agrees with the core tenets of a formal philosophy can be said to hold it as their philosophy. For example, someone who agrees with Aristotle on core issues like ethics and logic, but who rejects his cosmology, might still reasonably consider himself an Aristotelian. However, it is not necessary for a person to subscribe to a formal philosophy to be said to have a philosophy.

We have already said that as humans we have some fundamental psychological needs, including the need to understand ourselves, others, and the world around us.[iii] Thus, even if a person has never heard of the field of philosophy or of any particular philosophers, he can still have a personal philosophy. He himself can be the author of his own system of beliefs, by accepting some beliefs and rejecting others, creating for himself his own philosophy.[iv] Further, a person can hold any combination of formal philosophy

---

[i] The term "philosophy" comes to us, it is recounted by Will Durant (*The Story of Civilization, Volume 2: The Life of Greece*), because Pythagoras thought that the earlier term "Sophos" or "Wiseman" was pretentious and said that he was a mere "lover of wisdom."

[ii] Interestingly, "science" as we know it today started out as "natural philosophy." This is why those who earn the highest educational level in any field earn a Ph.D. or Philosophical Doctorate—because all fields started as a kind of philosophy (or love of wisdom, about different phenomena).

[iii] Religion, as a primitive form of philosophy, can also serve the same psychological needs that a true philosophy fills. (See: Rand, "Philosophy and Sense of Life," *Romantic Manifesto*, p. 25)

[iv] Which is not to imply that *every* belief I hold is part of my philosophy: *e.g.*, that I might believe my cat Panoply is the best cat in the world is not part of my philosophy.

and personal beliefs as their own personal philosophy. This, then, is a personal philosophy.

There are also two fundamental ways that a person can come to have a philosophy: they can consciously choose their beliefs and form their own judgements, or they can passively accept beliefs without critically examining them or forming their own judgements.[54] For example, in the former case we have the person who has taken great pains to work out his position on abortion and has independently concluded that he thinks that it is moral because a woman has a right to her own life and body, while in the latter case we have a person who thinks that abortion is moral because his girlfriend suddenly needs one and he is not ready to be a father. In reality, most people fall somewhere between these two positions: they think about some issues and default on others.[i] Consequently, many people hold a random assortment of beliefs from formal philosophy and their own personal beliefs, some of which are acquired consciously and actively and some of which are acquired passively, the sum of which is often contradictory and internally inconsistent. All of these beliefs, however, can impact our sentiments, as we have seen.

Our sentiments are capable of utilizing any of our beliefs in their responses, regardless of whether they come from our consciously chosen philosophy or we simply passively accepted them. Because of this, the degree to which a person consciously thinks about his beliefs and holds rational beliefs is the degree to which his reason and sentiments will be in unison. The degree to which a person arrives passively at his beliefs is the degree to which his sentiments will seem foreign to him: since he knows not their origin, he will experience them simply as "passions" which he passively suffers.

This means that philosophy is the principal foundation of our sentimental life, because philosophy is our way of gaining control of the most important of our values and beliefs, those that will have the greatest impact on our sentiments (including our metaphysical, epistemological, and ethical views).[ii] Because of this, it is important to make our personal philosophy as consistent as possible and to monitor our beliefs consciously. While it is true that our sentiments are responses to any of our beliefs, not just our philosophy, by making sure our most important beliefs are carefully cultivated and aligned with our conscious goals, we create for ourselves the best possibility of success. Since a person's philosophy is so critical to his life, and sentimental life in particular, let us look more closely at how a person develops his personal philosophy.

---

[i] The philosophy we hold will also impact what values we will choose: we will tend to pick values consistent with our beliefs.

[ii] It might reasonably be objected that our existing beliefs can influence which philosophic positions we *feel* to be correct and this might then become self-reinforcing. This is a possible danger, but, luckily, reason can save us from this trap. If we use our reason in pursuit of our philosophy, and not intuition or sentiment, then the trap can be avoided.

Development of a Personal Philosophy

Aristotle believed that "all men by nature desire to know"[55] and by this he meant that everyone has a natural curiosity about the world and a desire to understand it. All humans are born with this spark of curiosity and wonder about the world, but while some of us nurture it and keep it burning brightly throughout our lives, others allow their spark of curiosity to slowly burn out.[i] This sense of curiosity leads a person to try to understand the world for himself and to make his own judgements about the things he sees.

We see the difference in this natural curiosity most vividly among children who are just learning about the world. Most children have a continual string of questions that start with either "why" or "how" on seemingly everything they can think of. Some parents encourage their children to ask these questions and help them try to figure out the answers for themselves, while some parents yell at their children for being an annoyance or a distraction. These early developmental stages are crucial to a person's later philosophical attitude and if they do not, or cannot, question the world around them and the *status quo* (the ways things are), then they are more likely to tacitly accept the beliefs in the zeitgeist[ii] and less likely to look for answers for themselves.

In adolescence, a person starts to question some of the more complicated facts of the world such as social arrangements, religious beliefs, and personal identity. Adolescence is particularly hard because of the rapid physiological and mental changes a person undergoes at the same time. Not only is he forced to try to understand how his body is changing and what this means, but his rapid cognitive growth and change in social status from a child to a teenager forces him to start making judgements that are beyond any that he has made before. Through experience, learning about the world as he grows and matures, he begins to have a personal philosophy.

Cultivating Personal Philosophy

By the time we reach adulthood, most of us have become fairly settled in our beliefs. We have, one way or another, come to have a personal philosophy and it is this personal philosophy that is the principal source of our values and beliefs, and thus, our sentiments. While these aspects of ourselves are open to change, they are intractable and can require much concerted effort in order to

---

[i] Interestingly, Aristotle also thought: "It is for this reason that one always desires to live, because one always desires to know; and this is because he himself wishes to be the object known" (*Eudemian Ethics*, VII.12.1245a8). If this is true, our will to live is tied inexorably to our desire to understand the world and ourselves. Consequently, the death of our desire to know is also (to the same degree) a death of our desire to live.

[ii] "*Zeitgeist*" literally means "the spirit of the times" in German and is used in philosophy to capture the prevalent cultural ideas and attitudes at a particular time. I do not intend there to be any connection whatever with Hegel.

effect even a small change. We have also come to define the way in which we form our beliefs as either psychologically independent or derivatively through others.[i] The more consciously and deliberately we choose our beliefs (assuming, of course, that we are being rational), the more in line our reason and sentiments will be: the more firsthand our beliefs, the more our sentiments are ultimately authentic.

At the same time, our existing beliefs will play a role in what kinds of additional beliefs we accept: we tend to accept beliefs less critically if they conform with our existing beliefs. Part of this is just that our subconscious employs a coherence standard against our antecedent beliefs and if a new belief is found to be coherent, then we tend not to challenge it.[ii] Of course, if we are actively tending to our beliefs, then we can make this judgement consciously and not have to rely on our subconscious to do this for us.

Moreover, our existential orientation will dispose us to accept or reject certain beliefs if they support or challenge our views: someone who has an existential orientation that involves a sense of efficacy in the world will tend to reject beliefs that people lack control or are determined by forces outside their control. This leads to an interesting dynamic relationship where our existential orientation is determined by our beliefs and our beliefs are influenced by our existential orientation. This dynamic relationship also explains why certain people are "naturally" disposed to accept certain kinds of philosophy over others: people tend to accept whatever philosophy justifies their existential orientation, unless they are consciously and actively maintaining their beliefs and approaching them critically.

This, then, is our epistemic responsibility: we must, if we wish to live well, carefully tend to our philosophy and be active and conscious in forming and maintaining our beliefs. If we do this well, then we set ourselves up to live authentically and flourish. Moreover, through this, we can create true tranquility, because we will not have conflict among our beliefs or sentiments. Being a careful philosopher is the path to true and lasting tranquility.

Someone might think that this means that we are morally culpable for our sentiments, but this is not the case (at least not directly). When we experience an emotion (or other sentiment), this is simply a fact of the operation of our sentimental process, over which we have no volitional control over it. Thus, we cannot be held culpable for experiencing a sentiment. On the other hand, we *are* responsible for the beliefs from which our sentiments arise. If we know that we have shirked our epistemic responsibility, then we are culpable for this. We are also culpable if we have emotions or sentiments that lead us away from living well and we do nothing to work to change them. Changing these may not be a quick process and we may even need professional psychological help, but

---

[i] Compare with Chapter 1 "Universal values and Virtues" in the discussion of the virtue of psychological independence.
[ii] Which may be no more than confirmation bias at work.

as long as we are working to change them, then we are discharging our moral obligation (because this is as much as we *can* do). The experience of a sentiment is a fact and we cannot be judged, or judge ourselves, for it; however, we can be judged for what we do (or fail to do) with this information.

Summary and Conclusions

We started this chapter by noting how emotions historically have been considered impervious to reason, due to their complexity and their sometimes exogenous-seeming nature. It is now clear that not only is an answer to the question of emotions possible, but also that we have a robust framework to understand any kind of sentiment, their interactions, and even how to cultivate sentiments such that they will help us to live the best lives possible. Our new account of sentiments allows us to explain what was previously inexplicable. It is worth looking back at how we got here.

We started by drawing distinctions between emotions and other psychological phenomena, in order to get a clearer sense of our subject. We then moved on and, through several examples, saw that emotions are impacted by beliefs. This led us to a tentative definition of emotions, which was "emotions are a kind of mental phenomenon that operate as a response to our beliefs." However, it was clear that we had not grasped the essence of emotions and so we had to continue our inquiry.

We turned next to the emotional process, which underlies all emotions. We saw that the emotional process has three distinct phases (although it is always experienced as a totality), which are: identification, evaluation, and response. In identification, the object and its relation to our life are conceptually identified. In evaluation, our subconscious compares the object to our past network of values and beliefs (our evaluative framework) looking for relevance and, if it finds enough of a match, the emotional process moves forward to the third phase. In the emotional response itself, we experience the emotion, which is a way of orienting ourselves to the world with the potential for an affective response. By inquiring into the emotional process, we were able to articulate a more precise definition of emotions: "Emotions are a form of automatic evaluative awareness that orient us to their objects and are experienced as a cognitive conviction and often with attendant affect."

We then realized that emotions are not *sui generis*,[i] but are related to other sentiments (moods, existential moods, and existential orientation) through the same underlying process. Because of this, we realized we would have to rename the process the "sentimental process." To more fully understand this, we looked at each kind of sentiment in turn. We saw that moods had the indefinite object of how our lives are going right now and that their responses were

---

[i] *Sui generis* means "one of a kind" or something that is alone in its category.

broader than emotions. Existential moods also have an indefinite object, which is how our overall life is going and the response is broad and pervasive, affecting a person across their identity. Finally, for existential orientation, the object is all of reality, including our views about the nature of ourselves, others, and the world. Its response is pervasive and affects us at all levels, including making up the core of our personality. We also saw that the broader sentiments have a great impact on the other sentiments, such as our existential orientation setting the stage for which moods we are likely to experience.

We next turned to the issue of beliefs and philosophy, where we saw that everyone has a personal philosophy, whether they have a formal philosophy or not. We also saw that our sentiments can be responses to any of our beliefs. Thus, if we want to live well, then we need to carefully cultivate our beliefs to be in line with our conscious aims and to root out any discordant beliefs.

More broadly, we started this chapter without a firm idea of what an emotion was or how to begin to understand it. By contrasting it with other mental phenomena, we started to gain some insight into how it operated and we were able to discover its underlying process. Through this, we realized that emotions were part of the larger category of sentiments, all of which operated by the sentimental process. In Chapter 1, we saw that it was going to be important to have our sentimental life aligned with our ethical aims and now we have seen how this is possible and how to do so. Overall, we saw in this chapter that even though the sentiments are perhaps not simple, they are very much open to reason and can be understood via the sentimental process.

Our new understanding of the sentiments, both in their operation and importance for ethics, stands in marked contrast to the Abstinent and Resistant camps that we saw in the Introduction.

On our view, the sentiments are neither exogenous nor at odds with our "real self," nor are strong emotions and sexuality corruptions to be avoided. Rather, they are an important part of our human nature that we can align with our conscious goals to create tranquility and meaning in life. Thus, not only can we explain the sentiments, which the Abstinent and Resistant camps could not, but we can show their importance for a human life. So, not only were both of these camps wrong to disparage emotions, but the very problem that they sought to solve (that the sentiments were outside their control and inexplicable), was one of their own making.

We will see the importance of our sentimental theory and its explanatory power in the following chapters. More specifically, it will help us to understand love in Chapter 3, sexual attraction in Chapter 5, and sex in Chapter 7. While it may not yet be clear how our account of sentiments can shed light on these formerly impenetrable topics, we shall see that it holds the answers we need.

Chapter 3: Erotic Love

*One might complain that looking so closely at love spoils the magic,
but love is a pretty cheap trick if mere looking will spoil it.*[56]
~ Robert Solomon

*Those who have never known the deep intimacy
and the intense companionship of happy mutual love
have missed the best thing that life has to give.*[57]
~ Bertrand Russell

*Romantic love [is that] profound, exalted, life-long passion
that unites [man's] mind and body in the sexual act.*[58]
~ Ayn Rand

Love is one of the most expansive and profound emotions that a person can experience. Of all emotions, it is perhaps the most likely to be featured in works of art, such as paintings, books, and movies. Sadly, these portrayals of love often leave much to be desired. This is partly due to the complexity of love and the difficulty that many people have in thinking about emotions. Yet, it is also due to the existence of elements in our cultural mythology that have muddied the waters around love and made it harder to understand.

Thus, we must begin by stripping away these old myths and paradigms about love to get a fresh look at it. Once we have done this, we can use our new understanding of sentiments to help us understand the nature of love generally and erotic love more specifically.[i] We will explore the nature of erotic love and see its features and what role it can play in our lives. We will conclude by inquiring into what kind of person is capable of erotic love—a question that may have surprising answers.

---

[i] While love and relationships frequently go together, they are not necessarily connected and we need to understand each separately in order to understand how they should come together. Thus, we will explore the nature of love in this chapter and relationships in the next chapter.

1. Challenging the Old Paradigms of Love

Love is a constitutional value for most people and necessary for their flourishing[i], but it can be hard to understand why this is so from the conceptions of love that we have floating around in our culture. We have paradigms of love that ignore that we have bodies (Platonic Love), insist that we have no choice in the matter and that it has already been decided for us (soul-mates), think that love is best exemplified by suicidal teenagers (desperate longing), believe love happens for no reason at all (causeless love), and think love is no more than an illusion created by neurotransmitters (physicalism). How is love to survive in such a wasteland of bad philosophy? Because these mistaken ideals have come to permeate our culture as the "common sense" ways of thinking about love, we must first clear away the errors of the past in order to see why erotic love is so important and to start thinking about it in more life-affirming ways.

The Paradigm of Platonic, or Sexless, Love

Platonic love is a common paradigm of love, which says that love should focus only on the spiritual aspects of a person to the exclusion of any sort of sexuality. Not surprisingly, this conception of love comes to us from the philosopher Plato. Now, whether this is Plato's actual view is a matter of debate, but we can certainly say it follows directly from Plato's ideas and that it is a very influential view throughout the ages. To understand this view better, let us turn to some of Plato's views and see how this position arose out of them.

One of Plato's major ideas was that humans are just souls and that our bodies are not truly part of us, but a mere prison of flesh. He needs this view for his epistemology and his attempt to solve the "problem of universals"[ii]

---

[i] Having at least some kind of relationship with others, whether this be erotic love, friendship, or familial love, is necessary for all people to achieve happiness.

[ii] Historically, this was called the problem of "the one in the many." It is easiest to demonstrate the problem with an example: how is it that we are able to use the word, like "cup," when there are so many cups in the world which are different from each other? How do we know that they are all instances of cup? From the *many* cups in the world, there must be *one* thing to which we are actually referring among the many for this to be possible. If there is not, then language would be impossible and, yet, we know it works. Plato posited that the solution was that for any particular thing to be called a cup, it had to "participate" in, or be patterned after, a perfect form of "cup" that existed in a perfect world. The differences in the particular cups in our world, then, are simply copying errors or different combinations of substances that are taking on the form of cup. This is problematic for many reasons, not the least of which is that the only reason we have for believing in the realm of Forms is based on deduction from the "fact" that language would be impossible otherwise; yet, if any other alternative existed, then suddenly the edifice of the Forms would come crashing down. I, personally, think that Rand eloquently solves this problem with her theory of abstraction and measurement-omission in concept formation (See: Rand, *Introduction to Objectivist Epistemology)*. Aristotle also takes down

through the use of "Forms."[i] Plato relies on a theory of "recollection"[ii] that concludes that the soul must have existed before the body in the Realm of Forms in order to be able to recollect them in life. This means that the soul is separable from the body and sometimes exists in our world and sometimes in the true reality of the Realm of the Forms. Moreover, Plato thinks that the body is a corrupting influence on the soul because the body has needs and desires and keeps the soul trapped in our illusory world[iii] when it truly belongs in the Realm of the Forms, which is why he says in the *Phaedo* that: "The soul of the philosopher most disdains the body, flees from it, and seeks to be by itself".[59]

This view of the nature of man led Plato to take a strong stand against any idea of love that included the body, since it is, after all, merely a prison for our real selves. He argued that proper love should inevitably draw us away from the particulars of the body to the universals of the Forms.[60] This led to the modern idea of "Platonic love" as sexless love, because sex is necessarily bodily and we should be focused on the Forms. Thus, this position came to be characterized by its emphasis on "spiritual" love instead of sexual love and it became the ideal of sexless love of "pure souls." For Platonic love, to love an individual, especially for his or her body, is low and base. It is far better to love a person insofar as she participates in the higher Forms and to focus only on this to the exclusion of her base elements.

One problem (among so many others) is that this theory of personhood, where a person is "really" an immortal soul that just so happens to be trapped inside a body, completely denigrates what it means to be human. Humans have physical aspects and mental aspects, but they exist as an integrated unity. To divide a person into parts, as Plato does, and then to claim that some parts are real and pure while others are mere prisons for these real parts is to deny any importance to the other parts. Indeed, we can see this in Plato as he considers the body to be a prison of the soul. This denial of body in favor of the "soul" leads inexorably to his position on love: for why would anyone love the base element (body) instead of the divine element (soul)? In fact, Plato is explicitly arguing that we *should not* be so base as to love a body. Thus, this idea of "Platonic love" ends up being a hatred of what it means to be human, based on very dubious metaphysical claims. Although at first glance Platonic love may seem like a noble attempt to emphasize matters of character over physical beauty, in the end it denies, and indeed makes war on, our physical nature. If

---

the entire enterprise with his "third man" argument (*Metaphysics*, I.9.990^{b}15).

[i] The "forms" are the perfect archetypes of all existing things. See prior footnote.

[ii] Plato attempts to solve the question of how we know the forms, since they are in their own separate world, by saying that it must be the case that our souls must come to our world from the world of the forms and that, therefore, all learning about forms is merely a kind of "recollection" of what we knew before, but forgot due to the taint of the body. (*Meno*, 81d)

[iii] Plato thinks that our world is not the real world, but a mere world of shadows and argues for this in his "allegory of the cave" in the *Republic*, Book VII.

humans were non-corporeal beings, this might work; but since we are not, this ideal is a destructive one.

We will return to the issue of hatred of the body and this world in Volume 2, Chapter 9. For now, it is enough to note that this conception of love is very prominent, but that it is based on ideas that are not only false, but also incompatible with human flourishing. Unfortunately, this hatred of the body has found its way down through history in the Judeo-Christian-Islamic tradition. By taking the idea of a higher separable soul, they necessarily also had to take on the idea of a low and base body. This is the direct cause of the shame that those steeped in religious mythology feel and the source of many modern problems about sex and love.

Platonic love, as the ideal of sexless love, is an attack on the body, sex, and human nature. Platonic love represents a non-human ideal and thus, must be entirely abandoned if it is human happiness we seek.

The Paradigm of the Soul-Mate

The paradigm of the soul-mate again comes to us from Plato and the idea is that there is *one* perfect person for everyone somewhere in the world and all we have to do is find this "one and only" in order to have true love. Plato spells out this position through the character of Aristophanes[i] in the *Symposium* (or "drinking party"). The idea is that humans are fundamentally incomplete and that in order to fix this, we need to seek out the one perfect partner for us, who is somewhere in the world looking for us as well. Plato tells us that in the beginning, human nature was radically different than now:

> The shape of each human being was completely round, with back and sides in a circle; they had four hands each, with as many legs as hands, and two faces, exactly alike, on a rounded neck. Between the two faces, which were on opposite sides, was one head with four ears. There were two sets of sexual organs, and everything else was the way you'd imagine it... In strength and power...they were terrible, and they had great ambitions. They made an attempt on the gods...at last, after great effort, Zeus had an idea. "I shall now cut each of them in two...". Now, since their natural form had been cut in two, each one longed for its own other half...this, then, is the source of our desire to love each other. Love is born into every

---

[i] We should not confuse Plato's character Aristophanes with the poet by the same name from Plato's time. Indeed, these two men were antagonistic to each other and each mocked the other. For example, Aristophanes' *The Clouds* mocked Socrates, Plato's teacher and dear friend. This casts some doubt on whether Plato agrees with this position, but we are less concerned with Plato's position than with taking on the paradigm as it exists in our time.

human being; it calls back the halves of our original nature together; it tries to make one out of two and heal the wound of human nature. "Love" is the name for our pursuit of wholeness, for our desire to be complete.[61]

Of course, this origin story was not meant to be believed literally, but was intended as a parable to illuminate a difficult concept: how to account for how quickly love can form, how strongly love can bind people together, and why we all seem to be looking for some other person, our "other half" to (literally) "complete" us. These questions are important to ask and to seek the answers to, but making up stories as an answer is not the best way to address them.

Although this creation story from the *Symposium* is unknown to most people, the ideas in the story are very much still alive and influential in our time. This is due, in part, to this myth being incorporated into Christian mythology as the idea that the Christian god has a plan for every person to find the other person that he created just for them. While, today, no one literally believes they are looking for another half with whom they will fuse together, people are still very much committed to the idea that there is *one* special person out there for everyone and that, if we could but find this special person, we would fall instantly in love and have a perfect relationship. Indeed, people often talk about their partners as their "other half" or "better half" or use the language of their "soul-mate" or talk about how their partner "completes" them. This idea—that there is only one person in the world who we are capable of loving—is damaging to love. It causes people to throw away good relationships because they are not "perfect."

In addition, the idea of a soul-mate disposes people to passivity in love, because when we find our "other half," we are supposed to just know this and fall instantly in love. On this conception, there is nothing that we must do besides passively accept that we have found love. Problematically, love is not some kind of mystical force, but an emotion. As such, it operates like all other emotions and sentiments, via the sentimental process. Love never "just happens" to us; it is a response to our values in another person. Moreover, a good relationship with a lover is something that we must work to achieve and maintain (as we will see in the next chapter). Love requires us to be active: we must work to find it, kindle it, help it to grow, and maintain it. Love requires work.

Emotions are not mystical in the least and we do not need mythical stories to justify them. Furthermore, there is not just *one* person whom we are capable of loving, but rather there are many people who might be good romantic partners for us. We will shortly be addressing love in detail and how a person falls in love with another, but we need to stress here that the all-too-prevalent idea of there being only *one* perfect partner is as real as the myth that gave birth to it. There is no such thing as a "soul-mate" and if that is what we are seeking, what we will never find is love.

The Paradigm of Desperate Longing

The paradigm of desperate longing is the idea that love must be a desperate sort of longing to be real. It is best known in our culture through William Shakespeare's tragic love story about two teenagers, *Romeo and Juliet*.[i] In the story, Romeo and Juliet are both members of powerful families in Verona who are openly hostile to each other. They happen to meet fortuitously at a ball hosted by Juliet's family, "fall in love" with each other, and are married in secret shortly after. They are desperate for each other and their desperation leads them to make a series of bad decisions, which culminate in their mutual suicide. Their short relationship and untimely deaths have come to epitomize the paradigm of desperate love. Romeo and Juliet barely knew each other when they fell in love.[ii] They had hardly spent any time together before they died and certainly did not love each other for their virtues or character. Theirs was a love based on nothing more than attraction and fueled by a sense of desperate desire and longing. These kinds of relationships always end badly, although not usually so spectacularly.

The problem with Romeo and Juliet is that their story confuses passionate desire with love, but these are different. In fact, passionate desire is more like a kind of proto-love or something that could become love, if other things work out. This state of intense longing for another person is usually called infatuation or limerance, but some people today call it "new relationship energy." It is that excitement that drives us to find out as much as we can about another person so that we can see if we are compatible. To be fair, limerance can be an important step leading to real love since it encourages us to discover another person and open ourselves to the possibility of love. For most of us, limerance is the first experience we have approaching love and for those of us who are in love, we often remember that it started in limerance. Yet, insofar as it is a kind of love at all, limerance is an immature kind of love. Unfortunately, lots of people want the "intense" love they remember from adolescence, but mature love is not always intense. Mature love does not have this desperate passion to it, but that does not mean that mature love is not passionate. In fact, mature love can be more passionate than limerance, just not in this desperate way.[62]

The confused nature of desperate longing can also be seen when we consider what happens once the impediments to the desperate love are removed and the lovers are united. If the desperation that was fueling their love

---

[i] A story in which it is often overlooked that Juliet is thirteen and Romeo not much older: it is a love between adolescents.
[ii] Although they did not know it, we know they were experiencing an existential orientation attraction (see Chapter 5).

ends, since the impediments have been removed and they no longer have to be desperate, what will be the foundation of their relationship? Just as a house without a foundation will collapse, so too will a relationship.[i] We will explain what constitutes good foundations for a relationship in Chapter 4, but it should be clear even now that a relationship with no real foundation is doomed.

This is problematic if we are to use these stories to help understand the nature of love and how relationships function: especially since this paradigm is one of the primary ones seen in movies and books today. Think about it: stories are always about the struggle to get together. What happens once the lovers are united and the impediments are removed? "...And they lived happily ever after." We can all agree that the beginning of a relationship, especially when there is conflict to be overcome, is very exciting, emotions run high, and everything is very intense. But if we use this as the paradigm of love, then we have no guidance for more mature relationships. Worse, some people even create an ideal that *requires* conflict to exist. But what happens when there are no more external conflicts? This is one of the reasons why some people create conflicts in their relationships: in order to have their relationship conform to the ideal of desperate longing, which is the only way that they know how to love. Moreover, without conflict to rail against, they would come to see that their relationship had no foundation at all. Thus, the paradigm of love as desperate longing is just a confusion about what love is.

If we are to have good, mature, long-term relationships, we need to move beyond the paradigm of desperate love. This kind of love is immature, and only appropriate at the start of a relationship. The alternative is a deeper, more stable, connection with our partner that we will explore shortly.

Causeless Love

Causeless love is the common paradigm that love "just happens" and there is nothing more to be said.[ii] Yet, we have already seen that emotions do not "just happen" and that emotions are very much understandable. Thus, this view treats love as some sort of mystic phenomenon that cannot be questioned or understood. The person who firmly believes in causeless love wants to "just be loved," not for any reason, because that would be asking love to conform to reason, but just for the sake of being loved.

This view is championed in Erich Fromm's *The Art of Loving*, where he says: "To be loved because of one's merit, because one deserves it, always leaves doubt [...]—there is always a fear that love could disappear."[63] Yet, this does not convey the depth of the view. Ayn Rand perfectly portrays this view in

---

[i] Nietzsche says the following of too-quick-to-love relationships: "Sensuality often hastens the growth of love so much that the roots remain weak and are easily torn up." *Beyond Good and Evil*, aphorism #120.

[ii] I thank Robert Garmong for the suggestion to include causeless love as its own category.

Atlas Shrugged:

> "You don't love me or you wouldn't ask such a question."
>
> "I did love you once," she said dully, "but it wasn't what you wanted. I loved you for your courage, your ambition, your ability. But it wasn't real, any of it."
>
> His lower lip swelled a little in a faint, contemptuous thrust. "What a shabby idea of love!" he said.
>
> "Jim, what is it that you want to be loved for?" [...]
>
> "To be loved for!" he said, his voice grating with mockery and righteousness. "So you think that love is a matter of mathematics, of exchange, of weighing and measuring, like a pound of butter on a grocery counter? I don't want to be loved for anything. I want to be loved for myself-not for anything I do or have or say or think. For myself-not for my body or mind or words or works or actions."
>
> "But then...what is yourself?"[64]

The problem with causeless love, as the woman in the story fatally learns, is that it is *unearned* love. Wanting to have love for no reason destroys love. Love is a response to our values in another person. To insist that it should be a response to nothing is to destroy the very possibility of love.[i] If we want to have real love in our lives, it must be based in the reality of our partner and who they are as a person. Love is, then, our response to our values as instantiated in our partner.

Physicalism

The last paradigm that we will consider is that of Physicalism or the idea that love is just "chemistry." This is the idea that love is no more than a function of our glands and neurotransmitters: that what love "really is" is just a chemical response and no more, that love is "just animal attraction." The physicalist would decry an attachment to more robust ideas of love as wishful thinking and mischaracterizations of a simple chemical process. While this view is not as common as the preceding views, it is taken seriously in certain camps (*e.g.*, determinism in philosophy and behaviorism in psychology). It also manifests as a popular view that sex is purely physical pleasure and nothing else, since there is nothing else it could be. Or that love is an illusion and does not exist

---

[i] Rand believes that those who want unearned love are "spiritual moochers" who want the psychological benefits of virtue without having to earn them. She believes that these people operate on what she calls the "death premise" and that what they ultimately want, although they desperately try to avoid this knowledge, is the lack of any kind of responsibility for action that death brings. This is one of the major themes of *Atlas Shrugged*.

at all, but is merely attraction and arousal.

The problem with this account is that it must explain away our actual experience of the world, including the way we experience love. We know through direct experience that we make choices throughout the day: that we choose to have coffee now or read a book in the shade. We have direct experience of having affective states and then making choices about what to do about them. We can see our beliefs and values at play in our sentimental experiences. The physicalist must explain all of this away as illusory: everything that we think we are experiencing is just an illusion of experience and an illusion of choice. But, what possible reason could we have for believing this? Any such reason would have to be based in such experience and, thus, would reduce to the argument: we know through information gained from experience that our experience is an illusion. The contradiction is glaring.

Moreover, the fact that people have not been able to explain emotions and sentiments before now is not an argument against the reality of those emotions and sentiments. This is a classic case of the fallacy of the "argument from ignorance," which is where a person asserts that since their position has not been disproved, then it must be true. However, like phlogiston, just because a theory has not yet been proven false is no reason to believe it is true. For us to correctly believe something to be true, we must have reasons to believe that it is true. Although the argument from ignorance is usually reserved for imaginary beings (*e.g.*, you cannot prove that a god did not create the world, so therefore it is true), it can be used to posit causes in any area (*e.g.*, you cannot prove that it is not turtles all the way down, so it must be).

The physicalist account additionally makes the mistake of equating affective states with emotions or sentiments. As we have already seen in Chapter 2, while emotions and sentiments often are conjoined with affective states, they are not necessarily so and it is wrong to treat emotions as merely affective states. This also leads to the problem that we can be wrong about what emotion we are experiencing and this does not make sense if emotions are merely affective states. Love is not simply reducible to our serotonin, dopamine, and oxytocin levels, but rather is about our relationship with another person (including our shared history and our values) and none of this is reducible to neurotransmitters.

We cannot simply reduce emotions to brain states and we should be wary of anyone who attempts to explain away the world as we experience it and reduce the richness and beauty of human nature and experience to no more than chemical reactions. Indeed, in some ways this is the opposite of Plato, who tried to insist that we were simply souls and to explain away the body.

Moving Beyond the Old Paradigms

We have now seen all the ways that the old paradigms of love have failed and have learned important lessons for moving forward in our understanding of love. The paradigm of Platonic love denied that we have bodies. From this we learned the importance of understanding that humans are rational animals that have both mental and physical aspects. The paradigm of soul-mates took a creation myth too literally and insisted that there is only one person in all the world for us to love. From this we saw that there are potentially lots of people in the world whom we could love and that real love takes work. The paradigm of desperate longing made the mistake of judging all love by the intensity of limerance. From this we saw that even though it can look different, mature love can be even more passionate than new love. The paradigm of causeless love mistakenly insists that love must "just happen" in order to be love. From this we learned that love is, and must be, a response to our values manifest in another person. Finally, the paradigm of physicalism mistakenly tried to reduce the richness of life to chemistry and insisted that love was an illusion. From this we learned not to explain the world away and that love has a rich constitution that is more than simply our affective response.

The problem with all these paradigms of love is that they do not capture the real experience of what it is to be in love and they trivialize the human experience in favor of commitments to theoretical constructs. They do not represent the experience of being in love for actual people or over the long-term, with all of the other consideration that this necessitates. After all, the experience of newly burgeoning love is quite different from the less intense, but more profound, experience of mature love.

Having identified the major paradigms of love, at least in our culture, and having seen the ways in which they fail, we can begin to move beyond them and construct a theory that accounts for the reality of the human experience of love and its importance in a good life. It is time for us to rethink love and the role it should have in our lives.

2. The Nature of Erotic Love

Love is the expression of philosophy—of a subconscious philosophical sum—and, perhaps, no other aspect of human existence needs the conscious power of philosophy quite so desperately. When that power is called upon to verify and support an emotional appraisal, when love is a conscious integration of reason and emotion, of mind and values, then—and only then—is it the greatest reward of man's life.[65]
~ Ayn Rand

It is important to remember that we are inquiring into sexual ethics in order to live the best kind of life possible: that is, to achieve happiness. While we have already explored the nature of happiness in Chapter 1, there is much more that can be said about the relationship between love and happiness. Indeed, for most people the importance of love to happiness can hardly be overstated.

Love is also a crucial part of the meaning that most of us give to life. This is especially true of full-fledged erotic love, which is our subject here, as opposed to early love or limerance. Let us look briefly to the connection between erotic love and happiness, before we look at the nature of erotic love itself.

Recall that happiness is a state of living well for a person, of flourishing in life.[i] In order to flourish, a person needs well-defined *core values* (which define who he is as a person, give him purpose in life, and give meaning to his life), and *peripheral values* (which add to the richness of life). These values will be either *universal values*, which are the values necessary for happiness that are common to all people, *constitutional values*, which are necessary for some people based on their constitution, or *personal values*, which are not necessary for happiness, but which are chosen to enrich happiness. Among the universal values, are such goods as rationality, integrity, honesty, *etc*. On the other hand, erotic love is a constitutional value for most people, which means that most of us are constituted such that erotic love is necessary for our happiness. For those of us with such constitutions, erotic love is both necessary for happiness and a constitutive part of it, because for us erotic love is part of our happiness and not merely a means to it.[ii]

So, what does it mean to say that love is constitutive of happiness for most people? It means that love is necessary for their happiness and without it they would not be able to become truly or completely happy. Further, it means that they would not be able to live as well without love as they could live with it. It would be as though their happiness was a puzzle that was missing a piece and so the full image could not emerge: they would still be able to see much of the image, but the absence of the piece would disrupt it.

The idea that love is a part of happiness is hardly new. In fact, it dates back to the earliest days of philosophy, where both Plato and Aristotle argued for the necessity of love for happiness. We saw Plato's position earlier, with his allegory of the original humans and his idea of a soul-mate. Even though we reject the allegory, it is important to realize that Plato was still trying to elaborate a real human need. Aristotle, as is usually the case, does a better job of elaborating this than Plato and makes his case without introducing fanciful stories.

Aristotle argues that love is necessary for happiness because he thinks that a lover is, in a real sense, another self, because our lover shares many of our values and beliefs.[iii] This gives us a unique perspective on our values and beliefs

---

[i] Happiness is both the activity of living well itself and the self-reflective existential mood that comes from living well.

[ii] This, of course, applies only to adults as children do not need erotic love. Children need familial love and perhaps friendship as well.

[iii] Here I am reading the Greek word "*philia*" as "love" and not "friendship," because our modern idea of love is much closer to Aristotle's idea of friendship than our idea of friendship is. I will leave aside the issue of Aristotle's actual view here because this inquiry is into happiness and not Aristotle.

because we can see them acted on in the world through our lover: our lover acts as a sort of moral mirror for us so that we can see our own actions through theirs. Aristotle believed that this unique perspective on our moral character is so valuable that we cannot possibly live as good a life without it.[66] How is a lover able to do this? Aristotle did not work out a full account of this, but we can supply the missing pieces.

Our lover is uniquely able to become a mirror for us because part of what deep, mature love brings is intimacy. Intimacy is a real opening up of ourselves to our partner. This sets the stage for lovers to come to reciprocally internalize each other as a value and incorporate each other's values into their own hierarchy of values. This *co-internalization of values* is a major step to creating the shared identity that is part of erotic love (we will explore this more below). Our lover is also an embodiment of our values: since our sexual attractions and reasons why we love are rooted in our core values, our lover is a glimpse into our moral ideal (see Chapter 5 on sexual attraction). Because our lover is both a value to us, and an embodiment of our other values, they allow us to see our own values acted out in the world. Moreover, since our lovers are so closely tied in with our values and identity, they allow us to see our values in the world in a way that seeing a stranger acting from the same values in the world does not. Even though a stranger might share our values, we do not identify with them as we do with our lover. Our lover allows us to see our values acted on in the world as if we were doing it ourselves.

Additionally, our lovers also let us glimpse the world as we wish it were: living with our lover is like being able to enter our ideal world. With them, we create a mutually reinforcing environment where we both act according to our ideals and thus create a world in which our ideals can take on a life of their own. Through this, we can create a home that is an incarnation of how we wish things were in the world itself: we create a microcosm of the world as it might and ought to be, according to our ideals. To return to our original point, this world that we jointly create allows us to see our moral ideals in action and we can thus see their effect on our lives. This helps us to know whether our ideals are really helping us to live well or whether we have taken on false ideals that will ultimately harm us.

While having a lover is very important for this reason, love is not something that begins through conscious choice. In fact, we often do not know exactly what starts our interest in another person: perhaps it was because this other person was physically attractive or intellectually interesting, perhaps some trait sparked our curiosity and made us want to learn more about them, or perhaps we were struck by a *je ne sais quoi*. In these cases, what underlies our interest in the other person is their way of holding themselves, of speaking, of dressing, of engaging with us: their overall style of soul as manifested in a thousand little things about them. In short, our interest in a person starts at the *existential orientation* level (sexual attraction, including its connection to existential orientation, is discussed at length in Chapter 5). In order for love to progress from its early stages, or to progress from infatuation or simple desire, into full-blown love, we need to learn more about this person who sparks our interests. We need to find out who they are as a person, their character, and their values. However, it is important that we avoid the trap of situating love as either of the mind or the body: true love must be aware of the whole person.

We must aim for love of the whole person if we are to achieve erotic love and have the best kinds of relationships. Love, in this deep sense that includes the full range of what makes a person unique, is a response to a person's *chosen self* and to the values that underlie his character and by which he defines his life. A person's chosen self is constituted not only by his core values, but also his peripheral: by those things which give his life its meaning and richness, as well as make up his identity. The values that constitute our chosen self are the values that define who we are as people. Love is deepest when there is a robust value alignment between the partners.[i]

Value alignment is when two people share at least some of their values: the more values two people share, the stronger their value alignment is and *vice versa*. However, while having alignment generally between values is important, it is more important that there be alignment between their core values, rather than simply their peripheral values. Strong value alignment, especially of core values, leads to a more robust love that is less likely to change or fade over time. Furthermore, those who share our values are more likely to be a value to us in our lives, beyond our relationship with them, as they will be working to achieve the same ends. Value alignment is not necessarily holding the exact same values: it can also be holding complementary values. For example, valuing cooking is complementary with our partner valuing fine food and being a gourmand: although they are not the same values, they are related and complement each other. Value alignment is important, as two people who disagree on core values cannot maintain a long-term relationship, at least not without strife.

All of this, though, does not get to the core of the nature of erotic love, even if it does go a long way towards explaining how we experience love and how it functions in our lives. To remedy this, let us turn to the characteristics that make erotic love unique.[ii]

Reciprocity

Unlike some forms of love, such as love of an artwork or a hobby, erotic love is necessarily reciprocal. Before erotic love begins, if only one person has feelings that might otherwise turn into erotic love, then this is mere infatuation or desire. After erotic love ends, if only one person still experiences this

---

[i] In addition to value alignment, lovers should have a similar or complementary existential orientation.
[ii] These features are both necessary and jointly sufficient for erotic love.

emotion, then this is desperation or residue. Erotic love cannot be one sided. This will become plain as we look to its other characteristics.

Commitment

True love is not just some passing fancy: it is a real *emotional commitment* to our lover.[i] This involves intimacy and an unreserved opening-up to our partner emotionally. It also means making a decision that we want to be with our partner, which entails making our partner a value in our life and treating their ends as important. An emotional commitment is a promise to our partner that we will do what is in our power to maintain our emotional connection with them.

In addition to an emotional commitment, there is often a public commitment. Whether this is a more informal declaration of a relationship (that we are now "dating") or a formal declaration (that we are married or engaged to be married), the public act of promising ourself to our partner adds to the relationship. By committing to each other, in whatever way this is done, we give each other a level of certainty that we will not easily abandon the relationship and that we will invest time and energy in it to make sure that it works. This helps to build the kind of situation that makes it easier to commit to each other emotionally, since we have some certainty that our partner is likewise committed. Moreover, commitment is one of the reasons that a certain kind of relationship is so important for deep love, as we will see in the next chapter.

It is important that the commitment is not merely a "fair weather" affair, for that is no real commitment at all. We must be able to feel our partner's commitment to know that they will be there for us if times get tough. Indeed, weathering bad times together is an important part of learning about the relationship: we must *know* that our partner is committed to us and that we can rely on them, even in the worst of times. This kind of commitment allows us to be much less reserved with our partner and more open and authentic, because we can trust that they are committed to us. In this way, there is reciprocity between being open with our partner and commitment: openness fosters commitment and commitment allows openness.

Passion

There are several different, but connected, senses of passion[ii], which are

---

[i] It is worth reiterating that we are talking about deep and mature erotic love here and not simply whatever relationship a person might happen to be in. We emphatically should not do these things for a person just after our first date or for a person who is not a real value in our life: that is, who does not make our life better.

[ii] It should be understood that we are using "passion" here in its modern definition and not in its older meaning of "something suffered," even though this runs counter to the etymology of

all united around the idea of caring deeply about something and having a strong affective reaction because of it. This is what unites Juliet's passion and the passion that comes from caring about our life and making it meaningful. Let us briefly step back and look at passion before we look to why it is important for erotic love.

Passion is a sentiment (more specifically, an emotion) and, as we have seen, all sentiments orient us to their objects. In the case of passion, it is caring about the object and considering it important.[i] Through passion we become oriented to the object and it becomes a major part of our life and identity. Through passion we can experience our deep care for the object and its importance in our life: passion lets us *feel* this and this is deeply motivating. The things about which we are passionate define us and become part of our identity, because they are the things that we have chosen to care about as important.[ii]

Of course, we might be either positively or negatively oriented to the object: *i.e.*, we might be passionate about liberty or our hatred of irrationality. This latter example also shows another facet of passion: it can have the effect of modifying other emotions and causing them to be stronger. For example, if a person says "I hate John" versus "I passionately hate John," they are indicating that the latter hatred is stronger because not only do they hate John, but they also think that this is important enough to be part of their identity. While many people focus on the modifying feature of passion, its true core is the sense of caring and importance that lead it to be part of our identity.

As a constituent of erotic love, passion requires the choice to care about our partner and to hold them as important in our life. Through passion, our partner comes to be part of our identity because we care about them and are oriented to them as important and this orientation to them is part of what makes us who we are. Passion in erotic love requires specific actions, specific ways of caring, that are unique to it. It requires: holding our partner in a very high regard, being committed to them, working to maintain our relationship with them to the best of our ability, making them a priority in our life, and taking our responsibility to our partner seriously. This requires that we keep the value of our lover and our relationship in context, by thinking about the difference it makes in our life and the value it brings to it.

This last is important because it is all too easy to get lost in the mundanity of life and forget how important our lover is to us: to remember how they forget a chore, but not about how they make our entire existence better.

---

the Latin *pati*, "to suffer."

[i] Or, more specifically, we must choose to care about the object and internalize this care as well as hold the belief that the object is important and internalize this as well. Through these things, we will come to *feel* passionate about the object and orient ourselves to it. Of course, the orientation to it is partly our choice and partly the emotion.

[ii] Our passions tend to be core values or strong antivalues as we partly define ourselves through them. However, this is not to say that we are passionate about all of our core values and antivalues.

However, if we do this, we will not only kill the passion in our relationship, but also slowly the love itself as the little annoyances and resentments erode the foundations of love. It is important to keep the context of the value of our lovers in mind and to not let the mundane tarnish the important. This is keeping passion alive in love and through it we feel passionate about our partner.

Exaltation

Exaltation is a purposeful "raising up" of a value in our life due a strong belief that this is a value without which life would be less meaningful. Exaltation is a looking up to and an impetus for improvement. When we exalt our partner, we look up to their actions as a moral guide. Of course, this presupposes that our partner is a good person who is worthy of being looked up to. This "looking up to" should be mutual; we should each look up to each other and be a source of inspiration to each other through our actions and character.

Exaltation is important because one of the greatest benefits of love is its role as a moral impetus. When we exalt our partner, we hold them up as a moral ideal to work towards and be worthy of. In this way, we work harder than we would otherwise to improve ourselves and make sure that we are the kind of person worthy of love, because we have a goal and a strong motivation. This is tied to the issue of mirroring, which we will address in Chapter 4, where we can also see our actions as reflected in our lovers and their moral growth as partly a reflection of us.

A Profound and Selfish Joy

Erotic love is fundamentally selfish. It involves our happiness, our lover's happiness, our shared life, and the value we bring to each other's lives. It is selective and focuses only on us, ignoring all others. It contributes to our happiness and not to the happiness of any others. It is for us alone: a world that we share as lovers and this influences the way we see the rest of the world. When we are in love, our lives become better, our perspectives become more benevolent, and even the worst things are made better.

Love must be selfish. We cannot be in love with someone only for their sake, with no interest in the matter. Consider what this means concretely: we would open ourselves to them, try to take on their values and have them take on ours, and try to help them to be their best, all for the sake of what? Why would we care to do it? We care about our values and if the other person is not a value to us, we certainly will not go to these lengths for them and we should not do so, if what we wish is to flourish. Consider the perversity of loving someone merely for their sake and not for our own as well: they would be like a sympathy case to which we threw scraps of inauthentic love. No sane person should want to be in either position of this altruistic "love."

Shared History

While love can start without a shared history, it certainly cannot grow to maturity without one. This is because love requires knowledge of our partner. We need to know that our lover will be committed to us: that they will share our joys in good times and help us weather bad times. We learn a great deal about our lover from how they handle the events of life, large and small, good and bad. Through this, we learn that we can depend on each other. A good lover ameliorates the bad times and enhances the good. Through the experiences we share with our lover, we create a shared history together. Shared history is necessary for any kind of relationship: there is a real sense in which a relationship is defined by the values a couple shares and their history together.

Our shared history with our lover is even more than this, though. Our lives are constituted by what we have lived, chosen, seen, and experienced. The rich tapestry of our lives is woven through experience. When we share our lives with another, they are also woven into our tapestry. By living our lives together with a partner, and creating a shared history with each other, we create a shared life together. And there is something beautiful about sharing our life with someone special. Moreover, a shared history is one of the foundations of intimacy and of a shared identity.

Intimacy

Intimacy is one of the things that makes erotic love unique and not some kind of sexual friendship.[i] Intimacy is the opening-up of ourselves to our lover, the revealing of our innermost self. Intimacy is the unreserved embrace of our partner as part of our life. It is standing naked in soul before them and showing them our real and authentic self. All too many people wear metaphoric masks in their daily lives, but for intimacy to be achieved, we must unmask ourselves for our lover and show them our real self.[ii] By doing this, and by not holding anything back, we let our partner know who we really are and let them connect with us at the deepest level. This mutual and unreserved opening of ourselves to our partner creates intimacy. Of course, intimacy takes time to grow and develop; it is not an instantaneous process. This is why it needs commitment and a shared history to grow and blossom.

Nowhere is deep intimacy as possible as with erotic love. There are few

---

[i] There is a degree of intimacy in any kind of relationship. However, sometimes a difference of degree becomes a difference of kind and this is the case with the kind of intimacy between a good lover and a friend or family member. Even in the case of a secondary partner in a polysexual or polyamorous relationship, the degree of intimacy is different than with a partner with whom we have shared our life and co-internalized our values, creating a shared identity. This is not to say that a person with multiple primary partners could not have intimacy with each.

[ii] Compare with the idea of "psychological visibility" in Chapter 4.

situations where we can be as open and vulnerable as we can in a sexual situation. When we expose our bodies to our lovers, we are showing them something that we usually do not show others. When we bare our souls to our lovers in a sexual situation, then our lovers can see us completely unguarded. When we have sex with another person, we invite them to join with us in a literal way, but we can also invite them to join with us in a spiritual way (this will become clearer in Chapter 5). The intimacy of erotic love is different than sex in a one-night stand, because in erotic love we allow ourselves to be open and vulnerable, whereas in a one-night stand we usually keep much of ourselves reserved.

Shared Identity

Shared identity is one of the hallmarks of erotic love and involves all of the aspects that we have already explored. It arises from shared history, living a life together, opening up to each other, and being intimate. It is the coming together of two separate lives into a shared sense of identity: an identity that needs both lovers to define it. It is a broadening of our conception of our self, such that it necessarily contains our lover as well; that is, if we were to think of ourselves, we would also have to think of our lover. Or that any kind of explanation of who we are as a person would necessarily include our lover as well. With shared identity, an explanation of one of the lovers without the other becomes incomplete. Our lover becomes another self through our shared identity and we share a life together.

Erotic love builds, and thrives in, this environment of shared identity. However, it is not enough to simply have a shared history and open up to our partner to fully create a shared identity. We must also hold each other as a very high value and internalize each other's values as our own: that is, we must integrate our lover and their values into our own value hierarchy. Through this *co-internalization of values*, we create a shared identity: when our lover's goals are frustrated, we are frustrated, since we share our lover's ends. When our goals are frustrated, so is our lover, since they share our values. A shared identity brings us much closer together than we would be otherwise: it allows us to feel together, struggle together, and achieve together.

Sexuality is a necessary condition for co-internalization of values, because it gives us the intimacy and profound vulnerability that come from opening ourselves up to a lover. When we share each other's values in this way, we create a shared identity that deepens and enhances our connection with each other and is the deepest kind of intimacy open to two people. In this way, intimacy is both a precondition of the co-internalization of values and a consequence of it. Furthermore, through the co-internalization of values, the lovers become part of each other's happiness: they incorporate each other's ends into their own happiness, so that what is good for one lover is also good for the other. Thus, the lovers become part of each other's identity.[i] This is what Plato was hinting at with his allegory of the proto-humans: there is a sense of two becoming one when we create a shared identity with our partner. This is rich, deep, and mature love—that is, erotic love.

Irreplaceability

Our lovers are individual men and women with their own personalities, quirks, traits, characters, and histories. They are not a collection of traits that we love inhering in some body. Our lovers are *individuals*: unique, singular, and not interchangeable. When we love a person, we love them as a person and that encompasses everything about them. Not that we love everything about them, but we recognize our lover as more than just a collection of things that we love; we love the totality of who they are. Moreover, no one who was similar to them, even in every way, would be able to replace them.

Part of what we love about our lover is their individuality and uniqueness. We are all, in the way that we love, individualists. As our love grows and deepens, as we develop a (non-repeatable) past and shared history, and as we grow to have a shared identity through the internalization of each other's ends, our lover becomes *irreplaceable*. This is not to say that if we were to lose this lover that we could never take another lover. Rather, once a person becomes such a big part of our life, if we lose them, then we lose a part of ourself and no other person could ever fill that hole.[ii] Our lover becomes a part of us, a unique and irreplaceable part that will permanently be a part of our identity.

Erotic Love

These features constitute erotic love at its deepest level; they are the *sine qua non* of erotic love. Without any of them, erotic love loses the qualities that make it special (or even possible) and that make it an important part of happiness. While there is more that we can, and should, say about erotic love, it would help to first briefly turn to the question of love more broadly, because understanding this will help us to better understand erotic love in contrast.

Love, of course, is an emotion. Love is an intense form of caring for its object. Yet, this does not capture the richness of love. When we say that we love something, we are communicating more than that we have a high degree of care for it. The things we love are part of what defines us as people: the things we love are part of our identity. When we love something, it becomes

---

[i] This is why it makes sense to grieve a break-up when two people are very close: there is a sense in which the person we were has died and now we must reconstitute ourselves in the face of this.

[ii] This is, emphatically, not to say that we should never love again if we lose a lover. But, rather, it is to say that deep love is a permanent part of who we are, even long after that lover is gone.

one of our core values, which are the values we hold that define who we are as people and without which we would be different people.[i] Love, then, is caring about the object so much that it becomes part of our identity by being a core value and it carries with it the potential affects of warmth and positive regard that is characteristic of love. Or, if we prefer a standard form definition with a genus and differentia: love is an emotion where a person cares so much about the object that it becomes part of their identity.

Having now seen the nature of love, we are in a better position to bring together what we have learned about the nature of erotic love into a cohesive package, since erotic love is, after all, a kind of love. Erotic love is an orientation to its object (our partner) that is strongly positive and includes them in our identity. It is always potentially affective: if we choose to recall the reasons for our love and the value our partner has in our life, then we will feel the affects associated with love. Erotic love responds to our moral ideals in another person and, as such, it is both broad and deep in scope and so it is both expansive and profound (see Chapter 2). It is also a response to our partner's existential orientation and personality (see Chapter 5), beauty, and our shared history together—the life that we have created together. This new and unique account of erotic love does not fall into any of the pitfalls we identified with the old paradigms, since it includes lessons learned from them. Indeed, it is *only* this rich and deep kind of love that is constitutive of happiness because it allows us to experience our partner as another self and take pleasure in this. Moreover, erotic love serves as an impetus to happiness as well and drives us to be the very best we can be.

Let us now give a definition of erotic love to integrate all of this into a concise package. Erotic love is a joyful and passionately intimate form of reciprocal love that arises from a shared history and deep commitment to a partner we exalt and which leads to a shared identity through co-internalization of values. The standard form definition is: erotic love is a passionately intimate form of love.

Now that we have seen the nature of erotic love, we can understand why it is so important for happiness for most of us and we will return to this question in Chapter 7. Let us now turn to several related questions, before rounding out the chapter by looking into what sort of person is capable of erotic love.

Related Questions

Now that we know what erotic love is, we still have several questions to ask. One of the questions we should consider is whether other kinds of reciprocal love, such as friendship or familial love, can ever be as deep as erotic

---

[i] The degree to which a core value defines us, including our loves, will depend on the particular value and how important we consider it to our personal identity.

love. The answer is no: the depth of intimacy and vulnerability of erotic love, the creation of a shared identity and the co-internalization of values, are all unique to erotic love. To be sure, there is intimacy with friendship and familial love, yet we are not ever as fully ourselves with our friends and family because truly unreserved openness and vulnerability is only possible through sex. Moreover, while we do hold our friends and family that we love as values, we do not internalize their values as our own and they do not internalize ours (we hold *them* as values, but we do hold *their* values). This comes closest with parents and children, where some parents internalize their children's values as their own. This, however, is necessarily one-sided and should be so: a child should not live for the sake of their parents. Additionally, there is a danger here of attempting to live vicariously through one's child and letting go of the responsibility for oneself and one's life: the danger of inauthenticity. For these reasons, it should be clear that other kinds of love can never be as deep as erotic love.

Another question that we must consider is this: can it still be deep erotic love if it ends? We certainly do not want to make the case that, in order for it to be erotic love, it must be eternal. Indeed, this would be resurrecting the existentialist worry that we dispatched in Chapter 1, where we agreed with Aristotle that things that are white for a single day are no less white for not being eternally white.[67] So, too, love that ends is still love. Even deep, rich, mature love can end. Yet, it is still love.

There is also something better about erotic love that we do not get from new love or the love of friends. This is not simply due to its length, but depends on its features and its role in our happiness. Love needs time to grow and develop into the richness and depth of erotic love. It is the development of certain features, and playing a certain role in our life, that makes erotic love uniquely necessary for happiness for most people. We become part of each other's lives as we are slowly integrated into each other's value hierarchy and self-conception. Moreover, shared history deepens this sense of shared identity. These things cannot be rushed and there is no substitute for them that can bring the richness of erotic love.

The next obvious question is: can we have multiple loves throughout life? The answer here is: of course, we can. The only stipulation would be that erotic love needs time to deepen and mature and it is only this kind of love that is constitutive of happiness. Thus, if having serial loves leads to none of them gaining depth, then it would preclude the development of erotic love and prevent it from being part of happiness.[i]

On the other hand, sometimes we do achieve this deep kind of love and, sadly, our partner dies. The death of a good partner can maim and crush

---

[i] Having multiple concurrent loves at the same time is a more complicated question that we deal with at length in Chapter 13. However, we should foreshadow here that this is possible for some people to do morally, but if done poorly can lead one away from happiness.

happiness, making it impossible. Remember that happiness is an activity, not a state, so the question of whether we can be fully happy while missing a constitutive part of happiness is obviously no (of course, neither does this mean happiness is entirely closed to us). Moreover, the loss of erotic love is devastating: because of our shared identity, there is a real sense in which a part of us dies with our lover. No one could be happy during this kind of loss, nor should they attempt to be. There are simply times in life when happiness might be closed to us and there is an issue of moral luck here because this is real life and in the real world sometimes terrible tragedies happen that can bar someone from happiness.[i] At the same time, we can also find new love. This does not replace our lost love, which is forever a part of our history and identity. But by re-establishing erotic love with a new lover, if we choose to do this, we can come to rebuild happiness.[ii]

3. What Kind of Person is Capable of Love?

All love for others is an extension of the love one has for oneself.[68]
~Aristotle

One final question we must ask is this: What kind of person is capable of love? This may seem a strange question; after all, are we not all, insofar as we are all human, capable of love? Yet, on further examination, we shall see that there is merit to the question: that some of us are, in fact, *incapable* of love generally, let alone erotic love. Indeed, since love is caring so much about the object that it becomes part of our identity, it should be clear that love is a special kind of valuing. This is important because if a person did not hold any values or was incapable of holding values, they would be precluded from all forms of love.

In order to love, we must first value our own life. In order to value our own life, we must first, as Socrates commanded, "know thyself."[iii] Or, as Rand puts it: "In order to say 'I love you' one must first know how to say the 'I'."[69] There is simply no way for a person who does not know himself to value himself: a person cannot value the unknown. This point may seem trivial or

---

[i] For example, see Aristotle's example of King Priam in: *Nicomachean Ethics*, I.10.1100^{b}25.
[ii] At the same time, the death of an erotic lover can be utterly devastating. There are, in my estimation, few legitimate reasons for suicide, but this is one of them, given certain conditions. If we have had a long life with our lover, accomplished our major values, do not have children who are relying on us, and we think that finding erotic love again would be impossible, then this is one of the strongest cases for suicide. Moreover, that this particular situation is intolerable is evident by how frequently one elderly partner dies right after the other, because they do not wish to live apart.
[iii] Although this quote is frequently attributed to Socrates, there is significant evidence that the quote predates Socrates. Nevertheless, Socrates certainly pushed the idea forward in philosophy and emphasized it in his method of philosophic inquiry, making it his own, even if he is not its origin.

obvious, but it is very important. There are people who evade their true motivations and who cannot take an honest appraisal of themselves and of their beliefs and values. They may be holding implicit beliefs to which they would consciously object, but since they are not introspective, they are not aware of these. Indeed, it is primarily through introspection that we come to know ourselves and be "self-aware." At the same time, we also can learn about ourselves from a close friend or lover, but self-knowledge must precede this if we are to have the kinds of friends or lovers that can aid us in this. In this way, we must start the process of self-knowledge on our own, but we can use others to refine it and gain new insights.

A person must be willing to inquire about the reasons that he holds his beliefs and the motivations for his actions in order to be truly introspective. He must look at himself as though he were someone else and apply the same level of scrutiny to his own actions as he would to another's. In some ways having direct psychological access makes this process harder, as it is easier to be self-deceptive and rationalize our actions; but, if we are honest with ourselves, and practice consistent introspection, then the process becomes second nature and nearly impossible not to do. Some people do not want to be introspective because they are afraid of what they would find. However, the answer is not further self-deception, but to confront our contradictions head-on in order to resolve them and restore our integrity and authenticity. After all, if we cannot be introspective and cannot know ourselves, then we will never be able to love (among a whole host of other problems).

However, self-knowledge is just a starting point: we must also value ourselves if we are to value anything else.[i] The idea of values is necessarily empty to a person who does not value himself. What would be the point of having values if we did not care how our life went?[ii] Valuing ourselves in this way also creates the possibility of meaning in life and staves off the absurdity of a meaningless life. Valuing ourselves also means working to improve ourselves and make ourselves into the kind of people for whom life is rich and meaningful, the kind of person who aims at living a good life. In this way, valuing ourself also sets the stage for pride, or moral ambitiousness.

Valuing ourselves is also a pre-condition of being able to love ourselves. This is because being able to value is a precondition of love, since love is a response to values. If we cannot value ourselves, then we cannot love ourselves. If we cannot love ourselves, then we cannot love anyone else.

---

[i] Astute readers may notice an apparent contradiction here: if a value is that which furthers our life, then how can our life itself be a value? It should be recalled that there are two senses of value: the objective and subjective. While life cannot be an objective value, since it is the foundation of objective values, we can still choose to subjectively value our lives: that is, to care about our lives. In this way, we must value (care about) ourselves if we are to value anything else.

[ii] Those people who do not want to live are also incapable of love, because without wanting to live they can have no values and without values they could not love.

Loving ourselves entails deeply caring about ourselves and the way our life goes. Loving ourselves, as a practical matter, means working to create rich and full lives for ourselves, it means working to create happiness for ourselves. Loving ourselves requires a firm sense of identity and a developed character. In creating this good life for ourselves, we come to deserve our own love. It is for this reason that Aristotle says that: "A good man *should* be a self-lover."[70] Living a good life is more than merely acting correctly; we must also *feel* that we are good and loving ourselves in this way is one way of experiencing our own moral worth.

Loving ourselves also creates the kind of self that is capable of erotic love and worthy of it, where we can help a partner to live a good life and accept their help working towards our own. We must become morally good to be worthy of love: not only as an existential fact, but we must also *know* that we are good. Erotic love also requires us to be able to be open with another person, which means showing them our real self and being authentic. In doing so, we become vulnerable before our partner: we lay our defenses bare to accept them into our life and, in so doing, create the soil in which love can grow.

As we have seen, it is only through valuing ourselves that we create the possibility of valuing others and it is only through loving ourselves that we create the possibility of loving others. This concern about our own lives must precede love of others if we are to create the kind of self that is capable of love. These, then, are the minimally necessary conditions that a person must have in place in order to be capable of love: he must know himself and he must love himself.

Summary and Conclusions

> *There is little that is more definitive of a person and distinctive for that person over a long period of time than loving someone.*[71]
> ~ Robert Solomon

We opened this chapter by noting that even though love was one of the most expansive and profound emotions a person can experience, it was not well understood or well represented in art. This was largely the fault of old paradigms that obscured the real nature of love. Now that we have seen through these old paradigms, we have gained a much richer, and more realistic, view of erotic love. Let us briefly review how we got here, before looking ahead to where to go next.

We started this chapter by looking at the old paradigms of love that pervade our culture and pervert our ideas about love. We identified five major paradigms: Platonic love, soul-mates, desperate longing, causeless love, and physicalism. The first, Platonic love, is a position that denies the reality of human nature in favor of a theoretical framework for which there is no evidence. The second, the idea of a soul-mate, comes from a very dubious story and causes people to think that there can only be one "right" partner for them and if they cannot find that particular person, then they cannot find love. The third is the paradigm of desperate longing, which can lead to people creating conflict in their relationship to make it conform to this ideal. The fourth is the paradigm of causeless love, which is the desire for unearned love and, as a consequence, destroys love and makes it empty. Lastly, the paradigm of physicalism tries to reduce the rich experience of human life to an illusion arising from chemical reactions. These paradigms pervade our culture and we must move beyond them if we wish to live a good human life in the real world. Luckily, once we know the origin of these paradigms and their lack of support, moving past them is much easier.

Next, we looked to the nature of love itself. We saw that love is constitutive of happiness and makes up part of it, such that a person without love cannot truly be happy. There were many reasons for this, among which are that it allows us to gain a better perspective on our actions and beliefs and that it allows us to create a microcosm of our ideal world. Next, we looked at some of the unique features of love, such as: irreplaceability, emotional commitment, passion, exaltation, selfish joy, shared history, and intimacy. We concluded the section by addressing some questions, such as whether sex was necessary for erotic love. We saw that it was, because it creates a depth of intimacy that is not otherwise achievable.

We then asked what kind of person was capable of love. We found that it is only the person who both knows himself and loves himself who is capable of love. A person who did not know himself, could not value himself. A person who cannot value himself, cannot value others. A person who cannot value others, cannot love others, since love is a response to values and a particularly strong kind of evaluation. Thus, we saw that the only kind of person who can love another is the person who knows himself and loves himself.

Broadly, in this chapter we saw that our new account of love breaks away from past accounts that relied on mythology or faulty assumptions for their basis. By first clearing away the mistaken conceptions of love, we gained a much clearer picture of love generally, and erotic love more specifically, that allowed us to gain insight into these things and the roles they can play in our lives. This was facilitated by our new sentimental framework, through which we were able to understand the general nature of love and its operation. This allowed us to more thoroughly explore the specific nature and details of erotic love, without needing to get bogged down in its operation.

We have shown that our sentimental account from Chapter 2 can handle even the most complex emotions like love. We have also set the stage to understand relationships and the role they play in life in Chapter 4. More importantly, we have another major piece in place for Chapter 7, where we will see how everything ultimately comes together.

Chapter 4: Relationships

Love must feel the ego of the beloved person as important as one's own ego, and must realize the other's feelings and wishes as though they were one's own.[72]
~ Bertrand Russell

Love can flourish only as long as it is free and spontaneous; it tends to be killed by the thought that it is a duty.[73]
~ Bertrand Russell

Erotic love does not, indeed cannot, grow in a vacuum. It requires a certain kind of relationship in order to flourish and become the constitutive part of happiness that most of us want in our lives and need to live well. This relationship, the erotic relationship, provides the foundation for erotic love and is the rich soil in which erotic love can grow and develop. Without this foundation, love will never grow to reach the depth and maturity of erotic love. At the same time, while the erotic relationship and erotic love are conceptually separable, and must be analyzed separately to be fully understood, they are intimately connected in the world and neither exists on its own.

In this chapter, then, we will explore the nature of the erotic relationship and its role in our lives. We will also explore the differences between the erotic relationship and friendship in order to see how they are different in kind. We will then explore the institution of marriage and see when one should marry and how to know this. Finally, we will conclude the chapter by discussing divorce and when it is justifiable or necessary.

1. The Erotic Relationship

While erotic love is necessary for happiness for most people, and partially constitutive of it for them, it requires a certain kind of relationship.[i] The erotic

---

[i] This is not to exclude polyamorous relationships, but to point out that even there, love is

relationship sets up the conditions in which erotic love can flourish by having certain characteristics that facilitate intimacy and connection between the partners. In this section, we will explore the features of the erotic relationship that make it such fertile ground for erotic love.[i]

We will see how the features of the erotic relationship lay the foundation for erotic love. For example, we will see how mirroring is an important way in which we understand the implications of our values and beliefs. Or, through our partner being another self, we help to establish the co-internalization of values necessary for a shared identity. At the same time, we will also see how having the wrong partner could make a person's life much worse. Our inquiry is not an exhaustive exploration of the erotic relationship, but it does capture the most important features.

Through all these things, the erotic relationship creates the foundation that lets erotic love flourish. This kind of relationship allows the individuals in it to thrive and work to achieve the best kind of life possible.[ii]

Equivalence

In order to have an erotic relationship, the partners must be approximately equal, morally and intellectually. Morally, the partners must be comparably good and concerned about living a good life. One of them cannot be focused on being morally exemplary while the other is indifferent to morality. If the partners are too different here, it will end badly: one partner will be bothered by the other's indifference while the other may grow to resent the other. Even if they avoid this trap, having one partner become a moral coach of the other is not tenable long-term.[iii]

The partners must also be somewhat equivalent intellectually. A very intelligent person should want a partner with whom they can speak to as an

---

always between two people: If A loves both B and C, then it is the case that A loves B and that A loves C. It is not cogent to say that A loves "{B and C}," unless A's love of B is contingent upon his love of C and also that his love of C is contingent upon his love of B, which is surely never what we mean by "A loves B and C." This topic will be discussed at length in Volume 2, Chapter 13 on Polysexuality.

[i] I want to reserve the term "erotic relationship" for a relationship that has these features and provides the fertile soil in which erotic love grows. Thus, there are no instances of bad erotic relationships, but simply of bad relationships that failed to be erotic relationships.

[ii] The features we shall explore below are necessary for the erotic relationship. We have not, however, exhausted its features, but merely focused on the most important of these. At the same time, there is some overlap here between the features of the erotic relationship and erotic love itself and this is to be expected because while they are conceptually separable, they are necessarily connected.

[iii] Although it may not, at face value, seem problematic, this kind of moral asymmetry is toxic to erotic love because erotic love relies on intimacy, looking up to our partner, and creating a world of our ideals. Too large a difference between the partners makes erotic love impossible. Erotic love requires both partners to be morally good and working to live a good life.

equal—a partner who can *understand* them.[i] This is not to say that we could not love a person who is not our approximate intellectual equal, but that having a long-term relationship with that person will be very hard and it will be hard for the more intelligent partner to not be condescending, at least from time to time, or treat the partner as an inferior. It is important here, though, not to confuse *knowledge* with *intelligence*, since a disparity in knowledge will not cause the same sorts of issues.

None of this is to say that the partners must be the same in every respect. But, if one of the two partners differs greatly in either aspect, this will lead to a relationship where they will not be able to establish deep intimacy and will doom the relationship to fail. It is possible for the partners to have different strengths that complement each other, as long as neither is deficient in either area and the difference between them is not so great as to cause an imbalance where one becomes the tutor of the other.

The overarching point is that an imbalance in either of these areas creates an imbalance of power. The teacher always has more power than the student, if for no other reason than the knowledge and skill that the teacher has, which the student is trying to learn. If the imbalance of power is enough to make the partners less than approximately equal, then it will strain their relationship and prevent them from having deep intimacy.

Sexual Compatibility

Sexually, the partners must be compatible in terms of how they view sex: how frequently they desire sex, how long they enjoy engaging in it when they do have sex, and what sorts of sexual activities they are interested in.[ii] This can be harder to learn about our partner than other things, as often people do not understand themselves well sexually. Furthermore, people can change their sexual attitudes and preferences over time, in different contexts, or they may enjoy different things with different partners, depending on their level of arousal, their interaction, and their partner's preferences. Nevertheless, we must endeavor to learn as much as we can about a potential partner's sexual attitudes and proclivities before entering into a long-term relationship. It is for this reason that *pre-marital sex is morally obligatory*: we must learn whether we are sexually compatible with our partner or whether we can become sexually compatible with each other. Not knowing this going into a long-term relationship is folly and setting ourselves up to fail. It can also have damaging consequences on any future children who may have to endure the collapse of the relationship.

---

[i] The exact range of acceptable intelligence here is going to be determined by individual preference.
[ii] To be clear, the partners do not have to have the same levels of desire. They merely must be able to be non-sacrificially flexible with regards to finding a positive compromise position.

Mirroring

In his ethical writings, Aristotle identified an important part of the best kind of relationship, called mirroring.[i] Mirroring is being able to see and appreciate good moral action through our lover and involves three related elements: the external view, contemplation, and benefaction. We will deal with each in turn.

First, the external view. Aristotle observed that it can be hard for us to objectively judge our own actions as we can be too close to our reasons and our internal conflicts, but that we do not have this problem in judging others.[74] In fact, through our lover, we can see them living out their ideals and translating them into reality through their actions. We can, consequently, judge their actions and reasons objectively from the outside unburdened by having too intimate an access.

The external view is important, because the partners in erotic relationships should share their moral ideals and, thus, will be able to see these ideals in action in their partner. Because of this, our partner allows us to gain an external perspective on our actions by seeing ourselves through their eyes.[ii] The external view, thus, allows objective judgement of our actions through our partner. In this way, we can gain a better understanding of ourselves. Moreover, this creates a virtuous circle, because as we start to live better through our newfound perspective, we will gain the esteem of our partner and this becomes mutually reinforcing between the partners.

Second, contemplation. Aristotle observed that it is naturally pleasant to observe and contemplate good actions. Moreover, since our lover is like another self, their good actions will be even dearer to us, because we will identify with them and care about their ends, such that we will enjoy their good actions both as good actions and as contributing to their flourishing, in which we are invested.

Contemplation is important, because there is a great psychological and moral value in the contemplation of good action. It is simply pleasurable to see good people living well, especially when we care for them. Moreover, we said in the last chapter that our lovers allow us to glimpse a microcosm of the world as we wish it were. Part of how they do this is through exhibiting flourishing through their good actions. This allows us to contemplate their actions and see our moral ideals brought into the world.

Third, benefaction. Aristotle observed that the benefactor stands in a

---

[i] See: *Nicomachean Ethics* IX.7.1168^{a}5 & IX.9.1170^{a}13-1170^{b}17. While Aristotle limits his discussion to the love of friends, it is entirely appropriate to expand it to our modern-day conception of love. Our conception of erotic love is much closer to Aristotle's idea of character friends than it is to our contemporary conception of friendship.

[ii] Mirroring need not be passive: we can actively tell our partner the things that they are doing well or poorly.

special kind of relationship to the person whom he has benefitted: the benefactor is, in a sense, like a sculptor who helped to shape the character of the person he benefitted.[75] When we help our partner to become a better person, then we can see our good actions actualized through them: we can see the reality of our values as manifested through our partner as well as our effect on them.

Benefaction is important, because if we want to live well, then we must actualize our values in the world. Part of how we do this is through developing our own character, but it can be hard to see our own moral development. So, the other part of how we bring our values into the world is through helping other people, especially people we value, to develop good characters and to live good lives. This is naturally pleasant to us and we can feel pride in knowing that we had a hand in their goodness. Moreover, since our lover becomes part of us in erotic love, we have an added benefit: what is good for them is likewise good for us, since we share in happiness together. There is a great virtuous circle here: by helping our partner to live better, we actualize our best characteristics and can enjoy their goodness. At the same time, they can help us to live better lives as well, creating a self-reinforcing cycle of improvement. In this way, a good lover allows us to really feel pleasure in virtue and living well, to a degree not possible if we merely reflect on our own moral development.

At the same time, mirroring is not limited to morality: through the mirror of our partner, we can see our whole self. This includes our existential orientation and our sense of humor, what kind of art we like and what kind of movies, which activities we choose to spend our days doing and even how our overall life is going. Because our partner is like another self, we can see ourselves in, and through, them. Sometimes we are most opaque to ourselves and being able to understand ourselves through our partner's eyes can help to lift the veil and reveal us to ourselves. This, of course, can be hard to see, but we should never shy away from reality in order to save our pretenses. We must be careful, though, to make sure that our partner is actually seeing us for who we are and that they understand us, before we attempt to understand ourselves from their position as it is all too easy for love to become idealized and disconnected from reality.

When mirroring is done wrongly and reflects a distortion of reality, it can make things much worse. For example, if our partner is reflecting that we are living well back to us when they know that we are dishonest with others or vicious in general, then we may come to believe their reflection, especially if it helps us to ignore the parts of ourselves that we are trying to evade. However, when mirroring is done well, it is a great boon to moral development, as it will help the partners live well.

Being with a good partner is very beneficial to this end. When we are with a good partner, we each want to be the best that we can in order to impress our partner and to deserve their love and affection. Further, by being with a good person we learn together and what one of us does well, the other will learn to do well. If one of us is being morally incontinent, then the other can help. Our partner can tell us if we are making a mistake or encourage good behavior. In short, having a good partner makes it much easier to live well, because they can act as a second self who also propels us to live better.

Psychological Visibility

A closely related idea is what we will call "psychological visibility" and it is an idea that grew out of Aristotelian mirroring. The idea is this: it is important to be seen by our partner in the way that we see ourselves and that we want to be seen. For example, if we see ourselves as intelligent, then we want our partner to see us as intelligent as well. Psychological visibility is a reaffirmation of our self and of our connection to our partner. It is a need to be seen for who we really are and to be loved for that reason.

Psychological visibility is very important in a relationship: without it, we will think that our partner does not understand us or thinks of us as something that we are not. Unfortunately, this is fairly common. We have seen that erotic love is a response to values and character and if our partner misunderstands who we are, then they may not actually love *us*, but only the "apparent us," the "us" they think they know. This is a horrible position to find ourselves in: to think that our partner does not love us, but only loves a false image of us.

Because psychological visibility is a real need and an important part of relationships, it carries with it a responsibility to be open with our partner and to show them our real selves: to not hide the parts of us of which we are ashamed, but to show them fully who we are. This does not mean that we must be satisfied with who we are or static in our moral development, but it means we should not hide where we are in our moral development or that we are working on improving ourselves (if, indeed, we are). We must show our partner how we see ourselves and how we want to be seen, even if this is an ideal that we are working towards.[i]

To feel truly loved and connected to our partner, we must have psychological visibility. Without it, a relationship is doomed to suffer and will likely fail. Regardless of if it fails or not, without psychological visibility the relationship will certainly be of an inferior kind and will not help us to achieve happiness.

---

[i] It is worth pointing out that there is a significant difference between a person loving an overly idealized version of their partner that bears little relation to reality and including our partner's moral ideals in what we love about them. In the former case, we lose sight of reality and respond to a false conception of our partner. In the latter case, we recognize that people can become morally better and that working to do so is an important part of our ethical lives.

Respect

The *Oxford English Dictionary* defines respect in two different ways and they present an interesting contrast to each other. The first is "a feeling of deep admiration for someone…elicited by their abilities, qualities, or achievements" while the second is "Avoid harming or interfering with."[76] The latter use is important, especially when used in the sense of "respect my rights." However, while the negative use is important, it merely paves the way to happiness, but will not help us get there.[i]

The positive definition, on the other hand, captures the essence of the concept, which is admiration, or a "looking up to." We should think our partner is a good person and we should admire them for their ideas, their character, and their achievements. Our partner should embody our moral ideal or, at least, be working towards it. Their character should be good and they should care about this, because they want to be a good person. Our partner should be someone to look up to and emulate. Of course, that does not mean that we can be lax about our own character and moral development, but that each partner can be particularly excellent at different things and they can each look up to each other for different things. When we can look up to our partner, it helps to provide an impetus to improve ourselves and become better people. In this way, respect is important to eudaimonism, both in our respect for our partner and in our respect for our heroes.

Respecting our partner, holding them as a moral ideal[ii] and admiring them, is vital to having an erotic relationship. Of course, it is a demanding standard, but we are not looking to have lives that are merely decent. We are looking to achieve true and lasting happiness and that requires effort and exacting standards. When we hold up our partner as an ideal and respect them for what they have done, and they do the same to us, we will both be better people and our relationship will be much stronger.

Caring

In the erotic relationship, we should care about our partner for their own sake. This point sounds obvious, but it is a common pitfall. Many people, especially once they have been with a person for a long time, forget that our partner is a person who has their own values, ideas, character, and achievements. They start to think of them only relationally (*i.e.*, this is my *wife*), as though that captured all of what it means to be them. If we begin to think of our partner merely in this relational way, we lose sight of who they really are. This can happen when two people become too dependent on each other and

---

[i] While some people, especially in government roles such as the police, tend to think that "respect" means "to obey," this is wholly illegitimate.
[ii] To hold our partner as a moral ideal is not to insist that they be without fault.

lose sight of their individuality. When we care about our partner for their sake, we not only care about them for how they impact our life. We also care about their ends, such as: whether they are achieving the kind of life they want, whether they are achieving their goals, or whether they are pursuing their values.

There is an obvious connection here between caring and respect, as we tend to care more about the things that we respect and we tend not to care for the things that we do not respect. When we respect our partner, we are more likely to care for them for their own sake and not simply because they are our partner. The problem with caring for our partner as simply "our partner" is that it makes it all too easy to ignore the things that our partner cares for and values and, instead, worry about them only insofar as what happens to them effects only our interests and not their own. Yet this is a mistaken way of understanding the idea of shared values and of a shared identity. We should value our partner for their own sake and not simply value some of the benefits that they bring to us; otherwise we ignore their personhood, goals, and all the things that makes them lovable.

We must choose to care about our partner and their lives. This act of choosing to care about them is our choosing to value them and we must do this consciously and purposefully if we want to have a good relationship that will help us to achieve a good life.

Mutual Enjoyment

The best kinds of relationships should also be mutually enjoyable to both partners. This should seem obvious, but people sometimes feel that relationships should be a lot of work and that they do not necessarily need to be enjoyable, as long as they are helping us to achieve our goals. This is completely wrong. A relationship that is not enjoyable hinders us and will not help us to achieve happiness.

The mutual enjoyment should span many different aspects of the relationship, including sexual enjoyment, enjoyment of each other's company, enjoyment of mutual activities, *etc*. We should enjoy our partner's body, presence, and participation. We should not need to find other people whose company we enjoy to engage in the things most important to us. Of course, this is not to say that we must do everything with our partner or that our partner must fulfill our every need, but rather that we should enjoy our partner and our time with them.

It is important to point out that this also should not be taken to mean that we must do anything our partner might want. We should try to be open-minded and willing to do things with our partner, even if we do not love the activities ourselves. Except in the cases of harm to ourselves or our partner, this is an important part of a healthy relationship and making sure that each partner is getting their needs met. Of course, there may be things that we simply cannot or will not do for legitimate reasons and sometimes this means that our partner will have to get their needs met elsewhere. This is also fine and part of a healthy relationship. We do not need to be all things to our partner and the expectation that we should be can be damaging to a relationship.

Independence and Dependence

In the best kinds of relationship lovers become part of each other's identities and their lives become intertwined in myriad ways. Unfortunately, for some couples this spells the death of their respective individualities and they end up losing their identity to the relationship. We have all met people like this: people who lose their sense of identity and become whatever they think their partner wants them to be and their partner does the same, such that they end up being a "we" that obliterates both "I's." There is a careful balancing that must be done in relationships between being part of a relationship and being our own individual: straying too far in either direction will cause significant problems.

In good relationships, there is a sense in which the lovers are dependent on each other for happiness. Yet, they must not be dependent on each other for their identities: each partner must be complete in himself as a person, before he can truly enter an erotic relationship. A person who is not complete in himself will lose himself in the relationship and become a thin reflection of the relationship, thereby losing the value of the relationship. On the other hand, the partners should share in the development of new values that help to bind their relationship together, including things like shared activities, shared goals, or creating a family together.

However, if the partners in the relationship remain aloof from each other, in an attempt to gain a false sense of "independence" from each other, then the relationship will never work. This sense of being "independent" by defining ourselves against other people is a false sense of independence: it truly is a dependence on others and a derivative sense of self. Whether we define ourself through the rejection of others or by intentionally defying someone's wishes, we still gain our identity from others. True independence comes from acting on our own judgement and based on our own values.

To have a good erotic relationship, we must be able to be true to our values and self while letting our partner be a big part of our life. We maintain our independence by focusing on our values and character and making sure these only change when the change is for the better. We maintain our relationship by focusing on both the value of our partner and of the relationship itself, while also creating new shared values together with our partner. It is important to work together to create new values for the relationship. This must be a joint process that is neither dominated by one partner nor comes to consume either partner.

Now, it may seem like there is a tension here between how we have laid out our eudaimonistic account, with its emphasis on egoism, and how we have presented the ideal relationship in terms of the co-internalization of values and a shared life. There is, however, no tension here as both accounts are correct. Each person must pursue their own values and create their own lives and characters. At the same time, we also internalize our partner's values and they become part of our happiness. For this reason, pursuing *their* ends is also egoistic.

A relationship is, thus, like a kind of interplay between independence and dependence, where in the former case, we must create and maintain discrete selves in order to have a real relationship, and in the latter case, our happiness becomes bound up in another person. If we let our individuality fade away, then the very reasons our partner fell in love with us will disappear. If we try to remain distant from our partner because we fear the intimacy or shared identity, then love will never arise or will wither away. Yet, losing ourselves in the relationship spells the end of erotic love as well. Thus, we must find a path where we maintain our own individual identities as well as create a shared life and shared identity with our partner. Straying too far to either side will cause the love or relationship to fall apart. Yet, by walking just the right line, we can create a rich shared life where we develop a shared identity with our partner, where we develop new values with our partner, and, through doing so, develop the foundations for the erotic relationship and erotic love.

Erotic Love

We discussed erotic love at length in the last chapter and saw that it has certain characteristics, such as intimacy, irreplaceability, passion, *etc.*, that make it uniquely erotic love as opposed to other kinds of love such as friendship or familial love. There is a reciprocity between erotic love and the erotic relationship: erotic love encourages and nurtures the relationship in which it thrives and the erotic relationship creates the soil for erotic love to grow and prosper.

We shall explore this more in the next section, but erotic love is the most important bond for happiness for most of us. This is because it plays a larger role in the creation of ourselves, in our moral development, and in the very ways in which we experience the world than any other kind of human bond. It does this through intimacy, co-internalization of values, shared history and the creation of a shared identity, psychological visibility, mirroring, *etc.*

For these reasons, the erotic relationship is necessary to create and cultivate deep and mature love; that is, erotic love. And since erotic love is necessary for happiness for most people, as well as being partially constitutive of it, the erotic relationship is also necessary for happiness for these people.

The erotic relationship is a special kind of bond that incorporates so much of who we are as people and has deep and lasting implications for our lives. No other kind of human bond or relationship rivals the depth and importance of this one.

2. Friendship versus the Erotic Relationship

Some people think that the erotic relationship is akin to a kind of super-friendship and that our lover is no more than a very special friend. This is false. The difference is not merely in degree: it is a difference of kind. To see why, let us briefly compare the two.

We have already spent a good deal of time talking about erotic love and the erotic relationship, but let us briefly recapitulate to make the point as clear as possible. In an erotic relationship, the lovers develop a deep sense of intimacy and open themselves to each other, so that they are completely visible to each other. They have complementary existential orientations, share many core values, and have a deep congruence between their overall values. Furthermore, the lovers become part of each other's happiness, such that they incorporate each other's ends into their own happiness so that what is good for one lover is also good for the other. Thus, in a very real sense, the lovers become part of each other's lives and create a shared identity.

Friendship, even in its best instances, is somewhat different. While it is certainly true that good friends can become part of each other's lives, the sense in which this is true is more limited than it is with lovers. There is a sense of intimacy in friendship, but it is not the same degree as is possible with a good lover. The degree of intimacy we have with a lover comes from the co-internalization of each other's values and the creation of a shared identity, and the reciprocal relationship these things have. This is not the case in friendship.[i] Even though we may wish our friend well for their own sake and want good things for them, their goods are not ours. Even with our closest friends, while their pain is painful to us, this is different because it is not our pain as it would be if we shared a life. A friend's pain does not harm our life in a direct way, unlike a lover's. This is because friends do not internalize each other's values as their own: we wish our friend well for their sake. We wish our lover well both for their sake and ours.

The difference here is rooted in how we incorporate a friend or a lover into our hierarchy of values and, consequently, what kind of role they play in our life. Both friendship and erotic love are kinds of bonds and they are both a kind of love. With a very close friend, we care about them for their own sake (not merely because we find them pleasant to be around or useful for some

---

[i] This is not to say that any kind of sexual relationship is always more important than friendship. Certainly, a good friendship is much more important to happiness than a bad relationship.

ends)[i] and they care about us. Friends are a value to us in life and are necessary for happiness. However, while our friend is a value to us, their values are not our values. We care about whether our friend succeeds for their sake, but not for *ours*. Our friend's success is not, likewise, *our* success. In contrast, when our lover has successes, they *are* likewise our successes: because we have created a shared identity and because we see ourselves reflected in our lover and their good action. Our lover achieving their values is achieving our values because we *share* values through our co-internalization of each other's values. This depth of shared identity is only possible through deep intimacy and openness with each other. This deepest kind of intimacy is only possible through erotic love, because of its sexual component: it is only when we involve sex that we can be at our most vulnerable and most intimate, when we truly allow ourselves to connect with another person. In friendship, we do not take our friend's values into our self-identity in the same way, and thus, we do not share an identity as we do with a lover.[ii]

Although this may seem to be only a difference of degree, the difference is so great that it rises to a difference of kind. From a different perspective, we can say that while we are sad when we lose a friend, especially a very close one, we do not lose a part of ourselves when this happens. On the contrary, when we lose a lover, we do lose a part of ourselves in a very real way: part of our identity is ripped away with their loss. Even if we find a new lover, the impact of our former lovers will always be with us. This is not the case even with the best of friends, which is not to downplay the real loss that we would suffer at their death. Thus, lovers are different from friends: they are different in fundamental ways and fulfill different roles in our lives. Yet, for most of us, both are vital for happiness and we must seek both to live the best kind of life possible.

---

[i] These distinctions are based in Aristotle's account of friendship, which he elaborates in *Nicomachean Ethics*, Book VIII. See also Robert Mayhew's *Aristotle's Criticism of Plato's Republic* and his development of the idea of "character friends."

[ii] For more on this point, see Chapter 2, the end of Section 3. Moreover, this is not to say that any person we happen to date will be more important than the best of friends, but it is to say that the ideal lover and the ideal friend play different roles. In actuality, the role they play will be determined by all of the conditions we have outlined, such as the degree of intimacy, psychological visibility, trust, *etc*.

3. Marriage

> *Marriage: thus I name the will of two*
> *to create the one that is more than*
> *those who created it. Reverence for each other,*
> *as for those willing with such a will,*
> *is what I name marriage. Let this be*
> *the meaning and the truth of your marriage.*[77]
> ~ Nietzsche

We all have at least a vague and nebulous idea of what marriage is and what it should be. Children even talk about getting married and play at marriage in their games. But, all too often we get stuck in this vague childhood conception of marriage and few of us actually understand what marriage involves and what it should be. In order to remedy this, let us inquire into the nature of marriage.

Before we try to understand marriage in its current form, it makes sense to briefly consider how marriage arrived here. Indeed, our current conception of marriage is quite new. Historically, in most cultures around the world, marriage was an institution for guaranteeing lineage and bloodlines and making sure that property would pass to our genetic offspring. Marriages were often made for political reasons or to increase one's property and, for this reason, were often arranged.

At some point in history, marriage stopped being primarily about politics and property and started to be more focused on love, at least in most Western cultures. This started with the rise of "courtly love" which, for all its issues, had the virtue of treating love as a worthwhile end and not merely as a means to something else. This radical change paved the way for "romantic love" and the beginning of contemporary conceptions of love. These, of course, we have abandoned for our richer and more integrated conception of erotic love.[i]

Today, unfortunately, many people treat marriage as though it is just the last inevitable step in a natural progression of a relationship. However, marriage is not just a different kind of long-term relationship and cannot be simply this if we want a happy and successful marriage. Marriage must be a purposeful *choice* and entered into with the full knowledge of what it entails and requires: to enter into marriage simply because we have been with the same partner for a long period of time is foolhardy and immoral; that is, to do so is to set ourselves up for failure and to make our lives worse.

We have already seen the characteristics of the erotic relationship and a good marriage needs all of these as well. However, a good marriage has some further conditions that make it a unique kind of relationship and bond. Before

---

[i] For those interested in the history of love, consider reading Robert Solomon's *About Love: Reinventing Romance for Our Times*, particularly the chapter "The History of Love."

we elaborate these, it is important to point out that marriage may come before or after all of the conditions of an erotic relationship. That is, a couple need not wait until they have perfected their relationship before they marry, as long as their relationship is good, because the relationship can be perfected during the marriage. Sometimes people work to perfect their relationship first and sometimes they marry first; there is no necessary order. Often, the depth of the erotic relationship only happens after marriage as the couple lives their lives together. In fact, marriage may be the best arrangement to bring about an excellent erotic relationship, but it is not strictly necessary for it.

One of the things that makes marriage a special kind of bond is that it is a public commitment. In marriage, two people want to be publicly and legally recognized as sharing a life and creating a family together.[i] Marriage is, in this sense, both the social recognition of the relationship and a special kind of commitment. It is the recognition from others that our relationship is very serious and that we should be treated as a family. It is a commitment to intertwine our life with our partner with the wish that this fact be recognized by our friends, family, and society. It is a commitment to share our life with our partner, to live our lives together, and it should be entered into with the expectation that it will be life-long. Divorce should be reserved only for marriages that are no longer serving their function and enriching the lives of those in them. For a marriage to be truly successful, we must commit ourselves to it and to our partner without reservation.

Marriage is more than just wishing to be socially recognized as a family. It is also a legal contract between the spouses to join their property together. While, as a matter of fact, not all states recognize marriage as a contract, the state should do this because recognizing and protecting contracts is one of the legitimate functions of the state. Marriage, as a legal contract, provides legal recognition of the seriousness of the commitment and of becoming a family. Through this recognition of our special legal status, the state grants us a special set of rights that no other couples have, nor should they have.[ii] If a couple

---

[i] A "private marriage," that is known only to the couple, is not a marriage at all. Rather, it is merely a deep private commitment, even if it shares some features with marriage and the partners call it that. One of the essential features of marriage is that it is a public commitment and that the couple wishes to be recognized as a family by others to show how deeply committed they are to each other. The only exception here is if making the marriage public would harm the couple and they are forced to keep it a secret, including from legal recognition.

[ii] It is right that the state reserves special exceptions for married couples in light of their serious commitment to each other, such as the ability to speak for each other in times of medical emergency or inheritance of property. However, people should be free to marry the person whom they love and who makes their life better, regardless of their sex or orientation. Because bisexuals and homosexuals are simply people, they should enjoy all the same benefits of the law as anyone else, without any need to explicitly have the law name them as people. It is preposterous that we have arrived at a situation where it needs be pointed out that all people are people and that people have rights (an error, of course, caused by collectivism and their corruption of the idea of rights).

wishes to have the rights of married couples, then they must formally commit to each other through marriage.[i]

Beyond the social recognition and the legal contract, what makes marriage special is the depth of the commitment: marriage carries with it the promise to be life-long. This means that marriage should not be entered into lightly or with strong reservations, but with the intention to spend the rest of our life with our partner. This is a momentous decision. It entails a commitment to working to make the relationship work and to not simply allowing problems to continue or grow. It also entails being open and honest with our partner and with ourselves and finding ways for each person to grow and to grow together as well. Marriage is the commitment to work to build the kind of relationship that will last and help us to thrive.

One of the most important things that we must learn about is our partner's sexuality and our sexual compatibility.[ii] Since many marriages fail because of sexual incompatibility, to enter into a marriage in ignorance of our partner's sexual preferences and our compatibility is beyond foolhardy (which is why we said above that pre-marital sex is morally obligatory). We need to not only know about our partner's sexuality from experience, but we also need to have discussions about fantasies, future desires, and things that we each might want to try in the future. If two people get married and one person has the intention to have a threesome before they die and the other person does not know about that, nor would they approve or want to participate, then this person is setting himself up for problems in the future.

Sex is not the only important aspect of marriage, though, and it is important that we have conversations with a potential spouse about the kinds of things that can divide couples and about problems that frequently arise. We should discuss where we both want to live in the future, whether we want to have children, how we will raise and educate any potential children, how to handle finances, the boundaries of our obligations to birth families, *etc*. Again, to go into a marriage without having discussed beforehand some of the major problems that arise in a marriage is a mark of much folly. Further, to set ourselves up to fail through ignorance of these issues is not itself an innocent

---

[i] I also think that the state should allow more than two people to get married if they wish it. I think that in any sort of non-standard marriage, an explicit and legally binding marriage contract must be submitted by the partners to the court, which would serve to adjudicate any future disputes or issues. My position can be summed up to this: marriage is a legal contract and it is one of the proper functions of the state to protect contracts, but the state should have no role whatsoever in determining who can enter into marriage contracts and what their terms might be. Provided, of course, that all parties are legal adults, mentally sound, and acting of their own free will.

[ii] Sexual compatibility can change over the course of a relationship, but it is pure folly to at least not start on the same page. If it does change over time, the partners can try to accommodate each other or even open their relationship, depending on their sexual needs and other factors. See Chapter 13 for further discussion of this point.

error, but a moral failure, since we should know better.[i]

In order to know that we are compatible with our partner, we must really know them. But this can be hard. It is often the case that when we start to get to know someone, or begin dating, that we do not act authentically. Rather, to make sure the relationship works and that things go smoothly, we often present ourselves as we are likely to be best received. We hide our faults and put forward our best qualities. We also tend to focus only on the positives of our partner early on and minimize their negative aspects. While this is understandable from a psychological perspective, it can be disastrous if this is the extent two people have learned of each other when they start to consider whether to marry. If we still only know our partner on this superficial level, the criteria we use in our decision will not reflect who our partner really is and who they will be when the façade wears off and we suddenly find ourselves in a marriage with a different person. In order to avoid this outcome, we need experience of our partner in many different situations and over time.

Before we should consider marrying, we should know our partner well enough to be able to predict how they will respond to different things and *why* they respond the way they do. We should know their positions on major issues such as morality, religion, politics, *etc.*, and *why* they hold the beliefs they do. We should understand where we disagree with our partner, for what reasons, and whether this will be a potential source of conflict in the future. This, obviously, is no easy task, nor is it a quick one. This level of knowledge of our partner takes time and experience. But, it is necessary if we are to know whether our partner is the right person to marry.

So, how do we know *when* to marry? We will never "just know" when we have found the right partner to marry: there is no mystical sign from the heavens to watch for. It is, rather, a judgement we must make for ourselves. And, given what we now know about erotic relationships and about marriage, we have the foundation necessary to know what a good relationship is and how to work to achieve one. So, how do we know we have found the right partner? We know when our partner makes our life better than it would be without them and when we are with them, we feel happier and more capable than we would otherwise. If we can honestly commit to spending the rest of our life with them and working to make the relationship successful and we know that they can likewise commit, then we have found the right person to marry. In short, how do we know whether we should marry? We should get married if we judge that the relationship will contribute to our overall life and happiness.

If two people should get married, then this remains true even if they would face social censure for marrying: including couples who are same-sex or interracial and who worry about marrying because they fear backlash from those around them. Not marrying in this situation is a failure of integrity. We

---

[i] A relationship that is otherwise good but has a conflict in one of these categories can often benefit from couple's therapy to help the partners adjudicate the conflict.

should never allow our lives to be ruled by the irrationality of others (unless, of course, we risk physical violence and then it is no breach of integrity because we are being coerced). Furthermore, allowing ourselves to be cowed because of the pressure of others will not help anyone in the long-run. If we, instead, fight for our values, then people will eventually change and so will the culture. No one could have imagined, at the time of the Stonewall Riots, that same-sex marriage would be legal and as prevalent as it is today. However, through the persistence of those committed to their lives and happiness, society is changing for the better and same-sex couples are being accepted more and more. This is not to say that couples should martyr themselves, but that to the extent that they can live without fear of terrible reprisal, they should do so openly and proudly. If happiness is our goal and we have found a person who we need for our happiness, how could we do anything but fight to have them in our life?

4. Divorce

Unfortunately, even with the best planning, some marriages will fail. In general, the bond of marriage should be broken, all other things being equal, when it is discovered that the marriage is no longer contributing to the long-term happiness of the individuals that comprise it and that no remedy to this situation is possible. However, this is not always so simple.

There are many reasons why divorce might be necessary, but many of them stem from the same cause: lack of participation in each other's lives. People grow and change throughout their lives, all the way until death. While it is true that we are most open to change when we are young, this certainly does not mean that change is impossible as we age. In a marriage, the partners continue to grow as well. If they are not involved enough in each other's lives, then there is a real risk that they will grow apart and the things that were once important to them and that bound them together, may no longer be as important to them and may, instead, divide them. In order to make sure this does not happen, we need to be active in our partner's lives: we need to care about them, stay engaged with them and their development, and maintain open and honest communication with our partner about what is happening in our lives and about changes that may be occurring.

Beyond just growing apart and losing touch with each other, there are many things that can be done that will undermine and ultimately destroy a marriage. All relationships need trust, honesty, good communication, respect, and love. Any breakdown in one of these can cause the relationship to fail. Although it is not possible to create an exhaustive list of the reasons why marriages fail, some of the more common reasons, after growing apart, are: financial disagreements, sexual incompatibility, dishonesty, abuse, irrationality, and infidelity.[78] We have already explored some of these issues, but we have not yet explored the issue of infidelity, which has two primary forms: sexual infidelity and emotional infidelity.

Sexual infidelity is not conforming to our sexual agreement with our partner. While it is often thought of as simply having sex outside a relationship, this is a poor definition as some relationships allow for sex outside the relationship. The problem with sexual infidelity, or "cheating," is not that a person has had sex outside their relationship, but that, in doing so, they violated their partner's trust and broke their word. This is the real problem with sexual infidelity: it is the violation of trust that damages the relationship.

A closely related issue is emotional infidelity, where a person seeks the kind of deep intimacy of erotic love elsewhere and closes himself to his partner. In emotional infidelity, a person stops being emotionally open and honest with his partner. This erodes the intimacy of the relationship and will eventually destroy it. In both kinds of infidelity, the real problem is the violation of one's word and the damage to the foundations of the relationship.

What makes infidelity so very painful is that it comes from the person who should never be the one to hurt us. This is precisely why some people have such a hard time with the depth of vulnerability required for erotic love: it is a double-edged sword. The vulnerability allows us to love and be loved, but it also opens us up to pain and heartache. Yet, this risk is ultimately worth it, because love is so precious.

A question now arises: when is divorce justified? Or: When should two people get divorced? No matter how a relationship starts to fail, whether through growing apart, infidelity, *etc.*, there may come a time when divorce is the right thing to do. By what standard can we judge when it is right to do so? We must look back to the original reasons for marriage in the first place. Marriage is worthwhile because it helps to create the conditions in which we can achieve happiness. The standard to get married is whether it would help us achieve happiness. Thus, the standard for when to get divorced is this: divorce is the right thing to do when the marriage is no longer contributing to the happiness of the partners. If this seems simple, it is because it is: by having clear standards about when to marry and a clear ethical code, we remove many of the complications from thinking about this complex issue. Of course, the reality of this may be harder to judge, as we will shortly see.

Even though we have now clarified the field, we should still look at the error of divorcing too quickly or too reluctantly.

Marriage can be hard. It is hard to create a life together and it takes work and virtue to do it well. Some people see that it will be work and give up once it starts getting difficult. They get caught up in the old paradigms about love that we dealt with in the last chapter, such as the idea of "soul-mates" who will just naturally live "happily ever after." These people make the mistake of divorcing too quickly. Unfortunately for them, they will find that every relationship they will ever be in will require hard work and, thus, they frequently bounce from one short marriage to another, always expecting reality to conform to their mistaken beliefs about marriage and perpetually being surprised when it does not.

Just because a marriage gets hard, does not mean that divorce is the right choice. Whether a marriage is helping a couple to live better lives cannot be measured by a single day and often relationships are much stronger and more rewarding after a hard period when the couple puts in real work and recommits to each other and their marriage. It can be hard to tell whether a marriage has entered a "hard period" or is starting to fail. In order to ascertain which situation applies, one must look at what is causing the problems in the relationship. If it is disagreements about household matters or minor annoyances that have built into resentments, then it is simply a hard period. If the couple now disagrees about fundamental issues or there is a breakdown of mutual respect or care, the relationship may be over. This kind of thing can be very difficult to ascertain for those in the relationship and the outside perspective of a psychotherapist or psychologist can be very helpful. If the couple is able to resolve their problems, then they often have a much stronger relationship afterwards and they gain the added strength of having gone through a trial together.

At the same time, some people stay in relationships that are no longer contributing to their happiness. They might stay because they fear that they will never find another partner or they fear having to work to create their own individual identity.[i] Whatever the reason these people stay in the dysfunctional relationship, if it stops contributing to their happiness, they should leave it. A relationship that is no longer contributing to the couple's happiness is failing to be a worthwhile relationship.

In either case, the solution here is to look to the standard regarding when we should marry in the first place—whether it will contribute to our happiness—and judge whether divorce is appropriate based on this. This means that the individuals involved in the marriage must apply their *phronesis* and judge for themselves whether the marriage is contributing to their happiness or not.

Yet, even when there is good cause to end a marriage, there can be complications. The biggest complication is often children. It is not always clear what the best outcome is, with regard to children, even when there is good cause for divorce. However, it is better for children to be raised without their two biological parents being together than to be raised in a bad household where the parents are at odds with each other. Consider that for children, their parents' relationship is the first and usually only relationship that they have any familiarity with and this will give them their paradigm of what a relationship

---

[i] While some people today stay married for financial reasons, this is a poor choice. There are always ways to overcome financial issues, including taking on a new job, living with friends or finding a roommate, and scaling back one's expectations. If a person is willing to give up their happiness for money, then this is what they deserve.

should be and how people should treat each other. It is far better for the parents to separate and live happy, independent lives than for them to sacrifice themselves "for the sake of their children," when in the long run they are making their children's lives worse by showing them a bad example of a relationship and setting them up for future strife in their own relationships.[i]

It is important to point out here that just because a relationship ends, this does not mean that it has failed. People can change and they should not try to keep themselves stagnant to stay in a relationship that no longer works. This is not a failure of their relationship and the relationship should still be celebrated as an achievement if it was good and contributed to their happiness while it lasted.[ii] We must, here too, throw off Plato's error that only eternal things can be valuable or have worth and recognize that just because a relationship ends, does not mean that it did not have value while it lasted.

Summary and Conclusions

We have now seen how the erotic relationship provides the foundation for erotic love and serves as the fertile soil in which it grows. The erotic relationship is, in these ways, necessary for erotic love and these things always occur together. We have also seen how this relationship is unique among other human bonds and is capable of a greater depth of intimacy that other relationships. Let us briefly review how we got here before considering where we will head next.

We began this chapter by examining the nature of the erotic relationship, which we did by contemplating its major features. We found that it had features such as equivalence, sexual compatibility, mirroring, psychological visibility, care, respect, mutual enjoyment, and a balance between independence and dependence. We saw that through these characteristics, the erotic relationship was able to provide the foundation for erotic love, which is also part of the erotic relationship, as these things are not separable.

Next, we contrasted the erotic relationship with friendship and saw that there are significant differences, such that the difference between friends and lovers is more than a simple difference of degree. Our lover becomes a part of our life in a way that a friend cannot, due to the co-internalization of values and the creation of a shared identity in erotic love. Moreover, the level of intimacy possible in the erotic relationship is greater due to the element of sexuality, which creates a depth of intimacy that is not otherwise possible because we are not able to be as revealed and open with another person as we are in the sexual

---

[i] For an opposing view, see Bertrand Russell's *Marriage and Morals*, where he argues that marriage should be considered tentative until there are children and then it should be insoluble until the children are adults. Of course, I disagree with Russell on this point (among many others).
[ii] The American advice-columnist and podcaster Dan Savage is very good about emphasizing this point.

context. Thus, we saw that friendship and the erotic relationship were different in kind.

We next looked at marriage and found it to be a very important institution whereby we affirm the great value of our partner in our life and publicly ask others to recognize our shared life together. We saw that marriage is a promise we make to our partner to remain with them through the good times and bad, and to put forth effort to make the marriage work. For these reasons, we saw that the decision to marry is momentous and requires knowing our partner deeply beforehand, including our sexual compatibility and compatibility in other areas such as religion, finances, whether we want children, *etc*. Through our inquiry, we gained the knowledge we need to understand when two people should get married: when doing so contributes to each other's lives and happiness.

Finally, we saw that even with the best of intentions, marriages can fail. While this can sometimes be alleviated through psychotherapy, this is not always possible. We saw that the standard to use to judge whether divorce is the right course is the converse of how we know when to marry: people should divorce when their marriage is no longer contributing to their happiness and it is beyond their power to save. We also saw that some people are too quick to divorce, while others are too slow. People should not be too quick to divorce as relationships can be much stronger and more rewarding after trials, but should divorce when the relationship is no longer contributing to their lives and is irreparable.

Broadly, in this chapter we saw that the erotic relationship plays an important role in providing a foundation for erotic love and how these come together and contribute to the richness of our lives and happiness. Erotic love cannot grow in a vacuum and it needs the foundation of the erotic relationship to really flourish and become the constitutive part of happiness that most of us desire. Yet, it is worth remembering that the erotic relationship and erotic love always occur together and that we separated them only to facilitate our analysis.

We will now turn our attention more directly to sexuality in the next chapter and inquire into the nature of sexual attraction and sexual fantasy and see how they operate. Afterwards, in Chapter 6, we will explore the ideas of sexual identity and sexual orientation. Through all of this, and the work we have already done, we will be in a position to fully understand the role sexuality has in our lives in Chapter 7.

Chapter 5: Sexual Attraction & Fantasy

> *Tell me what a man finds sexually attractive*
> *and I will tell you his entire philosophy of life.*
> *Show me the woman he sleeps with*
> *and I will tell you his valuation of himself.*[79]
> ~ Ayn Rand

> *There is no need to pass moral judgment on our sexual imaginations.*
> *The creative mind demands a limitless field of possibilities that exists beyond*
> *the restrictions of reality and how we actually choose to experience sex. [...]*
> *Self-censorship [is] a brutal club that wounds our imaginations.*[80]
> ~ Betty Dodson

Most people think of sexual attraction as an irreducible primary that we can at best describe, but not understand. Yet, as we were able to find clarity with the sentiments in Chapter 2, so will we here with sexual attraction. Through looking at the operation of sexual attraction, we will be able to understand how sexual attraction starts, why certain people are sexually attracted to others, and the basis of this. We will find that the standard view is much too thin and fails to take into account the richness of sexual attraction.

Indeed, we will find that sexual attraction is a sentiment, and, as such, encompasses a whole range of things not usually thought to be connected with it, including our ethical beliefs. Our sexual attractions tell a grand story of who we are as people and how we view the very world itself. Through this richer and deeper view of sexual attraction, we will be poised to see how a person's ideas influence their attractions. Moreover, our more robust understanding of attraction will give us the basis to understand how to richly integrate sex into our live in Chapter 7 and will aid us in answering some of the complex questions in Volume 2. We will also briefly explore fantasy, how it operates, and its role in sexuality.

1. The Origins of Sexual Attraction

Sexual attraction does not seem like one of those things that we might need to define, as it seems so obvious. Surely all, or nearly all, of us have experienced sexual attraction. Yet, it can be hard to pin down the exact nature of sexual attraction. To complicate matters, something strange seems to happen when we start to look right below the surface at why a person feels sexual attraction. Let us start with some examples to get a handle on the phenomenon.

Let us imagine that we see a beautiful woman and we are immediately sexually attracted to her: we feel our heart race, our skin flush, and we cannot look away. In fact, we even feel sexually aroused. Now, what if we were told that this same woman had a deadly disease that is easily sexually transmitted. Would we feel the same sexual attraction? What if we found out that, instead of having a deadly disease, this woman was the mother of three children? Would we be more or less attracted to her than we were initially? Has anything changed about the woman?

Let us say that now we see a rather nondescript man and we feel no sexual attraction to him: he barely registers in our awareness and we do not give him a second glance. Would our sexual attraction to him change if we found out he was an extremely popular musician and very wealthy? What if our child were dying of cancer and we found out that this man had just found the cure that would save him and countless others? Would we find him arousing then? Did anything change about the man?

What if we meet a person through correspondence, whether by letter or online, and we are very attracted to his intelligence, his wit, and his ability to see the best in every situation, but find out (upon meeting him in person) that he is also frighteningly hideous. Would this effect our sexual attraction? What if, instead of being hideous, he lied and was actually female. Would this change our sexual attraction? What changed about the person? Does the fact that she lied matter for how attractive we find her?

There is something strange going on here: sexual attractions that appear at first to be solely physical are either heightened or reduced by intellectual judgements, while sexual attractions that appear at first to be solely intellectual are either heightened or reduced by physical considerations. The issue is not whether our personal sexual attraction actually changed, but the fact that such change is possible based on different kinds of judgements. This should remind us of something that we have already explored: sentiments. Indeed, sexual attraction is a sentiment (we will return to this point below, once we better understand sexual attraction).

However, let us take a step back. Although we all have some idea what sexual attraction is, we need to be clearer about our subject. We are not talking about sexual arousal, which usually includes physiological arousal and the body becoming ready for sexual activity, including erection, lubrication, tumescence, *etc*. While sexual attraction may lead to sexual arousal, the two are separate phenomena and surely all of us have had the experience of simple physical arousal that is purely physiological and not tied to anything deeper (we will explore sexual arousal more in Chapter 7). Sexual attraction is more of a sexual *interest* in a person or at least a potential interest. Sexual attraction is not simply a judgement about beauty and we may find things beautiful to which we are not sexually attracted and *vice versa*. Sexual attraction is also different from sexual desire, which is a wish to engage sexually with someone. While sexual attraction often leads to desire, it does not necessarily do so and we have all had the experience of finding someone sexually attractive, but not experiencing sexual desire for them for other reasons. Moreover, when we find someone sexually attractive and actually do have sex with them, our sexual arousal dissipates and our sexual desire is satiated, but our sexual attraction persists. So, let us posit a provisional definition of sexual attraction here: sexual attraction is a response we have to others that involves us being interested in them in a sexual way. Let us now dive into sexual attraction and see if we can flesh this out and understand it at a deeper level.

Sexual Attraction is not Simply to the Body

The view that sexual attraction is simply a response to physical characteristics is perhaps the most common view of sexual attraction, even though we have just seen that it fails. Now, it may seem that this idea, that sexual attraction is only to traits or physical attributes, is so facile that no one could seriously hold it. Yet even philosophers such as Kant seem to take such a view:

> Because sexuality is not an inclination which one human being has for another as such [*i.e.*, we do not desire *people*], but is an inclination for the sex of another [*i.e.*, we only desire their *genitals*], it is a principle of the degradation of human nature, in that it gives rise to the preference of one sex to the other and to the dishonoring of that sex through the satisfaction of desire.[81]

Let us agree with Kant that if this were what sex was, then it would be a degradation of human nature. Fortunately for us, the only perverse thing here is Kant's view of sex: his view of sexuality is both simplistic and misanthropic, but this is no surprise given his philosophy.

It is true that the body factors into our sexual attraction to other people, as Kant says. Certainly no one would dispute that the body is an important element of sexual attraction and the attractiveness of a person's body can be a reason to take a sexual interest in them in the first place. However, as we shall see, sexual attraction is robustly connected to the whole person and a person's body is only one part of this. Moreover, it is important to point out that while sexual attraction may start with physical characteristics, sexual attraction cannot *simply* be about these, because above we saw sexual attractions change based on beliefs and this would not be possible if sexual attraction were simply about physical characteristics. Thus, we need to let go of this view of sexual attraction as simply to the body if we are to find out its real nature.

The Greeks, in contrast to Kant, thought that love and sexual attraction began with the lover's gaze. This is because they considered the eyes to be the window to the soul and believed that a person could not be attractive without a noble soul (*i.e.*, a good character). The Greeks understood that love and sex are more than simply "bodily" things, that these things tie together the totality of our being and epitomize who we are as people. There is never a time we are more *ourselves* than when we are naked in body and unguarded in spirit: when we are totally open to our lover.

Much as we did with erotic love, in order to gain a richer understanding of sexual attraction, we need to understand it as a sentiment. We saw above that sentiments are a form of automatic evaluative awareness that orient us to their objects and are experienced as a cognitive conviction, often with attendant affect. Underlying this is the sentimental process, with its very specific automatic process of identification, evaluation, and response. Sexual attraction is a sentiment and operates this way. Sexual attraction starts by identifying an object. This object is compared, via subconscious evaluation, to a person's values and beliefs to see if a relevant match is found. If there is, then the person will experience sexual attraction. Like all sentiments, it can be best understood in terms of its object and the nature of the resulting response. Unfortunately for us, we do not yet understand sexual attraction well enough to fully understand these things and so we must proceed in our inquiry to understand it better first, before we can understand it as a sentiment.

Ignorant Sexual Attraction and Projection

One thing that complicates an inquiry into sexual attraction is that we sometimes feel sexually attracted to people whom we do not know. Indeed, sexual attraction usually starts before we know everything about a person and can even start before we know anything at all about a person. Let us call this "ignorant sexual attraction," when we know no more about a person than what they look like, using "ignorant" in its strict sense of "lacking knowledge." Yet, we know that sexual attraction must have some object more than simply the body to which it is responding, or else it becomes inexplicable how judgements can affect sexual attraction otherwise. How can we explain this?

One of the ways that we can be attracted to a person about whom we know nothing is via *projection*. In projection, we treat a beautiful stranger as a blank canvas onto whom we project the attributes to which we would be attracted if they were, in fact, instantiated in the person. Our response, then, is to these projected values *instead of* to the actual person.[i] For example, let us say that we see a woman who we find sexually attractive at a party, but whom we do not know. Consider that part of our sexual attraction is the assumption that she has the kind of values to which we would be attracted. If we value reading and education and we discover, upon talking with her, that she disdains reading and thinks the pursuit silly, then our sexual attraction will not remain the same. The reality of the woman will clash with the values we projected onto her and our sexual attraction will falter as the illusion cracks or even shatters. Projection relies on the façade of the projected values remaining firmly in place as the object of sexual attraction.[ii]

Alternatively, ignorant sexual attraction can be a response to a person's existential orientation; that is, a person's response to his views about himself, about others, and about the nature of the world. But, how can sexual attraction be a response to these things, when people often are not aware of their own existential orientation? It is because a person's existential orientation shows clearly in the way he carries himself, his gestures and mannerisms, the manner of his dress and speech, the way he grooms himself, and in a myriad of other little things. From all these things, collectively, a person's *style* emerges.[82]

Style

A person's style is the integration of the various ways that his existential orientation manifests across the different aspects of his life. Our existential orientation shows in myriad ways in our life, not only physically in the way we carry ourselves, gesture, or dress, but also in how we interact with other people, the way we conceptualize the world and respond to it, and even how we view our ability to deal with problems or engage with the world. Our existential orientation underlies everything about us and permeates us at all levels, from the deepest way we think of the nature of the world, to the type of clothing we prefer. All of these things come together in a person's individual style of soul. Moreover, a person's style, being an integration of the manifestations of his existential orientation, becomes a unifying element that makes a person unique.

While our style is the integration of the manifestations of our existential orientation, it is not simply reducible to our existential orientation. It is true

---

[i] Here, someone could reasonably object: "But why did you pick this particular person to project onto? Presumably because of their physical beauty." Let us hold this point for now and return to it below.

[ii] Because of this, projection is a form of self-deception. If we do not get to know a person better when we are sexually attracted to them, then we are left with nothing but to respond to their body and the values we project onto them. But we deceive ourselves that these really are their values and we respond to the illusion that we create in our minds of who we wish they were.

that the origin of our style is our existential orientation, but our style is so much more than just our existential orientation. It is all the various ways that our existential orientation has influenced us, the ways we have chosen to live, the ways that we have come to engage with the world, and the way that we embody our values and make them real. This is important, because while our ignorant sexual attraction is directed towards a person's existential orientation, we can never fully know another person's existential orientation. Because of that, when we experience ignorant sexual attraction, we are not directly attracted to the person's existential orientation *per se*, but to their *style*.[i]

When we meet another person, we are immediately aware of their style, even though this is not a conscious process, and we make an immediate judgement of whether we find the other person sexually attractive.[ii] This is what we mean when we say that sexual attraction is to a person's existential orientation, because a person's existential orientation manifests in all aspects of his life and this culminates in a person's style. But, it would be more precise to say that the immediate object of sexual attraction is a person's style.

That the immediate object of sexual attraction is a person's style is true for ignorant sexual attraction, but it is also an important element of *all* sexual attraction, such as in an ongoing sexual relationship or when we have a friend that we know well who transitions into a lover. In these latter cases, when we know more about a person, our sexual attraction broadens and takes account of more than projected values or style, as it does in ignorant sexual attraction.

Sexual Attraction is to the Whole Person

As we get to know a person, we learn more about them and come to understand who they are and who they want to be; that is, we come to understand their character.[iii] A person's character is the sum of their past choices, their conscious decisions about who they want to be in life and what they want out of life, and the values that they hold dear; our character is the way we live out our values and make them real in the world. Our character is, in a very real sense, the person we have chosen to be: it is our chosen self.

As we get to know a person at this deeper level, our initial sexual attraction is either dampened or heightened by our response to their character. The more we get to know a person, the firmer our sexual attraction can become, as it has a firmer basis in their character. For example, rational people look for qualities

---

[i] Style is also a major element of what underlies "types" of people we know.

[ii] One of the features of consciousness is selective focus, whereby we focus our attention on one thing and tune out others. As a result, we are consciously aware of the object on which we focus and less aware, or not aware, of other things. However, our brains are still getting information about things that we are not focused on and our subconscious can process this information and make it available to our conscious minds. Thus, even if we are not consciously thinking about a person's style, we are still getting information about it.

[iii] See Chapter 1 for more about character.

like honesty and integrity in a partner so that they know that they can trust what their partner says and that their partner's actions will be consistent with their beliefs. Without these things, it would be hard to have a real relationship with a person, as we would never know if we were getting the truth or how our partner would react.

That our sexual attraction is sensitive to a person's character is easy to see. Yet, as our sexual attraction to a person grows and we become aware of a person's character, we are still also aware of their body and their style. The combination of these things richly describes who we are as people. However, sexual attraction is not to each of these things in isolation, but to the whole person. For example, Diana is attracted to John as a whole person and not to something like the sum of his body plus his style plus his strong character. Her attraction, while it grew out of these things, is to *him* and not his features. Sexual attraction is to the full person and not merely to certain parts or traits of theirs.

Consider that this idea, that we judge the whole person and not attributes, was our underlying assumption in both kinds of ignorant sexual attraction. This is how we can explain beliefs modifying sexual attraction, which is apparently only to physical attributes. This is one of the major errors committed by those who argue that sexual attraction is only bodily and where they go awry: they focus on attributes instead of people. Sexual attraction is always to an entire person. Thus, even with "sexual attraction at first sight," our response will never be so thinly constituted as to be merely to their physical characteristics, but even here will also be sensitive to their style.

The contrast, between the idea that sexual attraction operates simply as a response to physical characteristics and our account that sexual attraction is to a full person, is illuminating. Certainly, sexual attraction includes awareness of physical characteristics, but these are not sufficient for sexual attraction, as we have seen. Moreover, and this is a subtler point, we have already seen how having a collection of attributes as the object of sexual attraction also fails. Why is this? First, as a matter of fact, people are not simply collections of attributes: for example, "brunette-ness" does not "inhere" in a person as an attribute they have but, rather, they are constituted such that they are brunette and this is a fact about them. For this to have been otherwise, they would have to have been a different person. Second, as we have seen in both the operation of projection and style-attraction, sexual attraction is always to the full person, and this is why as we learn more about a person our sexual attraction is either enhanced or diminished as a whole, but never do we develop multiple sexual attractions to the same person for different aspects. This can be seen with an example of how sexual attraction works in the world: let us say that we see a very beautiful woman who is currently quite viciously beating a child. We do not feel sexual attraction to her beauty, revulsion at her action, compare the relative levels of the two, and then act on whichever one is stronger. No, *either* we feel sexual attraction for her as a person or we do not (and, hopefully, we do not).

None of the foregoing is to insinuate that we can never experience conflicts in our sexual attractions. While we will primarily discuss this below, it is worth mentioning here that the fact that we sometimes have conflicted sexual attractions is not an argument against the fact that our sexual attractions are to whole people. Since our sexual attraction is a sentiment, it can respond to any of our values and beliefs. This can lead to us having sexual attractions that are discordant with our conscious convictions.[i] For example, we might consciously find ourselves sexually attracted to a person who is capricious and flighty and this might conflict with our conscious beliefs, but we might also hold the discordant belief that to be free of obligations is an ideal and so our sexual attraction becomes rooted in this. Conflicted sexual attraction is not our sexual attraction malfunctioning, since it can respond to any of our values and beliefs, but rather it is us being consciously displeased by our sexual attraction because it is discordant with our conscious convictions. As long as we hold discordant values and beliefs, we may experience discordant sexual attractions (or any other sentiment).

It is also true that when we have sentiments that are well entrenched, they do not always immediately change when we might wish they would. For example, if we have been with a person for a long time and are very sexually attracted to them, but they betray our trust and turn out not to be worthy of our affections, our attraction may not be immediately extinguished. It can take a while for sentiments to change as we have to internalize new information, and this takes time. Of course, sometimes our sentiments do change immediately if the situation is important enough: we might have our attraction entirely extinguished if we found our partner engaging in some heinous act. At the same time, we can also experience multiple different sentiments towards the same person: we might still feel sexually attracted to a partner who violated our trust and, at the same time, hate them for betraying us.

To return to our major point, when we say that sexual attraction is to the entire person, we mean that sexual attraction takes into account everything about a person, including their body, their style, and their character. Sexual attraction is to a person's complete self, including the parts that they have chosen as well as the parts unchosen. This much deeper sense of sexual attraction explains how sexual attraction is kept alive in long-term couples, which is quite perplexing to those who think of sexual attraction merely in terms of physical appearance. Not only does it explain how sexual attraction operates, but it also is instructive for us to think about how we can keep our sexual attractions alive and healthy as we age and our physical appearance changes.

Through the foregoing, we have seen that the object of sexual attraction is another person in a rich sense.[ii] We have also seen some of sexual attraction's

---

[i] Refer to Chapter 2 for a fuller discussion of discordant sentimental responses.
[ii] A quick note about the idea that "opposites attract." This is true, but only superficially. It is

sentimental nature, although there is still much more to say about sexual attraction. We need to explore the kinds of beliefs that are relevant to sexual attraction and its specific response, through which we will more fully understand its sentimental nature. This will help us to see the full picture of sexual attraction and to understand it at the deepest level.

2. The Nature of Sexual Attraction

Philosophy and Sexual Attraction

Now that we have seen that sexual attraction is to the whole person and that our character—our chosen self—is a big part of this, we will shift our inquiry to see how a person's beliefs and values impact sexual attraction, since it is these that underlie character. Of course, a person's beliefs and values constitute their philosophy and so we must understand the role of philosophy in sexual attraction.[i] This is important, because if a person's philosophy is contradictory, then this can cause discordant sexual attractions, as we have seen. Moreover, that our sexual attraction springs from our philosophy will have interesting implications for our responsibility for our sexual attractions. Let us begin, however, with a broader look at the connection between philosophy and sexual attraction: that is, we will focus more on a person's conscious beliefs and their influences in this section after having focused more on subconscious factors in the last section.

We have said that it is a person's beliefs and values that underlie his character and chosen self—and we have already shown how this is so. Now we need to show the connection between a person's beliefs and values, in the form of their overall philosophy, and a person's sexual attractions. While our discussion already brought some of this to light, this issue is subtle and requires care to understand. Certainly, it is not the case that if we simply know any particular belief a person holds, then we will know to what kind of person he will be attracted.[ii] Humans are complex and few people are so thinly constituted as to have only one deeply held value or belief.

On the other hand, few of us have robust systems of explicit philosophy. Indeed, maybe only philosophers do, and it is not clear that even among

---

true in the sense that we often look for a partner who exhibits characteristics that we wish we had, in the hopes that we will learn from them (*e.g.*, the shy man who is attracted to the outgoing woman, hoping that she might help him become more outgoing himself). On the deeper level, however, attraction to someone with the opposite existential orientation is rare and would not work well long-term, due to inevitable clashes in the ways that the partners would conceptualize themselves, others, and the world.

[i] Refer back to "Beliefs and Philosophy" in Chapter 2 for a refresher on the connection between beliefs, values, and philosophy.

[ii] If we were able to know *everything* about a person, then we would be able to know to whom they would be attracted. However, such is impossible, even with those closest to us.

philosophers this is the case. Most people have some explicit beliefs and hold the rest of their beliefs implicitly. Yet, holding beliefs implicitly can be a problem, because a person may not be aware he even has such beliefs. For example, a white person raised in the American South may have internalized beliefs[i] from childhood, such as the false idea that black people are inferior. He may, later in life, even consciously detest these beliefs and refuse to act on them, but they may persist and influence his emotional reaction, even contrary to his conscious beliefs. As long as the person continues to hold the beliefs at any level, they can influence his sentimental responses, such as causing discordant sexual attractions (*e.g.*, he might fetishize black women).

To the extent that a person is mentally focused and is actively thinking, his subconscious beliefs will follow from his reasoned convictions. To the extent to which a person is out of focus and does not think, his subconscious beliefs will simply be "truths" he has collected at random and about which he has never thought.[ii] This is important, because if our sexual attractions come from our deeply held beliefs and values and these are a mess of random platitudes, then our sexual attractions will be confused and may run counter to our conscious beliefs: that is, our sexual attractions may be discordant. If we want our sexual attractions to follow from the beliefs that we hold dear and from the convictions that we have thought about and judged to be true, then we must be very careful to not accept beliefs uncritically, without thought and judgement.

While we cannot reason from any particular belief a person holds to their actual sexual attractions, there are things we can say about the kinds of sexual attractions people would have if they accepted a philosophy completely. To show this, we shall sketch out just two positions and the differences in sexual attraction to which they lead, recognizing, however, that our examples will be oversimplified for the sake of elaboration.

Let us say there is a man named Paul who is a devout Christian.[iii] For purposes of our example, he is so devout that he has no other beliefs than

---

[i] See Chapter 2. Internalization is the process by which an idea becomes a part of a person's belief structure because it is either deeply held (accepted as true and important) or has simply been held for such a long time and accepted as true, that it influences a person's character and actions even though it may not be in conscious thought at the time.

[ii] This is not to say that the in-focus person will have no contradictions, but rather that his new beliefs will tend to follow his conscious convictions. While it is possible to change deeply held beliefs and patterns of thought, it is hard. If one wanted to do this, professional psychological help makes it easier (but not easy).

[iii] In Robert Solomon's *The Passions*, on page 105, he says that: "Frithjof Bergmann has written (quoting Hegel on Christianity) that behaviorism cannot be usefully attacked because 'no matter which version of it one assails, someone will always say at the end, that is not what he means by it.'" I have this same frustration when criticizing Christianity. The view of Christianity I present is the most consistent to their philosophic premises. (Note, that I could not find the original quote in Hegel and so I do not know whether Hegel ever made this point. Regardless, the point stands.)

these: there is a god and that god is the source of good and the only truly good thing in existence, that mankind has original sin and is wretched through and through, that there is a heavenly soul trapped inside the body which will return to a higher realm and its god after death, that bodily affects taint the soul and none does so more than sexual feelings (lust), and that the only worth a wretched human can attain is to sacrifice himself to his brothers and desecrate his prison of flesh. Insofar as Paul could succumb to his "base nature" and feel sexual attraction (although he should hate this), he would want a partner who is selfless and has a weak, amorphous character, who is not sexual, who desires no pleasure for herself but would dutifully please Paul if his base nature got the best of him, and who would be with Paul because of his need of her and not because she wanted to or had any interest in him.

As an alternative, let us say that there is a woman named Kira who greatly values human reason, who does not believe in any form of mysticism[i], who values her life and works to make it the best it can be, who does not think that others have an obligation to support her or her them, and who values honesty, integrity, and hard work. This woman will be drawn to a partner of strong character and conviction, a person who knows what they want out of life and acts to get it, a person who is reality oriented and who will try to get the most out of their life.

Now, obviously, no real people are so thinly constituted that this would exhaust their beliefs and values. Nevertheless, we can see that if we could know enough of a person's beliefs and values, we could understand to whom they would be attracted. The reason these examples seem so superficial is that real people have many more beliefs, but also that they do not have perfect unity in their beliefs and many people hold at least some contradictory beliefs and values, often derived from their experience and subconscious evaluation of it. We can see this if we look at our own beliefs and values and how they manifest in our sexual attractions.

The Cultivation of Sexual Attraction

While we tend to think of sexual attraction as something that just happens to us, we have now seen that this is not the case: we have some control over our sexual attractions, since our sexual attractions are responses to our values and beliefs. This control is not direct, but rather through our ability to cultivate our values and beliefs. As a consequence of this, we have a responsibility to be aware of the kinds of beliefs and values we hold, if we want our sexual attractions aligned with our goal of living well. For example, in our long-term erotic relationships, it is often the case that when we begin our relationships our partner's physical body is an important piece of our sexual attraction; yet

---

[i] Recall that the core idea of mysticism is that the law of identity (A is A) is mutable in some respect.

in long-term relationships, our bodies age and change. Given this, if we do not work to keep our sexual attractions age-appropriate (that is, to include others near our own age), then we will often have our sexual attractions dampened by time. We might also become fixated on youth as the paradigm of sexual attraction, since this is when we first develop our sexual attractions and this paradigm is prevalent in our culture. This is why some people constantly change erotic partners for younger ones, in order to satisfy their sexual attractions based on a mistaken belief that only young people can be sexually attractive. It should be obvious why this is disastrous for long-term erotic relationships. If we value our relationship, then we have an obligation to cultivate the beliefs that will lead to the kind of sexual attractions that will sustain it. Sexual attraction does not naturally fade with time; rather, we allow this to happen without careful cultivation of our beliefs. However, because we do not have conscious control of our sexual attractions, we cannot be held directly responsible for them. Yet, we are responsible for our values and beliefs and cultivating the kinds of sentiments, including sexual attraction, which leads us to live a good life.

This idea, that we have an obligation to cultivate the kinds of sentiments that will be beneficial to our life, is very important. The general idea dates back to Aristotle, who believed that children should be raised in particular ways as to cultivate the dispositions leading to virtue. However, it is new in the sense that we have now given an account of how the sentiments connect to a good life and have shown how they can be cultivated to specific ends, even as an adult, and even in very complex cases such as with sexual attraction. This is not limited to cultivating sexual attraction in long-term erotic relationships, but also to a general cultivation of our sexual attractions. If we want to only be attracted to our partner, then we should cultivate the beliefs that will lead to this. If, on the other hand, we want to have an erotic relationship in which we have other lovers as well, then we will need to cultivate different beliefs (we will explore the question of the morality of polysexuality in Chapter 13).

This cultivation of sexual attraction to be in line with our moral judgements is a boon to our overall goal of living the best kind of life possible: it integrates sexuality deeply into our moral enterprise and helps us to enjoy it in a robust way that also serves to enrich our lives. By working to cultivate sexual attraction only to those people who make our lives better, we improve our chances of achieving happiness. On the other hand, if we are sexually attracted to the wrong kind of people, people who make our lives worse, then we must work to change these discordant sexual attractions by identifying what beliefs they are a response to and then working on replacing these beliefs with more positive (*i.e.*, life-affirming) beliefs. We have a moral obligation to keep our sexual attractions in line with our overall life goals, if we want to have the best kind of life possible.

We should also be able to see now that a person who lacks strong values is an unattractive person: both to others and in their inability to be truly attracted to others.ⁱ They are unattractive to others, because they lack a firm chosen self to which we can respond in our sexual attraction. They have a hard time being sexually attracted to others because they do not have a firm enough sense of self to serve as the basis of the response. This is, in a way, the same problem we saw back in Chapter 3 with love and how only those who have done the work of creating their chosen self will truly be capable of love. Those who fail to do this work will fail in their love lives and with regard to sexual attraction. "The moral is the practical," as Rand would say,[83] and those who fail to create their chosen self in the right way will suffer the consequences of a life poorly lived.

As a final point about sexual attraction and philosophy, we must emphasize that it is not possible to simply take two people's conscious beliefs and see if these are compatible to understand whether they will be sexually attracted to one another: although sexual attraction is based in part on a person's character and ideas, it is certainly not true that any two people who believes the same things will be sexually attracted to each other. Sexual attraction is to the whole person and it is a mistake to try to limit this to just a person's conscious beliefs. The fact that we might believe the same thing as someone else does not mean that we will find them sexually attractive. We might not even like being around them if we have divergent existential orientations or styles. It is simply not true that just because two people believe the same things that they would be a good match for each other or should be sexually attracted to each other.

Sexual Attraction and Types

There is another element of sexual attraction on which we have not yet touched and that is sexual "types." Some people have certain types of people to whom they are attracted and use these types as heuristics (or cognitive shortcuts) in attempting to find partners. At first glance, this does not seem to conform to the account of sexual attraction that we have laid out. So, let us briefly explore this and see how it works as well as whether it presents a problem with our account.

People who have types that they find sexually attractive tend to think that certain types signal specific values or characteristics that they value. People tend to come to this in one of two ways: due to their experiences or through cultural stereotypes. In the first case, some people have had experiences that have led them to be disposed to think of certain physical attributes as indicative of deeper issues. For example, the first person they ever dated was a petite redhead who was always joyful and they overgeneralized this to the idea that petite

---

ⁱ I attribute the point that a person without strong values is an unattractive person to Patrick Ryan from our conversation regarding this section.

redheads are joyful and this became their type. In this case, people overgeneralize their experiences to create types: this can come from real experiences with partners or via exposure to fiction from which they overgeneralized. In the second case, some people have internalized cultural stereotypes and have formed types from this. For example, some people have blondes as their type because of the cultural stereotype that "blondes have more fun" or are attracted to people with glasses, because there is a cultural stereotype that these people are more intelligent. While the particular stereotypes will vary depending on the culture, there will be people in every culture affected by their cultural stereotypes.

No matter how a person ends up with one, types function the same way. They package together certain values a person might hold (*e.g.*, joyfulness or fun) and certain physical characteristics that the person thinks signal these values. The problem is that physical characteristics do not meaningfully stand in for values: a petite redhead may be joyful, but so may any other kind of person. This is not to say that it is wrong to use types and many of us have early experiences that served to partly shape our sexuality, but we must recognize the underlying values below the type and not unduly limit ourselves due to a lack of reflection on this point.

The real key to sexual attraction based on types is style. When a person becomes focused on a type, what they are really trying to track is a style and believe that all of the people who match a certain type will have the same or similar styles. Instead of focusing on the person's style directly, they substitute physical characteristics as a stand in. This is likely because many of these type attractions are formed when a person is young and they may believe there to be a causal relationship between the physical characteristics and the person's style and they believe that they can capture all of the latter with the former.

While types can be a semi-useful heuristic, they pose several dangers. First, while style does affect a person's physical appearance, style is much more than this. It cannot be captured by a reduction to physical characteristics such as hair color. Second, types can blind us to the world in favor of our own constructs.[i] When we focus only on our type (*e.g.*, redheads), we lose sight of the actual person in favor of their morally-insignificant physical characteristics. Third, types are a form of collectivistic thinking and if we indulge in such sloppy thinking, we run the risk of being led down the path to such immorality as racism.[ii]

None of this is to say that a person cannot have types without it becoming perverse, but that there is a real danger to type-based sexual attractions and we must be aware of this and seek to avoid it, if we wish to live good lives.

---

[i] In this way, types can form part of our surreality (we will discuss this in Volume 3).
[ii] Racism is the belief that a person's moral character is determined by their race. This is a vicious and appalling contradiction in terms: that which is not chosen is not in the realm of morality and, clearly, we do not choose our race.

Moreover, it is clear that our theory is again capable of handling even these complicated cases and helping us to understand them. When we hold high the torch of reason, we dispel the darkness of ignorance and irrationality.

Sexual Attraction and Beauty

There is one last element related to sexual attraction and that is beauty. We have already noted that one part of sexual attraction is our response to people's bodies. We have also discussed this in terms of types and how this can affect our preference for certain features. What we have not done yet is to show how beauty factors into this. While a full account of beauty is beyond our scope, we can nevertheless show how beauty factors into sexual attraction.

We will limit our discussion of beauty to living things, since only the beauty of living things will factor into our discussion of sexual attraction.[i] For living things, one aspect of beauty is being a good instance of its kind. For example, a "German Shepherd" is a kind of dog and the standards of beauty are set by the facts of its breed. A German Shepherd with back legs longer than the front would not be a beautiful German Shepherd, because it does not conform to the standards of beauty for being a German Shepherd. Another aspect of beauty is to live well for that species. Consider the case of two oak trees, one of which is large and green and the other of which is small and brown and failing. It is the large green tree that is beautiful, because the large green tree is a flourishing oak. Beauty for living things is being well-formed and flourishing.

Of course, human beings are richly constituted and it takes more than being symmetrical and well-proportioned for a human to flourish. Human beauty must also include psychological and moral facts, because humans cannot flourish without a good character, as we have already seen. Beauty, then, for humans is being well-formed overall, in our physical aspects and mental aspects, and flourishing in life. This is objective beauty for a human, if objective beauty is to truly have any meaning and be more than a statement of preference.

However, someone being objectively beautiful is different from us recognizing this. Thus, we must separate out our subjective response to beauty from objective beauty. Our response to beauty can be either a conscious judgement or a sentimental response. For example, sometimes when we see a new artwork, we have to consciously consider its merits, its composition, technique, message, *etc.*, in order to judge whether it is beautiful. Once we judge the artwork to be beautiful, then we often have a sentimental response to it and *feel* that it is beautiful. Other times, we simply have an immediate sentimental response to the artwork because we recognize moving themes in the artwork

---

[i] Paraphilias such as attraction to non-living things (*e.g.*, object fetishism) or to non-human living things (*e.g.*, zoophilia) require separate discussions and may be perversions (see Volume 2, Chapters 9 & 15).

to which we respond.

We are able to immediately recognize moving themes from art because proper art takes abstract concepts and concretizes them: it brings them onto the perceptual level and shows us justice incarnate as Lady Justice or the desire for an ideal lover as in Gerome's *Pygmalion and Galatea* (which graces the cover of this book).[i] This allows us to engage with them as a perceptual concrete, which is why we frequently have immediate responses to art: we do not need to think too much about the art, because we can *perceive* it.[ii] Of course, sometimes the themes of an artwork can be concretized, but still very complex and we may need to think about the artwork before we can grasp the themes and respond to them, as might be the case in Gerome's *A Roman Slave Market* where we might not immediately be aware that what we are seeing is a slave market and this will certainly impact our sentimental response.[iii]

There is a strong connection between our response to the beauty of art and the beauty of people. They both are responses to how we think the object should be and through our sentimental response to the object, we can see our ideals: beautiful art *represents* our ideals, whereas a beautiful person *embodies* our ideals. This is why our sexual attraction to beauty is so strong: since part of the strength of our sexual attraction is the degree that the other person embodies our values, seeing our ideals embodied leads to a strong response.

Of course, it is possible to not be sexually attracted to someone who we think is beautiful, as the sexual attraction does not *necessarily* follow. This may happen for many reasons, such as: the context would be inappropriate and so we suppress our sexual attraction as we might do with a beautiful colleague; we are not well integrated and so our sexual attractions are discordant with our conscious values and beliefs, leading us not to be sexually attracted to people we judge to be beautiful; we might find a person beautiful, but not be attracted

---

[i] This is part of how art can provide us with an extremely valuable experience that Ayn Rand calls "spiritual fuel," about which she says: "Since a rational man's ambition is unlimited, since his pursuit and achievement of values is a lifelong process—and the higher the values, the harder the struggle—he needs a moment, an hour or some period of time in which he can experience the sense of his completed task, the sense of living in a universe where his values have been successfully achieved. It is like a moment of rest, a moment to gain fuel to move farther. Art gives him that fuel; the pleasure of contemplating the objectified reality of one's own sense of life [existential orientation] is the pleasure of feeling what it would be like to live in one's ideal world. The importance of that experience is not in what man learns from it, but in that he experiences it. The fuel is not a theoretical principle, not a didactic 'message,' but the life-giving fact of experiencing a moment of metaphysical joy—a moment of love for existence." ("Art and Sense of Life," *The Romantic Manifesto*, p. 38) Art, in this way, can provide us with an existential moment.

[ii] This point comes from Ayn Rand's account of aesthetics in *The Romantic Manifesto*, particularly "The Psycho-Epistemology of Art." My account of aesthetics closely follows hers in many regards.

[iii] With respect to understanding artworks, I highly recommend Luc Travers' book *Touching the Art: A Guide to Enjoying Art in a Museum* (2010). With more complex art, understanding and appreciating it is a skill that must be learned, practiced, and refined.

to their style or even find their personality obnoxious, while still recognizing that they are beautiful; or they may be beautiful, but they are not our type and so we do not feel sexual attraction towards them. Nevertheless, we will *usually* be sexually attracted to people we think are beautiful and, in these cases, our sexual attraction will be strong because the beautiful person will embody our ideals.[i]

Our philosophy will have a major impact here as it will set the criteria for what we consider beautiful: what we think of as a beautiful person is someone who embodies our ideals, including our ideals about physical beauty, and our ideals ultimately come from our philosophy. Since eudaimonists have reverence for life and aim at happiness as their moral purpose, they will find people who are flourishing beautiful. Thus, for the eudaimonist, our subjective judgement of beauty and our sentimental response to it will be aligned with objective beauty, so that we will find beautiful what is actually beautiful. Moreover, when we find someone who embodies this perfect union, we will feel strong sexual attraction to them, all other things being equal. Thus, beauty is an important element of sexual attraction.

Sexual Attraction as a Sentiment

Now that we have robustly explored sexual attraction, we will round out this section by giving a fuller account of the sentimental nature of sexual attraction as well as a definition of it. This will help us to solidify our knowledge of it and better understand it. It will also help to integrate the features of sexual attraction we have seen so far through this chapter.

We can be more specific about sexual attraction than to simply say that it is a sentiment: sexual attraction is an emotion. We have already seen how emotions operate via the sentimental process in Chapter 2 and how this results in a way of being oriented to its object as well as certain affective states related to the object. Let us, then, flesh this out for sexual attraction.

Sexual attraction is a way of being oriented to another person: specifically, it is being sexually interested in a person, and carries with it the potential for sexual desire.[ii] Sexual attraction usually, but not always, leads to sexual desire and, as a consequence, sexual arousal. However, sexual attraction is a unique emotion that does not simply collapse into desire and is not reducible to it: sexual attraction is a rich spiritual experience that is more than just sexual

---

[i] Since beauty is partly our judgment that the person embodies our moral ideal, obviously people who have different moral frameworks will find different people to be beautiful. And, for the same reason, their response to art will differ based on their moral framework. However, we have already shown that the eudaimonistic framework is the right framework, if we want to live.

[ii] The object of sexual attraction must be a person. While a person can experience sexual desire related to an object, such as with a woman who has a favorite vibrator, to pick a non-person object for sexual attraction is perverse and represents a psychological problem.

desire. At the same time, sexual attraction does *usually* lead to sexual desire and sexual arousal, and we should take care not to divorce them in our effort to clearly delineate each.

When we say that sexual attraction is a rich spiritual experience, we need not overly elaborate this, since we have all presumably had this experience. Yet, an example will still help us to bring more clarity to the issue. Let us say that a man attends a gala and sees a beautiful woman there, to whom he is sexually attracted. He is attracted to her beauty and her style: the way she carries herself, the choice of her dress, her coiffure, the way she engages with others around her, *etc*. He feels interested in her and wants to know more about her. He sees her and wants to be seen by her. Let us say that he is bold and approaches her and they talk and find that they share many values and get along well. His sexual attraction may also give rise to sexual desire, especially if she reciprocates his advances or brings on her own.[i] Indeed, being seen as a sexually attractive person can even bring on sexual desire and sexual arousal, if we think that there is a real possibility of connection.

We have already seen that sexual attraction is to the full person, but it should now be clear that it also involves *our* full person as well. Sexual attraction involves our bodies and minds, existential orientation, values and beliefs, style, and character. Our sexual attractions are not only richly to another full person, but they are also richly from us as a full person. This explains the epigraph to this chapter from Ayn Rand: "Tell me what a man finds sexually attractive and I will tell you his entire philosophy of life. Show me the woman he sleeps with and I will tell you his valuation of himself."[84] If we truly understand a person's sexual attraction, then we will know his philosophy and valuation of himself.

Let us, now that we have seen all of the various aspects of sexual attraction, conclude this section with a definition of sexual attraction to help concretize our knowledge. Sexual attraction is a sentiment characterized by sexual interest in another person based on our response to their beauty, style, values, *etc.*, and with the potential for sexual desire. Or, the standard form definition is: sexual attraction is an emotion characterized by sexual interest in another person.

---

[i] While it is possible to feel sexual attraction for someone who does not reciprocate it, for most people this kills sexual attraction.

3. Fantasy

> *In the realm of the sexual imagination [...] we are more likely to throw off the restrictive effects of rules and taboos, including heartfelt ones, sometimes getting a thrill out of shocking even ourselves. Consequently, many people go much further in their fantasies than they would in real life.*[85]
> ~ Jack Morin

What is fantasy? At its root, fantasy is creating mental pictures or ideas; that is, fantasy is a type of imagination.[i] Yet, we will reserve the word fantasy to focus primarily on the sexual realm; thus, fantasy is fundamentally *sexual exploration in our head*. This is important not only for masturbation, but also for trying to understand our sexuality and our sexual compatibility with others. So, what things count as fantasy? There are four primary activities that come under fantasy: envisioning, testing, reliving, and the erotic shift. Let us briefly look at each in turn.

First, fantasy can involve *envisioning* new possibilities, such as new sexual positions, new sexual uses for mundane objects, or new and unique scenarios. For example, if we have only had sex in "missionary position," we might envision that there are lots of other positions that could be tried. Or, we might see a clothespin and realize, if we did not already know it, its potential utility in applying a little pain to the nipples or other parts. Envisioning can help us to come up with new sexual things we might want to try.

Second, fantasy can involve *testing* whether we want to do something new sexually, including things that we have just envisioned. For example, whether we want to have sex with a new person or whether a new sexual activity would be enjoyable. This can help us to understand whether an activity would be fun and pleasurable, without having to actually do it, giving us insight into our sexual desires and proclivities. However, there is a danger here of being rationalistic and thinking that because we cannot fantasize that something would be pleasurable, it therefore will not be. This makes as much sense as saying that we will not try Japanese food because we are used to Mexican food and we cannot imagine that Japanese food would taste good. We, thus, must take care to have real experiences in the world if we want to fully understand our sexuality.

Third, fantasy can also be *reliving* a past sexy experience. This function of fantasy may be most associated with masturbation, but it can also help us to develop our skills to think about how the sexual event went and how we performed. This is much more appropriate to do afterwards, as trying to put too much attention on the details during sex can lead us to treat it too

---

[i] Etymologically both imagination and fantasy mean having to do with images in our minds.

physicalistically or it can create performance anxiety.

Finally, fantasy can be used to create an *erotic shift* and help us to transition to an erotic frame of mind. Fantasy is one of the major elements of the "erotic shift," that moment when things go from being mundane to erotic and when we start to be open to the possibility of erotic delight.[i] In that moment, our fantasy comes alive with the possibilities of the situation and this shifts us to an erotic frame of mind. This is very important for any kind of eroticism as attempting to engage in eroticism when we are fully in a mundane frame of mind is not very sexually exciting and it can keep us from engaging with what we are doing or enjoying it.

Fantasy originates in our mind and sometimes we are directly in control of it and can make it exactly what we want, while other times we simply enjoy the fruits of our subconscious in the form of sexual dreams or daydreams. The downside to fantasy is that our imaginations are limited to our experience and what we can create from it: if we have no knowledge of a thing, then it cannot be part of our fantasy life.

We can increase the scope of our fantasies in several ways, such as through experiencing new sexual acts, new sexual partners, or even exploring sexual aids such as dildos, blindfolds, or restraints. On the other hand, we can seek out information in other ways such as reading books of erotica or watching pornography.[ii] While pornography and erotica can help us increase the scope of our fantasy and can be used in our fantasies, they are not a form of fantasy, because we are not the origin of them. However, there is a way in which they can help us to achieve the functions of fantasy (testing, imagining, reliving, or creating erotic excitement), because we can fantasize and imagine ourselves involved in the situation, whether as a participant or simply a spectator, or we can simply incorporate elements from them in our fantasies.[iii] The great advantage of this is that we can be exposed to lots of things we might not have tried, may never have thought of ourselves, may never have the opportunity to try, or may not even want to do in real life, but still find arousing. The downside to erotica and pornography is that we cannot control it and often the situations we find are not exactly what we want.

Fantasy is more necessary for our sexual lives than we might at first expect, including for our everyday sexual experiences. For example, through the erotic shift, fantasy provides some of "the spark" that makes our sex lives so much fun. Because it helps us shift to the erotic context, fantasy plays a large role in sexual arousal, and without it we would not become as aroused or become aroused as quickly. Fantasy is also often layered over our experience as it is happening.[iv] In the sexual moment, we are often thinking about the things we

---

[i] Other elements of this are sexual arousal and erousia.
[ii] We will deal with pornography and erotica at length in Volume 2, Chapter 12.
[iii] Much of our response to people in porn or erotica involves projection.
[iv] See Volume 3, Chapter 21, "On Surreality."

might do or will do before we do them and getting excited about the potential of what is about to happen, and all this at the same time as what we are doing.[i]

Fantasy is also that thing that makes masturbation so much fun. Few people enjoy, or would enjoy, masturbation without fantasy. For this reason, many people think that fantasy is a necessarily solo activity, but we can fantasize with our partner and this can make our sex life even more exciting. Indeed, sharing fantasies together can be extremely intimate. For example, a couple can fantasize about polysexuality together while only having sex with each other. We can also act out a fantasy through role-playing: many couples use role-playing to augment their sexual lives, by acting out fantasies such as "the naughty schoolgirl," "sex with a stranger," or "sex with a celebrity." Some couples also experiment with kink by role-playing and trying different aspects of BDSM to see if they enjoy it.

Someone might raise a question here about the moral bounds of fantasy: are there bounds to what objects we can fantasize about or ways of fantasizing that might be immoral? This kind of worry is understandable, but it stifles our fantasies and impairs our very ability to fantasize. With fantasy, nothing is out of bounds from a moral perspective, since we are not actually doing anything. However, there is one caveat: if we fantasize about something that would be immoral to do in real life, then we have to be careful to not cultivate a disposition to action for that thing in real life.[ii] As long as we carefully maintain a separation between fantasy and reality, nothing is out of bounds. Indeed, fantasy can properly include things that we might never want to do in real life, because in real life we must worry about considerations like disease, immorality, organization, time, consent, *etc*. In fantasy, however, we are free of these considerations and there are no limits to what we can do. In fantasy, the only limits are the limits of our imagination.

---

[i] Of course, there is a danger here if a person becomes too focused on his fantasies and forgets to engage with what is actually happening.

[ii] A person might reasonably ask how we prevent the cultivation of immoral dispositions. This is easy to explain, but is likely harder in practice. We must watch to see that we do not start thinking of the desires that we do not want to cultivate when we are not fantasizing. We must also watch to make sure that we do not start entertaining these desires in the real world. We must carefully separate reality from fantasy in our minds and not let the two bleed into each other.

Summary and Conclusions

> *Love is blind, they say; sex is impervious to reason*
> *and mocks the power of all philosophers.*
> *But, in fact, a man's sexual choice*
> *is the result and the sum of his fundamental convictions.*[86]
> ~ Ayn Rand

We said in the introduction to this chapter that: "Our sexual attractions tell a grand story of who we are as people and how we view the very world itself." It should now be clear that this is so. Our sexual attractions arise from the totality of who we are and they richly respond to other people as unified wholes. Indeed, sexual attraction is far from being unintelligible: it works through very clear means that we can understand if we look objectively and apply our sentimental account to their operation. Let us briefly review how we got here, before considering where we go next.

We opened this chapter by looking to the origins of sexual attraction and saw several examples showing a then curious connection between sexual attraction and a person's values and beliefs. We then challenged the idea that sexual attraction was merely a response to a person's body and showed how this contradicts the fact that our values and beliefs come into play. From there, we took on the issue that we can sometimes feel sexual attraction to people whom we do not know and showed how this ignorant sexual attraction can be caused by us either projecting our values onto someone else and responding to these in our sexual attraction or simply responding to another person's *style*, which is the rich manifestation of a person's existential orientation across all facets of their life. Finally, we saw that sexual attraction is to whole people and not simply their attributes and, moreover, that it involves much of ourselves and who we are as people. We, thus, rounded out our account of the origins of sexual attraction.

Next, we looked more deeply at the nature of sexual attraction. We started by looking at the connection between a person's philosophy and sexual attraction, since a person's conscious philosophy is the major source of their internalized values and beliefs and our sexual attractions are primarily grounded in these. We saw how, if we are thoughtful and in focus, then most of our internalized beliefs will be consistent with our conscious convictions. However, if we are not, then our values and beliefs can be discordant. This can cause our sexual attractions to be discordant or even perverse and so we saw that we have an obligation to carefully cultivate our values and beliefs. At the same time, we also saw how some people use "types" as a substitute for style and that, while this was not necessarily bad, it does present some perils. We then turned our attention to beauty and saw that objective beauty is being well-formed and flourishing, while we subjectively judge a person to be beautiful when they embody our ideals. We also saw how the eudaimonist position brings these together and unites objective beauty and our subjective response to it by aligning both in flourishing. Finally, we rounded out our discussion of the nature of sexual attraction by looking at its sentimental nature and how it is an emotion as well as giving a definition to help us to integrate and retain our new knowledge.

Lastly, we looked at fantasy and its role in sexuality, which we found to be more important than is commonly thought. We saw that fantasy has several important functions, such as testing, envisioning, reliving, and creating erotic excitement, each of which impacts our sexuality in important ways. Overall, we found that fantasy expands our sexual world and helps us to enjoy it more. We also saw that nothing is out of bounds for fantasy, unless it creates a disposition for action in the real world for something that would be immoral.

Broadly, in this chapter we saw that although sexual attraction is a complex sentiment that reaches to our very depths and is a rich response to another person, it is easily understandable using our sentimental account. We also saw the need to carefully cultivate our philosophy if we want to have our sexual attractions in line with our flourishing. Moreover, we saw that fantasy has a rich and important role in sexuality. All of this stands in stark contrast to the history of philosophy, which has treated sexual attraction as an irreducible primary or a mystical force and fantasy as philosophically uninteresting. These things are not only philosophically interesting, but they are also important if we wish to live well.

We have now almost come to the end of Volume 1. In the next chapter, we will explore the ideas of sexual orientation, societal sex roles, and sexual identity to round out our picture of a person's sexuality. Doing so will set us up to tie everything together in Chapter 7 and see fully why sex is so important for living well and, thus, why it is so important for ethics.

Chapter 6: Sexual Identity

> *What everyone forgets is that passion*
> *is not merely a heightened sensual fusion*
> *but a way of life which produces [...]*
> *an ecstatic awareness of the whole of life.*[87]
> ~ Anaïs Nin

In this chapter, we will call into question some of the ways that we think about sexuality and conceptualize ourselves as sexual beings. The problem is that some of the current ways we think about these things are incompatible with flourishing and may lead us to live derivative lives if we try to conform to standards that are not helpful to us. In order to do this, we will be exploring the idea of sexual identity, which we shall do by exploring sexual orientation, the societal sex roles, and erousia.

We will start with sexual orientation and see how the current *tripartite categorization system* has some insurmountable problems, such as that it does not track the reality of sexual orientation. To resolve this, we will propose a new system to understand sexual orientation. We will then turn our attention to the idea of gender and see that it, too, has insurmountable problems and propose the more useful concept of societal sex role. We will explore this as well as how it arises and perpetuates itself. We will then turn our attention to erousia, or the experience of our own sexuality, and how this underlies the societal sex role and impacts our experience of ourself. We will, finally, bring all this together in the final section to gain a better understanding of our sexual identity.

1. Sexual Orientation

Let us open this chapter by looking at the issue of sexual orientation. Currently, perhaps the most common way of conceptualizing sexual orientation is what we will call the *tripartite categorization system*, which classifies people into one of three mutually exclusive, and totally exhaustive, categories: heterosexual, bisexual, and homosexual. It is likely that most people today conceive of sexual orientation this way. Of course, some people treat each category as morally equal, while other people discriminate against certain categories, but it is rare (although less rare than it used to be) to find someone who does not agree with the categorization system itself. However, this way of conceiving of sexual orientation is problematic for a number of reasons. In order to understand why this is so, we must first turn our attention to the categories and underlying assumptions of the tripartite categorization system.

The Tripartite Categorization System

In the tripartite categorization system, a person is *heterosexual* if they experience sexual attraction exclusively to members of the other sex; this also entails that they try to be attractive only to, and only seek sexual encounters with, the other sex.

A person is *homosexual* if they experience sexual attraction exclusively to members of the same sex; this also entails that they try to be attractive only to, and only seek sexual encounters with, the same sex.

A person is *bisexual* if they experience sexual attraction to both sexes; this also entails that they try to be attractive to, and seek sexual encounters with, both sexes. However, even in the tripartite categorization, there are still some people who believe that bisexuality is either a transitional state that a person occupies when going between the "real" sexual orientations of homosexuality and heterosexuality or that bisexuality does not exist at all and that anyone who is attracted to members of the same sex in any degree must be homosexual. In effect, some people still believe in a bipartite categorization system.

The tripartite categorization system relies on some underlying assumptions about sexual orientation that we must also consider. First, the categories are mutually exclusive and, therefore, a person must fall into one category and only one category. Second, the categories are exhaustive and there are no other alternatives. Third, the categories are rigid and admit of no exceptions: that is, even a single thought can throw a person's orientation into question and a single action can change a person's category. Fourth, the orientations are categories of people (*e.g.*, a homosexual is not someone who engages in sexual activity with someone of the same sex, it is a kind of person).

Given that most of us have grown up in cultures that use the tripartite categorization system and we likely think about sexuality in these terms, it can be hard to see what the alternative is or why this system might be problematic. In order to see where to go from here, it would be helpful to gain a broader perspective on sexual orientation. One way that we can do that is to look at some other cultures and even other times to see how they conceived of sexual orientation and, if it was different, whether this can give us insight into the tripartite categorization system and whether other options are available. If they are available, then we must ask which way of conceiving of sexual orientation is the most helpful for us as we seek to live well.

Cultural Contrast

One very instructive cultural contrast is with the sexual practices of our philosophic forebears in Ancient Greece, particularly in Athens.[i] There are several significant differences between the Athenians and us. Two of the most notable are that high-class men had pederastic relationships and that they did not conceive of sexual orientation as a characteristic of a person, but simply of acts. Let us look to each of these to better understand them and their implications for the tripartite categorization system.

In Athenian culture, the practice of pederasty was widespread and everyone in the upper classes was expected to participate. Pederasty involved older men (*erastês* - "lover") taking younger men[ii] (*erômenos* – "beloved") into a mentorship that involved the older man teaching the younger about the ways of the world, about combat and gymnastics, and about politics and philosophy. In return, the younger man engaged in receptive anal sex with his *erastês*.[iii] The younger man was not simply an object of lust, but a charge and a future citizen whom the *erastês* had an obligation to mold into a good man.

At the same time, the *erastês* was expected to participate in, and engage with, society and to maintain a household.[iv] Part of maintaining a household was having a wife and a family, as well as maintaining his wealth and property. Thus, the Greek man was supposed to have both a wife and family as well as a young male lover. This was not considered "gay," "bi," or even "straight." The Greeks did not have sexual terms that described *people*, but rather only terms that described *actions* or *behaviors*.

The Greeks did have the term "*kinaidos*" that seems to stand in opposition to the idea that they did not have terms that described people. The *kinaidos* was

---

[i] For a fuller account of Greek sexual practice, the best place to begin is K. J. Dover's *Greek Homosexuality*. The information in this section is primarily gleaned from this source.

[ii] The "young boys" here were always adolescent, not pubescents or pre-pubescent children, and were usually 14-22. A boy was no longer eligible when he became a man or when he "grew his full beard." See Volume 2, Chapter 13 on "Children and Sexuality" for more on the distinctions between life phases and human sexuality.

[iii] This point is actually contested as it is known that receptive anal sex was considered, at least in some cases, to be demeaning to the receiver. Those who argue this point assert that the *erastês* would only ever engage in intercrural (between the thighs) sex with the *erômenos*, but this position seems weak for several reasons: 1) there are vases that seem to show immanent anal penetration and 2) the Greeks had a special pejorative term "*kinaidos*" for men who were exclusively anally receptive. Such a term would have been unnecessary if all anal sex was shameful.

[iv] As an interesting aside, the Greek word "*oeconomica*" means to "manage a household" and is the basis for the English "Economics."

a man who was exclusively anally receptive. The Greeks frowned on this for two reasons: first, because the man did not take his proper place in society and second, because his behavior was considered over-indulgent. The first problem is obvious, as societies have always frowned on their non-conforming members. It is the second objection that is more interesting. The Greeks did not think the *kinaidos* was an immoral kind of person. Rather, they thought that he could choose to be otherwise and was merely, although this might sound surprising to modern readers, succumbing to the pleasure of anal penetration in much the same way that we might look down on those who succumb to the pleasure of drugs[i] or the glutton who overeats. Thus, the *kinaidos* was so characterized because of his indulgence and lack of control over his actions. The Greeks would not have condemned him as irredeemable, but would rather have encouraged him to change his actions.

For the Greeks, having sex with men and women was not mutually exclusive and having sex with both was, in fact, actively encouraged.[ii] Manliness for a Greek was about having a good character, quick mind, and strong healthy body. It had nothing to do with whom a person had sex. Because of this, even if a person wanted to say that the Greeks were wrong about how they thought about sexual orientation, the fact is that they *did* structure it differently and this presents a problem for the idea that the tripartite categorization system is the only option.

Consider, also, that there are wide variances even between cultures contemporaneous to us. For example, the Sambia tribe thought that young boys would never grow up to become men if they did not ingest semen from the men of the tribe. Thus, younger boys would fellate the warriors in order to get their male essence (semen) from them: "Damei and another elder, Worangri…relate that only by ingesting semen can the lads grow truly masculine."[88] Fellating older men and ingesting their semen did not make the youths effeminate or homosexual: it is what turned them into men and secured their heterosexuality. This is radically different from how the tripartite categorization system would describe this.

Refuting the Tripartite Categorization System

This brief foray outside the tripartite categorization system has yielded some interesting contrasts.

---

[i] Although this is a facile understanding of addiction, which is fundamentally an improper way of coping with real psychological problems (which may also have an underlying genetic predisposition).

[ii] Lest we paint too rosy a picture of the sexual life of Ancient Greece, their treatment of woman was (generally) not good. There were many cities in which women had heavy restrictions and may not even have been eligible to leave the house without her father's or husband's consent or to own property. Thankfully, many Western cultures are much better (although not perfect) on these points today.

First, the ancient Greeks had no sexual terms to describe a *person*: their sexual terms simply described actions and behaviors.[i] If we were able to talk to an ancient Greek man and we called him a homosexual, he would not understand the predication of a sexual term to a person. It is not just that he would not understand the word, but he would be unable to understand the very intention behind the word. It would be as strange as someone calling one of us "a cunnilingus." What does it mean to be *a cunnilingus*? Is not cunnilingus something we *do*, not something we *are*? To the Greek person, sex was something a person did and could do with whomever they wanted; it was not a fixed aspect of their identity (just like we are not a cunnilingus). Because of this, they would reject the idea of categorizing persons.

Second, the Sambia also do not use the tripartite categorization system's categories. In fact, they think that part of what makes a man into a man is the ingesting of semen. While even if the men did primarily have sex with women later in life, the tripartite categorization system could not handle such a case.

These examples, and there are countless others,[ii] show that the tripartite categorization system is not the only framework to help us understand sexual orientation. Moreover, these other systems are a significant problem for the tripartite categorization system as their very existence presents an irreconcilable problem for the underlying assumptions of the tripartite categorization system. The sexual lives of the Greeks, and other cultures that do not buy into the tripartite categorization system, are very different from those who do buy into it and if the tripartite categorization is right that they are the only viable option, this should not be possible. That it is possible demonstrates that the tripartite categorization system is neither necessary nor natural. Moreover, it has other, deeper, problems to which we will now turn.

The tripartite categorization system has some deep internal problems that make it ultimately incoherent.

First, the emphasis on exclusivity and rigidity leads to facile worries about whether a person is "actually homosexual" if they ever have an attraction to someone of the same sex. The tripartite categorization cannot account for the fact that many of us have had at least one experience of feeling attracted to someone of the "wrong" sex. Yet, this should be impossible if the categories are rigid and mutually exclusive.

---

[i] Lest it be objected that Plato understood people categorically, as it may seem in his allegory of the proto-humans who were male/male or female/female and so who naturally sought that sex to be "complete," this objection falls flat. Plato would not describe them as "homosexuals," but as people who *preferred* to have sex with people of the same sex. The former is categorical, while the latter is about persons doing actions.

[ii] While a full elaboration of the differences in sexual practices is beyond the scope of *Eros and Ethos*, there are many good books on the subject and the broader one's perspective on sexuality, the more one can clearly see one's own sexual culture and better understand it. One good and easily accessible book, despite some flaws, is *Sex at Dawn*, by Christopher Ryan and Cacilda Jetha.

Second, the tripartite categorization cannot account for contextual orientation changes (*e.g.*, heterosexual boys engaging in same-sex activities only while at boarding school, the military, or prison) or that orientation can change over a person's life, and we know these things do happen.[i]

Third, the tripartite categorization system cannot account for how some people have one-time sexual encounters with the "wrong" sex for them and, yet, it does not change their orientation. One might think that the tripartite categorization system could simply say that the person who did this acted out of character. However, this would be impossible as character is a disposition to action and the tripartite categorization system is of people, not actions. It is right to say that a person can act out of character, but it is not a defense the tripartite categorization system can muster.

Fourth, the tripartite categorization system assumes that their division is natural: that it arises from nature and is so justified. It assumes that because it is natural, any other system would be unnatural and, by that fact, wrong. Yet, we have already seen that other alternatives exist and so this assumption is also wrong.

Lastly, and perhaps most damaging, is that conceiving of people categorically is simply unjustifiable.[ii] Thinking of people categorically fundamentally misunderstands human nature and action: people make choices and act in the world. People are not reducible to an action or pattern of action and attempting to do this obscures the real world in favor of theoretical constructs. If we want to live in the world, it behooves us to scrupulously pay attention to it and not lose sight of it for how we wish it were.

Many of these issues arise because the definitions and categories, indeed the very way of conceiving of sexual orientation, that the tripartite categorization system uses fail to track the way people actually engage in sex in

---

[i] Homosexuality can be both opportunistic and contextual. Lisa Diamond's *Sexual Fluidity* is a particularly good book on this topic.

[ii] Let us briefly note an interesting feature of the tripartite categorization system: it is a function of Christianity and their way of conceiving of the world. Or, a more salacious way to put it is: Christianity is the origin of homosexuality. Why? In a footnote in Chapter 1, we brought up Elizabeth Anscombe's brilliant essay "Modern Moral Philosophy" and her point that Christianity created the idea of the "sinner" or a person who was evil *in toto*. The "sinner" was not someone who merely acted badly, but was a "bad person"—the very first category of person. In their fervor to denounce that which they did not like, Christians created the "categorical person" and laid the foundation for this to be applied in the sexual realm by the tripartite categorization system. Of course, the arguments we have presented against conceiving of sexual orientation as categorical apply, *mutatis mutandis*, to ethics. Moreover, our eudaimonistic framework is grounded in the idea of *living well*, not of being a "good person" or "bad person." On our account, some people are living well and others are not. While we might call the former good and the latter evil, these are not categorical terms, but descriptions of how they are living. Thus, we must reject the idea of categorization of people across the board as being harmful to human life and flourishing: it is simply the wrong way to think about issues related to human action.

the real world. Moreover, it also fails to understand sexuality at a deeper level and so remains superficial.

Yet, someone might maintain that, although the tripartite categorization system is fundamentally wrong, it is still useful in order to quickly communicate information about our sexual orientation. Yet, even here, it fails. Consider that even though the tripartite categorization system can be used to communicate our sexual orientation, it does this in a very imprecise way. For example: is a heterosexual someone who *never* has sex with someone of the same sex or who has never felt desire for someone of the same sex? Is it both? How large is this category, really? If we say we are bisexual, what exactly are we communicating? What if we lean more toward one sex than the other? What if our overall level of sexual desire is low? How do we communicate that? How would we communicate that we are primarily heterosexual, but on occasion like to have sex with someone of the same sex? The tripartite categorization system merely *seems* to easily communicate information about our sexual orientation, but because of its deep problems, it fails to do even this.

Ultimately, we have to conclude that the tripartite categorization system fails, for all of the reasons that we have given. Yet, we still need a framework for thinking about sexual orientation. Thus, we must identify a new framework to help us to flourish. Let us turn to that now.

Sexual Orientation as a Disposition

Since we must abandon the idea of categories of people and focus instead on actions, we must start our inquiry afresh. If sexual orientations are not categories of people, then how should we think of them? Let us start by considering a slightly different question: what does it mean to have an "orientation" in the first place?

We might start by asking whether orientation is primarily about our *sexual attractions* or about our *actions*. It seems clear it is related to our sexual attraction, because people rarely have sex with people that they are not sexually attracted to and, indeed, most of us *only* have sex with people to whom we are sexually attracted. On the other hand, it also seems clear that orientation is related to action as well: it is about the sexual things that we *do* and not merely that we might want to do. Moreover, if a person makes a habit of doing some action, such as having sex with women, people can reasonably assume that this person will continue to do that in the future as well. Unfortunately, this leads us to a contradiction: it cannot be the case that both sexual attraction and actions are the primary focus of sexual orientation.

That both sexual attraction and action appear to be the focus of sexual orientation can be resolved by noting that there is another way out of our conundrum: that *neither* is the primary focus of sexual orientation. While both sexual attraction and the actions we take around sexuality are related to sexual orientation, these are peripheral issues. We have been led astray because we were looking at the consequences of sexual orientation and not at it, itself.

Sexual orientation is a *disposition* and it tracks which sex a person will usually want to engage with and what sorts of actions they like to perform. Because the idea of disposition can be confusing, let us compare it to a related case. Imagine a person who really values their health: they eat healthily, their friends have similar healthy lifestyles, and they exercise regularly. Moreover, they live in a culture in which this kind of action is encouraged. So, we might say that they are disposed to a healthy lifestyle. This does not mean that every meal they will eat will be healthy or that they will exercise every time they are supposed to, but it does mean that they will *generally* and perhaps even *usually* do so. They are *disposed* to do these things, but it does not mean that they will *necessarily* do them. This is similar to the way character works: we acquire habits through careful cultivation and we become disposed to not only act in certain ways, but to desire certain things. Our sexual orientation is not fixed and rigid, but is a disposition in the same way as the healthy lifestyle.

There are many factors that culminate in the disposition that is our sexual orientation. One factor is biological: sex hormone timing and amount seems to have a strong influence on which sex we will have a preference for.[i] The full extent of this effect is not known, but it cannot be doubted that there is a biological impact on our ultimate preferences. Nevertheless, this is not fully determining and there are other factors involved in the development of our disposition. Our sexual orientation is also influenced by factors such as the culture we live in, which determines what is culturally acceptable; the morality that we ascribe to, which determines which actions we think are moral; our unique histories and our responses to them; our existential orientation; and even our sentimental framework and how we feel about different sexual possibilities. Sexual orientation is a disposition that does not *determine* our actions or desires, but it does influence them, it does encourage them, it does nudge them; indeed, we might go so far as to say that it *orients* them. It points the way to our normal, or even usual, actions and desires. From it, we can have a pretty good idea about what we will probably do or desire, but we cannot know what we will *necessarily* do or desire: we have free will and can act contrary to our dispositions and even our nature.[ii] Sexuality is more dynamic than people

---

[i] For example, it has been shown that the timing of androgen exposure during fetal development in females is strongly *correlated* with which sex they will ultimately be primarily sexually attracted to and that females who are exposed to higher levels of androgens are more likely to be sexually attracted to other females. (Motta-Mena, N. V. & Puts, D. A. "Endocrinology of human female sexuality, mating, and reproductive behavior," *Hormones and Behavior*, Volume 91, May 2017, Pages 19-35, https://doi.org/10.1016/j.yhbeh.2016.11.012). For a more thorough treatment of this topic, see Simon LeVay's *Gay, Straight, and the Reason Why*, Chapter 6.

[ii] This should, *emphatically*, not be taken as an endorsement of "conversion" therapy, whereby people are psychologically tortured in an attempt to change their sexual orientation, or of any

think and much less rigid. Sexual orientation, then, is a person's general disposition to engage in sexuality and with which sex they tend to do this.

Sexual orientation impacts our sexual attractions, desires, and actions. This is why it is impossible to index our orientation to either sexual attraction or actions: that way of thinking completely misses the underlying disposition that is the ultimate cause of both. The actualization of this disposition does not directly lead us to be sexually attracted[i] to any particular person; rather, it sets the stage for what kinds of people we will be willing to consider as good candidates to be sexually attracted to or to sexually engage with. It manifests through our sexual attractions, through who we sexually desire, and through what we desire to do and actually do. In short, it underlies our sexuality and sets the stage for what we will be likely to do and who we will do this with.

Understanding sexual orientation as a disposition can also explain other problems. Some people argue that it is illicit to say that a person has a specific sexual orientation if they have never had sex or acted upon it. But, if orientation is a disposition, then that presents no problem whatsoever: it is simply an *unactualized* disposition. An example will help us to see this. Let us say that some woman has the potential to learn Attic Greek. If she does actually learn Greek, then she has the potential to speak Greek. At the stage where she knows Greek, but is not currently speaking Greek, she both actually knows Greek and could potentially speak it. Until she does, this is an unactualized disposition. This is very different than saying that she merely has the potential to learn Greek as once she has learned Greek, she could potentially speak it whenever she chose. A sexual disposition is similar: it is an actuality (a set of habits, beliefs, *etc.* as we have laid out, that influences our actions and desires), that in itself also has the potential to manifest in sexual desire, sexual attraction, and sexual action.[ii]

Moreover, thinking about sexual orientation as a disposition also allows us to easily see the answer to what were previously insoluble problems, such as the problem of the person who has an attraction to, or even sexually engages with, a person of the "wrong" sex: the answer is that there is no problem here at all. This is because our orientation does not determine our actions and thus we will sometimes experience sexual attraction to people of a sex we might not usually or we might even have sex with these people. This is only a contradiction if we accept the tripartite categorization system. On our conception, this is easily explainable as just one of the ways sexuality can go, since dispositions merely dispose us certain ways, but do not determine our path.

---

other attempt to change people's orientations by force in order to get them to conform to religious dogma.

[i] This does not change our analysis of sexual attraction in the last chapter in any way, but merely limits the scope of people one might consider in sexual attraction.

[ii] This follows Aristotle's distinction between what is traditionally called "Act 1" and "Act 2" from *De Anima*, 417^{b}1.

At the same time, this new dispositional account of sexual orientation can also accommodate people who do not fall into traditional sexual orientations like people who are asexual[i] or demisexual[ii]. For example, a person who is asexual is someone who is not, or only very rarely, disposed to sexual activity. Or, a person who is demisexual is only disposed to sexual attraction, sexual desire, and sexual action once they have formed an intimate connection with someone. Our new dispositional account of sexual orientation can handle and explain all these cases and show how they are all related to each other. Indeed, it can take the insoluble problems from the tripartite categorization system and easily show the way forward.

Now that we have disabused ourselves of the mistaken idea of the tripartite categorization system and come to see sexual orientation as a disposition, let us more fully explore this latter idea and see where it takes us.

Reconceptualizing Sexual Orientation

Sexuality permeates our lives. Our sexual identity, and with it our orientation, is more than a superficial description of us: it is a major component of who we are and how we understand ourselves. When we think of "who we are," we include facts about our sexuality, like our orientation, our desires, *etc.* While some may think that this is true only for erotic minorities[iii] (such as people who are LGBT, kinksters, polysexual, *etc.*), it is true even for those in the sexual mainstream. Consider that one of the first things we might ask of someone to try to get to know them is whether they are dating anyone or are married. While it would be considered improper to ask anything more, this still tells us quite a bit about their sexuality and how they structure their life.

Sexuality is an important part of our lives and we go to great lengths to structure our lives around our sexuality. Even societies are often structured around sexuality, as in the case of marriage, dating rituals, coming of age (sexual maturity) rites, *etc.* When we think of who we are, we think of things such as our accomplishments, our character, our values, and our sexuality. Most of us

---

[i] People who are asexual experience little to no sexual attraction to other people. This might be *total*, where they experience no sexual attraction, sexual desire, and take no sexual actions (including masturbation), or *partial*, where they still experience some sexual attraction, sexual desire, and may still masturbate or occasionally have sex with others.

[ii] People who are demisexual experience sexual attraction to others only in the context of intimacy. This might be *total*, where they cannot experience sexual attraction or desire outside of an intimate relationship, or *partial*, where they might rarely feel sexual attraction or sexual desire outside of an intimate relationship.

[iii] I first heard this term from Winston Wilde (although I do not believe him to be its origin). It captures those people who live outside of mainstream sexuality, like those people who are into kinks, fetishes, polysexuality, polyamory, homosexuals, bisexuals, transsexuals, *etc.* I particularly like this term and how it captures the element of commonality for those who stand outside the mainstream sexuality. On the other hand, if people were honest about their sex lives, we would find that mainstream sexuality is much less homogenous than people assume.

cannot even think of our identities without thinking about at least our orientation and desires. If we have a partner, they can come to be an integral part of our identity as we saw in Chapters 3 and 4.

Not only is sexuality an important part of our lives, but our sexuality comes from our deepest and most important parts of ourselves, as we saw in the last chapter. Sexual attraction is a rich expression of ourselves and our overall sexuality is no less so. Sexuality reaches all the way down to our core and affects how we live our lives. It forms a core part of our identity and it effects the way we groom ourselves and dress, the way we present ourselves to the world, the types of relationships we engage in, *etc.* Our sexuality is much broader than simply the biological sex of the people with whom we want to become intimate and engage in sex.

Because sexuality is so important in a human life, it would be useful to be able to quickly communicate information about our sexual orientation to other people. This was one apparent advantage of the tripartite categorization system. Unfortunately, it suffered from far too many problems to keep utilizing it for this reason alone and, even with communication, it fell flat. Thus, let us look to some new options that are capable of quick communication about sexual orientation, but which can also capture its dispositional nature.

Alfred Kinsey was the first person to try to seriously rectify the deficiencies of the tripartite categorization through his very good and clever Kinsey Scale. This scale is a continuum of sexual orientations from "0" to "6," where "0" is a person who only experiences sexual attraction and sexual desire for the other sex ("heterosexual"), a "3" is a person who experiences sexual attraction and sexual desire for both sexes equally ("bisexual"), and a "6" is a person who experiences sexual attraction and sexual desire only for those of the same sex ("homosexual"). The other positions along the continuum obviously indicate relative levels of preference for one sex or the other.

This continuum has distinct advantages over the tripartite categorization system, most particularly in its exactness and its ability to more comprehensively and accurately capture people's sexual attractions and desires. Moreover, it preserves the dispositional nature of sexual orientation and does not attempt to categorize people by their actions. This gives us a very good system to understand sexual orientation and it also allows us to both quickly and accurately communicate about our sexual orientation.

However, one drawback of the Kinsey Scale is that it only tracks *which sex* a person is sexually attracted to and sexually desires. It cannot track overall levels of sexual desire; that is, it only tracks how much a person desires someone of the same sex versus someone of the opposite sex, but it does not track how much sexual desire they experience overall (if any).

A new and better alternative is what we will call the *Triaxial Scale*. It is similar to the Kinsey Scale, except that the other axes allow it to be much more precise and to capture more information. The Triaxial Scale is based on levels of sexual attraction and sexual desire and tracks both how likely we are to engage in sexual activity and with which sex we will usually engage. This is in contrast to the Kinsey Scale, which can only track the *relative* level of sexual attraction and sexual desire between each sex. This will be clearer if we look more closely at the Triaxial Scale.

The Triaxial Scale tracks a person's sexual attraction and sexual desire to each sex on a 0-6 scale. Each number tracks the degree of sexual attraction and sexual desire from none to an intense desire for that sex. The first number represents a person's desire for males, the second number for those who are physically outside the male/female binary, and the third for females.[i] This second group is people who are intersex; that is, whose bodies have biological features of both sexes, whether they were born this way, developed these characteristics at puberty, or arrived at them through surgery.[ii] It is important that this group be represented, because by some accounts 1 in 25 people do not fit into the male/female dichotomy. [89] We must never attempt to turn away from reality in service to our theoretical constructs[iii]; rather, we should have our theoretical constructs match reality as closely as possible.[iv]

Thus, the scale can be represented as (M:I:F) and so a person who was (0:0:6) would be a person who has no sexual attraction to, or sexual desire for, males or intersex people, but a great passion for females. A person who was (1:2:1) would be a person whose overall levels of sexual attraction and sexual desire are below average, but shows some preference for intersex people. Someone who was (0:0:0) would have no sexual attraction or sexual desire for anyone and someone who was (6:6:6) would be a person who had a great amount of sexual attraction and sexual desire for males, intersex people, and females.[v]

The Triaxial Scale has many benefits compared to the scales that we have

---

[i] The Triaxial Scale simply tracks biological sex and not *gender* (or, to use a real concept, the *societal sex role*, which we will explore in the next section). Thus, it uses "males and females" as opposed to terms like "men and women" or other terms that may carry more meaning than physical sex.

[ii] I am sure that the decision to include intersex people in the scale will prove to be controversial, but the fact is that many people are born this way and others make choices to be this way. Thus, if we are to capture reality with our scale, we must look at how the world really is, and the reality of the situation is that these people exist and thus the scale should capture them as well.

[iii] This is not to say that we should not try to change the world! It is simply to say that we must first seek to understand the world as it really is, instead of blinding ourselves to it by trying to force upon it a framework like religion, which only allows us to see our framework and not the world. Seeing the world as it really is requires psychological flexibility and a constant testing of our beliefs against the world. (See Volume 3, on "Surreality" for more about this topic).

[iv] While Fausto-Sterling argues for five sexes, this seems unnecessarily complicated to capture in the scale.

[v] The positions can be thought of as: 0 – None, 1 – Low, 2 – Below Average, 3 – Average, 4 – Above Average, 5 – Considerable, and 6 – Great.

already explored. It has some modest advantages over the Kinsey scale, which cannot track levels of sexual attraction and sexual desire relative to physical sex, and thus the Triaxial Scale can capture a more robust picture of sexuality. It also allows the scale to capture people who exist outside the male/female binary, which the Kinsey Scale cannot capture. At the same time, the Triaxial Scale has great advantages over the tripartite categorization, such as that it preserves the dispositional nature of sexual orientation, does not categorize persons based on their actions, and tracks the way sexuality is actually experienced in the world.

The nuance of the Triaxial Scale and its emphasis on the dispositional nature of sexuality also allows it to be dynamic and account for changes in a person's sexual orientation. This can be a short-term change due to circumstances, such as we find in cases of "contextual homosexuality" in prisons or same-sex educational facilities, or long-term changes that happen over the course of a lifetime. In her book *Sexual Fluidity*, Lisa Diamond discusses the titular concept and demonstrates that these changes are a real part of sexual orientation for many people.[90] While this might have been complicated for older accounts, the dispositional nature of sexual orientation that underlies the Triaxial Scale can easily account for this as dispositions are not fixed and rigid, but are open to change and growth.

The flexibility of the Triaxial Scale may also have the side effect of encouraging sexual exploration and minimizing norming into a sexual category. It does the former by not forcing people to push themselves into rigid categories that may not represent the way they experience sexuality and thus leaves them free to explore the ways in which they actually do experience sexuality (instead of the ways that they think they *should* experience sexuality). It does the latter by lacking rigid categories and having many more options, which should reduce the group identification effect and attenuate hatred of other groups.[i] Thus, people will feel freer to explore their sexual orientation and be comfortable with wherever this leads them.[ii]

Overall, the Triaxial Scale preserves the dispositional nature of sexual orientation and does not burden it with unnecessary theoretical structures. Now, one might wonder, given the dangers we have shown with the tripartite categorization system, whether we ought not do away with all categorization. This worry, however, is confused. The Triaxial Scale is not a method of categorizing people at all, as we have shown, but a way of understanding their

---

[i] A full account of in-group/out-group psychology is beyond the scope of our purposes, but the basic idea here is that having more than two groups may attenuate hatred of those in other groups as this is more pronounced in binary systems. For more information, see the works of Henri Tajfel on "Social Identity Theory."

[ii] An unintended benefit of the Triaxial Scale is that a person's number does not necessarily change if a person has a sex-change, unlike the TCS where a person may suddenly go from "straight" to "gay" after a surgery.

sexual orientation. This is beneficial in understanding ourselves as well as helping us to easily communicate our preferences and typical patterns of actions to others, without the need to launch into a long story. The Triaxial Scale facilitates our ability to easily think about and discuss sexuality, and that is surely a boon.

Now that we have seen alternatives that better track human sexuality and do not suffer from debilitating internal contradictions, it should be clear that the tripartite categorization should be abandoned. Moreover, it should also be clear that utilizing it inhibits flourishing and will cause us to live less well. Minimally, we must abandon the rigid[i] tripartite categorization system and start thinking about sexual orientation as a continuum. Even using the Kinsey Scale would be much preferable to utilizing a system that is so robustly wrong, fails to capture the reality of the sexual experience, and carries with it too much philosophical baggage. It would be even better if we adopt the Triaxial Scale, which goes much farther towards capturing the reality of our sexual experiences and sexual orientation.

2. Societal Sex Roles

Now that we better understand sexual orientation and have given up the tripartite categorization system in favor of the Triaxial Scale, it is time to turn our attention to another problematic concept, that of "gender." After we inquire into gender, we will turn our attention to erousia, before bringing everything together in the last section on sexual identity.

Gender

The concept of "gender" has become pervasive in discussions of sexuality. Yet, it is not clear what this word means. In fact, it seems to have much more of a connotation than a denotation. Thus, it behooves us to critically examine this to see if there is any value to the idea of gender or whether we should reject it.

Historically, most cultures have maintained some kind of difference between a person's physical sex and their sex's "virtue" (or how that sex *should* behave); *i.e.*, between being physically male and "manliness."[ii] This is how it might be said that Alcibiades was particularly manly due to his courage on the battlefield: Alcibiades was not just physically male, but he showed virtue *as* a

---

[i] We should be wary of rigidity of thought, as it has been shown to be strongly correlated with mental health problems. Rigidity of thought should be understood as a failure to consider new evidence and always test our beliefs. Of course, we must never violate our moral principles, but this is not rigidity of thought.

[ii] In fact, we can trace the idea of virtue to this idea of the role a man should play, since etymologically "virtue" means manliness.

man.

However, the idea of "gender" is a relatively new development and the Sexologist John Money was one of the major forces behind it. In his 1955 work "An Examination of Some Basic Sexual Concepts: The Evidence of Human Hermaphroditism,"[91] he developed the idea of "gender role." This concept of gender role is a third term and tries to separate out the gender role from both physical sex and the sex's virtue; that is, it tries to capture "manness" as opposed to either being physically male or the sex's virtue (*i.e.*, "manliness"). With gender role, Money was hoping to capture what it meant to be a "man" or "woman" in itself:

> By the term, gender role, we mean all those things that a person says or does to disclose himself or herself as having the status of boy or man, girl or woman, respectively. It includes, but is not restricted to sexuality in the sense of eroticism. Gender role is appraised in relation to the following: general mannerisms, deportment and demeanor, play preferences and recreational interests; spontaneous topics of talk in unprompted conversation and casual comment; content of dreams, daydreams, and fantasies; replies to oblique inquiries and projective tests; evidence of erotic practices and, finally, the person's own replies to direct inquiry.

It is important to point out that Money did not intend this idea of "gender role" to be indexed in any way to physical sex, since it was amenable to both the perceptions of others and a person's own thoughts on the subject. Indeed, it not being indexed to physical sex was a marked break with the past, which had always clearly connected a sex's virtue to the physical sex.

Of course, people before Money did have at least some implicit idea of the roles men and women were supposed to play and these were often rigidly enforced, beyond the sex's virtue. But, these roles had not yet been given their own word: they had not yet been made concrete and rigid. What Money did was to try to subsume these social roles around sexuality under the concept of gender so that the male sex could be understood as having the male gender role and the female sex could be understood as having the female gender role. This was, in some ways, a big step forward in terms of utility in speaking about these ideas. Unfortunately, this conception came with its own problems.

One of the most problematic aspects of this idea of "gender" is that it is a strange amalgam of how we choose to identify ourselves and how others see us. This is easier to see with an example. Let us say that we wanted to assign everyone a value based on a beauty scale of 1-10, where 1 is very ugly and 10 is beautiful. Let us say that to arrive at a number, we would factor in both how a person viewed himself as well as how others viewed him. Of course, sometimes the two numbers would agree, but many times it would not. And how would we reconcile the fact that a person thought that he was an 8 while others thought he was a 4? What number is he? While this is a strange example, this is the same problem with gender. If it is both how others view us and how we view ourselves, then any cases of conflict between these are insoluble. And these conflicts arise all the time, rendering this conception of gender problematic.

This is the first major problem with the idea of gender. It attempts to package two essentially different things into a single concept. This is a classic package-deal.[i] There is no way to make a legitimate concept that contains both a person's perception of himself combined with the perceptions of others: unless we want to posit a world of absolute and perfect agreement in every instance of this. Of course, this would be absurd.

Regardless of whether Money intended it or not, gender came to be indexed to physical sex. Indeed, many people came to regard gender as directly following from physical sex and so their expectations about which gender a person should be became tied to what physical sex they thought a person was.

Thus, gender became an amalgam of a person's views about himself, how others view him, and his physical sex. This quickly devolved into new categories that people needed to try to fit themselves into. Of course, there had always been social expectations about how males and females should dress, comport themselves, and behave, but this gained a new rigidity by categorizing it into gender. Through this categorization of gender, people started to think of gender as some necessary, or perhaps even intrinsic, part of themselves.[ii] This, sadly, obscured the real nature of the phenomenon.

This is the second major, and more serious, problem with gender as we have it today: it obscures the real issue. The real phenomenon at play here is the conventional role of a particular sex. While a person can internalize this and abide by it, it is exogenous to the person and few people internalize every aspect of the role (if this is even possible). None of us are born with this role, even if we are raised into one and internalize aspects of it. Thus, calling it "gender" as though it may be part of a person obscures the real phenomenon: a social convention about the roles of the sexes, or what we will call the *societal sex role*.

We can gain a lot of needed clarity by abandoning the concept of gender and transitioning to the idea of the societal sex role. And clarity of thought is something that we should always strive for, as it is a critical component of our ability to flourish. Of course, while we have shown the problems with gender

---

[i] Recall that the "package-deal" is an informal fallacy identified by Rand, which is done by: "equating opposites by substituting nonessentials for their essential characteristics, obliterating differences." ("How to Read (and Not to Write)," *The Ayn Rand Letter*, p. 117.)

[ii] An additional harm is that people may try to force themselves to fit into a "gender" that does not accurately suit them and this can push them to live derivatively.

that led us to reject it, we have yet to make the case for the societal sex role and how it brings clarity and better helps us to understand sexuality.

Briefly, before we do this, it is important that we draw a distinction between three different terms: physical sex (*e.g.*, "male"), societal sex role (*e.g.*, "man"), and the societal sex role virtues (*e.g.*, "manly"). *Physical sex* is about a person's physical body and, as we discussed in the last section, there is good reason to minimally have three distinct categories: male, female, and intersex. The *societal sex role* is the conventional set of expectations in a particular culture for people of each physical sex. The *societal sex role virtues* grow out of the societal sex role and represent what the society thinks of as a particularly good instance of that sex role. The rest of this section will focus on elaborating the latter two terms, before moving on to see what underlies them in the next section.

Societal Sex Role

We have already said that the societal sex role is a conventional set of expectations in a particular culture. In order to flesh this out, let us first look at what kinds of things are parts of the societal sex role. The societal sex role encompasses many elements, such as: expression of the secondary sexual characteristics (*e.g.*, hair length, which physical attributes to accentuate), social roles (*e.g.*, equal vs. subservient, worker vs. homemaker), political rights (*e.g.*, suffrage, property ownership), stereotypical mannerisms, dress, acceptable hobbies, acceptable colors to favor, who should want sex more[i], *etc*. The particulars captured are going to be dependent on the society and the particular role they have for each sex.[ii] Many of these things remain invisible to those in a particular culture and are taken as "just the way things are." For example, in the US, prior to World War I, male babies were dressed in pink and female babies were dressed in blue. Before that, all babies wore white dresses, so that they could be easily bleached when they were inevitably soiled. The convention that male babies must wear blue and female babies pink is a recent one.[92] Nevertheless, the societal sex roles tend to be about the same sorts of features, even across cultures and times. They are things like: how people present themselves in society, what rights and responsibilities they have, what clothing

---

[i] Although it might seem strange to some readers, some authors argue that across the world until around the 1800's, women were considered to want and need sex more than men. If so, we can be sure that this shift to today's idea that men need and want sex more is not because of a change in our genetics. See, for example, Alyssa Goldstein's essay "When Women Wanted Sex Much More Than Men: And how the stereotype flipped" published on Alternet on April 19th, 2014 http://www.alternet.org/sex-amp-relationships/when-women-wanted-sex-much-more-men.

[ii] We are not going to discuss the particular societal sex roles for any culture as this is more of an anthropological and sociological question. We are seeking to explain the entire phenomenon.

they can wear, how they should try to make their body look, *etc*. Every society will have some regard for these categories, but the specifics will vary.

From these elements, societies will construct their specific societal sex roles. For example, in the United States, there are two primary societal sex roles: men and women. Men are males who are assertive, strong, quiet, and emotionless. Men who are particularly "manly" (who exhibit the societal sex role virtue) are called "masculine." Women are females who are docile, petite, nurturing, and emotional. Women who are particularly "womanly" (who exhibit the societal sex role virtue) are called "feminine." Now, obviously this is not an endorsement of these views (and we will return to the question of how to judge them shortly), but it does help to concretize the discussion.[i] At the same time, we do not want to spend too much time on the particulars of any one culture, because our goal is philosophical and we want to be able to understand any culture at any time and not be limited to understanding particular cultures.

Let us give a broad overview of how the conventions of the societal sex role work to keep the roles in place, through the example of female docility or submissiveness. Let us start by noting that everyone today is born into a culture and raised in a zeitgeist.[ii] A woman born today is, thus, exposed to many ideas as she grows up as well as the expectations of others such as her parents and friends. She sees docility modeled for her through her mother and other female figures. When she acts contrary to established norms,[iii] such as through being assertive, she is shamed (*e.g.*, through the use of the pejorative "bossy") and perhaps even punished (*e.g.*, for questioning her parents and not being "a good little girl"). Through this, she comes to internalize certain norms of behavior (*e.g.*, "I should be docile"). Of course, she also picks up on other norms through instruction, exposure to the ideas in the zeitgeist, through art, *etc*. Through internalizing certain norms (whether actively or passively) and being shamed when she does not correctly follow them, she comes to participate in the cultural conventions.[iv] Once she has come to participate in the cultural norms, she will both impose them on herself through rules, shame, and disgust, as well as impose them on others through shamenorming. She may also propagate the ideas directly through instruction or writing. In this way, she will eventually become an agent of the convention as well as participating in it.

A full account of the nature of social conventions would be required to fully ground our account of the societal sex roles; yet, such an account is

---

[i] There should be at least one more societal sex role to account for intersex people.
[ii] Recall that we are using the word "zeitgeist" to capture the prevalent cultural ideas that a person is exposed to, whether consciously or subconsciously. There is no connection to other philosophies intended or implied.
[iii] Whether these are of the culture at large or merely of a subgroup.
[iv] This is not to say that it is impossible for a person to ever consciously come to participate in cultural conventions, as a person can do this if they move to a new culture as an adult.

beyond our present scope. Consequently, we will simply assume the fairly noncontroversial point that social conventions exist. However, it behooves us to examine two elements that are particularly relevant to our discussion: the zeitgeist and shamenorming. These elements are more directly relevant to sexual ethics and we will see them again in Volume 2. Moreover, they are critical in understanding the societal sex role.

Societal Sex Role and the Zeitgeist

Most people start to collect beliefs about the societal sex role early in life. Societies are so inundated with societal sex role messages that we are confronted with them from the moment we begin to be aware of the world around us. These messages are everywhere, though their particular form will depend on the society in which they exist. For example, mommy and daddy dress differently and act differently and a child will pick up on this. Insofar as the child does not, the parents will often explicitly teach the child the norms. When a child enters school, the other children will collectively act to norm him into the proper societal sex role, including using ostracization and violence. The message to conform to his proper societal sex role will be all around the child growing up and even through adulthood.[i] The message exists in the zeitgeist and manifests in manifold ways: through art, literature, movies, people's existential orientation, *etc*. As we grow, our performance of the societal sex role is judged by others and we are normed into proper compliance.[ii]

Through being inundated with these messages since we are young, we will come to accept at least some of these ideas. Of course, as we discussed earlier in Chapter 2, it is important that we consciously work to develop our own views about important matters and not simply passively accept whatever ideas happen to exist in the zeitgeist. We must carefully cultivate our values and beliefs if we want to live well. Yet, it can be hard to change deeply internalized beliefs that we have had since childhood.

It would be helpful here to be clearer about the nature of the zeitgeist. The zeitgeist does not, *per se*, exist. It is a concept to help us understand the complicated interactions of ideas and actions across an entire culture. The zeitgeist is nothing more than the aggregate of all the ideas that people believe and act upon in the society. People come to these beliefs both through philosophy and through the zeitgeist into which they are born.[iii] In this way,

---

[i] The strength of the effect to conform to others will vary depending on the individual, but can be very strong. For example, in the Asch Conformity experiments, roughly 1/3 of people picked the wrong answer on an easy visual test in order to agree with others. The success rate when individuals were tested without group pressure was 99%.

[ii] While I am indebted to Judith Butler for the idea of "performance," our accounts are radically different and there is very little we agree on.

[iii] Someone might wonder about a time before the first zeitgeist. It is not clear that we can do anything but fruitlessly speculate about this as this existed long before written records.

the zeitgeist is self-perpetuating and is slow to change. It is, however, responsive to new philosophic ideas and often there are major shifts due to philosophic changes.

There are two striking examples of philosophic shifts in the zeitgeist. The first is the reintroduction of Aristotle's ideas through Thomas Aquinas (and Albertus Magnus). This had two major influences. First, it reintroduced a system of philosophy founded in reason instead of faith. Second, its effect on Aquinas himself led him to push the church away from the more virulent ideas like Tertullian's *"Credo quia absurdum"* ("I believe it [have faith] because it is absurd."). The combination of these things led to the Enlightenment and the decline of religion. This radically changed the zeitgeist. Of course, there was nearly a 400-year gap between the introduction of Aristotle and the enlightenment as the zeitgeist slowly changed. The second example is the publication of Locke's *Two Treatises on Government*. Locke spent the first treatise refuting Robert Filmer and the idea of the divine right of kings. The second treatise is more important as it deals with natural rights and property. This led, inexorably, to be the philosophic foundation of the United States of America, the only country ever founded on a philosophic ideal. This time, the time gap between these events is less than 100 years, but this is partly because the ground had already been laid by the reintroduction of Aristotle (it also helped that the printing press had been invented in the intervening time). The zeitgeist does change[i], but the timescale of this is long, and much of that is because people do not easily change their beliefs, especially when they only hold these implicitly, and so some of the change of the zeitgeist is inevitably the death of people and their replacement by those who were affected by the new ideas from a changing philosophy.[ii]

The ideas that are most prevalent in the zeitgeist are those that will ultimately determine the societal sex role because beliefs about the societal sex role tend to determine many people's actions about the societal sex role.[iii] This is not to make a case for strong determinism or to attempt something absurd like claiming free will is illusory. Rather, it is to acknowledge that many people do not live their lives in a state of conscious focus and instead spend a good

---

[i] Subgroups in the zeitgeist are more likely to experience rapid changes such as a religious schism splitting a religion into two sects or even fads that come and go. It is not possible to give a full account of the zeitgeist without a book-length treatment of it and the interaction with human psychology. I hope that another takes up this project.

[ii] Because of the large timescale effects in the zeitgeist, even if this present work is successful at freeing sexuality from the tyranny of mysticism and misanthropy, it is not likely I will live to see it. While easier flow of information does allow the zeitgeist to change more easily, sexuality is a particularly intractable topic. Nevertheless, I hope that it will one day show the importance of sex to human life.

[iii] This is a somewhat simplified picture of the zeitgeist and how its ideas will impact a person, because in reality the zeitgeist has many layers and people will participate in subgroups. They will also feel the pull between their subgroups and larger social groups. However, this complexity does not enrich our understanding of the general phenomenon.

deal of time in what we might call "autopilot," where they are not mentally present, not focused, and are not consciously choosing much of what they do. When we run on autopilot, we tend to simply follow our emotions or whims and these come from our values and beliefs (see Chapter 2). For example, if a man has never thought about why he should not wear a bright pink dress (which may be culturally inappropriate), then he simply will not wear one and would feel uneasy about it if someone pressed him to do so. If a person is living consciously, then they have chosen their beliefs and are choosing to act on them or not; yet, many people do not live like this or only do this in certain areas of their life. To the extent that a person is out of focus and on autopilot, they are at the mercy of forces they do not control and simply become agents of whatever conventions they happen to be exposed to.

Which ideas are most prevalent in the zeitgeist is a function of which philosophies have been most prevalent leading up to the time-period in question and may also be somewhat influenced by prominent contemporaries. For example, if the dominant philosophy is Christianity[i] and they hold that women are inferior to men[ii], then these ideas will be most common in the zeitgeist and that will influence the people in that culture. This will impact the societal sex role and will lead to women being seen as inferior and their roles will reflect this. Consequently, the societal sex role is tied to the particular philosophy and culture from which it arose and through which it is maintained. If the dominant philosophy were to shift, and with it the zeitgeist, then the societal sex role would shift.

While no individual can change the societal sex role directly, nor could they change any convention directly, it can be changed. However, it can only be done indirectly by changing the ideas in the zeitgeist. While this can be done by campaigning against certain ideas and trying to change them piecemeal, it is most effectively done by changing the philosophy to which the idea belongs. If the philosophy is one of the less impactful ones in the zeitgeist, then even if the philosophy can be changed, the new idea would still have to compete with the ideas from the dominant philosophy. If the zeitgeist can be changed such that the idea is no longer prevalent, then it will not be as likely to be picked up on by young people in the culture and some older people may also change. People act according to their values and beliefs and if we can change these, we can change their choices and actions.

---

[i] Religion should be counted among philosophies in this looser sense here; because, as Rand says, it is "a primitive form of philosophy" (*Romantic Manifesto*, 25) in that it seeks to explain reality through mysticism and faith instead of through discovery and reason.

[ii] This point, that Christianity is hostile to women, hardly needs to be argued, since it is so patently obvious. See, for example, Christianity blaming *all sin* on women (Eve and "the fall," *Genesis 3*) or even more explicitly "'Let the women learn in silence with all subjection. But I suffer not a woman to teach, nor to usurp authority over the man, but to be in silence. For Adam was first formed, then Eve. And Adam was not deceived, but the woman being deceived was in the transgression." (I *Timothy* 2:11-14).

While the foregoing may make it sound like the zeitgeist is an entirely passive thing from which people may end up getting beliefs, this is not accurate. People in a culture will actively work to make sure that others conform to their norms and ideals. One of the major ways that people do this is through shamenorming and so we will turn our attention to this now.

Shamenorming

People hate when their conventions are violated. When someone violates the conventions around the societal sex role, people tend to become angry and can even become violent in an effort to minimize the transgressions. For example, when Muslims stone women to death who have sex outside of marriage (including when they are raped), they are punishing the women to protect their social conventions around sex. This punishment arises partly from their ideas about the societal sex roles.[i] More relevant to our discussion, people attempt to use shamenorming to prevent these violations from happening in the first place or to try to reduce their occurrence.

We have already discussed the process of internalizing beliefs in Chapter 1, but there is a crucial difference between the standard internalization process and the process involved in the societal sex role, as much of the latter is also fueled by shamenorming.[ii] Shamenorming is an important component in how the societal sex role functions and spreads. The societal sex role is created and maintained by the individuals in the society internalizing the beliefs of the societal sex role through the zeitgeist and through explicit instruction from others (parents, peers, *etc.*) as they grow up. This inculcation of conventions and social norms lays the foundation for shamenorming. At the same time, no one will ever perfectly exemplify a particular culture's societal sex role. This will lead them to deviate from the acceptable societal sex role and this deviation will result in corrective action from those in the society: from disparaging looks to violence.

Given that we are dealing with enforcing norms through shame, it behooves us to briefly identify the nature of shame. Shame is an emotion that occurs when a person has both done something wrong and another has noticed this. This should be contrasted with guilt where a person knows they have done wrong, without a social component. A person cannot be ashamed of something that they do not think is right. For example, if a person is in a foreign land and does not know their customs and commits a *faux pas*[iii], they will not feel shame,

---

[i] One cannot be overly harsh in condemning this barbarism and blatant immorality. At the same time, Muslims should not be singled out as many religions and cultures have barbarous practices around sexuality. All of these practices, especially including genital mutilation of women *and men*, should be condemned as inimical to human life.

[ii] Shamenorming is also discussed in Chapter 16.

[iii] French is literally "false step" and serves to mean that a person made a social error (violated

because they do not know that they have done wrong. If they also believe that a person must conform to social conventions, then they may feel shame once someone points out their mistake to them. Shame requires that a person both knows and accepts the norms that others are attempting to hold them to, because they must accept that they have done wrong by violating them in order to feel shame. A person who does not agree with the conventions in question will not feel shame, even when confronted by others, because they do not accept the underlying norm and thus will not feel bad about violating it.

Shamenorming, then, is the use of shame to attempt to get people to conform their actions to social conventions. That is, when people deviate from the social conventions, then others will use shamenorming in an attempt to correct their behavior. This is especially evident in the societal sex role. Shamenorming uses any deviance from the societal sex role as the basis for corrective action. The source of shame here *is* the deviance.[i] By deviating from the societal sex role, a person has violated the conventions and they must be held accountable for this, minimally through social censure.

The ultimate goal of shamenorming is for individuals to internalize the beliefs, such that they control their own behavior through guilt if they violate the norms (because they will believe that they have done something wrong). The individual always knows whether he has transgressed and is in the best position to control his own behavior. Thus, if the societal sex role is well inculcated, then shamenorming is less necessary and only for rare slips. It is only when people violate the norms that shamenorming is useful as it is fundamentally about compelling the individual to internalize the norms and conform to them. If a person can be made to accept the conventions, then they will control their own behavior through guilt. If they violate the conventions, then others will shame them. This dual-pronged approach is the crux of shamenorming.

Shame is incredibly powerful. Most people would never consider violating their societal sex role. The very thought of it would cause them anxiety and dread. For example, most women in the United States carefully keep their breasts covered as is expected by their societal sex role.[ii] However, there is currently a movement in the U.S. right now called "Free the nipple" which aims to remove the shame and guilt about having one's breasts exposed in public. In order to do this, they are trying to reduce the stigma and shame around exposed breasts by having marches where women expose their breasts (but may still cover their nipples for legal reasons). This is an effort to change the societal sex role. In the U.S., women are supposed to keep their breasts and nipples covered and only reveal them to certain people, in certain situations. Why?

---

conventions).
[i] That people hate any kind of deviance is partly a psychological issue and stems from many things, such as Social Identity Theory, which we have already mentioned.
[ii] We will return to the topic of public nudity in Volume 2, Chapter 16.

"Because that's just how things are!"[i] While there is some support for this movement, there is quite a bit of backlash and even people who are not directly opposed to the movement are made very uncomfortable by it. Why? Because these are the ideas in the zeitgeist and people have internalized these and their emotional process is using these beliefs as the basis for their emotional responses. How is it that there are different people with different beliefs? Two reasons: first, people have free will and reason and can think and make up their own minds and second, the zeitgeist has lots of ideas in it and while the majority of people will take on the dominant ideas, this does not mean everyone will do so (some may take up ideas from a sub-group).

Of course, shamenorming can also be effective on people who are not from the same culture and do not share the same beliefs. In this case, it is still an effort to control behavior and instill the beliefs in the person, although it is harder if they do not have a common framework. At the same time, most people do not want to unnecessarily offend others and want to be respectful of other people's cultures, which makes this process much easier than it might be otherwise.

Now, it might sound like there is some large and nefarious actor at work here, directing the shamenorming. There is not. Shamenorming arises from individuals acting to preserve the social conventions and since they have the same ends, the actions appear coordinated. It is not, however, consciously led by anyone. Some people shamenorm others because they have really internalized the norms and want to uphold them. Others resent their own need to comply with the conventions and so they feel the need to make others feel the same way: "If I must suffer this, so must you." Regardless of their motive, by having the same ends, their actions will look coordinated. Shamenorming is much broader than simply the societal sex role and is used to correct any behavior outside the desired behavior in a group.

Of course, there are often more robust expectations for those in a society than the societal sex role itself. There are also the societal sex role virtues, to which we will now turn, after which we will bring our discussion back to gender and see the contrast and why we had to abandon gender as a concept.

Societal Sex Role Virtues

Let us now briefly turn to the societal sex role virtues.[ii] In contrast to the societal sex role *simpliciter* (*e.g.*, male, female, or intersex), the "role virtues"[iii] are

---

[i] While most people would simply appeal to the *status quo* for justification, the real answer lies in a denial of the body and this ultimately comes from Plato. See Volume 2, Chapter 9 for more on this.
[ii] I must credit Patrick Ryan for his help in thinking about the societal sex role virtues.
[iii] It should be noted that this use of "virtues" is loose and that these are not moral virtues.

society's ideals for the societal sex roles (*e.g.,* masculinity and femininity).[i] These role virtues are explicitly about the performance of the societal sex role itself and not about biological sex: *i.e.,* it is about how well a man is conforming to the ideal of the male societal sex role and not the size of his penis.

Consider that an archer is one who shoots a bow and a good archer is one who does it well, or a baker is one who bakes and a good baker is one who bakes well, or a lyre player is one who plays the lyre and a good lyre player is one who plays it well. It is illicit to use the same term for both simply performing an action and doing it excellently. The societal sex role virtues track this distinction.

The role virtues are the carrot to the stick of shamenorming: they provide a positive ideal for which an individual can strive (*e.g.,* "a real lady" or "a true gentleman"). Of course, achieving the full-fledged societal sex role virtue may be impossible depending on their constitution in any particular culture: that is, the role virtue may contain so many disparate elements (*e.g.,* great muscular strength, business acumen, social charisma, a good education, *etc.*), that no single person would be able to master the entire ideal. While the ideal is the goal and positive motivation, there's always the stick of shamenorming for those who are not striving for the ideal.

Participation in the Societal Sex Role

The fact that the societal sex role framework is a better way of thinking about these issues does not mean that any particular societal sex role will be good. We must differentiate between the conceptual apparatus for understanding the societal sex roles and the particular societal sex roles that exist in different cultures. Each societal sex role must be judged by whether it will help individuals to flourish or not. Or, rather, people should judge them this way if they wish to live well.

It is not up to us whether we will be subjected to the societal sex roles or the role virtues by others. A social role is a network of interconnected expectations that arises from cultural ideas in the zeitgeist through the expectations of other people and/or our own internalized beliefs and desires to conform to these. This is, obviously, largely outside our direct control. However, what is in our control is our own beliefs and our response to other's expectations; that is, what is ultimately in our power is whether we let this negatively affect our flourishing. Shamenorming can push a person to live derivatively[ii] to conform to other's expectations and can, thus, be a real impediment to authenticity and, through this, happiness. We must take care that we think critically about any social norms and whether following them

---

[i] Again, there needs to be an additional role virtue term for intersex people.
[ii] Recall from Chapter 1 that "derivativeness" is the vice associated with psychological independence, where a person allows others to define them.

would improve or harm our lives. Of course, if explicitly not following a social norm might endanger our life, then this must be taken into consideration as well.[i]

If we decide that the social norms would not benefit our lives (but that we are not in physical danger), then we have three choices: we can publicly rebel against the norm and openly violate it, we can publicly follow the norm while privately violating it, or we can attempt to subvert the norm by appearing to conform while actually violating the norm. This would be clearer with an example. Let us use the example of a societal sex role that required women to cover their faces around anyone who is not family. A woman could go out in public with no veil to openly rebel, she could publicly follow the norm but go unveiled at home even in front of non-family members, or she could attempt to subvert the norm by dressing as a man and trying to get others to see her as such. Even if we are limited to no more than rebellion against the norms in our hearts, this is still something and can be an authentic choice.

By conceiving of the problem of oppressive societal sex roles as a societal sex role instead of as something innate about us (as gender does), a possibility immediately presents itself to resolve some of the above issues: more societal sex roles could be created to better track the variety of human sexual experience and how people live their lives. While some in a society would resist this, if enough movement could be brought together and enough people participate in the new role, then it could gain enough traction to be recognized as a legitimate role. We can see a similar thing happen between the 1950s in the U.S. and present day, where now gay people are seen to occupy their own societal sex role, where no such role had existed before. Through the framework of the societal sex role, we can more clearly understand these issues and we can use this to seek out solutions to problems. This does not mean social change will be easy, but it is helpful to know that it is possible.

Societal Sex Role vs. Gender

Let us return now to the question of gender and its utility. Our new approach of understanding these issues through the idea of the societal sex role and the corresponding role virtues clarifies this field into easily understandable terms that we can apply to any society in order to understand it better. Now, someone might object and say that by societal sex role, we mean the same thing as is meant by gender. While there are similarities, there are fundamental differences between these ideas.

---

[i] If the norms are vicious enough and our lives are in danger, then fleeing may be our only option, such as was the case in socialist East Germany or in communist China under Mao. If history has taught us anything, it is that collectivism is one of the greatest threats to human life that humankind has ever known (see, for example, Hannah Arendt's *The Origins of Totalitarianism*).

As a concept, the societal sex role brings much needed clarity over the concept of gender, especially when it is recalled that gender has the two insurmountable problems we have already identified (*i.e.*, it is a package deal and it obscures the real issue). Moreover, by clearly distinguishing the societal sex role from its corresponding virtue, our new account makes it clear that there are three distinct phenomena and it gives us a way to understand each of these.

Moreover, not only is our account much clearer, we can also explain how the societal sex roles arise, how they can change, and why they vary between cultures. This is something that gender cannot do. In the next section, we will also show how our account of the societal sex role and the clarity it brings allows us to go even deeper and explore the underlying phenomenon beneath the societal sex role and the role virtues.

3. Erousia

The greatest virtue of our new account of the societal sex roles is that it helps us to get to a deeper kernel of truth. There is something deeper here than a mere social role, even though this can cut deeply in those people who have thoroughly internalized it. There is some common element in all societal sex roles, across all cultures, some kernel of truth that "gender" was grasping for. This kernel at the core of these issues is what we will call *erousia*.[i]

Erousia

Erousia is our *experience* of our sexuality, our experience of *being sexual*. Erousia is grounded in our sexual arousal[ii] and arises when we give our sexual arousal conscious focus.[iii] When we are sexually aroused, we can feel our bodies come alive with excitement, our every nerve taut with expectation, our mind racing with erotic possibilities. This is not simply a feeling of our body coming alive—*we* come alive. And we can feel the very life flow through us due to being sexually charged. This robust feeling of being alive, of being sexually aroused, allows us to experience the unity of our being. Moreover, erousia itself underlies the societal sex roles and through them we can see the reality that the societal sex roles were attempting to identify. In order to see all of this, let us start by looking more closely at the nature of erousia.

Erousia is not simply being sexually aroused. It requires us to be self-

---

[i] The neologism *erousia* is a combination of the Greek *eros* (passionate sexual love) and *ousia* (being) and thus means the state of being erotic. (I credit Tom Jones for helping me to come up with the word.)

[ii] Sexual arousal is itself a sentiment. We will explore sexual arousal more in Chapter 7.

[iii] This need not be the kind of sexual arousal felt because sex is immanent; it could just as well be the arousal of a new love blooming and the anticipation of future sex.

reflective in the moment while we are aroused, whether we are alone or with a partner, and to be aware of our own arousal. This self-reflective step, recognizing ourself as aroused and our bodies as alive, allows us to experience erousia. However, it should not be taken to mean that we should forget about the sexual activity in which we might be engaging and passively contemplate our arousal. Rather, it merely means that in order to experience erousia we must turn at least some of our attention to ourself and be aware of our own arousal. Without the self-reflective step, we will be focused on the object of our arousal and miss the experience of erousia.

While erousia requires that we be self-reflective in order to experience it, sometimes we can best see ourselves through the eyes of our lover. This can happen whether we have a new lover or through the rich intimacy of erotic love. Even with a new partner, we can learn quite a bit about ourselves in a sexual situation. Nagel, in "Sexual Perversion,"[i] elaborates this well: "Sexual desire involves a kind of perception, but not merely a single perception of its object, for in the paradigm case of mutual desire there is a complex system of superimposed mutual perceptions—not only perceptions of the sexual object, but perceptions of oneself."[93] Through the eyes of the other person, we gain perspective on ourselves, including through seeing our own reactions to them. This allows a person to become "conscious of his sexuality through his awareness of its effect on her and of her awareness that this effect is due to him."[94] Thus, through the eyes of even a new lover, we can gain quite a bit of self-awareness.

In the case of established erotic love, this goes much deeper, as not only do we have this self-awareness through the eyes of our partner, but we also have the deep intimacy of erotic love and a shared identity. Much as we saw in Chapter 3, where our lover helped us to see our values and beliefs, our lover helps us to see our sexuality. Through our lover, we can more deeply see our sexuality through our response to her, through the interaction between us, through our desires, and through our actions. We can see whether we are open and unreserved with our lover or whether we turn away and hide part of ourselves. We can see whether we explore our desires together or whether we are ashamed of our desires. We can see whether our desires are life-affirming or perverse, through our partner's response and its effects on our lives. Through our lover, we can more clearly see the nature of our erotic being, our erousia, because it will either be integrated and open or divided and guarded. Moreover, through this we also gain psychological visibility by being seen by our lover as desirable and causing desire in her as well.

Erousia is the experience of our sexual being and now we see how we come to have this experience: by giving conscious focus to our sexual arousal, which can be done alone or aided by a partner. There is, however, much more

---

[i] Our account of perversion (Chapter 9) will differ significantly from Nagel's.

to say about erousia. Through erousia, we can come to experience either the unity of our soul or its division and, either way, it allows us to experience the deep unity of our minds and bodies. Yet, before we can see this, we must turn our attention to two other matters to give us more insight into erousia: the erotic framework and the origins of erousia.

The Erotic Framework

We said in the last section that people internalize beliefs about the societal sex roles from the zeitgeist and those around them as they are growing up. We must now delve into this more in depth.

People's values and beliefs around sexuality comprise their *erotic framework*; that is, the erotic framework is the set of specifically sexual values and beliefs that underlies what we will find sexually arousing, sexually permissible, our sexual ideals, *etc.*[i] The erotic framework explains why we are aroused by some things and not others. Our erotic framework is much like the evaluative framework we explored in Chapter 2 when we were first attempting to understand the sentiments. It is filled with our values related to sexuality, our beliefs around sexuality, our judgements of sexuality, our experiences with sexuality and how we have conceptualized these, ideas we have accepted from the zeitgeist or from others, and so on.

We are not quite born a blank slate with respect to our erotic framework, because we are born with biological dispositions towards sexuality and some of us with strong dispositions to one sex or the other. We begin to fill out our erotic framework long before puberty; for example, a young child who discovers her clitoris and the pleasure it brings her may be stopped by her parents and even shamed about her behavior. Or another child who likes to be naked may be punished for this. These children will both internalize some message from these events, such as that self-pleasure is wrong or that nudity is shameful.[ii] It is interesting that the child who finds her clitoris does not know this is sexual, until the adults react to it and show her that it is somehow special through their actions. Children know only that genital stimulation feels good and no more. They do not know that it is sexual unless they are told. Even when they engage in age-appropriate sex-play, this is normal and healthy and an important step in learning about sexuality (we will return to the issue of children and sexuality in Volume 2, Chapter 13).

Our first exposure to the world of sex, even with only the idea of it, or our first experiences with sexuality, commences our erotic framework and

---

[i] This may be similar to John Money's "lovemaps," but I will leave it for someone better versed with Money's theory to make the comparison.

[ii] Even the mere act of hiding something that we like can make us feel ashamed, because we feel that these things must be bad if they must be hidden. Minimally, this will cause us to feel conflicted about the values in question.

starts us on the natural path to sexuality. This, obviously, varies quite a bit from person to person. Our erotic framework grows with us and our experiences, particularly how we conceptualize these. That is, our experiences do not directly come into our erotic framework; rather, what affects our erotic framework is how we conceptualize these experiences. For example, a woman who has an early partner who criticizes her for being too enthusiastic about sex can be shamed by this, take it as a mark of distinction, or something else. Her choices in the matter will determine how she conceptualizes this experience and how it impacts her erotic framework—and clearly those choices will have very different impacts.

Some of the most important experiences for shaping our erotic framework will be early ones, which then set the stage for how we engage in sexuality later. This may be our first experiences with masturbation or our first attempts at sex-play with a sibling, cousin, or friend.[i] The way we conceptualize these early sexual experiences will have a big impact on our erotic framework. Yet, it is not only our direct experiences that have an impact; we can also come to populate our erotic framework through fiction. For example, we might see a person tied up and struggling and find this particularly fascinating and exciting, but not yet know why. We start to create the erotic framework by "what works for us" (*i.e.*, what we find sexually arousing or exciting) and these things get reinforced as we do them and enjoy them. At the same time, our erotic framework is also populated by things we tried, but did not enjoy (similar to antivalues).

Our erotic framework also includes such things as whether we are attracted to certain types of people, things we might want in our potential partners, how we like to masturbate, what we fantasize about, which sex acts we enjoy and how we enjoy them, *etc*. It covers the range of sexuality, or, rather, it covers the range of sexuality that we have experienced or know something about, even if this information is mistaken (*e.g.*, men who "know" they would hate prostate play, until they try it). It includes our preconceptions and false beliefs. It includes the whole scope of our sexuality.

Our erotic framework does not exist in a vacuum: it will be influenced by our broader conceptions of ourself, our identity, and our sentiments, most

---

[i] Getting data on how common sex-play is among children is challenging for many reasons. Among them is the strong taboo against it, which makes people reluctant to admit that they have engaged in such behavior. There is also a failure among some researchers to differentiate consensual sex-play from non-consensual abuse or molestation. One study found that 10% of males and 15% of females had engaged in sex-play with siblings, but that 25% of this was nonconsensual (Finkelhor, D. "Sex among siblings: A survey on prevalence, variety, and effects." *Arch Sex Behav* (1980) 9:171. https://doi.org/10.1007/BF01542244) Of course, sometimes a person's first experiences will be abusive and involve molestation, including by a parent or care-giver. Our first experiences of sexuality are not always positive, but we need not be powerless in how we deal with these and they need not turn us away from sexuality forever.

particularly our existential orientation. Thus, things that are not sexual in nature can still have an impact on our erotic framework. For example, a person who is ridiculed and powerless to do anything about it in their non-sexual life may seek mastery over this shame through sex later in life, perhaps through BDSM and eroticized humiliation. Our erotic framework is a rich tapestry of our conceptualized experiences, thoughts, beliefs, values, and so on.

Even more broadly, our erotic framework is situated culturally and shaped by the beliefs we have internalized from the particular culture that we grew up in and in which we sexually developed, as we have already discussed with the societal sex roles. But, beyond these messages about the proper role of each sex, there are many messages in the zeitgeist about how we should think of sexuality, how we should act sexually, and even the proper ways to feel sexually. In this way, societies have a structuring effect on sexuality and this leads to social norming of sexual behavior and even influences our sexual self-understanding through its impact on our erotic framework. This affects which kinds of sex acts we might find desirable and even the kinds of emphasis that we will put on the secondary sexual characteristics (*e.g.*, Are breasts or buttocks to be accentuated? Should men or women have long hair? *etc.*). This even leads to limits on which sexual activities are socially acceptable and gives rise to taboos, such as those against anal sex or fisting.

Erousia is situated culturally because we internalize the beliefs of our culture (through the zeitgeist and other people) and this will have a structuring effect on our erousia through our erotic framework.[i] The social sexual mores that we internalize (whether we accept these or rebel against them) become part of our erousia.[ii] For example, if the culture into which a woman is born emphasizes a hairless body and she accepts this as a proper sexual characteristic, then she will feel more erotic when her body is hairless and less erotic when her body is hairy. If, of course, she accepts and internalizes this message.

While the particular society and its norms will affect a person who grows up in it, they will not necessarily internalize all of its norms. Moreover, sometimes a person will internalize a norm and choose to rebel against the norm instead of following it. One way to rebel against this that we have not yet discussed is through the transgression of these norms: some people find that transgressing the norms is one of the most sexually exciting things they can do. This is often called being "naughty" or doing something "dirty," but it really is just violating a social norm. Those who rebel against the norms in this way

---

[i] A question could be raised about why so many people care about structuring and controlling sexuality so much that whole societies take on these features through collective action. A full account of this is beyond the scope of our project here, but I think that the answer lies in the importance of sexuality and its power in a person's life. If their sexuality can be controlled, so too can they (*e.g.*, the story arc of Hank Rearden in *Atlas Shrugged*). This ties in with the sad fact that all too many people are derivative and want to control others. This creates a toxic combination.

[ii] The only way a societal sexual more will not affect our erousia is if we do not internalize it.

eroticize their transgression. We shall return to this in Volume 2, Chapter 15.

The erotic framework is also dynamic and can change throughout our lives. It is most malleable when we are young and for some may only change with extreme circumstances later in life. Our erotic framework grows and develops as we do: it grows out of our experiences and beliefs and it grows out of our developing desires and our responses to them. For this reason, it can vary quite a bit in different stages of our lives. At the same time, we can also cultivate the erotic framework by being mindful of what is in it, how we conceptualize new experiences, and working to correct things in the erotic framework that we do not want (although this may take professional psychological help to change).

Erousia and the Societal Sex Roles

Like sexual orientation, our erousia is not independent of the broader social environment in which our sexuality awakens and learns about itself. We have already briefly discussed how cultures have a structuring role on our erousia through their impact on our erotic framework. Now, let us turn to how they structure an individual's erousia, their experience of their own being erotic, into something formal and less connected to individual experience. Or, how societies take erousia and out of it they create the societal sex roles.

An individual's experience of himself as male and of his male erotic being is the kernel upon which masculinity is built.[i] Likewise, a woman's experience of herself as female and of her female erotic being is the kernel upon which femininity is built. For example, one of the principal ways that a man might experience his erousia is through his penis and erection. When he starts to become aroused, he might feel an overall sense of excitement throughout his body, an enlivening of his whole self. He might particularly feel this in his penis when it becomes hard and erect: his penis becomes the focus of his erousia and he might conceptualize his desire as a desire to penetrate, to use his penis to express his erotic being. Of course, the experience of erousia will vary from person to person, depending on how they conceptualize their erotic being. One woman might focus her erousia on her clitoris, while another may focus on the vagina. These individual experiences of erousia will become the foundation for the societal sex roles and their corresponding role virtues.

On these simple experiences of erousia, societies build the grand structures of the societal sex roles, populated by the society's mythology, its suppositions about sexuality, and beliefs about the nature of each sex and how they should behave. Societies, thus, attempt to structure erousia into its ideals;

---

[i] Recall that the male sex has the societal sex role "man" and its corresponding role virtue "masculinity" while the female sex has the societal sex role "woman" and its corresponding role virtue "femininity." We are using the role virtues here because they are the ultimate goal of the structuring and norming process.

for example, it takes an individual female's experience of erousia and attempts to turn it into femininity.[i] Societies do this in all the ways we have explained, such as through its impact on the erotic framework, shamenorming, *etc.* Each imposition on erousia takes us farther away from the reality of our experience towards the convention to which we are expected to conform.[ii]

Of course, erousia is a much broader experience than the societal sex role and the societal sex role is only one way that societies try to structure erousia. There is more in the zeitgeist than simply how each sex should behave. There is a robust (albeit piecemeal) sexual ethic, regarding such things as which sexual actions are permissible, how people should engage with each other, the conditions to be met before sexual activity is permissible, *etc.* Societies try to get individuals to conform to the societal sex roles and accept the other sexual mores as well, reducing the scope of erousia to socially approved boundaries. Thus, erousia can become weighed down with a society's ideals until it largely loses its individual nature. Yet, even with all this, our erousia is still fundamentally individual.

Since erousia is the kernel that underlies the societal sex roles (it is the real thing in which they are anchored), we can use this to understand how there can be so much variance in how people participate in the societal sex roles and even how people can participate in the societal sex roles in unexpected ways. Despite society's attempts to structure erousia, it is still fundamentally an individual experience and a product of a person's particular circumstances, choices, and beliefs. This explains how a person can still feel masculine or feminine without perfectly participating in the societal sex role: the societal sex role does not capture their erousia, the way they experience their sexuality, and so they seek to actualize their erousia in other ways. That is, they might feel like they are particularly male or female, even if they do not conform to the ideal.

This is not to say that these people are seeking to perfectly actualize the societal sex role virtue, failing, and, while aware of this, still using the title. Rather, by stipulating that people should express their erousia in certain ways, societies created the ideal of the societal sex role virtues and these are not always treated strictly in practice. That is, even if there is a firm conception of, for example, masculinity in any particular culture, this does not mean that a person who does not conform to this might not still feel masculine, because masculinity is grounded in erousia and this is individual. Thus "masculinity" and "femininity," or whatever a society called their societal sex role virtues, also became the term that people used to describe their experience of their erousia when they feel particularly of their sex.

---

[i] This agential way of speaking is merely shorthand and is not intended to actually impute agency to a collective process that arises through convention.

[ii] This is not some dubious "state of nature" account; rather, many people have experiences of their own sexuality that are not yet fully structured because the full force of the societal sex messages is often withheld from children and even adolescents.

Because society has stipulated that people should express their erousia through the societal sex role virtues, they do, even if they do not perfectly conform to the conventional role. Perhaps they take parts of the role virtues while rejecting others, or perhaps they rebel and create their own identity in opposition to the role virtues, or perhaps they develop their own erousia without regard to the role virtues. No matter the tack they take, since they understand masculinity and femininity as being an expression of erousia, they still feel masculine or feminine. This allows us to understand how a gay man can experience femininity: because he takes on part of the feminine role virtue as part of the structure of his erousia and experiences his erousia this way. Or how a lesbian can experience masculinity: because she takes on part of the masculine role virtue as part of the structure of her erousia and experiences her erousia this way. Or how a transsexual[i] person can experience masculinity or femininity, even if their body does not match.

Our account of erousia as underlying the societal sex roles and their corresponding role virtues also allows us to explain how these could be different in different societies and how there could be more than two of these. In fact, since there are at least three physical sexes (male, intersex, and female), there should be at least three societal sex roles with their corresponding role virtues, in order for the theoretical constructs to match up with reality.[ii] This is why we had to delve into erousia, because it is the foundation of the societal sex roles and their role virtues. Without understanding erousia, we would have been unable to really understand the societal sex roles at all. Erousia is what we are left with when we strip away all of the particularizing cultural constructs.

Our idea of erousia can help us to understand not only our own experience of being erotic, but it helps us to understand how this is situated in, and influenced by, our culture, past, and beliefs. This is one of the ideas that has been missing in historic inquiries into sexuality: a way of understanding our core way of being erotic that integrates everything about us as well as the world around us. Erousia is the real thing underlying a lot of the arbitrary stuff we have conventionally imposed through the societal sex role and the role virtues.

---

[i] One might wonder why the term "transgender" is not being employed. It should be obvious, given that we have already repudiated the idea of "gender," that we will no longer employ a term that relies on it. Moreover, on our account, people can participate in the societal sex roles in different ways, obviating the need for "transgender."

[ii] Transsexual people should also be accounted for, whether they are incorporated into one of the established societal sex roles or whether a new one is created for them. For my own part, I do not have a strong position on the issue of transsexualism, since I do not think the science on the subject is yet conclusive. However, I think the science starting to get there and there are some good works on the subject like Simon LeVay's *Gay Straight and the Reason Why: The Science of Sexual Orientation*. I can say, however, that regardless of how the science turns out, transsexuals are certainly still people and should maintain the same rights as anyone else and be free to pursue their own happiness.

The Experience of Erousia

Now that we better understand the origins of erousia, its underlying foundations in the erotic framework, and its grounding of the societal sex roles and the role virtues, it is time to round out our account of erousia by exploring the actual experience of erousia. There is a real sense in which the precise way a person experiences erousia is irrelevant: it is the *experience* of ourselves as an erotic being, not what particular experiences bring this about, that constitutes erousia.[i]

We experience erousia self-reflectively through our sexual arousal. It is the experience of our sexuality: the feeling of blood pumping through our veins, of the tumescence of our sexual organs, of our sexual desire. It is the joy of being alive and of being sexual. Feeling ourselves be aroused, feeling our bodies come alive with electric excitement, gives us the direct experience of our unity (we will return to this shortly). It is not simply feeling our *body* come alive—it is *us* coming alive.

Erousia, moreover, gives us access to further experiences, depending on our constitution. These further paths will depend on whether we are integrated in our soul or whether it stands divided.[ii] Being integrated or divided is dichotomous. A person can either be fundamentally well-integrated or not. If not, their soul is divided to at least some degree. Each of these constitutions will give us a different experience of our soul and, through this, of our total self. In order to see how this works, let us look at each in turn and the further experiences to which they lead.

We must start by being clear about what we mean by an "integrated soul." We said in Chapter 1 that: "The virtue of *integrity* is the commitment to achieve and maintain our unity of self. We do this in two ways: the commitment to the careful cultivation of our values and beliefs and the commitment to live by our values and work to actualize them." When we carefully cultivate our values and beliefs (specifically those in our evaluative framework) and live according to our values and work to actualize them, then we are fundamentally integrated, because our soul will be in harmony with itself and we will work to remove any discordance.[iii] Integrity of soul is not about having zero discordant values or

---

[i] The way we experience erousia can even change throughout our lives, especially as we learn more about who we are and authentically engage with the world. It might also need to change if our bodies change; for example, people with sexual difficulties or injuries are not barred from participating in erousia, but they may need to reconceptualize what this means for them: they may need to change the form of their erousia.

[ii] Recall that by "soul" we mean that part of us that is conscious, makes choices, feels, is self-reflective, *etc.*, the part of us that has our mental faculties and the richness of our inner experiences. We do not mean anything magical or mystical, such as some sort of separable and eternal substance, like Plato or the Christians mean.

[iii] It is specifically our moral beliefs, because these determine what we will choose to do, all other things being equal, and how we live. It is not as though we need to have no contradictions in

beliefs, but about the careful cultivation of our values and beliefs and the principled approach to these that does not allow the introduction of discordant values and beliefs and works to remove them when identified. This does not mean that a person must magically be able to instantly remove discordant values and beliefs, but that they will work to do so and work to not accept other discordant values and beliefs. This is what it means to be fundamentally integrated.

Our values are particularly in play in the sexual realm, in all of the ways we have already described, such as through sexual attraction, our sentiments, *etc.* Moreover, our values also come into play through erousia because erousia is based in our sexual arousal and sexual arousal has its foundations in our erotic framework.[i] Sexual arousal is both based in this framework and brings it to bear during arousal. When we are aroused by people who conform to our values, we have a sentimental response and feel good about this: we *feel* that it is right.[ii] When we act against our values, we also have a sentimental response and feel bad about this: we feel shame, guilt, or even disgust. When we act with our values, when we act with integrity, we can also *experience* the unity of our soul through this; that is, having an integrated soul lets us experience the unity of our soul. Erousia is one of the strongest ways that we are able to experience this. When we experience our soul being unified and at peace with itself, we experience our sexual arousal with joy and without any shame or guilt. Without an integrated soul, we will be cut off from this. This is just one more example that the moral is the practical.

Through erousia we can also *experience* our unity of self: the experience of our self as a unified being, both somatically and psychologically.[iii] That is, erousia leads us to the *experience* of the deep unity of mind and body through sexuality. The *experience* of unity of soul is both a precondition and constitutive part of this. When we are well integrated and our sexual arousal is aligned with our values, so that we do not feel shame or guilt about our desires, then we can directly experience the full unity of our self: we are able to *feel* our deep unity. The experience of being sexual (erousia), for those who are well integrated, *is* an experience of mind/body unity.

---

any of our knowledge. Although any belief is potentially morally relevant if it links up with otherwise moral beliefs in the right way (*i.e.*, if it suddenly has action implication for how we should live our lives), it is the beliefs that are in our evaluative framework that will be most impactful on our action. At the same time, our epistemic methods of acquiring and validating knowledge are also important (*e.g.*, reason or faith).

[i] Leaving aside simple physical arousal which neither involves values nor activates the body in the same way: a simple erection or lubrication does not engage the whole body, but just that particular organ.

[ii] Technically, this is a "second-order" sentimental response as it is a response to another sentiment.

[iii] Erousia is not the only avenue to experience unity of soul and unity of self, but it is a particularly poignant way.

When we have this experience of our unity of self, we do not think about our values or swollen sexual organs; instead, we are able to feel the oneness of ourselves. For the well-integrated person, erousia is the joy of being uniquely, and wholly, us: it is about savoring the experience of being ourselves.

Let us now contrast this with a person who has a divided soul, which will help us to more deeply understand this.

The alternative to unity of soul is a divided soul. A divided soul is one where a person has conflicting values and beliefs. This, of course, admits of degrees. There are two major kinds of division of soul: *internal discord* and *auto-enmity* (see Chapter 1). One of the greatest factors in whether a person is integrated or divided is their epistemic method (*e.g.*, reason or faith) of acquiring and cultivating their values and beliefs because values and beliefs do not come out of nowhere and it matters quite a bit how we acquire them and which ones we keep and which we reject.

Principled adherence to reason will lead us to be fundamentally integrated, even if we sometimes make mistakes, as it also provides us a method of testing and correcting our beliefs. Any other method (faith, intuition, mysticism, uncritical acceptance, *etc.*) will lead us to be divided, because we will be split between the framework we have chosen and the need to reason: we must reason to at least some degree because we must interact with reality to stay alive. Whenever anyone holds conflicting epistemic methods, it causes schisms of the soul: for example, the scientist who wants to use reason to engage with the world for his work and who also wants to use faith to justify his god has a division at the deepest level of his soul. He must carefully compartmentalize these parts of himself or else he would have to see his great hypocrisy and this contradiction would be debilitating until it was resolved. This compartmentalization is a fracture in a person's soul.

When we have discordant values and beliefs, our soul is pulled in different directions by them: the more divergent the values and beliefs, the greater the pull until the soul is pulled asunder and wars with itself. To use less poetic language, this means we will feel conflicted in our choices, our desires, and our sentiments. It will feel like one part of us wants to go one way and a different part wants to go another. The more we move away from reason as our method of gaining and validating our values and beliefs, the more discord we will have. Those who have some discordance in their values and beliefs will experience *internal discord*; that is, they will experience conflicts between their values and beliefs and will experience themselves being pulled in different directions. Those who have torn their soul asunder will experience *auto-enmity*; that is, they will experience deep conflicts in their soul and feel as though there are different parts of their soul that are fighting each other.

While it is true that many people have conflicts in their erotic frameworks, so that they experience mixed feelings about their sexual arousal or sexuality, for the person of reason this is resolvable because they have a method of adjudicating such things and a standard against which to judge their beliefs so that they can be culled if they do not help their life (this is simply stated, but by no means easy to do). For those people who have divided souls, they have no recourse against this and must suffer this division.

That erousia lets us experience the state of our soul and of our entire self is not necessarily a boon. While for people who are well-integrated, it is a wonderful gift, but for those whose souls are divided against themselves, this is a curse. It shows them clearly their split nature and the utter mess they have made of their soul. This is why some people recoil from sex or try to make it just about the body: they do not want to see the chaos that is their own soul.

When a person has a divided soul, he experiences his body or parts of his mind doing things that the part with which he identifies does not want; that is, he experiences desires that he does not want or is aroused by things that he wishes he were not. He will feel conflicts in his desires, doubt about his actions, guilt or shame for his sexual arousal, and feel torn in different directions. Such a person will feel out of control, because he has given up control. A person is only in control to the extent that they are integrated and acting in accordance with reason and out of control to the extent to which they are not. The divided person has given up control of his soul and his self.[i]

Now that we understand erousia, we can see how important this concept is and why its absence has held back our understanding of sexuality. Moreover, since erousia underlies the societal sex roles, we were unable to fully understand these without reference to it. It is worth pointing out that the range of behaviors in the societal sex norms, including the societal sex roles and their role virtue, may be incompatible with our authentic selves. For each of these things, we have to ask ourselves whether, if we participated in that convention, it would cause us to live better or worse. This eudaimonistic standard will help us to see which conventions to embrace and which to eschew. It behooves us, if we want to live well, to work to understand our own erousia and try to identify any contradictions in our values and beliefs that will lead us to be divided in our soul and in our desires. Understanding our erousia will lead us to live better lives as well as have better sex lives.

4. Sexual Identity

Now that we have explored sexual orientation, the societal sex roles, erousia, and the erotic framework, it is time to briefly turn to our last topic, that of sexual identity. Currently, the term "sexual identity" is used as a simple synonym for a person's sexual orientation. Yet, no one is so thinly constituted that their sexual identity can be identified by how disposed they are to engage with each sex. Thus, we need to redefine this term to make it useful again.

---

[i] Sadly, the fractured soul is the very paradigm of Freud.

Sexual identity is a rich idea that brings together everything we have been discussing. Many of us like specific features, or even types, that go beyond simply a person's physical sex: some people like brunette women, or men with strong backs, or a certain kind of smile. Moreover, most of us want more in our sexual partner than to simply have the right sexual organs. Indeed, for some of us, it is simply not enough that the other person has the right kind of body, but they must be engaging in the right kind of activities, have the right character, or be in the right outfit in order to really be sexually arousing. Since most of us have richer sexual desires than the kind of person we have sex with, using sexual orientation as a proxy to describe our sexuality is severely lacking.[i]

Thus, we will use the term *sexual identity* to capture the panoply of facts that paint the picture of who we are sexually: it is that rich confluence of things about us that creates a robust account of our *identity* as sexual beings. It is broader than our sexual orientation and includes much more of our sexuality, such as: whether we like kink, whether we are polysexual, whether we enjoy anal sex, how we experience our erousia, *etc*. Additionally, our sexual identity includes facts about our particular constitution and self-conceptions, including such facts as the societal sex roles in which we participate. Our sexual identity is more than simply *what* we do; it also includes the *why* we do it and *how* we understand ourselves in doing it. Consequently, our sexual identity is an important way in which we create, and maintain, our sexual selves. In this way, our sexual identity is an integration of our sexuality: it includes everything that makes our sexuality uniquely ours. Our sexual identity includes all these things because it is the expression of our erotic framework.

What does it mean that sexual identity is the expression of our erotic framework? It means that our sexual identity, who we are as sexual beings, is more than our orientation, more than our societal sex role, more than our erousia, *etc*. While all these things are important and connected, our sexual identity is the expression of our full erotic framework: of all the specifically sexual values and beliefs that we hold. It thus includes these things, but is not exhausted by them. Our sexual identity encompasses everything sexual about us: it is the particular form our sexuality takes.

This new understanding of sexual identity, as the expression of our erotic framework, might also mean that we have to give more than a one-word answer when asked about our sexual identity, such as: "I am a woman who is 2,1,5 and I am really into exhibitionism and fisting, but I sometimes also enjoy power-exchange." Of course, we might not want to share our full sexual identity with everyone, but it would be useful to be able to describe it to others sometimes and certainly it would be useful to be better able to formulate it for ourselves.

This latter point, that this new understanding of sexual identity will help us to better think about our own sexuality is important. Before, our "sexual

---

[i] Even with our much-improved conception of sexual orientation, there is much it does not capture (nor is it intended to).

identity" was wholly determined by our sexual orientation, but our sexuality is much richer than that: limiting it in that way cuts out much of what makes our sexuality uniquely ours as well as much of its richness and depth. It may be that our primary way of thinking about our sexuality is that we are a (2,0,4), but it might also be that we are kinky or that we are exhibitionists, *etc.*, and in limiting identity to orientation, all of this gets lost. In limiting our sexual identity to our sexual orientation, we limit the scope of our sexuality and unnecessarily restrict ourselves. And when we come to rigidly conceive of ourselves in a certain way, we *ipso facto* come to limit ourselves to the same degree. Sexuality is much too rich to have these artificial constraints thrust upon it.

Thus, we should work to develop an open mind about our sexuality: an open and compassionate look at the kinds of things we really enjoy, regardless of social pressure or the opinions of others. We should explore different possibilities and seek out information to learn about sex and all of its various expressions. We should not feel shame in our authentic desires, as long as they are not perverse and would inhibit our flourishing. Besides this, we should enthusiastically embrace our sexuality as the important part of our life that it is. And now that we have done away with the false ideas of sexual orientation and of gender, and have shed light on the nature of sexual orientation, societal sex roles, the erotic framework, and erousia, we can see our sexuality that much clearer and this will aid us in this process.

Summary and Conclusions

We can now see that we were right to call into question some of the ways that we think about sexuality and conceptualize ourselves as sexual beings. Indeed, at every turn in this chapter, we identified better ways of understanding sexuality. Through this, we gained some important insights. Let us briefly review what we learned in this chapter.

We started this chapter by analyzing the tripartite categorization system, which is currently the most common way of conceptualizing sexual orientation. We saw, partly through comparison with other cultures, that the tripartite categorization system had several insurmountable problems in that it relied on false assumptions and failed to track the way people actually engage in sex in the real world. We then saw how reconceiving sexual orientation as a disposition not only avoided the problems from before, but it more accurately tracked the reality of people's sexual experiences. Finally, we turned to see whether there were any ways of conceiving of sexuality in light of its dispositional nature and saw that both the Kinsey Scale and the Triaxial Scale were able to do this, but that the Triaxial scale was more robust and gave more information than the Kinsey Scale and so we proposed that it should be adopted.

We then turned to the idea of "gender" and saw that it too had irreconcilable problems such that we had to abandon it. We proposed to replace this with the idea of the societal sex role and saw how this better captured the reality of the phenomenon, including capturing the distinctions between a person's physical sex, the societal sex role itself, and the role virtue. We also saw how the societal sex role is conventionally determined and how this operates, including how shamenorming works and how it functions to preserve the societal sex roles.

Through our analysis of the societal sex role, we realized that there was a deeper phenomenon at play and inquired into the nature of erousia. We found that erousia is the *experience* of being sexually embodied: the experience of the self as a sexual being. We saw how erousia arises out of our erotic framework and is influenced by everything in the erotic framework, including by the culture in which a person lives. Moreover, we saw that societies try to structure a person's erousia into the societal sex roles and the potentially negative impact this can have on a person's life. We also saw how erousia lets us experience the integrity or division of our soul and even of our very self.

We lastly turned to the idea of sexual identity, which we saw was more robust than simply our sexual orientation. We saw how our sexual identity is the panoply of facts that paint the picture of who we are as sexual beings: it is that rich confluence of things about us that creates a robust account of who we are as sexual beings. We also saw that our sexual identity is very important and that we should take care in creating our sexual identity and in its maintenance.

Broadly, in this chapter we took a critical look at some of the concepts commonly used in sexual discussions, found them lacking, and introduced new concepts to pick up the philosophic slack. We also identified part of the deeper structures of sexuality through erousia and the erotic framework that helped us to better understand sexuality and its connection to our life than had previously been possible. Through all this, we gained the framework necessary to better understand our own sexualities and our sexual identities.

All of this, including the prior chapters, sets us up to conclude our inquiry in the next chapter as we tie everything together and come to clearly see sex's moral import.

Chapter 7: Sex and the Good Life

*To a rational man, sex is an expression of
self-esteem—a celebration of himself and of existence.*[95]
~ Ayn Rand

*The degree and kind of a man's sexuality reach up
into the ultimate pinnacle of his spirit.*[96]
~ Nietzsche

It should now be clear that sex is tied to the most profound and important parts of who we are as people. In this chapter, we are going to flesh out the rest of this connection and show the importance of sex for deep and lasting happiness, at least for those people who are constituted this way. Indeed, we shall see that our sexuality rises up from the very depths of who we are and propels us towards our ideals. Sexuality, properly integrated, is perhaps the greatest key to rich and lasting happiness.

To understand why this is so, we need to better understand the nature of sex itself, including the nature of sexual pleasure. Understanding sexual pleasure, and its differences from other kinds of pleasure, will help us to better understand the nature of sex. We will see how sexual pleasure is a sentiment and operates according to our beliefs and values. We will also closely examine the nature of sex and find that sex has no necessary ends in human life and so it is up to us to choose ends for it and to integrate it into our lives in healthy ways.

Through this exploration, we shall see that sex can become a great moral impetus. It can help us strive to reach the best things open to us and to become the best we can be. In this way, sex is both part of a rich and happy human life and a driving force for it. Let us turn now to see how this is so.

1. Sexual Pleasure

Someone might wonder why we are going to discuss sexual pleasure at all, since it may seem that nearly everyone agrees that sex feels good: that sexual pleasure is simply intrinsic to the act. But, of course, the story is much more complicated than this. For example, some women enjoy cunnilingus, while others do not. Some men enjoy scrotal pain, while others do not. Some people enjoy anal play, while others do not. Indeed, for any sexual act we might be able to name, we can find some people who enjoy it and some people who dislike it. Yet, how can this be if the pleasure of sex is intrinsic and just part of the act?

The solution to the paradox, of course, is that the pleasure of sexual activity is *not* intrinsic to the act. If it were, we would expect to find absolute agreement on what is pleasurable and what is not, at least among people with the same physiology. And, yet, we most certainly do not find this. Indeed, we find such a great variety in what people find sexually pleasurable that most of us have a hard time even understanding how anyone could possibly be interested in the sexual things in which we are not interested. For example, if we are not interested in erotic piercing or urethral sounding, then we may have a hard time understanding how anyone could be interested in them.[i] This lack of agreement about what is sexually pleasurable demonstrates that the pleasure of sex cannot be innate. If it is not innate, then where does it come from?

The Sentimental Nature of Sexual Pleasure

We can start to understand the nature of sexual pleasure by comparison to hunger and our appetites for food. While we all experience hunger, the range of things we think of as being good options to satisfy our hunger is given to us at least partly by our culture (*i.e.*, people in India tend to eat Indian food, while people in Japan tend to eat Japanese food). Even so, the particular things we want to satisfy our desires will vary: sometimes we will want to satisfy our hunger with a pizza and other times we will want it satisfied with tacos. And, indeed, we find that people in Japan often eat food that's not traditional Japanese food. While each culture has their own traditional foods and some people follow this exactly, others like to experiment with different foods. At the same time, some people like to cook from recipes and others do it by taste as they go. Moreover, some people could eat the same thing every day for years and be perfectly satisfied, while others want more variety in their meals. Some people eat nutritious meals that help them sustain their lives and some people harm themselves with their diets. Indeed, some people even eat things that are not actually food.[ii] Sex is similar.

---

[i] We will explore different kinks in Volume 2, Chapter 15.
[ii] This can be something as innocuous as swallowing chewing gum to the psychological disorder

The pleasure we get from eating or sex follows from our ideas about what is good and bad for us and about what things we should, and should not, seek as ends. If we think that fat is bad for us and that we should not eat it, it will not taste good. It is important to recall that it is not simply any ideas that we hold that deeply affect us, but those that we have internalized and made part of ourselves. Let us consider an example and three different responses. Let us say that a person tells us that sugar is bad for us and dangerous for our health. In the first case, if we do not believe them, then this will have no impact on our actions or desires. In the second case, if the person convinces us and we come to believe them, then we will avoid sugar, even if it might still taste good and sweet. In the third case, let us say that we remain convinced, but that we have had time to learn more and deeply internalize that sugar is dangerous for us, then it will no longer taste good. This is not to say that it might not taste sweet, but we will not perceive it as tasting good and we will not feel pleasure from it. Consider that a car's anti-freeze tastes sweet because of ethylene glycol. However, since we know that ethylene glycol is a deadly poison, even though it may taste sweet to us, it would not taste *good*, nor will we have pleasure from it. Indeed, we should be gravely concerned if we realize we had imbibed some antifreeze! Consider the parallels to rape: the same physical actions are happening as in consensual sex, yet even though the sensations might be counterfactually pleasurable (if it were consensual), because it is not consensual, the sensations are not pleasurable (unless there are other complex psychological phenomena at play). Our values and beliefs make all the difference.

Now, let us make the explicit claim that sexual pleasure is a sentiment and operates via the sentimental process: that is, our beliefs and values determine whether we will experience something as pleasurable, in exactly the same way that they determine our emotional responses and our sexual attractions (see Chapter 2). Sexual pleasure arises, not from the act itself, but as a response to a sexual act or situation based on our values and beliefs, specifically those in our erotic framework.

To see the explanatory power of our sentimental account of sexual pleasure, let us take a rather complex case like nonconsensual sexual activity. Imagine, for example, that it is dark and we wake up to someone stimulating our genitals. How does this feel? Is it pleasurable? Is it scary? To answer that, we might reasonably ask whether we know the person and whether we have consented to this. But, if pleasure was innate, why would this matter? If pleasure were innate, then the only relevant question would be whether the person was stimulating us *skillfully*. Yet, obviously, information about the situation matters quite a bit: it makes all the difference in the world whether it is our beloved partner or someone who has just broken into our home. If it is our partner stimulating us and they know that we would welcome this kind of

---

of pica, where people might eat hair, paper, glass, nails, or other objects.

thing, then it is going to be pleasurable. On the other hand, if it is a stranger sexually assaulting us, then this will not be pleasurable. Or, if we at first believe it is our partner, but then find out, upon fully waking up, that it is not, the pleasure will turn to horror (and *vice versa*). The exact same actions can feel radically different and we can easily explain why with our sentimental account of sexual pleasure.

In contrast, those who hold other views of sexual pleasure, such as the innate view, would struggle with this case and struggle more generally with cases of nonconsensual sexual activity and rape. For example, one of the more facile versions of the "pleasure is innate" view holds that if a woman feels any pleasure during nonconsensual sexual activity, such as rape, then it is not "really" rape: even if, on the whole, the experience was painful, scary, and humiliating. They are moved to this paradoxical position because they cannot reconcile their belief that pleasure is innate to sexual activity and that it can arise from something bad. Alternatively, they might be forced to commit to the paradoxical position that even though the person who is being raped does not experience pleasure, the activity *must have been* pleasurable if a woman lubricated or orgasmed.[i] This is absurd, but unfortunately all too common. While it is true that many women lubricate during nonconsensual sex, that is her body's way of protecting itself against physical trauma. Moreover, while some small percentage of women do report that they orgasm from nonconsensual sex, this can be a purely physiological response.[ii] Indeed, someone could electrocute a man's prostate and induce ejaculation (as we do with some farm animals), but this would not feel good if it were done against his will. Of course, if he desired it, then it might feel good—and even this is easily explained by our account.

Our sentimental account of sexual pleasure can even explain the very real, but often undiscussed, issue of how it is possible for a person to experience real pleasure from nonconsensual sexual activity: our sentimental responses can be to any of our beliefs and values and people can hold conflicting values and beliefs. They can also hold beliefs such as "sexual pleasure is a physical response" that can have very unexpected and undesired outcomes such as the possibility of feeling sexual pleasure from nonconsensual sexual activity. People can even hold very complex psychological beliefs like an internalized self-hatred that leads to a pleasure response from harm (*e.g.*, one of their beliefs may be "I hate myself, therefore anything bad that happens to me is actually good" or "I deserve this"). The beliefs and values to which pleasure are a response

---

[i] This is not to minimize male rape, but merely to acknowledge that rape of women is much more common. Rape is a vicious crime, no matter on whom it is perpetrated.

[ii] The orgasmic response is not always linked to pleasure and is outside our control. In the case of rape, the orgasm can be a response to the *physiological* arousal of adrenaline, stress, and fear. Sadly, many rape victims feel shame about their physiological responses, not knowing that they evolved as defense mechanisms, and instead think that they indicate that they "really wanted it." This is not the case. Since this is not talked about, they also feel isolated in their experience and betrayed by their bodies.

need not be simple and with more complex subjects, such as sexuality, it is more likely that there will be many beliefs and values at work and that they will be complex.[i]

The fact that people can hold conflicting beliefs and values is the reason they can experience discordant sentimental responses. This includes both people who experience pleasure in things they think are immoral as well as people who fail to experience pleasure in things that they think are moral. A good example of the former case is the man who is in a relationship with a masochist and experiences sexual pleasure from causing her pain, but believes that this is immoral. In this case, the man's conflict may be between the belief that it is not moral to cause others pain and the belief that it is good to enjoy his partner's pleasure. A good example of the latter case is the woman who leaves religion and now believes that masturbation is moral, but still does not experience pleasure from it. In this case, this woman likely still has deeply internalized beliefs that masturbation is immoral, and so even though her conscious assessment of it has changed, her sentiments have not caught up to her change in beliefs: they are still responding to her subconscious internalized beliefs. In both cases, the apparent contradiction is easily resolved by simply pointing out the conflicting beliefs and values.

The foregoing shows the robustness of our sentimental account of sexual pleasure: it can account for *all* cases, even the very hard ones we have just discussed. This is in marked contrast to other accounts that struggle to explain these cases or even simpler cases. Our beliefs, choices, and the person we have made ourselves into, our chosen self, affect us all the way down to our core. Now, of course, we do not mean our sense faculties themselves are affected: our senses tell us what is happening in the world, but our *response* to these things will depend on facts about us, like our particular beliefs and values.[ii]

Sensual Pleasure

Let us now, for the sake of clarity, draw a distinction between *sexual pleasure* on the one hand and *sensual pleasure* on the other. The difference we want to capture is between general bodily pleasure and pleasure that is specifically sexual. For example, the feeling of a cool breeze on a warm day can

---

[i] While this subject is important and interesting, it is beyond our present purposes. It is important to point out that no amount of explanation can fully capture the terror of sexual assault and the harm it can do, nor can it explain away sexual crimes. Victims of sexual crimes should be treated with sympathy and compassion. Yet, they should also want to overcome these experiences, which may require the professional psychological help.

[ii] On the other hand, I think that we often add a psychological overlay, such as our desires and fears, to our experiences so that we do not always have unfettered access to reality. Such direct access is possible if we work to recognize the distinction between our perceptions themselves and this overlay. See "On Surreality" (Volume 3, Chapter 21) for further discussion of this point.

be a sensual pleasure, a pleasure related to one of our senses. It is not, however, a sexual pleasure. On the other hand, the pleasure of our lover adroitly massaging our genitals is a sexual pleasure, since it is related to sexuality and our sex organs. Let us spell out this distinction more clearly.

Sensual pleasures, as their names suggests, are those pleasures related to our senses. This includes things such as the feeling of cool water when we are hot and thirsty, the smell of orange blossoms in the spring, or the sound of a babbling brook. Indeed, our bodies have many innate desires like hunger to help keep us alive. The satisfaction of these is naturally pleasant and it is for this reason that many of the sensual pleasures are common among different people and different cultures. For example, the warmth of a fire when we are cold is pleasant. At the same time, however, we must learn how to correctly satisfy our innate desires: a crying infant knows that he needs *something*, but does not yet know what hunger is or how to satisfy it.

The satisfaction of desire is naturally pleasant, but this is not the whole story: we must identify the desire, learn how to satisfy it, discover *good* ways to satisfy it, and then actually satisfy it.[i] It is here that our values and beliefs come into play. If we are lost in the woods while hiking and stumble across the corpse of a squirrel and eat its partially rotting flesh, our hunger may be satiated (and perhaps we will even survive this), but certainly no one believes that we will thereby feel pleasure in this meal. We *know* that eating rotting squirrel meat is not a good way to satisfy hunger because it can make us sick and kill us. Thus, if we value our life, then we will not feel pleasure about satiating our hunger in this way. Of course, we may feel pleasure that we will thereby survive, but this is different than pleasure at satisfying our hunger with rotten meat. Or, to take another example, we said earlier that the warmth of a fire when we are cold is naturally pleasant; yet, no matter how cold we are, the warmth of a funeral pyre for our children is not pleasant. While the pleasure from the satisfaction of a desire is innate, our sentimental response can *override* innate pleasures or pains, which explains why the warmth of the funeral pyre is not pleasant.[ii]

---

[i] This can be more complex than it sounds. Consider that I might have a desire to be more intimate with my partner while we are in a public setting. Once I correctly identify my desire (if I am not introspective, then I may not know what I am experiencing), then I can go about trying to find ways to satisfy it. Of course, given the context of being in public, there are many ways that would not be socially appropriate to satisfy it. I might, then, decide that holding hands would be a good way to meet my desire. Of course, I will have beliefs about how best to do this: the shape of my hand, whose hand should be on top, whether my hand should be dry, *etc*. Thus, I might even correctly identify the desire, correctly identify what to do about it, correctly identify good ways to achieve it, and actually achieve it, but still not feel pleasure because my hands were sweaty and I find that embarrassing.

[ii] We must also draw a distinction between two different kinds of sensual pleasure. The first we will call desire-based sensual pleasure and these are when we desire some sensual pleasure, such as water to quench our thirst or shade and a cool breeze to relieve us from the hot sun. The second we will call unexpected sensual pleasure, which are sensual pleasures that we experience without antecedent desire for them or seeking them out, such as when we

It should now be clear that what makes sexual pleasure so different from sensual pleasure is that sexual pleasure is dependent on our values and beliefs and has no innate forms, unlike sensual pleasure.[i] Sexual pleasure is a sentiment and all expressions of it will depend on our values and beliefs. This is why there could be no such thing as "innate" sexual pleasure, since there is no such thing as sexual pleasure apart from our beliefs and values.

Of course, there are connections between sensual pleasures and sexual pleasures. A sensual pleasure might become a sexual pleasure as when, for example, a massage between friends takes a surprising turn. Moreover, sometimes the same action could be a sensual pleasure in one context and a sexual pleasure in another: for example, a man holding the hand of his young son might be experiencing (among other things) a sensual pleasure, while holding the hand of his wife might be a sexual pleasure if it portends delights to come. Even though they are both instances of "hand-holding," they are experienced very differently. This is why our beliefs and values make such a difference. Moreover, even holding his wife's hand can be either a sensual pleasure or a sexual pleasure depending on the context: it is not as though every time a couple hold hands they have sex. Sometimes they simply enjoy the sensual pleasure of holding each other's hands.

Sexual Pleasure and Sexual Arousal

It is important to be clear, though, that while we have been discussing sexual pleasure as a sentiment and focusing on its connections to values and beliefs, we have done this because this is the element that has historically been misunderstood. It was not meant to imply that this is all there is to sexual pleasure: indeed, sexual pleasure always involves the body and the senses. Sentiments impact the body and are impacted by it; for example, we are not prone to excitement when we are tired or as easily annoyed when we are well-rested. Moreover, sexual pleasure (a sentiment) requires sexual arousal (a bodily

---

unexpectedly smell sweet flowers or the cool breeze finds us when we were not yet aware that we were hot. Since there are two different kinds of sensual pleasures, there are two ways that our values and beliefs impact sensual pleasures. In the case of desire-based sensual pleasures, values and beliefs can come into play in either the identification of the desire's satisfaction or as an override. In cases of unexpected sensual pleasure, values and beliefs only come into play as an override.

[i] A careful reader will notice a possible flaw with this argument: infants and children do seem to be capable of experiencing innate sexual pleasure without having developed an erotic framework. Indeed, fetuses are even sometimes observed stimulating their genitals *in utero* and we can be pretty confident that at least they do not have any values and beliefs. However, these cases are easily explained in that they are experiencing sensual pleasure from their genitals, but not yet full-blown sexual pleasure. Indeed, there is a marked phenomenological difference between these two kinds of pleasure. Once a child hits puberty and their bodies start developing, then they can start experiencing real sexual pleasure. Thus, while our account focuses only on adults, children pose no problem to it.

state) in order to arise. Sexual arousal marks the difference between sexual pleasure and sensual pleasure; that is, some degree of sexual arousal is a necessary precondition, or *sine qua non*, of sexual pleasure.

In order to understand this, we need to start by drawing a distinction between sexual arousal and simple physiological arousal. Physiological arousal is the body preparing for sex, including: increased heart rate, increased blood pressure, rapid breathing, flushing of the skin, *etc*. It also causes the tumescence of the sexual organs, including erection of the penis and tightening of the scrotum for men and erection of the clitoris and vaginal lubrication for women, among many other effects. This gets our bodies ready for sexual activity and creates the possibility for sexual pleasure. Whereas simple physiological arousal is caused by hormones and has no object, sexual arousal is more involved.

Sexual arousal usually, but not always, includes physical arousal.[i] However, unlike simple physiological arousal, sexual arousal is a sentiment (more specifically, an emotion). It orients us to its object through sexual attraction and sexual desire and with the intention of sexually engaging with a particular person. Or, in the case of masturbation, it involves sexual desire and self-love. Sexual arousal is based in the erotic framework, which makes it a specifically *sexual sentiment*,[ii] as opposed to other sentiments that are based in the evaluative framework. The difference here is that while the erotic framework is primarily a subset of the evaluative framework, it also includes things not found in the evaluative framework, such as sexual types, favorite sexual acts, *etc*.

We said that sexual arousal is connected to sexual desire, but we should say more about this. As adolescents, we frequently experience simple physiological arousal; that is, we feel "horny" due to raging hormones, and we have desires that we do not yet understand and have a hard time controlling. These nascent sexual desires are, at this point, merely an unfocused disposition to action. They take on their specific forms as we learn about sexuality, begin to experience it, and form beliefs and values around it. In our early sexual desires, our body simply knows that it "wants something" and we must learn to identify this desire and good ways to satisfy it. This is similar, to return to an earlier example, to how infants suffer from incomprehensible feelings of desire until they understand that the feeling means they are hungry and need to eat. Then, as they grow, they develop tastes around which foods are good to satisfy these desires. This process of sexual discovery is a major part of constructing our erotic framework.

As we grow and mature, our hormones settle down and we learn to identify certain desires as sexual desires, what satisfies them, and how we enjoy sexuality. By the time that we are adults, our sexual desires take on specific

---

[i] Many things can cause physical arousal to not follow from sexual arousal, as it usually would. Among these are illness, infirmity, and old age. Indeed, many people in their older years lament the onset of this disconnect.

[ii] Other sexual sentiments include sexual attraction and sexual desire.

characteristics. These are shaped by our erotic framework: *e.g.*, a person's sexual desire might manifest as a specific desire to engage in bondage. Sometimes substitutes are acceptable in sexual situations if we have learned there are many ways to satisfy certain desires, but sometimes our desires are firmly for a particular thing like bondage and something else, like *irrumatio*,[i] would not suffice. In this way, our erotic framework both grows out of learning about our sexual desires as well as shapes our sexual desires, in a process that is both dynamic and reciprocal.

Sexual desire is a wish to engage sexually with someone and this usually brings on sexual arousal. Sexual arousal creates a shift in our experience of the world,[ii] the erotic shift: from the everyday world to the world of sexual possibility. It also awakens our bodies to sexuality and sets the stage for the possibility of sexual pleasure. These things all come together for sex to take place. While we have been treating them separately for clarity, we must remember that in reality, they interact with each other and sometimes the lines even begin to blur as when sexual arousal itself gives us sexual pleasure.

In conclusion, let us now restate more clearly the point we have been considering: the sexual pleasure of a kiss is only partly in the lips, the sexual pleasure of fellatio is only partly in the penis, and the sexual pleasure of sodomy is only partly in the anus.[iii] In fact, the sexual pleasure is our response to these things, based on our erotic framework. In this way, the answer to the question of what makes certain acts sexually pleasurable to some people and not to others is that they are different people with different erotic frameworks. There is, thus, no real mystery at all. Moreover, since sexual pleasure necessarily involves the unity of our physical and spiritual aspects, it is another instance of the deep unity of being human.

2. The Nature of Sex

The nature of sex, or "what sex is," is an interesting question for humans and it is the topic to which we must now turn. While it may seem, *prima facie*, to be an easy question, it is more complicated than it may seem.

Historically, one of the most vocal groups on this topic has been the Catholic Church. The side of the Catholic Church championed by Aquinas is part of the Resistant Camp and they believed that sex had one function, which was reproduction, and that any use of sex outside this "natural function" was

---

[i] Or, as we might say in English, "face-fucking." While I am aware that it could also mean oral-rape, this is not the usage here.

[ii] As we have already said, fantasy is also part of this erotic shift.

[iii] Although in the contemporary U.S. the word "sodomy" means only anal sex, it has meant different things at different times. See Volume 2, Chapter 14 for a longer discussion of sodomy.

sinful and against their god's will.[i] Unfortunately for the Catholics, this does not track the reality of human sexuality and it does little to help us understand the nature of sex.

Human Sexuality is not Primarily for Reproduction

Human sexuality is not primarily about reproduction. Some facts about human sexuality, and its comparison to other species, will clearly show this.

Humans have sex dramatically longer than other mammals. Sex, for most mammals, involves a simple insertion of the penis briefly into the vagina and insemination, which is usually over in several seconds: for example, chimps have sex for 7 seconds before the male ejaculates and bonobos have sex for 15 seconds.[97] This is markedly different than in humans, where the average time of sex from penetration to ejaculation is 5.4 minutes.[98] That means humans have sex 46.3 times longer than chimps and 22.6 times longer than bonobos! And these are our closest genetic relatives.

Human sex is also unusual in that we do not have mating seasons. In most mammals, sex only happens during mating season when the female is fertile and exhibits this to the male. For example, female dogs will only allow a male dog to mount them when they are in heat and male dogs will only try to have sex with a female dog that is in heat.[ii] The only animals that consistently have sex outside of a female's heat are dolphins, bonobos, and humans.[iii]

Sex for humans is also terribly inefficient, if we assume reproduction is its end, with a live birth rate of less than 1 for roughly every 1,000 sex acts.[99] If we contrast that with other primates such as the orangutan or gorilla, where there are fewer than 20 sex acts per live birth, we can see that in some species sex is closely tied to reproduction and in others, like ours, it is not.[100]

For these reasons, we can say that human sex is markedly different from other animals. Moreover, if we assume that sex is just for reproduction, it is inefficient to the point of absurdity. Thus, we must reject the idea that sex is only for reproduction, although certainly reproduction is one of the ends of sex. At the same time, we must point out that calling human sex "animalistic"

---

[i] The waning Catholic Church relaxed this position in 1992 under Pope John Paul II, through his *Catechism of the Catholic Church* and its revision of Catholic doctrine. The revised position allows Catholics to (moderately) enjoy (only) penile-vaginal sex as long as it is reproductive *or* it brings the (married) couple closer together. (Catechism 2351: "*Lust* is disordered desire for or inordinate enjoyment of sexual pleasure. Sexual pleasure is morally disordered when sought for itself, isolated from its procreative and unitive purposes.")

[ii] It should be noted that both male and female dogs hump each other (and sometimes human legs) to show dominance. This is not (usually) a sexual activity.

[iii] Which is not to say that other animals *never* have sex outside heat, since homosexual behavior has been observed in as many as 450 different animal species. See, for examples, Bruce Bagemihl's *Biological Exuberance: Animal Homosexuality and Natural Diversity* (St. Martin's Press, 1999).

is not only misanthropic; it is factually false. Human sex is fundamentally nothing like sex for most other animals, which is merely for reproduction and no more.[i]

Choice is the Origin of our Sexual Differences

We have shown that human sex is fundamentally different from sex for most other animals. But why is this? What makes sexuality different for us? The difference is *choice*. Humans have the ability to make choices about what they will do. Not only can we choose what we will do right now, but we can also make long-term plans and even choose ends for the overall course of our lives. Moreover, we can act in ways that can either harm or improve our overall lives. What makes sex different for humans is that we have choice and can determine the function we want sex to have in our lives.

While this may not seem like it would make a big difference, it makes all the difference in the world. It frees us from the biological determinism that controls most animals and allows us to choose which ends we want to give to sex; that is, we get to choose how we want to incorporate sex into our lives. This puts sex firmly in the moral realm. Because of this, we need to ask what possible ends sex has and then look to see which of these will help us to live well, if this is what we seek.

Sex has many possible ends.[ii] Of course, one possible end of sex is reproduction and we should all be thankful for this fact, since it brought us into being. However, sex has many other ends such as pleasure, bonding, intimacy, reducing stress, relieving headaches, exercise, as an aid in getting to sleep, and generally just makes us feel better. At the same time, sex can also be used for evil ends, such as rape, assault, intimidation, betrayal, and retribution. Some of the ends of sex we might call "natural" in that they follow from having sex, regardless of other ends we attribute to it, such as how many men become sleepy after orgasm and this happens whether they choose this end or not. Reproduction might be another "natural" end in that we must take action if we want to be sure that pregnancy does not occur (although the odds of a woman getting pregnant from any particular sex act are very low). On the other hand, these ends are not inevitable as some men do not become sleepy and there are both women and men who are infertile. Thus, "natural" here does not mean "necessary," but rather "generally follows from the act, whether chosen or not,

---

[i] Barring the handful of counter-examples already mentioned. (The broader point about human sex not being animalistic from Long's *Sane Sex Life and Sane Sex Living*, 38-39.)

[ii] This is in contrast to the case of artifacts (man-made things) which have an end given to them *qua* artifacts and which can then be used in accordance with this end or "used for" other ends. Sex, however, does not have a unitary function and can be used for many ends, none of which are *determined*, so it does not make sense to have the contrast here be between "the natural function" of sex and the ends we choose.

depending on a person's constitution."

It is clear that sex can be used for many different ends. The question facing us now is which of these ends will benefit us and help us to live well. If we are to incorporate sex into our lives and we wish to live well, the ends that we give it should align with our goal of creating a rich and happy human life. After all, we are not inquiring into sex simply to understand it, but also to live well. However, in order to decide what ends to give to sex, we must come to better understand it first, so that we can make a good decision.

What is "Sex"?

We have been discussing sex and things related to it, such as sexual pleasure for some time relying only on our vague and perhaps nebulous understanding of sex. While this works on some level, we would be better served by more clarity on the topic. So, let us turn now to see what "sex" is.

The first thing that most people think of when they think of "sex" is that act that we do to reproduce as a species: a male puts his penis into a female's vagina, thrusts vigorously (for an average of 5.4 minutes) because it feels good, and then ejaculates semen so that an egg may be fertilized and the species continued. Certainly, this has a lot of intuitive appeal for the paradigmatic sex act for a sexually-reproducing species such as humans, especially because there are so many other species for whom this is the only possible sex act.

However, as we have already seen, humans do not primarily have sex for the sake of reproduction. Indeed, the primary reason most people seem to have sex is because it feels good: sexual pleasure is the usual draw to sexual activity. Consequently, our paradigmatic sex act should not include "for the sake of reproduction," but "for the sake of pleasure." Thus, the paradigmatic sex act is a male and female coming together and conjoining their penis and vagina, for the sake of sexual pleasure. Our paradigmatic case, then, arises from the nature of our species. Yet, certainly we do not yet have a full picture of sex and need more depth in our inquiry to fully understand sexuality.

The question we must now turn to is how other things that we might think of as "sexual" are related to the paradigmatic case. Or, whether there are other sexual acts at all and, if there are, what makes these things "sexual." We are going to suggest that the element that makes something "sexual" is the specific kind of pleasure that arises from the paradigmatic sexual act. That is, what makes something sexual is whether it involves, or aims towards, this kind of pleasure, which we will call sexual pleasure. That sexual pleasure underlies what it means for something to be sexual comes partly from its conjunction with the organs involved in the paradigmatic sex act and partly from sexual pleasure's unique constitution. So, let us turn to the nature of sexual pleasure to see how it can do this.

We have already discussed the sentimental nature of sexual pleasure at length in the last section. But sexual pleasure is also, pardon the pun, intimately tied to bodily touch. Indeed, we are going to see how there is an inherent intimacy to touch that arises from our physical constitution. This intimacy of touch is an important element of sexual pleasure. Let us turn to this now, so that we can round out our conception of sexual pleasure and see how it is able to underlie and define sex.

The touching of someone else's body is generally thought to be an intimate act, for good reason.[i] We do not generally touch strangers, unless custom compels us as in the case of handshakes, and would likely find an unknown person coming up to us and touching us to be offensive and a violation of our personal boundaries.[ii] Consider that we do not even hug many people, even though hugging generally involves very little touching while wearing clothes, because it is intimate by nature. We do not let people touch our necks or caress our ears and we do not generally expose our bodies to others so that they can see it or touch more of it.[iii] This is because bodily touch is necessarily somewhat intimate.[iv]

Part of what makes the touching of our bodies intimate is that we are vulnerable to be harmed and when someone touches us, we must trust that they will not harm us. Certain areas, especially those where we are most vulnerable, are more intimate than others because of their vulnerability. Consider that it is particularly easy to kill a human if we have access to their neck. Because of this vulnerability, allowing someone to touch our neck is more intimate than allowing them to touch our hand.

While the touch of our bodies is necessarily intimate, this does not necessarily mean that it is sexual. Hugging our child is an intimate act, as is rubbing their back while they try to go to sleep after a nightmare, but these are obviously not sexual acts. What is the source of the difference between an intimate act and a sexual act? Let us now turn to this question.

We have already discussed how vulnerability underlies intimacy, but the most vulnerable areas are those where the barrier between the outside world

---

[i] Even though sex is necessarily intimate, this does not mean that we will *experience* it as such. Many of us spend so much time closing ourselves off psychologically in an effort to protect ourselves that we have a hard time letting go of our defenses and feeling vulnerable, which we must do if we are to experience intimacy.

[ii] The limits of this will be determined by a combination of cultural custom and personal preference.

[iii] Consider, too, that people who make a career out of touching bodies tend to stand apart from society and are treated differently in their professional capacities. Consider that what makes it acceptable for a doctor to touch our bodies is that he is professional and the touch is not intimate, it is purposive and its end is to heal the body. In this way, we accept that there are limited people who we need to touch our bodies, as in the case of the doctor, and for this reason we suppress our natural disinclination to be touched and allow this, even if this does cause some people discomfort.

[iv] The necessary intimacy of physical touch is why assault, besides harming us, is also *defiling*. We are being touched against our will and, by this very fact, our will is also damaged.

and the inside of us is capable of being crossed. That is, the most intimate areas are where things can go into our bodies, such as the vagina and anus.[i] These areas also have the most nerve endings (along with our hands, which is one of our main ways of interacting with the world), so that we can be aware of any sort of danger. This sensitivity also evolved so that we would be moved to have sex in order to help continue the species and making it very pleasurable is a good way to help encourage this. This explains why the penis has a high level of sensitivity, even though it is not a barrier area in quite the same way.[ii] It also explains why even though certain other areas, like the nose, are very sensitive, they are not sexual. Because of the great sensitivity of these sexual areas, their touch moves us more than touch in other areas, and they have the greatest potential for pleasure.

Thus, certain organs, let us call them the "sexual organs," are uniquely pleasurable because of their vulnerability and/or evolved sensitivity and, for these same reasons, are also deeply intimate by their nature. Thus, the sexual organs, such as the vulva, vagina, penis, testicles/scrotum, breasts, nipples, and anus, are the primary avenues to sexual pleasure. This also entails that giving someone sexual pleasure is a necessarily intimate act: part of what makes sexuality special is that we do not just let anyone touch our bodies (especially our sexual organs) and we rarely let anyone come into us. Moreover, this means that sexual pleasure is linked to these sexual organs.

We have now started to understand some of the deeper nature of what makes things "sexual." We started with the paradigmatic case based on biology and how the species reproduces, and then observed that given the incredibly small number of births to sexual acts, that reproduction could not be the driving force of sexuality for humans. We then assumed that it was a certain kind of pleasure, sexual pleasure, which underlies what we think of as "sexual" and started to explore this. We noticed that there was something inherently intimate about bodily touch and especially so regarding the sexual organs, which evolved to be particularly sensitive and connected to sexual pleasure. Thus, it seems our assumption that sexual pleasure was the deeper underlying factor was correct. Let us, then, attempt a working definition of "sexual" based

---

[i] While the penis and testicles are *particularly* vulnerable, they do not offer an obvious physical entrance into the body and this may be why some men feel that sex is not that intimate: because they do not see the penis as an intimate area of their body. (As an aside, the external nature of the testicles, necessitated by sperm needing to be slightly below body temperature, is strong evidence against "intelligent design.")

[ii] The *glans penis* is a mucous membrane and in an unmutilated penis, the presence of the foreskin enclosing the *glans* makes the glans itself an internal organ (enclosed by the *dermis*). Thus, the penis is a barrier in the sense that it is a mucous membrane and is capable of letting infection into the body. Incidentally, the internal nature of the *glans* is why the ancient Athenians considered an exposed *glans* to be indecent, while an exposed penis and testicles were not. (This tracks the way that some think of a dog's penis as just "part of the dog," unless it becomes erect and the penis protrudes from its sheath.)

on this: an act is sexual in nature if it causes or aims at sexual pleasure, which is a unique kind of pleasure that arises from the sensitivity of certain organs and their inherently intimate nature.

However, there is a strong caveat here: consent is required for an act to be sexual. This can best be seen through an analogy: we do not include both rape and consensual sex together under the same concept for the same reason that we do not include both stabbing and surgery under the same concept, even though they both involve using a knife to cut someone. Our intentions make all the difference in human action and, in this context, differentiate an action between sex on the one hand and rape, sexual assault, or molestation on the other.[i] Without consent, the actions that might otherwise have been sexual become perverse and harmful.

In light of this constraint of consent, let us give a revised definition: Sex is any consensual activity that causes or aims at sexual pleasure. This new definition will include many things besides the paradigmatic sex act. Indeed, any consensual activity related to the sexual organs and which causes, or aims to cause, sexual pleasure will be included in this new definition.[ii] Moreover, so will masturbation, the pleasure of anticipating future sexual pleasure, and even the pleasure of eroticized pain. It will even include things that are not obviously related to the stimulation of the sexual organs, such as the pleasure of a gentle caress on the back of the neck as a prelude to sex, which is sexual because of the pleasure of anticipation and what it portends.

More on the Nature of Sex

Even though we now know that what makes something sexual is its consensual connection to sexual pleasure, this still leaves out one piece of the puzzle. If we want sex in our lives, we must still choose how to incorporate it into our lives. In order to see how to do this, we need to look at the rest of the nature of sex.

Although we have been emphasizing both that sex has no necessary ends, and so we must choose the ends that sex is to have in our lives, and also that sex responds to our values and beliefs, this does not mean that sex has no nature. Quite the opposite, in fact. We have just seen that sex is necessarily connected to sexual pleasure, intimacy, and vulnerability. We could not choose for these to not be part of sex as they are part of its nature[iii]; as opposed to even

---

[i] While we may still use the word "sex" (*e.g.*, sexual assault), this is only to point to actions that would counterfactually have been sexual if they had been done with consent.

[ii] It is worth pointing out that sexually pleasurable touch is rarely an accident, but rather a conscious choice to touch someone or ourselves in a certain way. That is, we usually have to intend to give someone sexual pleasure and this intention to give sexual pleasure is part of what makes an act sexual in nature.

[iii] While we cannot disassociate intimacy from sex, we can certainly tear our soul apart in the attempt to do so, as we shall see in Volume 2, Chapter 9.

a natural end like reproduction, about which we can make a choice and forestall with contraception if we choose. Moreover, it is part of the nature of sex to be responsive to our values and beliefs: the great variety of sexuality is evidence of its responsiveness to our values and beliefs. As we have already seen, everything surrounding sex, including even sexual attraction and sexual pleasure, depends on our values and beliefs, especially those in our erotic framework.

To say that sex is responsive to the values and beliefs in our erotic framework does not go far enough. Part of the nature of sex is that it lets us not only directly *experience* the reality of our values and beliefs, but also the necessary unity of our minds and bodies.[i] Whether this is a boon or not will depend entirely on our character and constitution: on whether we have created a good self or bad self. For those people who have taken the time to create good characters and live well, sex will be deeply pleasurable (all other things being equal). On the other hand, for the vicious person who engages in irrationality, sex will be (at best) a mitigation of his negative existential moods such as angst or anxiety.[ii] The person who values things which do not further his life may experience momentary pleasure from sex or just a sense of the lessening of the negativity in his life. At worst, sex will throw his viciousness into stark relief and show him the reality of his life and choices as it lets him have a direct experience of his values. While we are free to subjectively value anything we might wish, if we do not align our values with objective values (that is, value correctly), we are not free to escape the sentimental consequences of this. If we are not working to live well, our sentiments will reflect this and we will feel our moral failure: it is for this reason that sex for the vicious person is not a pleasure. In this way, sex lets us *feel* whether our ethics works or not; that is, it is another part of the nature of sex to be like a moral barometer.

Erousia is a major way in which we are able to experience our values and beliefs through sex. This rich experience of the deep unity of personhood sets the stage for a much more profound experience of sexual pleasure, because it has already stressed the unity of mind and body and, thus, created a more robust foundation for sexual pleasure. This makes the connection between our values and beliefs much more evident and easier to see and experience. This point, that part of the nature of sex is that it has a deeply unifying aspect to it,

---

[i] Regardless of the state of our soul (whether it is integrated or divided), sex still gives us the experience of our deep mind/body integration, such as how the arousal of the body is caused by the mind and sentiments in the mind are tied to the body and affective responses. And this is a terrible experience if we are afraid of death as it shows the necessity of our embodiment. It is also a terrible experience if we hold the irrational idea that the soul is separable and, through this experience, we can experience the deep connection of mind and body, which might make us feel trapped, as though in a prison of the flesh, as Plato feared.

[ii] The vicious person does not experience a life of tranquility, but a life of inner turmoil that merely calms somewhat if something positive happens to him. The vicious man is barred from experiencing happiness by his own values and action. (This is not to say that all people who experience anxiety are vicious.)

is critical for understanding the importance of sexuality in a good life: it is unifying because it stresses the unity of personhood and puts it in stark relief for us to see and, hopefully, cultivate.

It is worth emphasizing that one of the things that makes sexual pleasure so intense, and so intensely human, is that it highlights the unity of our minds and bodies to an extent that other pleasures are not capable of. This is precisely because sexuality has its roots in our values and who we are as people, which enables it to show the connection of our minds and bodies in a way other pleasures could not. When we have sex, we are not merely experiencing the physical pleasures of sex, but we are also experiencing psychological pleasure or what might be called spiritual pleasure.[i] Sexuality unites our minds and bodies in the sexual act and allows us to experience the totality of our humanity: the values to which sexuality responds are the deepest and most important to who we are as people.[ii] This is why sexual pleasure has this unifying effect in a way most sensual pleasures do not: while we might love the taste of espresso, the sight of a vibrant sunset, or the feeling of a cool breeze on a hot day, these things do not allow us to experience the totality of our being in the way sex does.[iii]

Sex is able to do all this because so much of ourselves comes to bear in the sexual act: sexuality comes from the most fundamental aspects of ourselves, such as character and sentiments, and so we can safely say that sex is tied to who we are in the deepest way possible and to the most fundamental parts of our self. Sex ties together our values, beliefs, character, choices, experiences, aspirations, and ideals. The nature of sex is rooted in the deepest parts of our humanity, in the very foundation of who we are as people.

3. Integrating Sex

The noble soul has reverence for itself.[101]
~ Nietzsche

We have seen how sex is ethically significant, pleasurable, and valuable. Now

---

[i] Indeed, there seems to be little difference between calling something "spiritual" or "psychological," given that the origin of "psychology" is "*psuche*" — which means "soul" in Greek. Regardless, we mean our mental faculties and the richness of our inner experiences, whatever we want to call it.

[ii] Moreover, this close integration between our minds and bodies is also highlighted by sexuality through our sexual responses. When we try to engage sexually with a person who does not conform to our values and with whom we do not share values, then we will have either a muted sexual response or none at all, depending on the situation. In fact, many people experience this if they try to have sex that violates their values and find that they do not become physically aroused and cannot get an erection or lubricate. Some might call this "sexual dysfunction," but it is, truly, our sexual organs functioning correctly.

[iii] In allowing us to directly experience our values, sex is much like art.

that we understand the nature of sex, we must integrate it into our lives in order to maximize our happiness. Of course, as we have already discussed, sex is a constitutional value and so this discussion will primarily apply to those people whose constitution necessitates sex for their happiness. Yet, some people who are not constituted such that they *need* sex to be happy may well still choose to have it in their lives, and this discussion will include these people as well. It will have little to say to those whose constitution does not require sex and who do not choose to have it in their lives.

Nevertheless, for those of us who require sex in our lives or choose to have it, we must be deliberate in how we integrate it into our lives. So, we will conclude our project by inquiring how to do this. There are four key elements to this: identifying the ends we will choose for sex, integrating sex into our lives in the right ways, cultivating the right dispositions to sexuality, and thinking about sex in the right ways; all of which is supported by creating and maintaining a good character. Yet, before we do that, we must quickly dispel one last major problematic way of thinking about sex.

Contra the Thin Conception of Sex

What we consider to be "sex" will greatly impact the way we think about sex, as might be expected. The problem is that there are many people who take a thin view of the paradigmatic sex act and then reduce all of sexuality to this: that is, they consider sex is a one-off act of a man putting his penis in a woman's vagina, and think that this exhausts "sex." This may well be sex, but it does not exhaust sex or sexuality (as we have already shown) and is, moreover, a rather *impoverished conception of sex*. This impoverished conception of sex is largely the result of the major camps of sexual ethics that preceded us (the abstinent, resistant, and indulgent). They have all weakened and limited sex in various ways and worked to reduce its importance for human life.[i] This was helpful to achieve their theoretical ends, but not helpful for us in our quest to live well.

This thin conception of sex does not represent the richness of sex nor its connection to the most important parts of who we are as people. If we allow ourselves to be guided by this thin conception, we will surely be led astray. Thus, when we say that sexuality is necessary for happiness for most people, we do not mean that any particular sexual act is necessary for happiness. Rather, we mean the whole rich phenomenon, and all of its deep connections to the

---

[i] This culminates in someone like Alan Goldman, in his "Plain Sex" theory, claiming that sex has *no* particular moral relevance at all: "There are no moral implications whatever [to sex]. Any analysis of sex which imputes a moral character to sex acts in themselves is wrong for that reason. There is no morality intrinsic to sex, although general moral rules apply to the treatment of others in sex acts as they apply to all human relationship." This position could only be held by someone with such a myopic view of sex that it is hard to believe they can see it at all. (Alan Goldman, "Plain Sex," *The Philosophy of Sex*, p.66).

various aspects of human life, are necessary for happiness.

In order to show this, we must focus on the richer phenomenon of sex and so let us draw an analogy to a related phenomenon: the sentiments. We have already shown that the sentiments are a core part of human nature and that they give rise to meaning in life. That being the case, it makes as much sense to take such a thin conception of sex and reduce it to a particular act as it does to reduce the richness of the sentiments to a particular moment of sadness. While it is true that sadness is a sentiment, taking a particular instance of sadness as exhausting the sentiments is to miss most of what makes them unique and important in a human life. To reduce them to a thin conception is to lose the richness of the sentiments. It is the same with sex.

If we make the mistake of reducing sex to a simple physical act, we will lose sight of its richness and its deep connections to the most important aspects of our lives. If we tear sex away from the sentiments like sexual arousal, sexual attraction, and sexual desire; tear it away from erotic love and the erotic relationship; tear it away from its ability to give us the experience of our selves; tear it away from our identity and self-conception; tear it away from all the things that make it what it is, whatever it is we are left with, it is not sex. Moreover, in reality, sex cannot be separated from all these things: there is no such thing as a pristinely disconnected sex act. All we could do is to choose to ignore or evade these things and then claim that sex is impoverished—we cannot actually make it so. Thus, we must reject the thin conception of sex and always recall that sex is a rich phenomenon with deep connections to many different parts of a human life.

We Must Choose the Ends of Sex

Sex is a complex phenomenon, which has its origins in an innate biological drive for reproduction. Yet, by the time *homo sapiens* evolved, this drive had been decoupled from reproduction as we have seen. The drive for sex, however, remained. Because it does not always, or even usually, result in pregnancy or birth, we had to give the continued drive new ends; that is, since clearly people were not just having sex to have children, they must have had some reasons to keep doing it. For many people, this reason was no more robust than that sex felt good and so they did it. Some people did it to feel more powerful. Some did it to feel connected to others. Some people allowed their cultures to define sex for them. Because sex lost its necessary end for our species, its end opened to our choice. As a consequence, if we want to have sex in our lives, we must choose how to integrate it. There are three major things that we need to think about in this process: our overall way of engaging with sexuality, the ultimate ends we want sexuality to have in our lives, and the immediate ends we will choose for any particular sex act. These three factors will determine how sex fits into the overall course of our lives.

The overall *way* that we engage in sex will be influenced by both the ultimate ends and the immediate ends we choose for sex, but also by our existential orientation, personality, and the dispositions we cultivate around sex. The way that we engage in sex is not usually something that we consciously consider, but such consideration is valuable and we can change the way we engage in sex if we wish. Let us be more concrete to better understand this issue. We can engage in sex joyfully or somberly, inquisitively or disinterestedly, reverentially or disdainfully, excitedly or resignedly, actively or passively. We can be enthusiastic about anal sex or reluctant about it. We can be sensitive to our partner's needs and pleasure or indifferent to them. We can be flexible and experimental with sex or fixed and rigid about it. We can allow ourselves to be open and intimate in sex or try to close ourselves off and try to make it a mere physical act. We can choose partners with whom we share values and who would be a value in our lives or we can try to ignore the character of our sexual partners and engage with whoever is willing to engage with us. All of these choices, whether consciously made or not, will affect how we integrate sexuality into our lives. It is not primarily the particular acts we engage in, but the *way* we choose to engage in sexuality overall and over the long-term that will create our habits around sex and determine how sex fits into our lives. These choices of how to engage in sex overall are also influenced by how we choose to integrate sex into our lives more broadly, as well as by the immediate ends we choose for sex.

The *immediate ends* we choose for sex are what we want this particular sex act to mean, right now. There are many possible immediate ends of sex, some of the more common ones are pleasure, connection with our partner, and reducing stress. While these will usually be in line with the ultimate ends we choose for sex, they need not necessarily be so. We can choose other ends for our immediate end as long as they do not *contradict* our ultimate ends. For example, a person might choose reverence for life as the ultimate end of sex, but they might be having sex this time simply in order to help them go to sleep and that is fine. We might also choose bad immediate ends if we fail to keep the context of our ultimate ends in mind, become overwhelmed with sexual desire, evade the implications of our actions[i], or even suffer *akrasia*. For example, a person who has the overall ends of sexual pleasure and connecting with their partner could still choose to cheat on their partner and violate their trust by having sex with a co-worker because they wanted the "thrill" of doing something illicit, even though this will thwart their ultimate ends and may destroy their relationship. Thus, while our immediate ends should be in line with our ultimate ends, it is no problem if they occasionally are not, as long as they do not contradict our ultimate ends.[ii] Our immediate ends will also be

---

[i] After a person has deeply cultivated evasion of the intimacy of sex, they may lose the ability to be able to experience intimacy or they may require psychological help to undo this.

[ii] This is how a person can have an ultimate end of sex of intimacy with their primary partner

influenced by the overall way we choose to engage in sex. For example, a person who has cultivated the habit around sex of caring for their partner's pleasure is unlikely to pick an immediate end that is indifferent to this. While our immediate ends can have grave moral consequences (*e.g.*, rape), their moral impact is usually in the habits we cultivate through them and in how they affect the overall course of our lives, including how they impact the ultimate ends we choose for sex.

The *ultimate end* we choose for sex is the larger role we want it to play in our life. This could be that we want sex to be part of our happiness, we want to use sex to keep a partner, or that we will only have sex to make offspring. The choice we make for our ultimate end will be influenced by the choices we have made about our immediate ends and the way we have chosen to engage in sex; yet, we should still pick our ultimate end consciously, if we want sex to be part of happiness. If not, we will still end up with an ultimate end, but we will have had little conscious control over it. This will happen because the immediate ends we choose for sex do add up over time into ultimate ends through the habits we thereby cultivate. If we, thus, consciously choose the ultimate end of sex as intimacy with our partner, but we always choose immediate ends that seek to give us a false sense of self-esteem through sexual "conquest," then we will end up with the ultimate end of sex as a way of gaining this veneer of self-esteem, whether we wanted this or not. Indeed, it is unlikely that most of those who end up incorporating sex into their lives in evil ways did this on purpose, they most likely defaulted into their position by evading their responsibility of choice of ultimate ends (or in their lives more generally) and created their ultimate end through the habits of their immediate ends.[i]

How sex fits into the overall course of our life results from the ultimate ends we choose for sex, the habits we cultivate around the particular sex acts we engage in, and how we otherwise treat sexuality. The choice we make for the ultimate end has to be backed up in our action, if it is to have any meaning. Moreover, the habits we develop around the particular act will affect how we incorporate sex into the overall course of our lives, whether we want it to or not. While the one-off act does not change our habits, the acts we regularly choose and the way we choose to engage with sexuality will become our habits and who we are. In this way, there is a great deal of dynamic interaction between the ultimate ends we choose for sex, the immediate ends we choose for sex, and the way we typically engage in it.

---

and yet sometimes have sex with others without compromising their overall ends (as we will explore in Volume 2).

[i] Some people, however, do choose evil ends. For example, there are some men who feel entitled to sex and consciously think of it in these terms. The coward who perpetrated the "Isla Vista Shootings" in Santa Barbara in 2014 stated in his "manifesto" that it was partly because he felt entitled to sex and women were not giving it to him. Feeling entitled to anything from another person is a recipe for disaster: we are entitled to no more than the basic respect that others not violate our rights.

If we choose to have sex at all, we cannot help but to have ends for it. These ends should be consciously chosen, if we want sex to be a positive force in our lives. Yet, even if we do not consciously choose the ends, we will end up with some ends through the habits we cultivate around sexuality. We can choose not to have sex, but we cannot choose not to have ends for sex if we choose to have it in our lives.

If we want sex to be part of a flourishing life, then we need to choose ends that will help it to be so. Moreover, we have to be sensitive to its nature. While sex does not have an innate end, it still has a nature. If we try to act contrary to this, we will only bring ourselves to grief and fail to flourish. Moreover, we must be conscious and focused in our choice of the ultimate end of sex and not simply default into it, if we want to achieve happiness and live well.

Integrating Sex into Our Lives in the Right Way

If we want to have sex in our lives, and most of us will likely choose to do so, then one of the most important things we can do is to create a good erotic relationship full of erotic love and deep intimacy.[i] While we have already explored these things at length individually, it is worth briefly looking at them again to see how they fit together to help us achieve a good life.[ii]

One of the most important things sex does is to create intimacy and connection between people. Sexuality provides intimacy between a couple and if they nurture this intimacy, it will continue to grow and sex will continue to not only provide intimacy, but also push the partners to deepen their connection with each other.[iii] Moreover, sexuality creates the passion to sustain the intimacy and relationship and, thereby, keep the fire of love burning brightly. This is the kind of deep relationship that Plato was hinting at with his

---

[i] This is not to deny that some people are capable of having multiple intimate relationships at once, but it is to say that even here each relationship is its own individual thing. Moreover, the number of possible intimate relationships is necessarily small and if a person attempts too many, then they shall achieve intimacy in none of them.

[ii] It is worth reiterating that we cannot have a good relationship unless we are at least working on our own moral progress. While a relationship where both people are working on their moral improvement together can be successful, if both partners do not share this goal, the relationship will fail.

[iii] A friend recounted to me that when Viagra was first introduced, there was a news segment in which they interviewed a couple in their 60's. The couple seemed to be happy together, but their body language was of a pair of good companions: they sat on the couch, a foot apart, and looked mostly at the interviewer. The next morning, after trying Viagra, there was a follow-up interview and they looked like a totally different couple. They sat with their legs touching, and they kept glancing at each other in a way that they had not done the night before. He said that while it was possible that this was staged, it looked quite natural and the news reporter did not comment on the difference, but just focused on how Viagra had worked for them. He said that he could not help but notice that amazing difference in body language. This is the power of sex and its impact on intimacy.

allegory of the proto-humans and idea of the "soul-mate": the kind of relationship that fulfills our deep need for connection with another person. An erotic relationship requires more than just living together or spending lots of time together: it requires that we open ourself to our partner during sex. Since sex is necessarily intimate and integrates all of the deepest parts of us, this creates the perfect combination for developing deep intimacy.

This deep intimacy sets the stage for our partner to become "another self," as we develop a shared identity over time through coming to internalize each other's values and ends. This opens the possibility of our partner becoming a psychological mirror for us and gives us an outside perspective on ourselves, which lets us see our actions better and greatly aids our living well. Moreover, this also opens the possibility of being psychologically visible to our partner and being seen and loved for who we really are.

This sense of shared identity is also a unique and profound pleasure in life. In addition to it being a pleasure in itself, once we achieve this kind of relationship sex takes on the added role of being a *celebration* of our values together, of our values as embodied in each other, of each other, of our lives and how they are going, and ultimately, a celebration of the world as we want it to be. Moreover, because in the erotic relationship, our partner's pleasure is our pleasure as well,[i] the depth of pleasure, both physical and spiritual, is much greater than it could be otherwise. Indeed, it is one of the greatest pleasures possible in life. This kind of shared life with another self, with shared identity, intimacy, and value co-internalization, is what it takes to keep passion alive for each other over the course of a life and it serves to help us create true and lasting happiness. This not only fulfills a deep psychological need, but it is also a great moral boon.

It is a great moral boon because sex becomes a moral impetus that drives us to be the best we can be. Not only do we want to be our best possible selves for our partner, but we also want this for ourselves as well so we can experience our chosen self through sex. Because of this, sex becomes a driving force for our happiness and creates a strongly virtuous circle of living well. As a result, sex becomes both a moral goal as well as a driving force: the drive to achieve our best and to experience one of the highest things open to us. Sex is, thus, both an impetus to living the best life possible and a powerful way of experiencing this in our lives.[ii]

Cultivate the Right Dispositions Towards Sexuality

To integrate sex into our lives in healthy ways, we must cultivate the right kinds of dispositions towards it. While these dispositions will be affected by

---

[i] Some people call taking pleasure in one's partner's pleasure "compersion" and this is a trait we should work to cultivate in ourselves, whether we are naturally disposed to it or not.
[ii] In this way, sex is connected to pride and moral ambitiousness.

our existential orientation and personality, they are still open to our conscious choice and we have the ability to change them if we need to do so. We should cultivate dispositions for *reverence*, such as: for our life and the self we have created, for our humanity, for reason and our body, for the capacity of sex to let us experience our values and character, and for our partner and their chosen self. We should cultivate dispositions for *intimacy*, such as: allowing ourselves to be vulnerable, acknowledging the inherent intimacy of sexuality, and being open and honest with ourselves and others. We should cultivate dispositions for *healthy sexuality*, such as: sexual curiosity and willingness to explore, a laissez-faire attitude with respect to others' (non-harmful) sexuality, the attitude that pleasure (that is consistent with our ends) is worth pursuing, the ability to feel pleasure in our partner's pleasure, and the embrace of our own mortality so that we do not try to push away the body. Cultivating these dispositions also entails not doing their opposite, but there are several that are worth stating on their own, such as: never using sex to harm someone else, never letting sex conflict with our living well, and never forcing sex upon anyone else.

Cultivating these dispositions is a personal endeavor and requires *phronesis* and experience to get right. That is, we should hold these goals in mind and engage in sexuality in a way consistent with them until we develop the habits and dispositions that will make them automatic and part of how we engage in sex. This also means that if we make a mistake, we should work to correct it and to keep developing the right dispositions. Through doing so, we will ultimately cultivate the dispositions that will help us to engage in sex in life-affirming ways that will help us to live well.

Think about Sex in the Right Way

We have already discussed the importance of the ends we hold for sex for how it fits into our lives and whether it will help us to achieve happiness. But, the ends we hold for sex are also important for the way that we think about sexuality. Indeed, the way we think about sexuality is critical for whether it will be able to help us to live well.[i] The overall way that we think about sexuality is the result, not just of the ends we hold for sexuality, but of the beliefs that we have in our erotic framework.

Our erotic framework is full of beliefs about sex, some that we have consciously chosen and others of which we have simply defaulted into. Because the way we think about sex comes from our erotic framework, we must carefully cultivate it so that we can have sex in our lives in

---

[i] The character arc of Hank Rearden in Ayn Rand's *Atlas Shrugged* is all about unearned guilt and how by accepting the wrong sexual premises, a person can be morally cut in half. Moreover, it also demonstrates that by accepting the wrong moral premises about sex, we will be led down the wrong moral path, even if we consciously have some of the right moral premises, because sex is such an important part of who we are.

positive ways. This includes watching for negative thoughts about sex, such as that it is "only bodily," "dirty," or "dangerous" as these all signal incorrect beliefs about sex that will make it harder for sex to be part of our happiness. These thoughts may arise from consciously held beliefs or from subconscious beliefs. They could even arise from the beliefs we have from the ways that we have conceptualized our past experiences. We must be careful that the beliefs we hold in our erotic framework are true and will help us to integrate sex into our lives in healthy ways.

We must work to be able to challenge any negative thoughts through developing good introspective skills, such as being honest with ourselves and thoughtful about our lives. We must also be able to talk about sex openly and honestly, as this is one of the best ways to gain perspective on our own beliefs and to challenge any beliefs that are at odds with our goals in life. This also helps us to see whether we are holding fixed and rigid ideas about sexuality or whether we can change them in light of new evidence. Overall, we must take care in the way we think about sexuality if we want it to contribute to our happiness.

Learn about Sexuality

While the most important part of sex is spiritual, we cannot ignore the physical act of sex; the ideal of "virginity" or ignorance about sexuality is perverse and will not help us to live well. For this reason, if we want to integrate sex into our lives, it behooves us to learn as much about the physical act of sex as we can (being careful not to reduce sex to simply the physical act). While awkward enthusiasm is much sexier than indifferent skill, a partner who is both skilled and enthusiastic is the best.

First, we should *learn sexual anatomy and morphology*. It is important that we find good anatomical diagrams and learn the parts of the body.[i] We should learn about female anatomy, including: the difference between the vulva and the vagina, the structure of the clitoris and how it is mostly hidden, the uterus and ovaries, and the structures of the breasts including the difference between the areola and nipple. We should learn about male anatomy, including: the penis and its structures such as the frenulum and foreskin, the testicles and scrotum, and internal male anatomy such as the prostate and its role in orgasm. We should learn about sexual morphology and similarity between male and female bodies and how all humans begin as female. We should learn about intersex

---

[i] We should also make sure that our information is accurate. For example, while many people think that the average penis size is 8," studies show that it is 5.165" (SD=0.653") meaning that 68.3% of men have a penis between 4.512" to 5.818." (Veale, D., Miles, S., Bramley, S., Muir, G. and Hodsoll, J. (2015), Am I normal? A systematic review and construction of nomograms for flaccid and erect penis length and circumference in up to 15,521 men. BJU International, 115: 978–986. doi: 10.1111/bju.1301002)

bodies and the differences between them. We should also learn about the anus, the dual anal sphincters, the rectum, and the sigmoid colon.

Through learning these things, we should also realize that there is great variance between human bodies in things like breast size, areola size, nipple size, outer labia size, inner labia size, clitoral size, penis size, length of foreskin, size of testicles, length of scrotum, *etc.* The human body varies quite a bit between people and this should be a source of celebration of their individuality and not a source of disappointment by holding impossible ideals. Moreover, this variance is not only in our physical constitution, but also in how different people like being touched and what they sexually enjoy.

Second, we should learn about the *orgasmic response*. We should learn about the orgasmic response cycle and what happens at each stage of the cycle. We should learn about what happens to the body when it becomes aroused and how it changes with arousal. We should learn about the refractory period, including our own refractory period, and how it varies between people. We should learn about our own orgasmic response and the various kinds of orgasms we can have and learn the same for our partner. We should learn about orgasmic manipulation and ways to change, extend, or ruin an orgasm. Even if we do not want to engage in orgasmic manipulation, knowing about it will help us to better understand sex and help us to avoid the things we might not want to do.

Third, we should learn practical *sexual skills*. We should learn how we like to be touched through masturbation and sexual self-exploration. We should understand how to stimulate a clitoris or penis, how much pressure, what speed, and in what way a partner likes to be touched when they are not aroused, becoming aroused, fully aroused, and nearing orgasm. We should learn about different sexual acts and try things that we have never done before. We should understand that each of our sexual partners will have different preferences and that our own might even change with different partners or in different stages of a relationship.

Fourth, we should learn about *pregnancy and reproduction*. Although the birth rate per sex act is very low for humans, it is foolish to take no action to prevent pregnancy if we do not want a child and engage in the kinds of actions that may result in one. We should learn about the various forms of contraception and the advantages and disadvantages of each. We should learn about the options for abortion, whether or not we would want to exercise this option. Children can be a great value in life, but a person should not have them if they are unable to support them or unwilling to help them grow and mature.

Fifth, and finally, we should have *fun with sex*. Sex is a serious matter in a human life, but it should also be a source of fun and joy. We should enjoy our bodies and the pleasure they give us. We should enjoy our partner and their pleasures. We should celebrate different bodies and not become overly focused on a single ideal of physical beauty. One of the best ways we can show reverence for life is to find joy in good sexuality.

Develop a Good Character and Self

While we spent Chapter 1 detailing how to develop a good character and self, let us give some last brief remarks on it at the close of our inquiry. After all, if we fail in developing a good self, the rest of it will be in vain.

We must learn to always think for ourselves, practice *phronesis*, and take charge of our lives. There is *nothing* worth giving up our integrity, authenticity, or independence for. We must cultivate the virtues and practice them until we have them fully automatized and we rarely need to think about them: the virtues serve us best when they are not deliberate.

We must be true to our reason, it is what differentiates us from the lower animals and it is our means of survival. Moreover, no matter how intelligent or not, how virtuous or not, how well our lives are going or not, we are all capable of being reasonable and it is never worth turning against this best element within us.

We must cultivate the right kinds of relationships: we are social animals, neither gods nor beasts. Yet, we must be careful whose company we keep: while good people will improve our lives, bad people will make them much worse. We must take care to minimize our association with bad people and maximize our association with good people. This certainly includes our birth families, which may be of either kind.

Intellectual honesty is one of the most important traits we can cultivate: knowing what we know and what we do not know and being honest with ourselves and others about this. We should never be embarrassed by ignorance, but we should work not to remain in such a state.

Finally, we should cultivate tranquility and not hold conflicts in our soul and spend our days torn apart. Most of these conflicts arise because we do not bring our desires in line with our reason. This is made worse when we fail to recognize the difference between what is open to change and what is not.[i] All of these conflicts can be removed from our lives. If we follow reason, we will have few conflicts.

Conclusion

The choice of how to integrate sexuality is ultimately up to each person, but if we want sex in our lives and want to live well, then we should choose ends that cultivate reverence for our lives, that bring us joy, that make us glad to be human, and that help us to achieve happiness. All of the various parts of

---

[i] Ayn Rand has a particularly good discussion of this in "The Metaphysical Versus the Man-Made," from *Philosophy: Who Needs It*. We might also think of Epictetus's injunction in the *Enchiridion* to recognize what we have control over and what we do not.

our life are connected and we must work to bring each area in line with our conscious goals. Sex is an important part of ethics because it is an important part of who we are. It is not some separate thing from ethics that is also important.

There are no secrets and no shortcuts. While we are alive, we should struggle to make the most of our lives, because this is all we have. We can either suffer it or enjoy it. I suggest we choose to enjoy it and seek happiness.

Summary and Conclusions

It's a rare gift, you know, to feel reverence for your own life and to want the best, the greatest, the highest possible, here, now, for your very own. To imagine a heaven and then not to dream of it, but to demand it.[102]
~ Ayn Rand

We opened this chapter by saying that sex was both a driving force for happiness and a necessary part of it for most people. We have now demonstrated how this is so: we have seen how sex is a great moral impetus that also forms part of happiness. Let us briefly review what we saw in this chapter, before we turn to our final remarks in the Conclusion.

We began by exploring the sentimental nature of sexual pleasure. We saw that since sexual pleasure is a sentiment, it is dependent on our erotic framework (which is, itself, the result of our own past experiences, our culture, and family, among other things). This means that, as a sentiment, the ends we pick for sexual pleasure, and our particular erotic framework, will determine the pleasure of sex. We also showed how this new understanding of sexual pleasure was able to solve complex problems related to things like nonconsensual activities and conflicting values. We then contrasted sexual pleasure and sensual pleasure and saw how sensual pleasure is related to our senses, such as the feeling of warmth when we are cold, and it tends to be common among people and across cultures (as opposed to how sexual pleasure is a sentiment and is dependent on an individual's erotic framework). We also saw that unlike sensual pleasure, sexual pleasure requires at least some sexual arousal to arise.

We then turned our attention to the nature of sex and saw that human sex was markedly different from other animals: while, for most animals, sexuality was deeply tied to reproduction, for humans this was not the case. We saw that since sexuality has no necessary end for humans, how we integrate it into our lives is open to our choice. However, we realized that we needed to better understand sexuality in order to make a good choice about how to integrate it into our lives. We thus explored the nature of "sex" and saw that what makes something sexual at all is its relation to a specific kind of pleasure that we called "sexual pleasure." We saw that sexual pleasure was tied to the intimacy of touch and the vulnerability of our bodies, especially including our sexual organs. From this, we identified that sex is "any consensual activity that causes or aims at sexual pleasure." We also saw that sex throws the necessity of our mind/body unity into stark relief and allows us to experience whether we are living well or not, much as a moral barometer. It is able to do this because sex brings so much of ourselves to bear and comes from the most fundamental parts of us: because sex is rooted in the very foundation of who we are as people.

We concluded the chapter by rejecting the thin conception of sex: sex is not some impoverished thing and is not reducible to a simple act in the same way that the sentiments are not reducible to a simple act of sadness. We saw that, for most people, sex is an important moral impetus for happiness and losing out on it would harm their ability to achieve happiness. We also saw that the end of sex is open to our choice and that we must choose how we want to incorporate it into our lives, which includes choosing ultimate ends, immediate ends, and the way in which we engage in sex. From this, we looked at some broader points for integrating sex into our lives. We saw that one of the most important ways to integrate sex into our lives is through a good erotic relationship. Through this, a couple can cultivate intimacy and experience the profound pleasure of another self and of the celebration of their lives together through sex. We also saw that in order to make this possible, we need to cultivate the right dispositions towards sexuality, including: dispositions for reverence, intimacy, and healthy sexuality. We saw how all of this was supported by thinking about sex in the right ways, which is facilitated by careful cultivation of our erotic framework. We also saw how learning about the practical side of sexuality greatly facilitates integrating it into our lives, including learning about anatomy, morphology, orgasm, sexual skills, reproduction, and learning to simply enjoy sex. Finally, we saw how all of this was supported by developing a good character and self.

More broadly, in this chapter we brought everything together. We saw that since sexual pleasure, like sexual attraction, is a sentiment, and responds to our erotic framework (including our values and beliefs about sexuality), it thereby shows our ethical self through what we find sexually pleasurable. This highlights the inescapable connection between sexuality and who we are as people, which should come as no surprise as sex is an important part of human nature. We also saw how sex is not only necessary for happiness for most people, but also a strong moral impetus to achieve it. Moreover, sex allows us to directly *experience* the greatness of this, which is its own source of pleasure and provides another drive to live well.

We said in the introduction to this chapter that sex is both part of a rich and happy human life and a driving force for it for most people. This should now be clear. It should also be clear why accounting for sex is *necessary* for a rich system of ethics: omitting sex is omitting a very important part of most people's lives, a necessary piece of their happiness, part of how they experience their happiness, a major source of richness, and a strong moral impetus.

We should now be able to see why any system of ethics that does not include sexuality must, necessarily, fall short of a full system of human ethics: it simply misses too much of what it means to be human and too much of human happiness. For these reasons, and, indeed, for everything that we have said until now, we can finally say that, for most people, sex is one of the most important keys to happiness.

Conclusion: The Sexual Ethics Revolution

> *Intellectual honesty consists in taking ideas seriously.*
> *To take ideas seriously means that you intend to live by,*
> *to practice, any idea you accept as true.*
> *Philosophy provides man with a comprehensive view of life.*
> *In order to evaluate it properly, ask yourself what a given theory,*
> *if accepted, would do to a human life, starting with your own.*[103]
> ~Ayn Rand

Let us conclude this volume on a revolutionary note; because, truly, in many ways our eudaimonistic account of sexual ethics is revolutionary. It is both a revolution *against* the past systems of sexual ethics as well as a revolution *for* a future that includes a pro-life sexual ethic. We will wrap up the conclusion by looking at philosophy more broadly and its place in a human life.

1. A Revolution Against the Past

> *Nothing is more powerful than an idea whose time has come.*[104]
> ~ Victor Hugo

We opened the present volume by identifying three historic camps of sexual ethics (the Resistant, Abstinent, and Indulgent) and their positions. We have now elaborated our own theory and we are ready to respond to each of the camps and show not only how they fail, but also how our account is uniquely equipped to deal with sexual ethics. Let us start, however, with a broad response to the various philosophic positions that underlie the older sexual ethics.

Broad Responses to the Past

First, against the *thin conception of sex*. This premise is utilized by all three camps. It treats sex as a simple physical act, disconnected from any spiritual element and all of its psychological ties (as we saw in Chapter 7). In so doing, it takes on a strange strawman of sexuality, instead of that rich phenomenon that is part of human life. However, as we have already shown, sex is connected to the deepest and most important parts of who we are as people and is one of the most morally profound acts we can perform. To fail to account for such an important element of human life is to miss the mark entirely and any system that does so cannot be said to be a system of *human* ethics at all.

Second, against *mind/body dualism*. This premise is utilized by all three camps, with the resistant and abstinent taking the side of the soul and the indulgent taking the side of the body. It treats a person as being fundamentally disjointed, with certain parts being more real or more important than others. This is a fundamental denial of human nature and of the real world. Humans are not a weird amalgam of a this-worldly body and an other-worldly soul, but unified beings that have physical aspects and mental aspects. Until some evidence of this fundamental disjunction can be presented, we must reject it as arbitrary and at odds with the real world.

Third, against the idea of *emotions as necessarily in conflict with reason*. This premise is utilized by all three camps. It treats emotions (or the "passions") as an almost exogenous thing thrust upon us and necessarily in conflict with reason. We have shown, however, that *all* of the sentiments, including our emotions and sexual attractions, proceed from our values and beliefs in our evaluative and erotic frameworks, and are ultimately all the product of reason. This includes discordant sentiments, which are merely responding to discordant values and beliefs. This means that instead of the sentiments and reason being opposed to one another, the sentiments follow from reason (or should if we are living well) and that there was never a conflict here at all.

Fourth, against the idea that *sex is not worth moral mention*. This premise is utilized by the Resistant and Abstinent camps. It is the idea that sex is not really part of morality and has no proper place therein; it is merely a moral danger to be either resisted or abstained from. Yet we have shown that sex is, in fact, an important part of morality, not only in its connection to human nature and our ethical selves, but also in its ability to be a moral impetus and help us to achieve happiness.

Fifth, against *mysticism*. This premise is utilized by all three camps in various fashions. The core idea of mysticism is that the Law of Identity (A is A) is mutable in some respect and that, at least sometimes, a thing can be other than what it is (A is ~A). This premise is held for different reasons, but ultimately boils down to some version of "a mind has causal power to change the world," whether that mind is a "god" or simply a person having "faith." However, such a thing is impossible and amounts to no more than wishful thinking on the part of those who hold it. There is no other source of truth than reason and no mind has direct causal power in the world (and there has never been any evidence to the contrary).

Sixth, against *duty and rule-based ethics*. This premise is utilized by the Resistant and Abstinent camps. It is the idea that ethics must be constructed as a system of rules to which a person has a duty. Yet, as we have seen (in Chapter 1), there can be no such thing as a system of ethics based on rules, as they all ultimately reduce to a system of commands backed by punishments. These rule-based systems are about control and will never help us to live a good life. If we want to be happy and live well, we must reject these systems and embrace eudaimonism as the only ethical system whose goal is our happiness.

Response to the Resistant Camp

The Resistant camp worries that if we cannot control the black horse of the passions, our chariot will be pulled astray. Yet, it is they who go astray in thinking that reason and the sentiments are necessarily at odds. On their account, there is no way to truly bring the sentiments in line with reason because they did not understand the nature of the sentiments and so were powerless before them. Yet, now that we understand the nature of the sentiments, we can see how they can be integrated with our reason so that they work together. A life of pure reason would be cold, meaningless, and unmotivated. A life of pure sentiment would be out of control, directionless, and animalistic. Luckily for us, a human life is instead a unified life of reason and the sentiments.

Response to the Abstinent Camp

The Abstinent camp worries that if we have strong sentiments or indulge in pleasant things, such as sexuality, then we will grow to be unfit for our duty to follow the moral rules. They go astray in thinking that the idea of "moral rules" is cogent: it is a contradiction in terms, as we have seen. The Abstinent camp also goes astray in thinking that we are somehow a duality of soul and body and that our sentiments come from the body and corrupt an otherwise pure soul. Yet, as we have also seen, our sentiments are inexorably both of the "body" and "soul" at the same time, because we are single, unified beings. Moreover, as we have shown, our sentiments are an important part of human life. They are necessary for ethics and give meaning to our lives. To abstain from them is to necessarily impoverish our lives and move away from happiness.

Response to the Indulgent Camp

In the Introduction, we begged off our critique of hedonism until we had made our own positive case first. It should now be clear why this was necessary: we needed to understand sentiments and the nature of pleasure to show the great irony of the hedonist position. They assert that the standard of morality is pleasure, without being aware that pleasure is not a primary, but a response to our own values and beliefs. Their advice, such as it is, amounts to this: the standard of good is whatever you already happen to believe, because it is this to which your pleasure will respond. It is, thus, nonsensical to try to make pleasure the source of ethics, because part of the nature of pleasure is to be a response to our ethical beliefs! Thus, the great paradox of hedonism: pleasure cannot be a moral standard because it is dependent on our moral values. This holds even for a more sophisticated hedonist like Epicurus. Any theory that places a sentiment as its moral standard will fall to circularity. Because of this, it is worth pointing out that "happiness," while our end, is not primarily a sentiment, even though it has a sentimental component. The sentimental component is not the goal of eudaimonism, but arises out of our living a certain sort of life, which is the actual goal.

Revolutionary Eudaimonism

In contrast to the past, we offer a viable ethical theory. Eudaimonism is both internally consistent (coherent) and tracks the real world (referential). It functions without any irrational assumptions, intuitive leaps, or mystic revelations to make it work. Moreover, it does not require us to deny parts of reality or human nature (*e.g.*, the sentiments or sexuality).

In contrast to the past, we offer reasons to be moral: choosing to live morally will lead us to happiness and help us to acquire the goods of happiness. Through achieving happiness, we can secure tranquility and peace for ourselves. We can also secure our unity of soul and of our being. We can even directly experience the joy of this through sexuality and erousia.

In contrast to the past, we offer the possibility of a good human life. We offer: the *shameless* joy of sex and bodily pleasure, the enjoyment of healthy sexuality, the joy of internal peace and tranquility, pleasure at our own existence, and the pleasure of using our minds and bodies to strive for the best things open to us.

Finally, we offer a theory that is uniquely capable of handling the complexities of sexuality. We have already seen how eudaimonism is capable of handling current debates and we will explore this more in Volume 2. But it is also capable of handling debates that we have not even conceived of yet, due to its principled nature and emphasis on human flourishing. As long as there are living humans, our philosophy will still be viable. It is only our eudaimonism that can support a human sexual ethic; we cannot rely on the false ethics of rule-based systems. No other ethical system has as its end the long-term happiness and flourishing of the individual. And, if this is the end we want, a life well-lived, then eudaimonism is the kind of ethics we must embrace.

2. A Revolution for the Future

> *The ideal frames the debate.*
> *And he who frames the debate, wins the debate.*[105]
> ~Alex Epstein

If we want to secure the future for our eudaimonistic ethics and work to make the world a better place for sex, then we must lay the groundwork for that revolution now. A real "sexual revolution" is a long-term project that will be won inch by inch. It will not be swift or glorious, but it will slowly become inevitable. For our revolution to work, there are three critical elements that must all come together to make it happen: reframing the debates, becoming moral exemplars, and shifting the zeitgeist. Each of these will impact the others and make them easier to achieve. These things will allow us to change the landscape of sexual ethics and shift the future in our favor and towards human life. At the same time, we should not place our focus on the change in the world that is outside our control, but only on the factors within our control. If we focus too much on the things over which we have no control, we give up our tranquility to no gain.

Reframe the Debates

For too long the sexual ethics debate has been framed by the Resistant and Abstinent camps and their ideals that sex should be resisted or abstained from. Because these were the primary moral positions, they defaulted into the moral high ground. This led to the bleak landscape that heretofore existed, where the field of sexual ethics was no more than prohibitions against this and condemnations about that. This is, obviously, a problem for anyone who thought that sexuality could have a positive role in human life, as we were forced to fight an uphill battle against these entrenched ideals. These ideals eventually became the only real options and dominated the debate.

We cannot yield the moral high ground and expect to ever win an argument. If we want to win, we must stop arguing from a position of disadvantage. How do we do this? The first step is that we need to reframe the moral debate.[i] This is important, because it is impossible to win a moral debate on the defensive. This is the problem of the current "sex-positive" movement: it has no firm philosophic foundation and so is forced to argue defensively and often from a subjectivist position. There is no way they will be able to win the debate without adopting a better philosophic foundation. No one will ever be convinced by the argumentative tack of: "yeah, sex is immoral, but it sure feels

---

[i] I must thank Alex Epstein his work on this topic and demonstrating the approach in his book *The Moral Case for Fossil Fuels*.

good." However, the debate has now changed with the introduction of our new theory of eudaimonism and its emphasis on the importance of sexuality for a good human life. Now that we have a robust philosophical framework from which to argue, we are no longer at a disadvantage. In fact, we are now at a great advantage as we offer something that these older systems did not: the possibility of a good human life. Yet, it is not enough to simply have our new theory—we must apply it to the problems of sexual ethics and reframe the debates on our own terms.

So how do we go about reframing the moral debate? We have to argue that our position is morally right, that it will lead to a rich and happy life, and that the competing theories will fail to do this. We must reframe the debates in terms of the fundamental ethical systems and what they represent. Our eudaimonism represents a rich and happy human life and we must frame the debate in these terms.

It is not even necessary that we explicitly formulate the debate in contrast to the Resistant and Abstinent camps. While it is helpful to be able to identify the opposing philosophic positions in order to argue against their theories, we need not do this in order to win the debate. Instead, we will win the debate by showing our eudaimonistic ideal in positive terms and letting people decide for themselves which ideal they want to pursue. Yet, this is all rather abstract. It would be clearer if we showed actual examples of historic and entrenched debates and how reframing them can help us to resolve them. This is the work of Volume 2, but let us give a quick example here.

The current debate about abortion has been particularly intractable.[i] In its current manifestation, the debate is between the "pro-choice" and "pro-life"[ii] (more properly called "anti-abortion") sides. The first, pro-choice, argues that a woman should be free to choose whatever she wants with her body and that, therefore, abortion is not wrong, or perhaps that is it a necessary evil. The second, anti-abortion, thinks that the fetus is a person with full rights from the moment of conception and that, therefore, the mother has no right to murder the fetus.

Our position is different. Even if the anti-abortion side was correct that the fetus was a person (which is not true), it still would not prove their case. No one would have the right to abduct someone off the street and hook themselves up to them in order to live, not even if it were a short length of time.[iii] It is no different if the fetus were a person: they would still not have the right to force the mother to sacrifice herself to support them.

On our eudaimonistic account, a woman has the unequivocal right to determine the course of her life and has no obligation to sacrifice herself to

---

[i] We will deal with the topic of abortion at length in Volume 2, Chapter 11.
[ii] The irony of this name ("pro-life") must be lost on that side, given that they are not advocates of human life, but of sacrifice and of death (which they call the "next life").
[iii] I am indebted to Judith Jarvis Thomson's "A Defense of Abortion" for this point.

anyone, including a potential person growing inside her or a full-grown adult living down the street who will die without her aid. Thus, on our account, we can say firmly, and with no caveats, that a woman has the right to her own life. If we grant that there are some conditions on which she must sacrifice her life, then we are stuck splitting hairs about when and how she must give up her life. If we reject the entire premise of sacrifice in favor of life, then we can reject all demands for sacrifice and show them for exactly what they are: a call for death. Moreover, we can say something stronger than "abortion is not always immoral" we can say "abortion can be a fully moral choice."

In order to successfully reframe a moral debate in general, we must frame it in terms of *eudaimonism* and show how our position leads to the best life possible. This also allows us to clearly show the contrast between eudaimonism and the Resistant and Abstinent camps, which neither lead to happiness, nor do they intend to. This contrast will make it plain that if what they seek is happiness, they must come to eudaimonism. It is not enough that we win the theoretical case for sexual ethics; we must make ethics understandable and show people the practical value of it.

More broadly, we want to reframe the overall debates about sex from how to resist it or abstain from it to how to integrate sex into our lives so that we can achieve happiness. We want to insist that sexuality is an important part of a human life and that any ethical theory that fails to account for this is not appropriate for humans. This drives us to reframe the debate around sexuality as fundamentally a debate about whether happiness is our goal or not. If happiness is our goal, then most of us need to integrate sexuality into our lives in certain ways. If happiness is not our goal, then we do not.

Reframing the practical moral debate has several real advantages, as we have shown. Moreover, by reclaiming the moral narrative, we can help to reclaim sexual ethics from those who hate the body and our enjoyment of it. This will make the world a friendlier place for sexuality and will indirectly improve our sex lives, since there will be fewer sex-negative messages in the zeitgeist and people will have fewer sex-negative beliefs. Reframing the debates will allow us to make real headway in the culture. We may not be able to change everyone's mind, but we can win what we really want: a world where sex is a real value in human life.

Ultimately, reframing the moral debate amounts to showing that eudaimonism is a moral ideal for which we should strive if we want to live good lives. Through doing this, we can change the debate from "Well, yes, sex is bad, but..." to "Sex is moral and an important part of a rich and happy human life for most people. Here is why...". This is all made possible by our new eudaimonistic account of sexual ethics.

Living Moral Exemplars

Reframing the debates is an important first step in the revolution. However, one of the most powerful arguments that can be given for an ethical position is to show that it actually leads to a person living well. Even most people who hold views opposed to eudaimonism, such as altruism and its standard of sacrifice, do not actually want to live bad lives. They just mistakenly think that they must, in order to appease their god and have a good time "after death." If we can show them, through our own lives, that our theories really do work and that they do lead to happiness, we can make a powerful point for eudaimonism and the importance of sexuality. Demonstrating this in real life is the most powerful argument we can make. Yet, being a moral exemplar is no easy task. Moreover, in a culture that is dominated by the Resistant or Abstinent camps, it is quite the revolutionary act. Given all this, how do we become living moral exemplars?

First, we must learn the eudaimonistic ethics and work to master its various aspects. We must internalize these so that we will be motivated to be good and feel good about our ethical choices. We must develop our *phronesis* through experience and work to create the habits that are the virtues. This does not mean that we cannot make mistakes, but that we will focus on doing our best and correcting any mistakes that we do make. In fact, admitting mistakes and working to correct them is an important part of the process. All of this comes together to create our character.

Second, we must work to cultivate reverence for life. Like happiness, this cannot be aimed at directly, but emerges from living in a certain way. In order to cultivate reverence for life, we must start by recognizing the good things we have in life, even if they are few. We must recognize when goods things happen to us and give no more attention to bad things than we must. We must recognize how wonderful life is and how great it is that we get to be alive at all. Through all this, we should focus on the things that we enjoy and improve our lives. Once we have done all this, from time to time we will directly experience reverence in little moments and also through existential moments: those moments in life where we can directly experience the course of our lives, as we can through sex and erousia. These moments will help us to feel the reverence for the life we have created. Finally, it is important that we keep in mind that we will all die and that it will all end, so that we do not forget to cherish what we have while we have it.

Cultivating reverence for life makes one more apt to recognize the goods of life and to hold reverence for other things as well. Indeed, reverence for life in general is a major element of richly loving our own lives. At the same time, reverence for life requires reverence for our own lives, which we must earn through the cultivation of a good character and living well. There is a reciprocal relationship here between reverence for life in general and reverence for our own lives: as we cultivate one, we likewise cultivate the other. Moreover, once we cultivate reverence for our own lives, we will experience joy at our existence.

Third, we must work to cultivate meaningfulness in our lives. We discussed this in detail in Chapter 1, but let us briefly reconsider it in overview here. In order to create meaning in life, we need to care about our life and how it goes. Meaning arises when we set purposes in our life. This involves choosing a central purpose in life around which to structure our lives. Once we have done this, we must establish a hierarchy of values and be clear about what our values are and how they relate to each other. This also involves aligning our subjective values with objective values so that we will care about things which actually improve our lives. And, of course, our values must align with human nature, given that we are human. Once we have done this, working to achieve our purposes brings meaning to our lives and it is one of the most powerful ways in which we are able to do this.

Fourth, we must cultivate tranquility. Tranquility arises when our soul is at harmony with itself (unity of soul) because we have a clear central purpose in life, a well-defined hierarchy of values so that we do not have conflicts in our values, well-cultivated values and beliefs so that we have few to no discordant values and beliefs, and when our sentiments are in harmony with themselves and with our conscious purposes because we have well-cultivated values and beliefs. It is important to stick to our hierarchy and only care about the things that are important to us and eschew meaningless things, because otherwise we will be led astray. We need not be perfect to experience tranquility: as long as we work to cultivate tranquility and do the best that we can, we will still experience tranquility, because we will know that we are masters of our own souls.

Fifth, for those of us who will have sex in our lives, we must cultivate a fun and healthy sex life. We can do this by learning to enjoy our bodies, enjoying our partner's body, and enjoying sex together. We must learn how to do all this without shame or guilt, which may involve letting go of: cultural norms that do not serve our lives, moral rules, and ethics not aimed at human happiness. It will most certainly involve learning all we can about sexuality, including about things that we may not like currently, and experimenting with sexuality with an open mind, since not all learning comes from books and we cannot rationalistically know what sexual things we will enjoy *a priori*.

Living good lives on our own will exemplify good action, but also be "permission giving" by showing people that there are other and better ways to live and that they, too, have permission to live well. While there are far-ranging social and political implications of our theoretical revolution, we must take care to put our primary focus on integrating sex into our lives in the right ways, knowing what we know now, in order to start living richer and happier lives. We should be living moral exemplars: not to sacrifice ourselves so that others may succeed, but because we ourselves want to live well. By so doing, we will start to shift the zeitgeist.

Shift the Zeitgeist

As we said in Chapter 6, the zeitgeist is the sum of ideas that people hold and act on in a culture and which are treated as "just the way things are." The zeitgeist does not *per se* exist, but arises from the interaction of individuals, conventions, and even social institutions, much as a market does and, indeed, it is something like a marketplace of ideas. The zeitgeist cannot be changed directly, because we cannot directly change what ideas people hold and which are represented in a culture through such things as their art, music, *etc*. We can, however, still shift the zeitgeist, even if indirectly.

The zeitgeist changes every time a new comprehensive philosophic system is introduced and at least some people start to acknowledge and accept it. If only a small number of people adopt it, the change might be small or may take a long time, whereas if a large number of people accept it, the change may be quick. This is precisely what we are doing with our new account of eudaimonism and of sexual ethics: we are starting to change the zeitgeist. As we accept these new theories ourselves, work to reframe the debates and become living moral exemplars, we will change the zeitgeist.

We can accelerate the rate of the change by focusing on certain ideas, such as the cultural ideas about what is "normal" with respect to human sexuality. The very idea of "normal" is problematic, because it is a positive concept (about what people *are*) used as a normative concept (about what people *should be*). Nonetheless, since so many people focus on it, we must address it. We should do this in two ways to be most effective: try to abolish normality as a moral standard and try to change what people think is normal for sexuality.

We should, first, push for people to drop "normal" as a moral standard and, instead, adopt the eudaimonistic standard. Why should we want to be like everyone else? Our goal is to live a good life, not to conform to others. Indeed, being like everyone else is no moral standard at all. True, people tend not to like people who are different, whether they are better or worse than average, and people can become aggressive or violent when they are trying to force others to conform to their ideas, but being "normal" is no sure path to living well. Moreover, by pushing the eudaimonistic standard, we will reduce the aggression and violence of unreflective people as we show them that what they hold is no real standard.

Second, we need to push to change the ideas about what is "normal" for humans with regards to sexuality. We have already shown that sex is a part of a good and healthy human life and this challenges the idea of what is "normal" for sex for those in the Resistant and Abstinent camps. However, we need to argue for more specific positions as well, such as that masturbation is not gross or immoral (the sin of "spilling seed")[i], but an act of self-love that is fun and pleasant and good for our health, both physically and spiritually. Or that "pre-marital" sex is not immoral, but the right thing to do if we want to live well. Indeed, we must push the principle that for most people, sex is an important part of a human life.

If we are able to start making changes in each of these three primary areas, then the revolution will begin. Cultures are slow to change, but if we can keep making an impact in each area, then change will happen. Yet, as we warned in the introduction to this section, we must be careful that we do not become consumed by the revolution. Instead, we must focus on our own happiness and moral development. After all, ours is not a philosophy of duty, but a philosophy for life.

Each element of the sexual ethics revolution is mutually reinforcing with the other elements: as we begin to reframe the ethical debates and convince people of our position, the zeitgeist will start to change. This change in the zeitgeist will make it easier to win the next debate. Progress in one area will facilitate progress in the other areas. As the zeitgeist shifts to embrace our ideas, it will be easier to live as moral exemplars as this is much easier in a culture that endorses the framework by which we are trying to live. This is why all of these elements need to happen together: they are mutually reinforcing and together they will have a much larger impact than any element would separately.

3. A Philosophy for Life

> *The life of reason makes brothers of its lovers*
> *in all times, and everywhere.*[106]
> ~ Will Durant

We warned in the last section that our primary goal should not become the revolution itself, but our own moral development. Indeed, if we give up our happiness for the revolution, the revolution is thereby lost. Philosophy is not primarily for changing the minds of other people, or for argumentation and debate. Philosophy is primarily for *living* and its practice is how we work to develop ourselves and engage with the world. Because this is a rather controversial claim, given that most people think that philosophy is the most esoteric of subjects with little applicability to the real world, we shall briefly explore this as the ultimate conclusion to this volume.

---

[i] It seems that Onan's "crime," as it were, was not masturbation at all, but pulling out of his brother's widow and ejaculating on the ground. It is not clear how this became the sin of masturbation. (Genesis 38:8-10)

Philosophy's Fundamental Divide

Whether or not the revolution happens in our lifetimes, by engaging in philosophy, we will become better people and live better lives. Philosophy, as a subject, was born in Ancient Greece. Before that time, there were many religions that attempted to provide a comprehensive worldview, but which approached this endeavor through mysticism and faith. Philosophy was born when the Greeks attempted to gain a comprehensive worldview through the use of reason. This does not mean that every Greek philosopher did a great job (*e.g.*, "the swerve," "all is fire," or "everything is flux"), but they did lay the groundwork for later philosophers. Socrates was one such philosopher who gave us two great gifts: the idea that we should live examined lives and the idea that nothing was beyond the bounds of questioning. Plato, one of Socrates' students, formulated the fundamental questions of philosophy, even if his positions were rather mystical (perhaps due to being influenced by Pythagoras and the mystery cults).

Aristotle was the first philosopher to firmly insist that reason was our only source of information about reality and that we had to engage with the world in order to understand it; we could not merely sit in armchairs and try to deduce it. This is not to say that Aristotle was perfect and that there were no elements of mysticism still in his works (*e.g.*, "The Prime Mover," natural place, the motion of the heavens, forms as existing in particulars in his hylomorphism, *etc.*). Nevertheless, it was Aristotle who sent us down the path to the modern world by insisting on reason and on engaging with reality (creating whole new fields of science, such as biology).

There are, fundamentally, two radically different approaches to philosophy: the Platonic approach and the Aristotelian approach.[i] In the Platonic approach, a person looks inward first, sees how the world should look, and then uses reason to justify whatever conclusions he already has. In contrast, in the Aristotelian approach a person looks outward first, sees reality as it is, and then uses reason to try to understand the world and live in it.[ii] To be fair, there have also been some mixed bags, like the Stoics, who were fundamentally religious, but who also had great insights into the nature of psychological processes and emotions. Indeed, the Stoics should be considered the very first psychologists.

Some philosophers like Kant are very explicit that they are on the Platonic

---

[i] This is beautifully shown in Raphael's "School of Athens," which prominently features this divide. At the center of the painting stand both Aristotle and Plato. Plato is holding his *Timaeus* and pointing up to the world of the Forms. Aristotle, in contrast, is holding his *Ethics* (presumably the *Nicomachean Ethics*) and holding his hand straight out to insist on this world.

[ii] Ayn Rand would call the Platonic approach "primacy of consciousness" as it holds that some consciousness has causal power over the world, while she would call the Aristotelian approach "primacy of existence" as it holds that reality exists independently of any consciousness. (See "The Metaphysical Versus the Man-Made," *Philosophy: Who Needs It*).

side ("I had to deny *knowledge* in order to make room for *faith.*"[107]) as are the religious philosophers like Duns Scotus, William of Occam, Abelard, *etc.* Other philosophers strove to be reasonable, but ended up relying on mysticism anyway, such as Aquinas and Descartes. Few philosophers actually managed to be fundamentally reasonable and follow in Aristotle's path, such as Rand and Locke. Nevertheless, every philosopher pushes philosophy forward to at least a small degree, even if sometimes it is by learning what not to do.

Philosophy is for Living

Philosophy is the art of life. While few contemporary philosophers would recognize this, many of the Greeks would have, which is why we opened this volume with a quote from Epicurus about the necessity of philosophy throughout life. Of course, today many people think that philosophy is not necessary, but to them Rand would say: "The men who are not interested in philosophy need it most urgently: they are most helplessly in its power."[108] This is because such people are simply passively accepting ideas from the zeitgeist and do not even realize that they are not fully in control of their lives.

So, let us ask what it means to engage in philosophy and how this will help us to live. To start with, we must strive for objectivity; that is, we must always ask "What is true?" instead of "What do we want to be true?" Objectivity amounts to taking a reality-first stance and seeking to know the way the world really is. This requires us to think critically about everything and make sure that we truly understand things and never accept them on faith or because we wish they were true (although these amount to the same thing). This is greatly facilitated by striving for clarity, both in our thoughts and in our speech. In order to have clarity, we must know both what we know and what we do not know. We must understand how we arrived at our knowledge and whether we are justified in it. We must also understand context and how all of our knowledge is contextual. We must, therefore, work to integrate our knowledge so that we can understand the world as best as we are able. We must also, as we have been stressing here, examine our own lives and carefully cultivate our values and beliefs. Philosophy is, thus, a way of living and of being oriented to the world.

All of these things are facilitated by the study of philosophy, even philosophy with which we might not agree. To really engage with philosophy, we must read the old masters, not to memorize them or become their students, but to engage with some of the most profound ideas humans have ever had. This is best done by engaging with the primary texts and reading a philosopher's own words. While secondary sources may help us to understand texts sometimes, they are never a substitute for engaging with the originals. Indeed, reading philosophy is like having a conversation with the best minds of the ages and we should want to have this conversation directly. There are few things in life better or more important for our moral development than being well read.

Philosophy is exercise for the mind. It sharpens our mental skills. It pushes us to become better: clearer in our thought and deeper in our questions. It forces us to engage with ideas that are new and complex. It helps us to clarify our values and goals. It shows us what people have tried in the past and whether or not it worked. Philosophy is not always easy, much as going to the gym is not always easy, but in both cases we become stronger through so doing and are capable of living better lives as a result.

This is why it is particularly tragic that philosophy is often treated as a game today by philosophers and of no consequence by regular people who (understandably) do not see any connection between the abstract games philosophers play and their real lives. This dolorous situation is the fault of philosophers such as David Hume who was only skeptical until it was time to play backgammon with his friends and then all his skepticism seemed ridiculous.[i] Even though he saw that his theorizing needed to be abandoned to live in the world, he did not seem to think this particularly relevant to his theories. This radical disconnect between philosophy and real life is a mistake and a perversion of the field. Philosophy is for living a human life, not for simply seeing who can make the most convoluted theory that bears the least relation to reality.

We have demonstrated herein that philosophy is not a game, but a powerful tool to help us understand the world and how to live in it. Indeed, as we have shown, Rand was right to insist that "the moral is the practical"[109]—that ethics is a powerful tool to help us live well. Not only does philosophy help us individually to become better, but it also helps us to become better as a society. There is great value in living in a world of good and rational people, who can help us to make the world a better place. Moreover, each of us has certain skills and cultivated powers, but none of us has the ability to do everything. We are much stronger when we work together. This is only possible when we all embrace reason and live examined lives.

Durant observed in the *Story of Civilization* that in the battle between philosophy and religion, "religion won because Philosophy was a luxury for the few, religion was a consolation for the many."[110] We have now demonstrated that good Philosophy is no luxury, but a practical necessity of human life. Let us hope, then, that its practice spreads far and wide.

---

[i] "Most fortunately it happens, that since reason is incapable of dispelling these clouds [of skepticism], nature herself suffices to that purpose, and cures me of this philosophical melancholy and delirium, either by relaxing this bent of mind, or by some avocation, and lively impression of my senses, which obliterate all these chimeras. I dine, I play a game of back-gammon, I converse, and am merry with my friends; and when after three or four hours' amusement, I wou'd return to these speculations, they appear so cold, and strain'd, and ridiculous, that I cannot find in my heart to enter into them any farther." David Hume, *Treatise on Human Nature*, Volume 1, Part IV, Section 7.

Bibliography

Aristotle. *Categories*; from *The Complete Works of Aristotle: The Revised Oxford Translation*. (Ed. Jonathan Barnes). Princeton, N.J: Princeton University Press, 1984.

——. *Eudemian Ethics*; from *The Complete Works of Aristotle: The Revised Oxford Translation*. (Ed. Jonathan Barnes). Princeton, N.J: Princeton University Press, 1984.

——. *Magna Moralia*; from *The Complete Works of Aristotle: The Revised Oxford Translation*. (Ed. Jonathan Barnes). Princeton, N.J: Princeton University Press, 1984.

——. *Metaphysics*; from *The Complete Works of Aristotle: The Revised Oxford Translation*. (Ed. Jonathan Barnes). Princeton, N.J: Princeton University Press, 1984.

——. *Nicomachean Ethics*; from *The Complete Works of Aristotle: The Revised Oxford Translation*. (Ed. Jonathan Barnes). Princeton, N.J: Princeton University Press, 1984.

——. *Poetics*; from *The Complete Works of Aristotle: The Revised Oxford Translation*. (Ed. Jonathan Barnes). Princeton, N.J: Princeton University Press, 1984.

——. *Politics*; from *The Complete Works of Aristotle: The Revised Oxford Translation*. (Ed. Jonathan Barnes). Princeton, N.J: Princeton University Press, 1984.

Bacon, Francis. *Novum Organum*. Cambridge, UK: Cambridge University Press, 2000

Baker, Robin. *Sperm Wars*. New York, NY: Basic Books, 1996.

Beck, Judith. *Cognitive Behavior Therapy: Basics and Beyond*. New York, NY: Guilford Press, 2011.

Diamond, Lisa. *Sexual Fluidity: Understanding Women's Love and Desire*. Cambridge, MA: Harvard University Press, 2008.

Dickinson, Emily. *Complete Poems*. (Ed. by Thomas H. Johnson.) London, UK: Faber & Faber, 1976.

Dodson, Betty. *Sex for One*. New York, NY: Three Rivers Press, 1987.

Dover, K.J. *Greek Homosexuality*. Cambridge, MA: Harvard University Press, 1978.

Durant, Will. *The Story of Civilization, Volume 2: The Life of Greece*. New York, NY: Simon and Schuster, 1939.

Ellis, Havelock. *Studies in the Psychology of Sex, Volume 1: The Evolution of Modesty*. Philadelphia, PA: F.A. Davis Company, 1910.

Epstein, Alex. *The Moral Case for Fossil Fuels*. New York, NY: Penguin, 2014.

Fromm, Erich. *The Art of Loving*. New York, NY: Harper, 1956.

God, The Judeo-Christian. *The Bible*. Standard English Version. Wheaton, IL: Crossway Publishers, 2002.

Gottman, John. *The Seven Principles for Making Marriage Work*. New York: Three Rivers Press, 1999.

Gould, Terry. *The Lifestyle: A Look at the Erotic Rites of Swingers*. Toronto, ON: Vintage Canada, 1999.

Kant, Immanuel. *Lectures on Ethics*. Translated by Louis Infield. New York: Harper and Row, 1963.

Kant, Immanuel. *The Metaphysics of Morals*. Translated by Mary Gregor. Cambridge, Eng.: Cambridge University Press, 1996.

LeVay, Simon. *Gay, Straight, and the Reason Why: The Science of Sexual Orientation*. New York, NY: Oxford University Press, 2011. Kindle Edition.

Locke, Ed and Ellen Kenner. *The Selfish Path to Romance: How to Love with Reason and Passion*. Doylestown, PA: Platform Press, 2011.

Long, H. W. *Sane Sex Life and Sane Sex Living*. Teddington, UK: Echo Library, 2007.

Mill, Jonathan Stuart. *Utilitarianism*; from *John Stuart Mill on Liberty and Other Essays*. (Ed. John Gray). Cambridge, MA: Oxford University Press, 1991.

Morin, Jack. *The Erotic Mind*. New York, NY: Harper Collins, 1995.

Nagel, Thomas. "Sexual Perversion." *The Philosophy of Sex: Contemporary Readings* (Ed. Alan Soble and Nicholas Power). Lanham, MD: Rowman & Littlefield, 2008.

Nietzsche, Friedrich. *Beyond Good and Evil*; from *Basic Writings of Nietzsche*. (Trans. Walter Kaufman). New York, NY: The Modern Library, 1992.

———. *On the Genealogy of Morality*. (Trans. Maudemarie Clark and Alan Swensen). Indianapolis, IN: Hackett, 1998.

———. *The Gay Science*; from *Basic Writings of Nietzsche*. (Trans. Walter Kaufman). New York, NY: The Modern Library, 1992.

———. *Thus Spoke Zarathustra: A book for None and All*. Trans. Walter Kaufman. New York, NY: Penguin, 1978.

Peikoff, Leonard. *Objectivism: The Philosophy of Ayn Rand*. New York, NY: Meridian, 1991.

Plato. *Meno*; from *Plato: The Complete Works*. (Eds. John M. Cooper and D. S. Hutchinson). Indianapolis, IN: Hackett Pub, 1997.

———. *Phaedo*; from *Plato: The Complete Works*. (Eds. John M. Cooper and D. S. Hutchinson). Indianapolis, IN: Hackett Pub, 1997.

———. *Republic*; from *Plato: The Complete Works*. (Eds. John M. Cooper and D. S. Hutchinson). Indianapolis, IN: Hackett Pub, 1997.

———. *Symposium*; from *Plato: The Complete Works*. (Eds. John M. Cooper and D. S. Hutchinson). Indianapolis, IN: Hackett Pub, 1997.

Rand, Ayn. *Atlas Shrugged*. New York, NY: Signet, 1997.

———. *For The New Intellectual*. New York, NY: Signet, 1961.

———. *Introduction to Objectivist Epistemology*. New York, NY: Meridian, 1990.

———. *Philosophy: Who Needs it*. New York, NY: Signet, 1982.

———. *Playboy Interview* (Pamphlet). Irvine, CA: Ayn Rand Institute Bookstore, 2004

———. *Return of the Primitive*. New York, NY: Meridian, 1999.

———. *Romantic Manifesto*. New York, NY: Signet, 1971.

———. *The Fountainhead*. New York, NY: Signet, 1993.

———. *The Objectivist*. New Milford, CT: Second Renaissance Books, 1971.

———. *Three Plays: Night of January 16th, Ideal, Think Twice*. New York, NY: Signet, 2005.

———. *Virtue of Selfishness*. New York, NY: Signet, 1964.

———. *We The Living*. New York, NY: Signet, 2011.

Ray, Darrel. *Sex and God: How Religion Distorts Sexuality*. Bonner Springs, KS: IPC Press, 2012. Kindle Edition.

Russell, Bertrand. *Marriage and Morals*. New York, NY: Liveright, 1970.

———. "Our Sexual Ethics." *Why I am Not a Christian*. New York, NY: Simon and Schuster, 1957.

Ryan, Christopher and Cacilda Jetha. *Sex At Dawn: The Prehistoric Origins of Sexuality*. New York, NY: Harper Collins, 2010.

Smith, Tara. "To Imagine a Heaven." Irvine, CA: Ayn Rand Institute Bookstore, 2011.

———. *Viable Values*. Lanham, MD: Rowman & Littlefield, 2000.

Solomon, Robert. *The Passions*. Indianapolis, IN: Hackett, 1993.

———. *About Love*. Indianapolis, IN: Hackett, 1994.

———. "Erotic Love as a Moral Virtue," from *Virtue Ethics Old and New* (Ed. Stephen Gardiner). Ithaca, NY: Cornell University Press, 2005.

Thoreau, Henry David. *Walden*. New York, NY: Dover, 2012.

Travers, Luc. *Touching the Art: A Guide to Enjoying Art at a Museum*. Self-Published, 2010.

About the Author

Jason Stotts is a philosopher and psychotherapist who has long been interested in the intersection of philosophy and psychology that is sexuality.

He received his Master of Arts in Clinical Psychology from Brandman University in 2015 and his Bachelor of Arts in both Philosophy and Economics from Denison University in 2006.

In terms of his philosophic work, Jason is primarily interested in sexuality and ethics, but is also very interested in philosophy of emotion, philosophy of psychology, and epistemology. In terms of philosophers, he is primarily interested in Ayn Rand and Aristotle, but also enjoys Ancient Philosophy more generally. Jason is a member of the Society for the Philosophy of Love and Sex (SPLS) of the American Philosophical Association.

In terms of his psychological work, Jason specializes in sex education, sex therapy, relationship therapy, and general psychotherapy. His work is primarily grounded in Cognitive Behavior Therapy (CBT), but he is also very interested in Philosophic Therapy (the good life, virtue, the role of other people, *etc.*) and Existential Therapy (meaning in life, death, *etc.*).

You can find out more about Jason, as well as his blog, at his website **www.JasonStotts.com**

Endnotes

1. Morin, Jack. *The Erotic Mind*, p. 312.
2. Russell, Bertrand. "Our Sexual Ethics," *Why I am Not a Christian*, p. 170.
3. Seneca. *Moral Epistles*, CVI "On the Corporeality of Virtue."
4. Solomon, Robert. "Erotic Love as a Moral Virtue," from *Virtue Ethics Old and New* (Ed. Stephen Gardiner), p. 93. Referencing Kant's *Lectures on Ethics*, trans. Infield (Indianapolis: Hackett, 1963), p. 164.
5. Nietzsche. *The Gay Science*, aphorism #173.
6. Nietzsche. *Thus Spoke Zarathustra*, "On Poets," p. 128 (paraphrase).
7. Aristotle. *Nicomachean Ethics*, I.4.1095^{a}25.
8. Russell, Bertrand. *Marriage and Morals*, p. 268.
9. Ellis, Havelock. *Studies in the Psychology of Sex, Volume 1 The Evolution of Modesty; The Phenomena of Sexual Periodicity; Auto-Erotism*, General Preface.
10. Epicurus. *Letter to Menoeceus*, 122. Trans. Nussbaum (As found in Nussbuam, *Therapy of Desire*, p. 115.)
11. Russell, Bertrand. *Marriage and Morals*, p. 5.
12. Solomon, Robert. *The Passions: Emotions and the Meaning of Life*, p. 7.
13. Dickinson, Emily. *Complete Poems of Emily Dickinson*, poem 1741.
14. Aristotle. *Eudemian Ethics*, I.2.1214^{b}6.
15. Thompson, Hunter S. *Letters of Note: Correspondence Deserving of a Wider Audience* (Ed. Shaun Usher), Letter #021 "A Man Has to Be Something; He Has to Matter."
16. Plato. *Protagoras*, 358c.
17. Aristotle. *Eudemian Ethics*, I.8.1218^{a}12.
18. Solomon, Robert. *The Passions: Emotions and the Meaning of Life*, p. IX.
19. Rand, Ayn. *For the New Intellectual*, p. 179.
20. This list generally follows Aristotle; see *Nicomachean Ethics*, I.8.1099^{b}1.
21. See, for example, *Eudemian Ethics*, II.1.1219^{a}35. "Therefore happiness would be the activity of a complete life in accordance with complete excellence."
22. Aristotle. *Nicomachean* Ethics, IX.7.1168^{a}5.
23. Aristotle. *Nicomachean* Ethics, VI.13.1144^{b}25.
24. Aristotle. *Nicomachean Ethics*, IX.8.1169^{a}12.
25. Rand, Ayn. *The Virtue of Selfishness*, p. ix. My argument here follows Rand's closely.
26. Seneca. *De Ira*, 3.43. Trans. Nussbaum (As found in Nussbaum, *Therapy of Desire*, p. 429.)
27. Aristotle. *Nicomachean Ethics*, II.2.1103^{b}27.
28. Aristotle. *Nicomachean Ethics*, II.6.1106^{a}27-^{b}25 & II.7.1107^{b}9.
29. Aristotle. *Nicomachean Ethics*, IV.3.

30 Aristotle. *Nicomachean Ethics*, II.6.1107a5.
31 Aristotle. *Politics*, I.2.1253a25.
32 Aristotle. *Nicomachean Ethics*, II.6.1106b28.
33 Bacon, Francis. *Novum Organum*, Book I, Aphorism 3.
34 Aristotle. *Nicomachean Ethics*, IX.7.1168a5
35 Rand, Ayn. *The Virtue of Selfishness*, p. 29 (quoting *Atlas Shrugged*).
36 Rand, Ayn. *The Virtue of Selfishness*, p. 29.
37 Aristotle. *Nicomachean Ethics*, IV.3.1124a1.
38 Rand, Ayn. "The Age of Envy," *Return of the Primitive*, p. 130.
39 Thoreau, Henry David. *Walden*, 1-A, #9.
40 Rand, Ayn. "Philosophy and Sense of Life," *The Romantic Manifesto*, p. 27.
41 Aristotle. *Eudemian Ethics*, I.3.1215a11.
42 Aristotle. *Nicomachean Ethics*, II.6.1106b16.
43 Aristotle. *Nicomachean Ethics*, I.10.1100b20. Priam was, of course, the King of Troy when it fell during the *Iliad*.
44 Paraphrase of Glaucon's arguments around the ring of Gyges. *Republic*, 360b.
45 The Christian Bible, Matthew 16:26, English Standard Version.
46 Rand, Ayn. *Atlas Shrugged*, p. 925.
47 Rand, Ayn. "The Objectivist Ethics," *The Virtue of Selfishness*, p. 27.
48 Solomon, Robert. *The Passions: Emotions and the Meaning of Life*, p. 194.
49 Rand, Ayn. "Philosophy and Sense of Life," *The Romantic Manifesto*, p. 25 (paraphrase).
50 Ayn Rand makes this point in multiple places, see for example: *For The New Intellectual*, p. 55 and *The Virtue of Selfishness*, p. 32.
51 Rand, Ayn. "Philosophy and Sense of Life," *The Romantic Manifesto*, p. 25.
52 Beck, Judith. *Cognitive Behavior Therapy: Basics and Beyond*, p. 32. Judith Beck is referencing her father Aaron Beck's book *Cognitive Therapy of Depression*, where he first used the idea of "core beliefs."
53 Solomon, Robert. *The Passions*, p. 109.
54 Point broadly taken from: Rand, Ayn. "Philosophy: Who Needs it," *Philosophy: Who Needs It*, p. 5.
55 Aristotle. *Metaphysics*, I.1.980a25.
56 Solomon, Robert. *About Love*, p. 32.
57 Russell, Bertrand. *Marriage and Morals*, p. 123.
58 Rand, Ayn. "Of Living Death," *The Objectivist*, p. 531.
59 Plato. Phaedo, 65d.
60 Plato. *Symposium*, 211c.
61 Plato. *Symposium*, 189d-194e.
62 See, for more on the idea of mature love: Robert Solomon's *About Love*.
63 Fromm, Erich. *The Art of Loving*, p. 41.

64. Rand, Ayn. *Atlas Shrugged*, Part Three, Chapter 4, p. 809.
65. Rand, Ayn. "Philosophy and Sense of Life," *The Romantic Manifesto*, p. 32.
66. Aristotle. *Nicomachean Ethics*, IX.9.1169^{b}30 and IX.9.1170^{b}7.
67. Aristotle. *Eudemian Ethics*, I.8.1218^{a}12.
68. Aristotle. *Nicomachean Ethics*, IX.4.1166^{a}10.
69. Rand, Ayn. *The Fountainhead*, p. 376.
70. Aristotle. *Nicomachean Ethics*, IX.9.1169^{a}11. (And again on 1169^{b}1).
71. Solomon, Robert. "Erotic Love as a Moral Virtue," from *Virtue Ethics Old and New* (Ed. Stephen Gardiner), p. 86.
72. Russell, Bertrand. *Marriage and Morals*, p. 127.
73. Russell, Bertrand. *Marriage and Morals*, p. 140.
74. Aristotle. *Magna Moralia*, II.15.1213^{a}13-26.
75. Aristotle. *Nicomachean Ethics*, IX.7.1168^{a}5.
76. "Respect." *Oxford Dictionaries Online*. Oxford University Press. August 23rd, 2013. http://oxforddictionaries.com/
77. Nietzsche, Friedrich. *Thus Spoke Zarathustra*, "On Child and Marriage."
78. Some studies show as many as 80% of marriages end because of the couple growing apart. See: John Gottman *The Seven Principles for Making Marriage Work*, p. 16.
79. Rand, Ayn. *For the New Intellectual*, p. 99.
80. Dodson, Betty. *Sex for One*, p. 132.
81. Solomon, Robert. "Erotic Love as a Moral Virtue," from *Virtue Ethics Old and New* (Ed. Stephen Gardiner), p. 93. Referencing Kant's *Lectures on Ethics*, trans. Infield (Indianapolis: Hackett, 1963), p. 164. (Comments added.)
82. I took the term "style" from Ayn Rand's essay "Philosophy and Sense of Life" (*Romantic Manifesto*, p. 32), although the work elaborating it is my own. It is not clear whether she would have endorsed my account.
83. Rand, Ayn. *The Letters of Ayn Rand*, p. 355.
84. Rand, Ayn. *For the New Intellectual*, p. 99.
85. Morin, Jack. *The Erotic Mind*, p. 90.
86. Rand, Ayn. *For the New Intellectual*, p. 99.
87. Nin, Anaïs. *Diary*, Vol. 5. (As found in Robert Solomon's *The Passions*, p. 23).
88. Herdt, Gilbert. *Sambia Sexual Culture: Essays from the Field*, p. 101.
89. Fausto-Sterling, Anne. "The Five Sexes: Why Male and Female Are Not Enough," *The Sciences*, March/April 1993, p. 20-24.
90. Diamond, Lisa. *Sexual Fluidity: Understanding Women's Love and Desire*.
91. Money, John; Hampson, Joan G; Hampson, John (October 1955). "An Examination of Some Basic Sexual Concepts: The Evidence of Human

Hermaphroditism." *Bulletin of the Johns Hopkins Hospital (Johns Hopkins University)* 97(4): 301–19.

92 Maglaty, Jeanne. "When Did Girls Start Wearing Pink?" *Smithsonian Magazine*. Smithsonian Institution, April 7, 2011. Web, accessed September 12th, 2017.

93 Nagel, Thomas. "Sexual Perversion." *The Philosophy of Sex: Contemporary Readings* (Ed. Alan Soble and Nicholas Power), p. 36.

94 Nagel, Thomas. "Sexual Perversion." *The Philosophy of Sex: Contemporary Readings* (Ed. Alan Soble and Nicholas Power), p. 37.

95 Rand, Ayn. "Of Living Death," *The Objectivist*, p. 530.

96 Nietzsche, Friedrich. *Beyond Good and Evil*, aphorism #75.

97 Ryan, Christopher and Cacilda Jetha. *Sex at Dawn*, p. 236.

98 Waldinger M. D., Quinn, P., Dilleeen, M., Mundayat, R., Schweitzer, D. H., Boolell, M. (2005). A Multinational Population Survey of Intravaginal Ejaculation Latency Time. *The Journal of Sexual Medicine*. Vol 2, p. 492-497.

99 Ryan, Christopher and Cacilda Jetha. *Sex at Dawn*, p. 230. (Note also that Chimps and Bonobos have the same rate of sex per live birth.) Referencing: Dixson, A. F. (1998). *Primate Sexuality: Comparative studies of Prosimians, Monkeys, Apes and Human Beings*. New York: Oxford University Press.

100 Ryan, Christopher and Cacilda Jetha. *Sex at Dawn*, p. 230.

101 Nietzsche, Friedrich. *Beyond Good and Evil*, Part IX, #287.

102 Rand, Ayn. *We the Living*, p. 117.

103 Rand, Ayn. *Philosophy: Who Needs It*, p. 16.

104 Hugo, Victor. "The History of a Crime." Loose (but common) translation based on the original French "On résiste à l'invasion des armées; on ne résiste pas à l'invasion des idées." This literally translates as "An invasion of armies can be resisted; an invasion of ideas cannot be resisted."

105 Epstein, Alex. "How Republicans Can Make Energy a Winning Issue In 2016," *Forbes*. Forbes, April 6, 2016.

106 Durant, Will. *Story of Civilization, Volume 2: The Life of Greece*, p. 436.

107 Kant, Immanuel. *Critique of Pure Reason*, p. Bxxx.

108 Rand, Ayn. *Philosophy: Who Needs It*, p. 6.

109 Rand, Ayn. *The Letters of Ayn Rand*, p. 355.

110 Durant, Will. *Story of Civilization, Volume 2: The Life of Greece*, p. 578.

www.ingramcontent.com/pod-product-compliance
Lightning Source LLC
Chambersburg PA
CBHW030903080526
44589CB00010B/128